Real Estate Planning and Development

EDITORIAL ADVISORS

Rachel E. Barkow
Vice Dean and Charles Seligson Professor of Law
Faculty Director, Zimroth Center on the Administration of Criminal Law
New York University School of Law

Erwin Chemerinsky
Dean and Jesse H. Choper Distinguished Professor of Law
University of California, Berkeley School of Law

Richard A. Epstein
Laurence A. Tisch Professor of Law
New York University School of Law
Peter and Kirsten Bedford Senior Fellow
The Hoover Institution
Senior Lecturer in Law
The University of Chicago

Ronald J. Gilson
Charles J. Meyers Professor of Law and Business
Stanford University
Marc and Eva Stern Professor of Law and Business
Columbia Law School

James E. Krier
Earl Warren DeLano Professor of Law Emeritus
The University of Michigan Law School

Tracey L. Meares
Walton Hale Hamilton Professor of Law
Director, The Justice Collaboratory
Yale Law School

Richard K. Neumann, Jr.
Alexander Bickel Professor of Law
Maurice A. Deane School of Law at Hofstra University

Robert H. Sitkoff
Austin Wakeman Scott Professor of Law
John L. Gray Professor of Law
Harvard Law School

David Alan Sklansky
Stanley Morrison Professor of Law
Faculty Co-Director, Stanford Criminal Justice Center
Stanford Law School

Real Estate Planning and Development

Barlow Burke
Professor of Law and John S. Myers and
Alvina Reckman Myers Scholar
Washington College of Law
American University

Copyright © 2022 Barlow Burke.

No part of this publication may be reproduced or transmitted in any form or by any means, electronic or mechanical, including photocopy, recording, or utilized by any information storage or retrieval system, without written permission from the publisher. For information about permissions or to request permissions online, visit us at www.AspenPublishing.com.

To contact Customer Service, e-mail customer.service@aspenpublishing.com, call 1-800-950-5259, or mail correspondence to:

Aspen Publishing
Attn: Order Department
PO Box 990
Frederick, MD 21705

Printed in the United States of America.

1 2 3 4 5 6 7 8 9 0

ISBN 978-1-5438-3282-2

Library of Congress Cataloging-in-Publication Data

Names: Burke, D. Barlow, 1941– author.
Title: Real estate planning and development / Barlow Burke.
Description: Frederick, MD : Aspen Publishing, 2022. | Series: Examples & explanations | Includes bibliographical references and index. | Contents: Land acquisition—Contracting to acquire project property—Environmental concerns—Acquisition techniques other than executory contracts—Forming and capitalizing an entity for acquiring title—Taxes and investments in real property—Preparing for construction—Construction lending agreements—Equity financing and investors—The permanent mortgage—Leasing the project—Planning to exit a project. | Summary: "This book is intended for students in upper level, elective courses in real estate planning, finance, and transactions. It focus is on the development of new commercial real estate projects—office buildings and retail shopping projects. Its Chapters follow the sequence of development–acquiring a project site, negotiating the acquisition sales contract for it, choosing the entity to hold title to it, then taking title to it, hiring and dealing with architects and construction contractors, financing construction, finding permanent mortgage financing for it, dealing with equity investors, leasing the completed project and, when the time is right, exiting the project. Thus the text discusses the various persons and professionals who play a vital part in the development process and whom attorneys for developers should come to know, and, I hope, admire"—Provided by publisher.
Identifiers: LCCN 2022026930 (print) | LCCN 2022026931 (ebook) | ISBN 9781543832822 (paperback) | ISBN 9781543832839 (ebook)
Subjects: LCSH: Real property—United States. | Land tenure—Law and legislation—United States. | Real property and taxation—United States. | Vendors and purchasers—United States. | Mortgages—United States. | Real estate business—Law and legislation—United States. | Commercial real estate—United States. | Real estate development—Law and legislation—United States.
Classification: LCC KF570 .B87 2022 (print) | LCC KF570 (ebook) | DDC 346.7304/3—dc23/eng/20220729
LC record available at https://lccn.loc.gov/2022026930
LC ebook record available at https://lccn.loc.gov/2022026931

About Aspen Publishing

Aspen Publishing is a leading provider of educational content and digital learning solutions to law schools in the U.S. and around the world. Aspen provides best-in-class solutions for legal education through authoritative textbooks, written by renowned authors, and breakthrough products such as Connected eBooks, Connected Quizzing, and PracticePerfect.

The Aspen Casebook Series (famously known among law faculty and students as the "red and black" casebooks) encompasses hundreds of highly regarded textbooks in more than eighty disciplines, from large enrollment courses, such as Torts and Contracts to emerging electives such as Sustainability and the Law of Policing. Study aids such as the *Examples & Explanations* and the *Emanuel Law Outlines* series, both highly popular collections, help law students master complex subject matter.

Major products, programs, and initiatives include:

- **Connected eBooks** are enhanced digital textbooks and study aids that come with a suite of online content and learning tools designed to maximize student success. Designed in collaboration with hundreds of faculty and students, the Connected eBook is a significant leap forward in the legal education learning tools available to students.

- **Connected Quizzing** is an easy-to-use formative assessment tool that tests law students' understanding and provides timely feedback to improve learning outcomes. Delivered through CasebookConnect.com, the learning platform already used by students to access their Aspen casebooks, Connected Quizzing is simple to implement and integrates seamlessly with law school course curricula.

- **PracticePerfect** is a visually engaging, interactive study aid to explain commonly encountered legal doctrines through easy-to-understand animated videos, illustrative examples, and numerous practice questions. Developed by a team of experts, PracticePerfect is the ideal study companion for today's law students.

- The **Aspen Learning Library** enables law schools to provide their students with access to the most popular study aids on the market across all of their courses. Available through an annual subscription, the online library consists of study aids in e-book, audio, and video formats with full text search, note-taking, and highlighting capabilities.

- Aspen's **Digital Bookshelf** is an institutional-level online education bookshelf, consolidating everything students and professors need to ensure success. This program ensures that every student has access to affordable course materials from day one.

- **Leading Edge** is a community centered on thinking differently about legal education and putting those thoughts into actionable strategies. At the core of the program is the Leading Edge Conference, an annual gathering of legal education thought leaders looking to pool ideas and identify promising directions of exploration.

Summary of Contents

Contents		*ix*
Preface		*xv*
Acknowledgments		*xvii*

Chapter 1	Land Acquisition	1
Chapter 2	Contracting to Acquire Project Property	15
Chapter 3	Environmental Concerns	47
Chapter 4	Acquisition Techniques Other Than Executory Contracts	69
Chapter 5	Forming and Capitalizing an Entity for Acquiring Title	111
Chapter 6	Taxes and Investments in Real Property	133
Chapter 7	Preparing for Construction	147
Chapter 8	Construction Lending Agreements	191
Chapter 9	Equity Financing and Investors	225
Chapter 10	The Permanent Mortgage	245
Chapter 11	Leasing the Project	265
Chapter 12	Planning to Exit a Project	329

Index	*363*

Contents

Preface		*xv*
Acknowledgments		*xvii*

Chapter 1   Land Acquisition   1

Approaching the Landowner	2
Letters of Intent	3
Options to Purchase	7
A Right of First Refusal	11

Chapter 2   Contracting to Acquire Project Property   15

A Note on Drafting	15
The Executory Period	16
The Due Diligence or Study Period	18
The Purchase Price	19
A "Break-Up" Clause	21
"Subject to Financing" Clause	22
Warranties and Representations	29
"Subject to Rezoning" Clause	31
Marketable Title Clauses — Express and Implied	34
"Time Is of the Essence" Clause	39
Anti-Assignment Clause	41
Remedies for a Breach	42

Chapter 3   Environmental Concerns   47

Contract of Sale Disputes	47
Marketable Title	48
Deed Warranties	48
Title Insurance	48
Mortgage Disputes	49
Hazardous Substances	50
CERCLA	50
Indemnification Agreements	56
Insurance	57

ix

Contents

Insurance Policy Terms	57
Environmental Audits	59
Phase I	59
Phase II	60
Environmental Consultants	60
Enforcement	61
CERCLA Defenses	62
Lender Defenses	62
Site Owner Defenses	64
The Tax Status of Cleanup Costs	65
Brownfields	65
Other Hazards	66
Asbestos	66
Lead	67
Endangered Species	67
Radon	67

Chapter 4   Acquisition Techniques Other Than Executory Contracts   69

Installment Land Sale Contracts	69
Creditors' Rights to Reach Contract Interests	72
Mortgaging the Purchaser's Interest	73
Bankruptcy	74
Remedies	75
Closing an Installment Contract	75
The Measure of Damages	76
State Legislation	81
Ground Leases	82
Ground Lease Negotiations	83
Take-Back Financing and the Subordination Agreement	97
Subordination Lien Circuity	102
The Wraparound Mortgage	105

Chapter 5   Forming and Capitalizing an Entity for Acquiring Title   111

The Limited Liability Company	113
An LLC Compared to a General Partnership	115
An LLC Compared to a Limited Partnership	115
An LLC Compared to a Subchapter S Corporation	116
Forming an LLC	117
A Developer's Use of These Entities	120
Partnership Taxation	121

Contents

	Drafting an LLC's Operating Agreement	122
	A Developer as a Fiduciary	128
	Securities Acts' Liability	130
	Investment Trusts	132

Chapter 6   Taxes and Investments in Real Property   133

Tax Events	133
Deferring the Recognition of Gain	136
Business or Investment Property	136
Depreciation	137
Passive Losses	138
Investments in Real Estate	139
Examining the Setup for a Project	140
The Difference Between Income and Cash Flow	145

Chapter 7   Preparing for Construction   147

An Overview of the Construction Process	147
Documenting the Process	148
Project Planning and Design	149
An Architect's Duty to Prepare Plans and Specifications	152
The General Contractor	160
Selecting the General Contractor	161
Project Inspections	161
Construction Contract Agreements	162
Warranties	168
Other Provisions in Construction Agreements	170
General Conditions in Construction Agreements	173
The Role of the Subcontractor	173
Mechanic's Liens	175
Scope and Inclusiveness of Mechanic's Lien Statutes	177
Stop Notices	177
Enforcement	177
Surety Bonds	181
Builder's Risk Insurance	185
Green Buildings	187
An Updated Construction Process	188
A Final Note	190

Chapter 8   Construction Lending Agreements   191

The Construction Lending Process	191
Construction Lending	191

Contents

Types of Construction Lenders	192
The Permanent Lender	194
Appraisals of Commercial Real Estate	196
Nonrecourse Mortgages	197
The Construction Loan Commitment Letter	200
Reverse-Engineering: Doing the Deal Backwards	206
The Construction Loan Agreement	206
The Construction Note and Mortgage	212
The Note	212
The Construction Loan Mortgage	213
Business and Financial Covenants	219
Protecting the Construction Lender	222

Chapter 9   Equity Financing and Investors   225

Mezzanine Financing	225
Waterfalls for Commercial Real Estate	226
The Position of the Mezzanine Financier	228
Securities Acts' Exemptions for Equity Investors	243

Chapter 10   The Permanent Mortgage   245

An Assignment of Rents	245
Mortgagee in Possession	250
Receiverships	253
Loan Participations	259

Chapter 11   Leasing the Project   265

Shopping Centers	267
Office Buildings	267
The Parties to the Lease	268
The Premises	268
Rent and Square Footage	272
Possession and the Commencement of the Term	277
Rent	283
Rent Escalation Covenants	286
Percentage Rents	287
Expansion Rights	291
Contraction Rights	293
Subordination and Nondisturbance	293
Telecommunications Access	298
Assignments and Subleases	299
Work Letters and Tenant Improvement Allowances	303
Compliance with Statutes, Laws, Ordinances, Etc.	305

xii

Contents

Leasing Shopping Center Space	307
Use Covenants	312
Restrictive and Exclusive Use Covenant Remedies	316
Continuous Operation Covenants	318
Other Lease Covenants	323

Chapter 12   Planning to Exit a Project   329

The Sales Contract	334
Deed in Lieu of Foreclosure	336
The Sale-Leaseback	344
Tax-Free Exchanges	349
Converting Business Property into a Residence	356

Index	*363*

Preface

This book is intended for students in upper level, elective courses in real estate planning, finance, and transactions. Its focus is on the development of new commercial real estate projects — office buildings and retail shopping projects. Its chapters follow the sequence of development — acquiring a project site, negotiating the acquisition sales contract for it, choosing the entity to hold title to it, then taking title to it, hiring and dealing with architects and construction contractors, financing construction, finding permanent mortgage financing for it, dealing with equity investors, leasing the completed project and, when the time is right, exiting the project. Thus the text discusses the various persons and professionals who play a vital part in the development process and whom attorneys for developers should come to know, and, I hope, admire.

When reference is made to basic matters in the field that may have been introduced in other real estate courses, a brief, refresher in those matters has been provided, either in the text or a footnote.

Citations to cases is limited to either leading opinions or more recent opinions both summarizing needed law and giving guidance to other authorities. All citations to statutes are intended to be illustrative of others enacted with a similar pattern.

Frequent Examples are provided after a summary text on a subject. They are intended to illustrate the rules given in the text and sometimes to suggest how the rules might be used in negotiating documents necessary for a development project to proceed. Examples involving those documents suggest methods for handling those negotiations. Suggestions are just that, and no more: a development project is like a jigsaw puzzle whose shapes are not constant, but evolve to fit a unique pattern that will allow the project to take shape and form. The developer's attorney must have a knowledge of the law that is "a mile wide and an inch deep." He or she knows when to consult with specialists, what the needs of an opposite party require, and from what default rule of law the negotiations should proceed.

Explanations follow each Example. Before you read them, it is advisable first to think of your own explanation so that it can be compared with what I provide. If an Example asks you to take a point of view — that of a

xv

Preface

developer's attorney, or that of a lender's, architect's, or general contractor's attorney — think first of the opposing interests involved before you answer in your own mind. All of the parties presented in the text want to "do the deal," not walk away from it. That's true in life, and in these pages.

Barlow Burke
March, 2022

Acknowledgments

This book owes much to my students enrolled in my courses. They are too numerous to mention, but their research done in response to my prodding questions contributed much to my understanding of this subject. Week by week during a semester, they researched and wrote about matters on which they had not come to class expecting to become experts. I am immensely grateful for their flexibility and work ethic.

Over the years, my teaching this subject evolved into a case study approach, much like the one used in many business schools. Students were called to work in teams on a project, much like associates in a law firm. That evolution would not have been possible without the presentation and writing skills of one of my co-teachers. While Philip Horowitz, Esq., conducted a busy practice with integrity and good humor, he also found the time to write many of the case studies on which this book is based. Once a year, over thirty years, he worked them up to reflect the most recent legal, market, and project trends in the real estate industry. I cannot thank him enough for that effort, and for a succession of his firms, most notably Venable LLP, for giving him the time to spend with me and my students. All his students are in his debt, and many are working in this field of practice, as a result.

CHAPTER 1

Land Acquisition

The acquisition of a project site is a tricky business. Why? Because the buyer and the seller's aims are basically antithetical. The buyer wants to purchase at the lowest price while the seller, realizing that the buyer sees the land as a presently undervalued commodity, wants to obtain the highest price possible for it. The situation is the perfect set-up for "seller's remorse"—the idea that "I should have held out for more."[1] Moreover, if the land is already improved, with an office or retail building on it, the seller is likely to operate the property for the highest return possible during any period when it is up for sale.

Thus the buyer wants control as quickly and as cheaply[2] as possible. At the first and earliest stages in acquisition, the developer buying a site (land and/or buildings) seeks to control it just enough to exclude competitors from obtaining the same opportunities that the developer sees for it. Second, at the same time, the developer won't yet really know if the project he has in mind makes business sense and is economically feasible—and doesn't want to spend the money (which he might not yet have) to find out. Third, the developer knows some—but not all—of the business and legal

---

1. That is, in a rising market, a feeling of regret, disappointment, or sadness about having made a decision that for some reason or another is with hindsight seen as unwise, "I should have waited, raised the price, or looked around for a better offer." In a falling market, it might be, "I should have taken the last offer."

2. Buying cheaply is the first of many times in the development process that the developer will think, "spending as little of my money now will maximize my profits later." This is the first instance of the concept of leverage encountered in this book—gaining control of a site or project while paying as little cash as possible.

1. Land Acquisition

risks involved in the project. (This is where the developer's attorney enters the picture—to warn the client of the unknown, known unknowns, and perhaps unknowable risks, and to provide guidance and a "trip-tik" through those risks. And fourth, the developer wants to keep it simple, dealing with the risks one or two at a time, but not letting the attorney swamp the seller with knowledge of them and causing the seller to back off or lawyer up.

APPROACHING THE LANDOWNER

Why might the prospective land buyer/developer be hesitant to approach an owner about selling land? Consider that a developer might have

- taken a public position on land use issues the owner disagrees with,
- argued with the owner in the past,
- competed with him for a public project and won, or
- bought land from his neighbor who bad-mouthed him.

Imagining the variants on each of these situations and others make a developer hesitant to make a direct approach. Consider the following illustrations:

1. Alex Gomez owns several adjacent office buildings in an old area of downtown. He purchased the land and constructed the buildings decades ago; they are producing considerable income for Alex, who is living very comfortably on the cash flow the buildings generate. Alex has been generous to his two children, neither of whom has shown any interest in their father's real estate business. How should the developer interested in redeveloping Alex's properties approach Alex?

2. Ted White and his sister own several buildings—several low-rise retail buildings, and a five-story office building. All are located on land near a public transit station. They are rented to long-term tenants with whom Ted and his broker have had warm relationships. Recently the city council enacted new zoning regulations for the land on which the buildings are located, permitting more intense commercial development around transit stations. How should a developer interested in redeveloping these properties approach Ted?

3. Robert Poole is interested in developing a corporate office park in the suburbs. Nicole owns an old orchard of nut trees with more than enough acreage for Robert's needs and adjacent to a recently constructed residential subdivision and a riding stable. Harvesting the nuts involves shaking the trees, generating lots of dust that often blows through the subdivision. How should Robert approach Nicole?

The choice of the initial document a developer might use to approach the landowner and gain control of the site is typically unaided by the

I. Land Acquisition

attorney. After all, it is the developer who has made contact with the seller and who is best able to assess the seller's willingness, readiness, and ability to sell. So making this choice is that first of many times when the attorney should defer to the developer as a client.

This initial choice involves four alternative documents: a letter of intent, an option to purchase, and a contract of sale—the last to be discussed in a later chapter 2 of this book.

Letters of Intent

Such letters are a form of nonbinding, preliminary agreements. See Cochran v. Norkunas, 919 A.2d 700, 707-709 (Md. 2007). Developers often refer to them as comfort letters. The purposes of such a letter are several. It might show that the parties have agreed on the price and other material business terms of a purchase and sale. It might also prevent the seller from shopping the deal, while not preventing the buyer's further exploration of the business risks involved. It might further satisfy the Statute of Frauds' essential terms requirement.[3] It might include a confidentiality clause[4] and exclusivity clause, but still state that it is not binding on the parties.[5] That is, the letter can state that it is not binding, but also include some exceptions to or "carve outs" from the nonbinding clause for exclusivity in dealing, confidentiality, rights to information or inspection, with a duty to indemnify for damage and governing law. See Georgette Poindexter, Letters of Intent in Commercial Real Estate, 28 Real Est. L.J. 195 (2000).

The parties to it may incur costs and want to share them and the information produced, set deadlines for further negotiations for a contract, and guarantee best efforts and good faith bargaining.

---

3. By stating the partyies' names, identifying property, stating the agreed on purchase price, and the other business terms thought material at the time the letter is signed. See Tamir v. Greenberg, 501 N.Y.S.2d 103 (N.Y. App. Div. 1986).

4. That is: "This letter is confidential and shall not be disclosed to anyone other than the parties to it, their employees, accountants, attorneys, and possible lenders."

5. By stating this expressly it will assure the seller that signing the letter is a small step in the right direction, and here the attorney for the developer might pile it on by adding: "This is not a contract. It is not a legally binding contract. It is a nonbinding letter of intent. It contains provisions that might be the elements of a possible sale, and is for discussion purposes only." Or, "These terms are not binding unless they are set forth in a written contract signed by . . . " "This letter does not mean that the attached terms are or ever will be binding. . . ." See generally Harris Ominsky, Counseling the Client on the "Gentleman's Agreement," 36 Prac. Law. 25 (Dec. 1990). One opinion suggested the following: "The purpose of this document is to memorialize certain business points. The parties mutually acknowledge that their agreement is qualified and that they, therefore, contemplate the drafting and execution of a more detailed agreement. They intend to be bound only by the execution of such an agreement and not by this preliminary document." See Goren v. Royal Investments, 516 N.E.2d 173 (Mass. Ct. App. 1987).

1. Land Acquisition

The parties to the letter of intent cannot be held to it unless they intend to be bound. To determine intent, the language, its context, the open terms, any part performance, and the need to put the agreement in final form, are the factors for consideration. See Norris Wolff, Letters of Intent, Preliminary Agreements, and Binding Acquisition Agreements, 111 Banking L.J. 292 (1994).

Examples

Example 1

A letter of intent states that "this letter is an agreement to negotiate your usual contract of sale." Are courts likely to enforce the letter as they would a binding contract?

Explanation

No. Enforcement is unlikely. Why? This language creates a strong inference that the agreement is preliminary and nonbinding. (1) Courts will find it difficult to devise and enforce a remedy when they have no way to know the final agreement. However, this rationale is a weak one. (2) Enforcement requires a remedy. Here damages might be awarded; they might be based on the reliance of the injured party, not any lost expectation damages. However, the relying party seeking enforcement will have a heavy burden of proof. (Only a claim of unjust enrichment favors the use of expectation damages.) Less definiteness will be demanded with the plaintiff seeking reliance damages. (3) A better explanation for nonenforcement is that the court will not know what is required of parties whose dealings are incomplete and scant — it will be hard to tell what fair dealing means in this context.[6]

On the other hand, some courts have ruled that while such language is evidence of an intent not to be bound, it is not dispositive of the issue. See Prant v. Sterling, 753 A.2d 758 (N.J. Super. Ct. Ch. Div. 1999). Whether the agreement is binding is typically an issue of fact for a court. When all significant economic issues are resolved in an agreement, additional matters with which the purchase and sale contract treat — such as "the state of the title, conformance with local law, condition of the premises, extension provisions to allow seller time to remove title defects, buyer's right of election to accept a deficient title, performance to be merged in delivery of the deed, use of purchase money to clear title, maintenance of insurance . . . ,

---

6. See E. Allan Farnsworth, Precontractual Liability and Preliminary Agreements: Fair Dealing and Failed Negotiations, 87 Colum. L. Rev. 217 (1987).

I. Land Acquisition

assignment of insurance, closing adjustments, holding of deposit by broker, and disclaimer of implied warranties"—while "not without importance "and occasionally "the subject of further bargaining" are "subsidiary matters for which norms exist for their customary resolution." See Goren v. Royal Investments, 516 N.E.2d 173, 175 (Mass. Ct. App. 1987) (enforcing a letter of intent on this basis). Moreover, the phrase "your usual" contract of sale indicates that the coming contract is a formality and that it is mutually acceptable to the parties. Id., at 176, n.4.

Example 2

A letter of intent states that "the parties will make every reasonable effort to agree and to negotiate exclusively with each other." What does such language add to the letter? Who benefits from its insertion?

Explanation

This language sounds like "an agreement to agree." It should not be used alone. It should only be used as an addendum to a duty to negotiate, that is, as an addendum to language such as: "The parties agree to negotiate a contract of purchase and sale of the property to completion, at a price of _____." As a practical matter, buyers rather than sellers benefit from letters of intent. If the buyer wants to walk away from the transaction, the letter will probably provide ambiguity enough to make litigation over it problematic, and if the buyer wants to enforce it, then the litigation itself can tie the seller's hands and the title to the property for the time it takes to litigate. A letter provides a basis for a tort suit, its breach being an interference with an economic advantage if the seller breaches an exclusivity clause by selling to a third party. For a developer, it might be the basis of a conversation with a mortgage lender or investor (if the confidentiality clause permits) that might otherwise not be interested in discussing a loan. If all else fails, the overriding issue is whether the parties reached a meeting of the minds, and this issue is one of fact that insures the litigation will survive summary judgment. See Dennis v. Kaskel, 950 N.E.2d 68, 72 (Mass. Ct. App. 2011).

Example 3

Will the stage of the negotiations matter?

1. Land Acquisition

Explanation

Yes, courts are less likely to enforce a letter that emanates from the early stages of negotiations. Another rule of thumb might be that the more a letter includes, the more likely it is that a court will enforce it.

Example 4

A buyer's letter of intent states that the parties have a duty to negotiate, but "are not bound to negotiate in good faith and can end negotiations at any time." What might a seller wish to add to such language?

Explanation

This language gives rise to an inference that the duty to negotiate will be difficult to enforce and that the agreement is not binding. See GMH Assocs. v. Prudential Realty Grp., 752 A.2d 889 (Pa. Super. Ct. 1989) (reversing a trial court award of damages for breach of a letter agreement). A seller might add that "negotiations will be completed within 90 days or the agreement is null and void" in order to cabin an exclusivity clause. See Fredo v. Wright, 1998 Conn. Super. LEXIS 1729 (Conn. Super. Ct. June 19, 1998). Both parties might agree on something similar to the following: "Until a definitive agreement is executed, neither party may rely on this letter and neither shall have any legal or equitable obligation or remedy against the other, whether under this letter of intent or on any other grounds, including but not limited to, a legal duty to negotiate or to continue negotiations to reach a definitive agreement, and either may discontinue such negotiations at will and for any reason whatsoever."

Example 5

Should a buyer offer the seller some monetary consideration for the letter?

I. Land Acquisition

Explanation

Why not? It cannot hurt, and might more easily provide a basis for obtaining (as an encumbrance on the title) a *lis pendens* in any litigation over it as well as a basis for damages in a suit for its breach.

The literature on letters of intent is extensive. See generally Thomas Homburger & James Schueller, Letters of Intent—A Trap for the Unwary, 37 Real Prop. Prob. & Tr. J. 509 (2002); Matthew Franger, Real Estate Law Issue: Fine Print, 20 Los Angeles Lawyer 28 (1998) (suggesting two letters, one on the major business points of a proposed transaction, and another on terms such as an exclusive negotiation period); Herbert Bernstein and Joachim Zekoll, The Gentleman's Agreement in Legal Theory and Modern Practice: United States, 46 A. J. Comp. L. 87 (1998); J. B. Heath, Letters of Intent: Are They Binding?, 24 Colo. Law. 2367 (Oct. 1995).

OPTIONS TO PURCHASE

Options are a right to buy property, an irrevocable promise on the part of the owner executing the option—a/k/a the optionor—giving the prospective buyer—a/k/a the optionee – the right to have the promise specifically performed, It is not subject to specific performance by the optionor. In other words, the optionor cannot call on the option holder to buy, but the holder can call on the owner to sell: it is thus a "call" option, not a "put" option. As with any contract, its holder—the optionee—must give consideration[7] for the privilege of buying. An option typically is exercisable only within a short period of time. The consideration is forfeited if the option is not exercised. By definition and often by express language, the right to buy is a right exclusive to the optionee. The optionor takes the property off the market for the period the option is in effect. Thus, an optionor "gives and grants an exclusive and irrevocable right and option" to buy to an optionee. See Gregory Gosfield, A Primer on Options, 35 Real Prop. Prob. & Tr. J. 129 (2000).

If the period of time the option is in effect is particularly short, a provision might be made for extending it. Why? Because the holder of the option while interested in the property, is likely to want to do some due diligence regarding it during the option's life. If expenses are incurred in performing this due diligence, it's all the more important to have the right to buy be an

---

7. If the option is exercised, the consideration given for it will normally be treated as a component of the purchase price and become part of the buyer's tax basis in the property.

I. Land Acquisition

exclusive one; otherwise the optionee won't get the benefit of the information generated by the due diligence effort.

Examples

Example 6

The owner of a low rise apartment house has expressed a willingness to execute an option. The person seeking the option offers as consideration an amount of money for the option equal to the rent roll of the property for the period of time the option is outstanding. How might the owner respond?

Explanation

By recalling that the optionee is seeking the right to buy the property, not rent it. Thus, the owner might propose that the option price be credited toward the purchase price of the property and be set as would a first payment on a down payment for it. This gives the optionee an incentive to exercise the option, better reflects the purpose of the option, and is consistent with the income tax treatment of an option once exercised.

Example 7

A developer needs to assemble 3 land parcels – abutting parcels A, B, and C — for a project. The owner of parcel A executes an option to sell and stipulates that the contract of sale contain the following provision: "I promise to sell for a price of $100,000 and if you buy either parcel B or C, at more than $100,000, you will remit to me the difference(s) between my purchase price and the price either parcel B or C. Is the option enforceable?

Explanation

Yes. There is no requirement that an option price be paid all at once. Here the developer is getting control of parcel A and its owner is assured that the price at which she sells will reflect the true, development market value of her parcel. This avoids "seller's remorse" as to price. The provision is a win/win for both parties — for the buyer early control of parcel A and for the seller market assurance as to price. See Dodek v. CF 16 Corp., 537 A.2d 1086, 1095-1096 (D.C. 1988).

1. Land Acquisition

Example 8

When negotiating with an owner for an option, a developer proposes that the amount of time the option is outstanding be a reasonable time, not a fixed time period. The developer explains that she doesn't know how long her due diligence will take. How should the owner respond?

Explanation

By resisting the proposal. While some jurisdictions will imply that a contract with no time frame for performance lasts a reasonable time, others will find that such an option violates the common law Rules against Perpetuities. See Dorado Ltd. P'ship v. Broadneck Dev. Corp., 562 A.2d 757 (Md. 1987). To avoid such uncertainty, options traditionally have a fixed term and most courts will imply that time is of the essence in exercising the option. See Dixon v. Haft, 253 A.2d 715 (Md. 1969).

Example 9

Optionor and optionee execute an agreement entitled "Option to purchase Blackacre." It is effective for three months. Does it satisfy the Statute of Frauds? Is it recordable?

Explanation

Good question! An option, while a separate agreement, is essentially a promise to sell. It will be effective in doing so only when it results in a contract of sale for Blackacre. So it should be drafted as if it is a contract of sale, but subject to a one-sided right to specific performance. Attaching a contract the optionee intends to use to it and incorporating it by reference will both satisfy the statute and make it recordable. Once recorded, it might be interpreted as a real covenant running with the land[8] for a fixed term—hence the "gives and grants" language suggested in the initial discussion of options—the granting referring to the use of a deed for realty.

An option does not create an interest in real property in its holder. Unlike an executed contract of sale, it is not subject to the doctrine of

---

8. For example, a covenant in a lease involving an option to expand the premises or renew the lease would typically be regarded as a real covenant (one that runs with the land and binds remote parties), here benefitting sub-lessees.

1. Land Acquisition

equitable conversion and does not create an equitable interest in property in the optionee. See Shaffer v. Reed, 437 So. 2d 98, 98 (Ala. 1983). It instead creates a contract right to enforce the optionor's promise to sell. As a contract right, it can't be mortgaged, most jurisdictions won't give an optionee standing to file a land use proceeding, and most property insurers won't regard its holder as having an insurable interest. Unexercised, the right will be regarded as an executory interest under the Bankruptcy Code and subject to rejection by a optionor's trustee in bankruptcy.

Like any contract and absent language to the contrary, an option is assignable, though its exclusivity clause might imply otherwise. So its assignment should be expressly prohibited or limited to the optionee's business entity. The prohibition should include the situation in which the option is exercised and then immediately assigned—otherwise the prohibition will mean nothing.

Once terminated, an option should deal with due diligence reports and the issues of whether the information in them might be disclosed to the optionor and at whose expense disclosure occurs. When the option contains a break-up fee, its amount should be pegged either to the loss of marketability of the property or to the due diligence expenses incurred. If a real estate broker procured the option, the issue of whether a brokerage commission is due the broker, on either exercise or termination of the option, should be dealt with as well.

Example 10

Ben, a prospective buyer of Blackacre, gives Sid, its owner, $100,000 and receives Sid's receipt for the money. On the receipt, Ben promises Sid in writing that, in exchange for the $100,000 to be credited toward Blackacre's $500,000 purchase price, Ben will buy Blackacre using the attached contract of sale within 90 days. The attached contract is executed 60 days later. It provides that, if no closing occurs, Sid's sole remedy is retention of the $100,000. The contract is never closed. Ben sues Sid for the return of the $100,000. Will Ben win the suit?

Explanation

No. The provision in the contract nullifies the promise in the receipt. It is the last and controlling word in interpreting the intent of the parties. The buyer has the right to refuse to pay some portion of the purchase price and has no liability except forfeiture of the $100,000, while the owner has no recourse but retention of the $100,000, so this receipt and the contract together constitute an option. See Green Manor Corp. v. Tomares, 295 A.2d 212 (Md. 1972).

I. Land Acquisition

Example 11

A corporation with a healthy economic outlook seeks to construct its corporate office complex on farmland in a developing suburb. Its officers approach the not-quite-ready-to-retire farmer, seeking an option to buy the farm. The farmer responds to this approach by offering to sell the one third of his acreage abutting a major highway using a 90 day "call" option, and to sell another third of the farm in 5 years, and the rest of the farm 10 years from now: all 3 sales "shall be at an appraised price and at the land's then market value" and in the last 2 sales, the corporation "gives and grants the seller (the farmer) the sole, exclusive, and irrevocable right to sell at the appraised price." Is this option enforceable?

Explanation

Yes. The first sale is initiated by a call option. The later two sales have the rudiments of a "put" option — that is, the right of an owner to force a sale at a predetermined, exercise, or strike price that is the result of a fair market value appraisal. Each option has a definite term that lies within the time for vesting permitted by the common law Rule Against Perpetuities. In this put option, the corporation accepting the option is obliged, if the farmer desires, to buy the underlying acreage from the farmer at the farmer's request at a stipulated time during the life of the option, at the strike price. Like all options, put options require consideration when given and have expiration dates. Here the farmer/owner obtains an assured market for a sale of the remaining two thirds of the farm and the corporation acquires room to expand its corporate offices as its business increases. As with other options, the farmer need not "retire" the remaining two thirds of the farm from agricultural uses, but the corporation must buy.

A Right of First Refusal

The holder of a right of first refusal (ROFR) has an inchoate or conditional option. It is conditioned on the decision of the owner of property to sell it. The ROFR's holder is first in line to buy. She has the right to receive an offer to buy land from its owner. See generally Robert Wise, et al., First Refusal Rights Under Texas Law, 62 Baylor L. Rev. 433 (2010) and David Walker, Rethinking Rights of First Refusal, 5 Stan. J. L. Bus. & Fin. 1 (1999). An option gives its holder the right to force an owner to sell land solely by calling on the owner to perform the option and fulfill the owner's promise to sell. A ROFR typically needs a "trigger." It is triggered by an owner receiving a third-party offer to buy and "ripens" into an option once its holder receives the details of that offer (typically a contract of purchase and sale)

I. Land Acquisition

and makes a good faith decision to match it. See Van Dam v. Spickler, 968 A.2d 1040, 1045-1046 (Me. 2009) and A.G.E., Inc. v. Buford, 105 S.W.3d 667, 673 (Tex. Ct. App 2003). It is not triggered by involuntary sales. Nor is it typically triggered by sales between affiliated legal entities.

The ROFR in effect forces an option on the owner. Before matching the offer received by the owner, the holder must be given enough information about the terms of the offer to make an informed choice of either to exercise the right or to acquiesce in the transfer of the property to the offeree. See Koch Indus. v. Sun Co., 918 F.2d 1203, 1211-1212 (5th Cir. 1990). Once a reasonably detailed disclosure of the terms had been made, the holder of the right has a duty to undertake an investigation of any terms that are unclear. See *Koch*, 918 F.2d at 2112.

Like an option, a ROFR should be time-limited so as not to violate the Rule against Perpetuities. Cf. Martin v. Seeley, 142 N.Y.S.3d 252 (N.Y. App. Div. 2021) (validating a ROFR under the Rule when it was not assignable and was personal to the right holder). In a few jurisdictions, options and a ROFR are exempt from the effect of the Rule, but a majority of jurisdictions considering the issue hold that both are subject to the Rule: thus to avoid it, the right to exercise should be time limited to up to 21 years after the death of the holder when the holder is a legal entity or made personal and nonassignable when the holder is a natural person.

Thus a ROFR "limits an owner's right to dispose freely of his property by compelling him to offer it first to the party who has the first right to buy." See Mazzeo v. Kartman, 560 A.2d 733 (N.J. Super. Ct. App. Div. 1989). It is sometimes referred to as a First Right to Buy or Right of Preemption.[9]

Examples

Example 12

The person granting a ROFR rejects the third-party offer and makes a counter-offer. Is the ROFR still effective?

Explanation

Yes. The rejection of the offer by the owner does not excuse a failure to report it to the RPFR's holder. Indeed, the ROFR might be said to be revived by the rejection of the offer, so that any revised offer by the same third party must be reported.

---

9. A variant on a ROFR is a right of first offer (ROFO). It is the right to match any good faith offer made by an owner before it is made to a third party. It will typically contain a time period during which the owner can see whether better offers are obtainable — and then the right holder will have to match the better offer.

I. Land Acquisition

Example 13

Andy holds a ROFR granted by Blackacre's owner. It "shall terminate 60 days after the receipt by (the owner) of a good faith contract to purchase" Blackacre. The owner is offered a binding contract to purchase, accepts the offer, and signs the contract—and, 30 days later, the contract offeror rescinds the offer. Is the ROFR still exercisable?

Explanation

Yes. Once triggered, the ROFR ripens into an irrevocable option to purchase so long as the ROFR's term lasts. See Glick v. Chocorua Forestlands LP, 949 A.2d 693 (N.H. 2008). However, the cases on the issue are split. The contrary view is that the holder's option is exercisable only so long as the first offer is in existence: once notice of the offer and disclosure of its terms is given, the owner has fully performed his agreement; indeed, further notice is impossible—one can't give notice of an offer not in existence. See Shower v. Fischer, 737 P.2d 291 (Wash. Ct. App. 1987). Here, the mandatory nature of termination at the end of 60 days supports adoption of the former position: no matter that the contract offer is terminated, the right "shall" run for 60 days. The owner's acceptance of the contract offer, not its termination, is the proper focus.

Example 14

A ROFR provides that, "within 30 days of receipt of a good faith offer to purchase Blackacre," the right holder must match the offer. The owner with such an offer argues that the matching offer must be net or more than her tax liability on the sale. Is this argument likely to succeed?

Explanation

No. Absent an agreement to the contrary, it is the purchase price in the third party offer, and not the net amount the owner receives, that must be matched. Otherwise, the right would be ambiguous, unenforceable as an indefinite contract, and inconsistent with the parties' reasonable expectations. It would also permit the owner to subtract many costs of the sale, such as brokerage commissions. Here, the wordings' focus is on the offer, not the money received. Finally, the wording could clearly be otherwise, providing that the purchase price in the offer is "net to owner." See Fallenius v. Walker, 787 P.2d 203, 205 (Colo. Ct. App. 1999). Here it is not so clear. The holder of the right must match the offer, meaning that she must buy on the same terms and conditions as the offer received. See St. George Dragons

1. Land Acquisition

LP v. Newport Real Estate Grp. LLC, 971 A.2d 1087, 1098-1101 (N.J. Super. Ct. 2009).

Example 15

Len is leasing one half of Greenacre. The lease contains a ROFR to buy the leased premises at its then appraised fair market value. Greenacre's owner has accepted a sales contract to sell all of Greenacre. Is Len's ROFR triggered by this sales contract?

Explanation

Yes. The sale of the property burdened by the ROFR as part of a larger property sale triggers the right. (Note: some jurisdictions have decided otherwise.) The exercise of the right is consistent with the intent of the parties when negotiating it. However, permitting the right holder to exercise the right at the fair market value of one half of Greenacre's worth is to give the holder a windfall when the leased half is more valuable than the rest. Better to give the right holder an action in specific performance for the burdened property alone at a price allocating the fair market value of the leased property. See Country Visions Coop v. Archer-Daniels-Midland Co., 2021 Wis. LEXIS 54, text at nn. 10-11 (Wis., Apr. 21, 2021). Jurisdictions deciding otherwise might permit the right holder to enjoin the sale of the whole of Greenacre and leave it to the parties to negotiate the value of the injunction. See Bernard Daskal, Rights of First Refusal and the Package Deal, 22 Fordham Urb. L.J. 461 (1995).

* * *

While the largest developers might have an inventory of possible project sites, smaller ones work the field one project at a time, chary of committing both time and money except to a site where an investment might, more likely than not, pay off.

CHAPTER 2

Contracting to Acquire Project Property

A NOTE ON DRAFTING

When beginning to draft a contract of sale, and after writing the word "Contract" on the title line, the developer's attorney should think first about the prospective seller who will read it.[1] Starting with a simple standard form is best, remembering that a "standard" form is by definition one that has been worked over enough times, over a long period of time, to become standard. It may have been written over time by a partner in your firm that saw problems you won't encounter and tried to write solutions into the form. It could be a "tie the opposing party in knots" form or a form trying to meet every contingency and risk the drafter ever encountered. So start with a simple form. Then,

- Avoid "or" and "ee" words when they are confusing and sound pompous: "transferor "and "transferee" are confusing and likely to be transposed, "vendor" and "purchaser" less so; "buyer" and "seller," better still.
- Avoid words like "heretofore" and "herein": they are fuzzy cross-references. As a matter of fact, avoid cross-references altogether!
- Spell out numbers, and then in parentheses, use arabic numbers.

---

1. In a residential purchase and sale contract, many jurisdictions today have "subject to an attorney's review" clause in the contract; not so for commercial transactions because the attorney is either the drafter of the contract or has negotiated for it with the seller/landowner.

15

2. Contracting to Acquire Project Property

- Use no adjectives, no adverbs.
- Include blanks for the date, signatures, and initials on each page.
- Plain language is best; drafting isn't like a law school exam and the drafter doesn't want to sound pompous.

THE EXECUTORY PERIOD

The period of time between the completion and execution of a contract of sale for real property and the closing or settlement of the transaction is known as the executory period. It commences when the parties sign or "execute" the contract. It is a time when the contract is not yet fully performed — that is, it is subject to contingencies and "subject to" clauses. The buyer is most likely to apply for a mortgage loan, have the property inspected and appraised, and deal with attorneys searching the title and determining its marketability. All this cannot be done overnight. The usual executory period is 45 to 90 days long. The modern contract of sale for real property is replete with "subject to" clauses — as in "the closing of the title involved in this transaction is subject to" or "only to be held when the following conditions are met." The contingencies become preconditions to a closing. A precondition is an event not certain to occur that, unless its occurrence is waived, excuses further performance of a contract.

"Contingencies" is a word of double meaning. A contract provision may state, "this contract is made subject to the ability of the buyer to fund this purchase, and if he is unable to do so, this contract shall be null and void." First, this language is more precisely defined as a condition — that is, it defines an event annulling the contract. Moreover, it is a condition subsequent — that is, it states that the buyer has a contractual interest in the seller's property until he fails to fund the purchase, but that meanwhile that interest continues. In this instance, the funding occurs at closing, so the contract remains binding during the whole of the executory period. Defining a contingency as a condition subsequent may have important consequences for the buyer if (say) the improvements on the property burn to the ground while the interest continues. In a majority of states, by placing the risk of loss on the buyer, the doctrine of equitable conversion operates even though the purchaser's interest is subject to a condition subsequent.

Other cases interpreting contract contingencies have assigned them a second meaning. A contract provision may state, "this contract is made subject to the rezoning of the property from residential to commercial use." Most courts would interpret this provision to mean that the buyer, the party to benefit from the rezoning, is under an obligation to pursue the rezoning application. The basis for such an obligation is an implied covenant of good

16

2. Contracting to Acquire Project Property

faith and fair dealing. Breach of such a covenant can be the subject of waiver (by the party benefitted) or an action for breach of contract, while the occurrence of a condition subsequent is not. Its breach or performance is a precondition to the sales contract; upon its breach, there is no sales contract on which to base a suit. In some jurisdictions, unperformed contingencies of the second type delay the applicability of the doctrine of equitable conversion. However, the traditional rule is that a contract with unperformed contingencies that are nonetheless capable of performance does not prevent an equitable conversion.

In a developer's contract of purchase, where the developer is interested in either obtaining a construction loan for unimproved land, or a renovation loan for a building already built upon land, the developer's attorney will guide the developer to reduce the risks associated with the purchase.

Such a contract deals first with the business and economic risks associated with the project the developer envisions. "Envisions" is perhaps the wrong word here, because envisioning a project involves economic and market projections that the project is feasible, but what if

- the project's *pro forma* analysis does not hold up,
- the developer does not secure equity investor(s) to pay its initial costs,
- the governmental approvals needed are not obtained,
- the project is late to the market and its target customers are fewer,
- the economy around it changes, or
- the developer's creditworthiness precludes financing.

In all of these situations, the developer will want to pull out of the contract with the least financial damage.

Other risks, more particularly associated with the land or property itself, will require documents that the developer can readily anticipate. For instance, if the property does not carry zoning intense enough to justify the financial analysis, a land use procedure is in order to obtain the proper zoning classification. The developer's land use counsel can opine on present status of the land under applicable zoning and land use codes. If the public access is doubtful, or there are no utility service easements on site, reports from transportation officials and utilities on the costs of obtaining these is in order. Likewise, a geologist's or environmental report will be necessary to determine if the soil will support the intended construction, or if environmentally sensitive conditions (wetlands, protected or endangered species, preservation easements, cemeteries, contamination by hazardous substances or other pollutants, etc.) exist. Some of these may be deal-killers — particularly pollutant contamination of the land — putting the development out of reach or, more particularly, beyond the developer's economic horizon or timeline for its completion. Developers are in this instance typically not interested in proceeding under indemnity agreements with sellers, warranties

2. Contracting to Acquire Project Property

and representations that the property is free of pollution, or environmental insurance.

THE DUE DILIGENCE OR STUDY PERIOD

For these reasons, a developer's executory period is typically divided into two stages. The first is a due diligence[2] or study period, during which a developer will have access to the property and can investigate the environmental, business, and physical/geologic/ land use risks the contract must foresee. To wit: "Buyer shall have a period from the date of this contract to 5 p.m. on [day and date inserted] within which to undertake such investigations and inspections regarding the property as Buyer deems advisable." To start, the seller provides financial records, zoning and building permits, surveys,[3] his title insurance policy,[4] property and casualty insurance policies, and any existing environmental reports. The developer is likely to order his own, environmental Phase I report: this will detail whether the property contains any toxic or hazardous substances or is the subject of any environmental liens for cleaning up ("remediating" in the jargon of many environmental statutes) the site. He might also check for rights affecting the land that will not be the subject of a normal investigation of the property's title, such as public rights, natural rights (say, riparian rights), or those based on custom and usage by the public.

The contract will be "soft" during the study period, allowing the developer to either withdraw at the end of it without penalty, with a break-up fee, or by forfeiting the payment of small amounts of the earnest money or down payment for the property.[5]

---

2. As used here, due diligence is a process of investigation into the feasibility of a project. It requires that the developer be given a license, for as long as the process lasts, to enter the land free of liability for trespass.

3. The survey should show the project property's boundaries, the location of its improvements, access and utility easements, and when appropriate, areas for outlying lots, parking and recreational facilities, in sufficient detail to satisfy a mortgage lender, equity investor, and title insurer. The last will want to approve the survey when asked to eliminate the standard survey exception to its title policy. The developer should insist that old surveys be redone using newer surveying techniques and when discrepancies arise between old and new surveys, have the landowner quitclaim title using the new survey as well as warrant title using the old survey. The ALTA/NSPS Land Title Survey should suffice in this regard.

4. Unlike other forms of insurance, title insurance is a one premium agreement to indemnify an insured policy holder, in amounts not exceeding the face amount of the policy (usually set as the insured's purchase price), for actual losses caused by either on-record or off-record defects in title found to have existed on the date the policy is issued. It protects a title, not the right to possession. It does not insure against post-policy defects.

5. Issues of who holds the deposit, whether it is paid in cash or with a letter of credit, whether it will be held in an interest bearing account, and whether it is refundable in whole or part or not, are typically negotiated at this stage.

2. Contracting to Acquire Project Property

Past this first stage, the contract is "hard" or binding. In this second stage, more similar in subject matter and procedure to residential transactions, financing, surveying, and title investigations are conducted.[6]

THE PURCHASE PRICE

If a letter of intent or option has preceded the contract, a purchase price will most likely have already been negotiated and agreed on. The common law rule is that "in gross" or "per acre" or unit purchase price is to be paid in cash at the closing. The contract might additionally provide that the cash will be given to the seller by wire transfer through the Federal Reserve's electronic transfer system to a named account.

When unimproved land is the subject of the contract, the per acre or (in urban settings) the square footage of the land is often the basis for setting the purchase price as, for instance, so much per acre. A square foot measure of the price is often necessary because of zoning and land use requirements: the zoning "envelope" for the land may impose a floor area ratio—that is, one that limits the size of the improvement and prescribes a ratio of developed to open space footage on it.

Likewise, when a project property needs rezoning of some type, the purchase price at closing may vary, up or down by agreed increments, depending on the number of lots or units possible under local land use ordinances and regulations. See, e.g., Wodzisz v. Live Oak Land, LLC, 948 So. 2d 875 (Fla. Dist. Ct. App. 2007).

Not typical in good economic times is a contract provision calling for the assumption of the seller's mortgage obligations for the land, or a provision for seller's taking back a mortgage financing a portion of the purchase price. Such provisions are more common when capital markets for mortgage loans are tight.

When the purchase price for project property is stated as a whole or "in gross," the risk of a deficiency (even if substantial) in the acreage or square feet contained within the legal description or described in the contract is on the buyer. The in gross price indicates that the buyer regards the acreage or square footage as immaterial to the closing. See Turner v. Ferrin, 757 P.2d 335, 337 (Mont. 1988); Hilburn v. Brodhead, 444 P.2d 971, 974-975 (N.M. 1968), and Perfect v. McAndrew, 798 N.E.2d 470 (Ind. App. 2003). Including the term "more or less" in the legal description is a bad idea from the buyer's

---

6. Many of the provisions in a commercial real estate contract of sale will track standard provisions in any residential contract. The provision of a legal description and the allocation of the risk of loss, are illustrative. This chapter highlights some (not all) provisions likely to be contentious in the commercial setting.

19

2. Contracting to Acquire Project Property

perspective; its inclusion throws the unassigned risk of a deficiency on him. See Marcus v. Bathon, 531 A.2d 690, 694 (Md. App. 1987), cert. denied, 547 A.2d 189 (Md. 1988). When the sale is in gross, the buyer is not entitled to an abatement in the purchase price to take account of the deficiency.

On the other hand, if the purchase price is stated on a *per acre*, area, or square foot basis, the risk is on the seller; such a statement indicates that the buyer regards the acreage as an essential term of the contract. If the deficiency is substantial and a price *per acre* is stipulated, the buyer can decide to reduce the price proportionately and sue for specific performance at the abated price. He might also sue for damages or to rescind the contract, although these remedies may be more difficult to obtain. See Hinson v. Jefferson, 215 S.E.2d 102 (N.C. 1974). Why? Because here rescission must be based on a mutual mistake of fact. Turner, *supra*, at 153 ("Equity will provide a remedy when by mutual mistake the land contains materially more or less acreage than the parties believe. A slight disparity will justify equitable relief if the sale is by the acre, but, if the sale is in gross a great disparity must exist to authorize relief.").

If the price is stated in gross but the parties agreed to compute it on an acreage, area, or square foot basis, parol evidence is admissible to show the true nature of their agreement. In this regard, the need for public rezoning and subdivision approvals may present surrounding circumstances indicating the true nature of the transaction. For instance, a developer's purchase of an unimproved urban lot might be subject to floor area ratio or density regulations. In such circumstances, the contract is not inconsistent with the area computation, and parol evidence can explain how the parties arrived at the price. Use of parol here is particularly useful when urban commercial space is involved and the price is computed on a square footage basis. Similarly, the sale of land in an unbuilt residential subdivision may be on the basis of the number of buildable lots involved — a fact to be determined by subdividing the property in some way that must be approved by municipal land use officials. Likewise, a legal description including the footage of lakefront or shoreline property may indicate that such footage is essential to the development of the property.

Any representation by the seller as to the acreage will often change the results of these rules. The same is true as to seller's representations about boundaries.

Examples

Example I

Buyer and seller execute a brief but enforceable contract for lakefront property. The purchase price is "$500 a front foot, or $250,000." When surveyed, the property is found to have only 400 front feet on the lake. Should this price statement be treated as an in gross price, or not?

2. Contracting to Acquire Project Property

Explanation

If this property is undeveloped land, the arguments for treating the price as if it were stated on a *pro tanto* basis, not in gross, are substantial. This would force the seller to reduce the price to $200,000. On the other hand, if the property has a residence on it or has picturesque geographic features, treating the price as if it were stated in gross is preferable. Which will be used is a matter of ascertaining the intent of the parties as a matter of fact, and because the contract is ambiguous on this point, extrinsic evidence will be admissible to show this.

A "BREAK-UP" CLAUSE

At the end of the first stage of the acquisition contract, the developer/buyer may want to walk away from the contract. He or she would then prefer to do so without any financial liability. Thus a provision might read:

> "Buyer's obligation to purchase is effective only when the buyer determines, in his sole and absolute discretion, that the project is not suitable for the buyer's intended use."

Without any financial penalty, a court in many jurisdictions is likely to find that the "contract" is in effect an option and without consideration.[7] Taking another tack, a court might find that the "discretion" referred to is back-stopped by an implied covenant of good faith and fair dealing, limiting the discretion to "reasonably exercised discretion" and thus requiring a developer to justify its decision-making process.

A developer might add to the quoted provision: "This determination shall be made within 180 days of the execution of this contract." Such a lengthy due diligence period will likely provoke a seller's response: "let's make that 90 days." And negotiations over the length of the due diligence period will ensue.

Negotiations over the "unsuitability" referenced in the quoted clause will lead the seller—or seller's attorney—to ask for the specific risks

---

7. Except in California. See Steiner v. Thexton, 226 P.3d 359 (Cal. 2010) (finding consideration in due diligence actions of benefit to the seller: preparing reports on soil capacity, governmental approvals, or surveys performed). The holding in *Steiner* rests on the more widely applicable premise that the seller has constituted the developer his agent to procure these benefits in good faith and transfer them to the seller when the developer decides not to go forward with the purchase. However modest in amount, some nonrefundable money—perhaps $1,000 or so—should change hands as consideration before due diligence investigations begin.

2. Contracting to Acquire Project Property

the developer has in mind. A list of these risks might be a long one, but the developer is really being asked which risks he thinks most seriously about. If the land is undeveloped and in a burgeoning suburb, the list will likely be longer than it would be if the land was urban and in a built-out neighborhood. Do they pertain to the physical condition of the land? To its soil's capacity to bear the intended project? To an unfavorable environment report? This will likely prompt the developer to share his due diligence plan with the seller. Thus, the developer might be pushed to limit the scope of the determination made at the end of the due diligence period to, for instance, environmental conditions, soil capacity, or more generally, physical conditions.

"SUBJECT TO FINANCING" CLAUSE

Perhaps the next most contentiously negotiated and certainly the most litigated contingency clause is a "subject to financing" clause, in which the buyer typically agrees to close only after he has applied for and received a lender's commitment for a type of mortgage financing outlined in the clause.

Without such a clause, the default is, "all cash at closing"—that is the transaction won't close without the developer paying the purchase price in full.

The developer will pay close attention to this clause. In it he will outline the mortgage financing needs for his project. In some instances, he may be hesitant about including its provisions into a document that will be shared with the seller. Hence a need not to share too much, just enough to make the clause the subject of either a condition subsequent to the contract, or to give the developer a means to waive its benefit and close with cash without annulling the whole contract.

This type of clause is generally of benefit to the developer; he is presumed to have been its drafter, so its provisions will be construed against him. Waiving its benefit would mean at a minimum agreeing to close with cash instead of the proceeds of a mortgage loan. But the clause may arguably benefit the seller as well: obtaining a mortgage loan commitment assures him of the developer's financial ability to close the transaction. It also puts "fresh eyes" on the contract, particularly as to the purchase price. In a commercial transaction, moreover, the seller will be interested in the lender's appraisal of the property as an assurance that the purchase price is market-based.

The parties will likely negotiate the time given the developer to obtain a commitment. The seller will want a shorter time, the developer a longer one. If no time is specified, a reasonable time after executing the contract

2. Contracting to Acquire Project Property

will be implied. Better is that this clause should provide that a commitment be in the seller's hands within (say) 30 days, with further assurances of the smooth underwriting of the loan to follow.

The usual material terms of this type of clause are (1) the amount of the mortgage loan to be obtained; (2) the term of that loan, stated as a minimum term acceptable to the developer; and (3) the maximum interest rate acceptable (acceptable here may mean, in conformance with the developer's *pro forma*). These three terms are necessary to avoid a finding that the clause is void for vagueness, indefinite, or ambiguous in its provisions. Such a finding results in the parties being able to rescind the contract, and rescission will require the other party to tender back any benefits received under the contract, including the developer's deposit.

The basic triad of terms for the loan is subject to some modification without impacting the developer's *pro forma*. For instance, a lower interest rate means that a larger loan principle becomes feasible for the developer. A longer loan term means that the amortization of the loan over the term will result in lower monthly repayments. In many instances, the actual loan obtained by a developer will vary in its terms but have substantially the same financial effect on his project plans. Extended to the purchase price, this attitude gives rise to saying: "I'll pay anything for a property as long as the financing's right."

Other terms might include a maximum amount payable in closing costs on the loan, a maximum amount necessary to satisfy the lender's requirements for a mortgage escrow account for real property taxes and property hazard insurance, and a maximum amount necessary each month to repay the loan.

Executing a contract with a subject to financing clause, the buyer undertakes the implied obligation to make a reasonable effort to obtain the outlined financing. See Williams v. Ubaldo, 670 A.2d 913, n.1 (Me. 1996). Often the developer will apply for a preapproval of a mortgage loan application before executing a contract; such an early application has been held to be good evidence that the developer has shown good faith to the seller, making an effort to satisfy his part of the bargain here. Often it is held that the seller may, but need not, search for the purchaser's financing, too, but the seller may not force the buyer to accept financing not called for in the clause. See Binford v. Shicker, 553 N.E.2d 845 (Ind. Ct. App. 1990). Much depends on the words of the clause. Some Examples follow.

Examples

Example 2

Seller and developer execute a brief, enforceable contract of sale for Blackacre for $375,000. The contract provides in part "if developer is unable to obtain this loan [described below] within 60 days from this date, the developer's deposit will be refunded to him in full; otherwise the deposit

2. Contracting to Acquire Project Property

is nonrefundable." The contract is further conditioned on developer's ability "to borrow $300,000 at a conventional, fixed interest rate of 4%, for 20 years." The parties reduce the contract price in the contract to $350,000 but do not otherwise change the terms of the contract. The developer files a mortgage loan application. In response, the lender appraises the property and offers a commitment for a mortgage loan whose principal amount is $280,000 and whose interest rate is 4.25%. Ninety (90) days after the date of the contract's execution, developer walks away from the contract and requests the return of his deposit. The seller refuses. The developer sues the seller for its return. What result?

Explanation

Judgment for the seller, who is entitled to keep the deposit. While the seller will concede that the benchmark for buyer's satisfaction of the clause is a commitment for a loan, the seller has at least three arguments to make: (1) that the risk of not procuring the required loan in 60 days is the developer's; (2) that, as to the amount of the loan, considering the declining contract prices that this transaction reflects, the reduction in the purchase price implicitly amends the subject to financing clause, reducing the principal of the required loan to an amount bearing the same loan-to-price ratio as $375,000 is to $300,000 — 80%. The same ratio is maintained with a price of $350,000 and a loan amount of $280,000 — 80%. So as amended, the loan amount is satisfactory and the developer should accept it; (3) that, as to the interest rate, the seller can argue that application to only one lender cannot establish a conventional interest rate.

As to the third argument, courts have validated subject to financing clauses that provide for financing "at prevailing conventional rates and terms." Such language applies to all the terms of the financing, not just the interest rate. How are such rates and terms to be ascertained? In a majority of jurisdictions the answer comes through the good faith, reasonably diligent efforts of the buyer seeking the loan. Such an effort becomes the subject of an implied covenant attached by many courts to this type of clause. If the buyer makes a good faith effort to obtain financing and the transaction does not close due to the seller's default, the buyer recovers the deposit; on the other hand, when no good faith effort is made, the seller not otherwise in default may retain it. See Manning v. Bleifus, 272 S.E2d 821 (W.Va. 1980). Only one of the parties — the nondefaulting one — will "win" the deposit when satisfying the good faith covenant is the issue. In contrast, if the clause were to be found indefinite and the contract null and void on that account, the deposit would be returned to the buyer.

Another answer is that for purposes of fleshing out the contract as to this term, the developer becomes, upon the execution of the contract, the seller's agent for the purpose of establishing what a conventional interest

2. Contracting to Acquire Project Property

rate is. Here the good faith covenant is an implied term of the agency. This agency argument may at first seem strange to you: Why should parties who are in an adversarial relationship when negotiating a contract suddenly become principal and agent for purposes of carrying it out? The answer lies in their mutual interest in implementing the contract and the narrowness of the scope of the agency. As an agent, the buyer owes a fiduciary duty to act in good faith for the principal. This duty is breached when only one financing application is filed. So an application must be filed with a reasonable number of lenders and until the buyer does this, or else shows why one application and long discussion with a commercial lender is reasonable, he is in breach and not entitled to the deposit. See Liuzza v. Panzer, 333 So. 2d 689 (La. App. 1976).

Example 3

Would the result change if the contract called for buyer's filing only one loan application with a named conventional mortgage lender?

Explanation

No, arguably because once the agency is created its duties can supersede the contract's words, which in any event can be taken to mean that the parties intended that the agent's duty is to apply, not just to the one named lender named, but also to lenders like the named one. The support for such a view is not overwhelming and does not involve commercial transactions. See Kovarik v. Vesely, 89 N.W.2d 279 (Wis. 1958).

If the clause does not contain all of the definitive material terms for the loan, the effect of establishing the buyer's becoming an agent is that the filing of an application has the effect of providing material terms for the contract. Without it, the time and manner of the payment of the purchase price — an essential term for the contract of sale — become uncertain. The application can then be incorporated into the contract for two purposes: to satisfy the Statute of Frauds and to supply material terms for the contract.

No matter what it provides, this financing condition cannot be unconditionally fulfilled. Why? Because while a "commitment" is the benchmark for performance, the commitment will have other terms and conditions. The lender will want to oversee many steps in the prospective borrower's acquisition of the title securing its loan; it wants the title searched, appraisals done, and so forth. The terms in the contract are unlikely to cover all the ground the commitment will.

Once a mortgage commitment is obtained, the buyer/borrower is under a duty not to hinder the closing on the mortgage loan. See Bruyere

2. Contracting to Acquire Project Property

v. Jade Realty Corp., 375 A.2d 600 (N.H. 1977) (holding that when the commitment was withdrawn, the buyer breached the financing clause).

Example 4

Buyer and seller execute a brief but enforceable contract for the sale of Greenacre, containing a brief but enforceable subject to financing clause. Buyer writes a letter, asking the seller to add terms to and to approve a modification of the clause. The seller construes the letter as an anticipatory repudiation of the contract, noting that the letter does not deal with any term already in the clause. Is the seller correct?

Explanation

Yes. The contract has been repudiated or rescinded by the buyer. Be careful what you let a client write. The buyer should have written, "If you can't modify the clause, I will be forced to withdraw from the contract," indicating that he has not already done so.

Example 5

Buyer and seller execute a brief contract of sale for Blackacre. The contract conditioned the closing on "buyer's obtaining satisfactory financing." Is this contract unenforceable on account of this language? What other language might be substituted?

Explanation

Yes. Again, obtaining a commitment is the benchmark, but "available financing" would be better. From the seller's perspective, words like "satisfactory" or "suitable" are ambiguous, indicating either financing offered by the mortgage market or financing that the buyer can afford. Any meaning encompassing the buyer's financial ability gives him too easy an out; such words connote the exercise of discretion. Availability, on the other hand, is a standard subject to verification in the marketplace and, further, need not depend on the personal ability or satisfaction of the buyer with what's offered. See Gildea v. Kapenis, 402 N.W.2d 457 (Iowa 1987). "Conventional financing" is another term achieving the same result. See Stackhouse v. Gaver, 801 N.W.2d 260 (Neb. Ct. App. 2011). Both terms provide an objective,

2. Contracting to Acquire Project Property

rather than subjective, standard for fulfilling the clause and are more likely to pass judicial muster on issues such as indefiniteness and mutuality of obligation; both avoid the buyer's good faith in satisfying the clause from becoming an issue. Moreover, "satisfactory" financing makes the contract resemble an option.

Example 6

Buyer and seller condition closing their contract on "Buyer's applying for available financing from an institutional lender within 10 days of the execution of this contract." The next day buyer fills out an application, gives it to a mortgage broker to submit to a qualifying lender, and does nothing more. Ten days later, the broker submits the application to the lender, who 30 days later rejects the application. Has the buyer satisfied the clause?

Explanation

No. A mortgage broker is not a lending institution. The language here implies that the buyer will be dealing directly with the lender(s) — promoting speedy responses to lender inquiries, and so on — so the buyer makes other arrangements at his peril. What the broker does, as the buyer's agent, is imputed to him. See Vafa v. Cramer, 622 N.Y.S.2d 567 (N.Y. App. Div. 1995), discussed at 17 Cardozo L. Rev. 299 (1995). The buyer has not satisfied the clause. It is no longer a precondition to a closing. The buyer now has either to bring cash to the closing table or else the seller can declare the contract null and void.

When the time provided in the clause runs out and the buyer does nothing, the deposit is forfeited as liquidated damages. See Sanjana v. King, 101 N.Y.S.3d 289 (N.Y. App. Div. 2019) (absent a mortgage commitment satisfying the clause, it is deemed waived and the buyer must proceed with or without a mortgage or forfeit the deposit). Thus, when the buyer is a developer, the clause must clearly provide that if it is not satisfied, either the contract is (1) terminated automatically, becoming null and void, or (2) at the option of either party, subject to cancellation, or (3) in effect and the executory period continues to run and the developer will have to produce cash at the closing. In the latter instance, the seller's attorney will likely ask for a "proof of funds" letter.

Better yet, the developer's attorney should either bargain for an extension of the period in the clause during which a financing commitment may be secured or (when an all cash closing is required) bargain for an extension of the executory period, postponing the closing until cash is available for the acquisition, the developer can assume the seller's existing financing, or the seller provides a bridge loan in the meanwhile.

2. Contracting to Acquire Project Property

Example 7

Buyer and seller agree that "the obligation of Buyer to purchase under this contract is conditioned upon the issuance to Buyer of a firm written commitment for a first mortgage loan within 45 days of the execution of this contract. If at the end of 45 days, Buyer has not obtained such commitment, then either party may cancel the contract." What further changes would you suggest for this language?

Explanation

Several problems with this language might be addressed.

(1) It does not take account of the possibility that a firm mortgage commitment might be withdrawn or contain conditions that Buyer is not able to meet in good faith. (If nothing is said in the clause, the Buyer would be allocated the risk that the commitment conditions cannot be satisfied.) Thus the developer's attorney might bargain further that, in the event the commitment is withdrawn or subject to conditions Buyer cannot meet, the clause becomes unsatisfied and Buyer has the right to rescind the contract. See Seven Star Props. v. Edgewater 880 Assocs., 2020 N.J. Super. Ct. Unpub. LEXIS 1899 (N.J. Super. Ct. Sept. 29, 2020).

(2) A seller's attorney might ask that the developer agree to notify the landowner in writing that the required commitment has been obtained and continues in force up to the closing. See Penny's Inv. Corp. v. Gasamanes, 230 So. 3d 130 (Fla. Ct. App. 2017).

(3) After the 45 day commitment-seeking period, when no commitment is forthcoming, either party has the right to cancel the contract. The developer's attorney might explain this language further: in a jurisdiction in which the financing clause is intended to be of benefit to both parties, the developer will not be able unilaterally to waive the benefit of the clause. Why? Because that action would be unilaterally to waive another's benefit. See, e.g., Medina v. Dankowski, 2019 Ill. App. Unpub. LEXIS 447 (Ill. Ct. App. Mar. 20, 2019) (holding that when a financing clause is not for the buyer's sole benefit, the buyer may not unilaterally waive the clause). Thus the clause should be clear that both parties must either mutually agree to the cancellation, or else the seller should agree to adding " . . . or Buyer has the right to cancel the contract" at the end of the existing language. See Lobo IV LLC v. V Land Chi. Canal LLC, 138 N.E.3d 824 (Ill. Ct. App. 2019)

(4) In a clause of this type, the loan principal amount might be stated as "eighty percent (80%) of the purchase price." The interest rate might be stated as "a rate of interest not to exceed one hundred twenty five (125) basis points over the rate in a ten (10) year U.S. Treasury bill." The term of the loan might be stated as "ten (10) years, amortized over thirty (30) years." Stating the principal this way would eliminate the problem presented

2. Contracting to Acquire Project Property

in the first Example in this section. Further, the interest rate and term statement are in line with commercial practice and both can be determined from objective, third-party sources, avoiding charges of indefiniteness.

(5) The clause is adaptable for a permanent loan for already improved property. It is not easily adaptable to the situation in which the property is underdeveloped or unimproved and a construction loan commitment will be needed to satisfy the clause. For the latter situation, more will be said infra, Chapter 8.

WARRANTIES AND REPRESENTATIONS

The developer's attorney will want many warranties, representations, indemnities, and covenants from the seller, all reflecting the developer's due diligence and the reports produced as a result. In contrast, the seller will typically ask little of the buyer. This asymmetry reflects the level of work each performed during the preliminary stage of the contract: a lot by the buyer, little by the seller. Moreover, the buyer's attorney will typically want representations that not only will be true and accurate when made, but also will be true and accurate at the closing. Thus a procedure for updating them during the course of the executory period will be necessary.

Some representations and warranties even concern post-closing events. For instance, a buyer will often request a representation that no real estate brokers (other than those named in the contract) were involved in the transaction, should any appear post-closing and demand a commission. This representation is particularly important in jurisdictions where real estate listing and commission agreements need not be in writing. Seller will be asked to indemnify[8] the buyer for an such unexpected demand. Similar representations will be asked to the effect that there are no options, rights of first refusal or offer applicable to the property.

The seller will want to cure any representation that changes after it is initially made. The buyer on the other hand, may see some continuing representations as essential to purchasing the property and ask that any material adverse change give rise to a right not to close. Thus negotiations as to when the seller may withdraw from the contract when the accuracy of a representation changes, what representations are essential preconditions to a closing, and what remedies are available to each, will be protracted. A representation of continuing accuracy puts a burden on the seller unmatched by any on the buyer.

---

8. Any indemnity agreement intended to include attorneys' fees, must be clear and specific on this issue. See Cracker Barrel Old Country Store v. Epperson, 284 S.W.2d 303 (Tenn. 2009).

2. Contracting to Acquire Project Property

A seller's attorney may respond to the asymmetry by adding materiality and knowledge limitations to any and all representations, and by limiting the buyer's remedies to the rescission of the contract—in effect making the contract "nonrecourse"—that is, offering no further remedy. This response in effect gives the buyer the right to waive enforcement of any inaccurate representation. Another seller response is to lengthen or broaden the due diligence period: with such a response, the seller avoids giving a representation of a fact by giving the buyer time and opportunity to confirm it for himself.

Examples

Example 8

In light of the many representations likely required of the seller, what representations will the buyer make?

Explanation

A buyer's representations will confirm the existence of the buyer's legal entity both when the representation is made and at the time of the closing, and of the entity's authority to purchase and close the transaction, as well as its obligation to disclaim any objections to closing due to the nonexistence of the entity or its authority to sell and close the transaction. The inaccuracy of such representations should give the seller the right to withdraw from the transaction, but the worth of such a closing condition is of little value compared to the worth of a buyer's withdrawal rights.

Example 9

When the buyer is granted a right not to close when a "continuing accuracy" representation is found inaccurate, what further bargaining might the seller engage in?

Explanation

An eager seller might bargain for the right to have the property appraised with an eye to adjusting the purchase price up or down as appropriate. A similar adjustment might also be written into the financing clause.

2. Contracting to Acquire Project Property

Example 10

When the seller is nominally a single purpose legal entity with limited assets, the buyer's damages remedy for inaccurate representations may be worthless if its assets are disbursed right after the closing. What further remedies might the buyer negotiate for in this instance?

Explanation

Further remedies might include third party guarantees, letters of credit, or an anti-merger clause[9] in the contract, along with the ability to hold back a part of the purchase price for a post-closing period sufficient to compensate the buyer for losses due to the breach of some or all representations.

"SUBJECT TO REZONING" CLAUSE

If the developer needs to rezone[10] the property, the contract should make the closing conditional on obtaining the needed change. Otherwise the law presumes that the parties have executed the contract recognizing the present zoning and the developer will bear the risk that an existing zoning regulation does not permit the future use that he wishes to make of the property. The contract should specify the type of zoning classification sought and the use permissible after the rezoning is obtained.

Such a clause, when drafted as a condition subsequent in the contract, gives the developer standing in the legislative and administrative zoning bodies hearing the rezoning. The developer's equitable property interest is the basis for such standing. (An option to purchase, being merely a contract interest, does not confer standing.)

Obtaining a rezoning often involves negotiating with zoning officials and their staffs, so rezoning clauses should reflect the fact that many

---

9. An anti-merger clause is a provision in a contract which has the legal effect of precluding another contract provision from merging into the deed given at closing in such a way as to extinguish or otherwise eliminate the enforceability of the latter provision.

10. For purposes in this section, the terms "rezone" and "rezoning" refer broadly to any type of legislative or administrative action, at either the municipal, state, or federal level of government, pertaining to a land use or environmental statute or regulation affecting a developer's project. Thus, administrative actions involving a variance or special exception before a zoning board of appeals or adjustment, as well as a municipal legislative action for a change in the land use designation of a property (what is customarily referred to as a rezoning by land use attorneys), is included in this discussion.

2. Contracting to Acquire Project Property

rezoning applications are not denied, but are granted with conditions attached. See Steele v. Pack, 674 S.E.2d 134 (Ga. App. 2009) (rezoning not "denied" under a rezoning clause even though a condition made its satisfaction impossible). Nothing is more vital to this type of clause as a clear and objective statement of what type of governmental action removes the contingency. See Wodzisz v. Live Oak Land, LLC, 948 So. 2d 875 (Fla. Dist. Ct. App. 2007) (denying summary judgment because of a dispute of the waiver of the clause). If possible, a specific rezoning application should be incorporated by reference.

Rezoning property can be a lengthy process. Thus a developer might seek to record the contract of sale when a rezoning procedure is of uncertain outcome. Provisions in the contract for removing it from the public record might satisfy a seller's likely strong resistance for recordation. As a compromise, recording an agreed memorandum of the contract may be possible in some jurisdictions. This will maintain the confidentiality of some of the contract's provisions. However, the developer's attorney must take care that either the contract of the memorandum is in recordable form, e.g., acknowledged by the parties before a notary.

If the zoning ordinance applicable to the property subject to a contract of sale is amended or changed during the executory period, judicial opinions divide on whether the parties are excused from the performance of the contract or are presumed to have contracted with the knowledge that the zoning might change. The latter view rests on the doctrine of equitable conversion. The former depends on contract theory: if the parties are deemed to have contracted in light of existing regulations without at the same time allocating the risk of a change, the continuance of that law becomes an implied condition of the contract. Both of these theories are well established — thus the need for an express provision allocating the risk of an unforeseen change in zoning during the executory period.

Examples

Example 11

Knowing of a developer's interest in a property, a municipal legislature publishes a notice of a public hearing affecting the permitted uses of the very property a developer has eyed for a project. Days later, a developer and the property owner execute a contract for the property. At the hearing, the use of the land that the developer proposes is changed from a permitted to a prohibited use. The effectiveness of the use change relates back to the date of the notice of the hearing. The contract is silent on the allocation of the risk of a rezoning. The developer sues the landowner to rescind the contract. In this suit, what result?

2. Contracting to Acquire Project Property

Explanation

Judgment for the defendant landowner. The traditional rule applies even here. The risk of a rezoning during the executory period is on the purchaser. The legislative action is one neither party can control. However, say the courts adopting this traditional view, the purchaser is in the best position to know the use that he plans to make of the property and whether that use is permitted by the ordinance: his due diligence should include legislative receptiveness to his project. The fact that the purpose of the rezoning was to block the developer's use of the property is irrelevant: legislative motive is irrelevant and not the subject of judicial inquiry. See PH, LLC v. City of Conway, 344 S.W.3d 660 (Ark. 2009) (holding that judicial review of a legislative rezoning is limited to whether it is arbitrary and capricious and that a *de novo* review would be an unconstitutional usurpation of legislative power). The experienced developer will realize that the power of zoning officials is the power to say no.

Example 12

Same facts as in the previous Example, except that the landowner knew the developer wished to use the property in a way possible at the time of the execution of the contract but impermissible after the rezoning. Same result?

Explanation

No. Judgment now for the developer, on the grounds of a mutual mistake of fact. The facts underlying the traditional rule are distinguishable from this case. See Dover Pool & Racquet Club, Inc. v. Brooking, 322 N.E.2d 168 (Mass. 1975); see generally Restatement (Second) of Contracts §§151-152 (1977). The developer's informing the owner of his due diligence in this regard is an important step in making this "subject to rezoning" clause effective as a condition subsequent in the contract.

* * *

In addition to legislative actions, the types of land use regulations are many: they might concern the common administrative actions for a variance,[11] a special exception or a conditional use,[12] or an application for a

---

11. A variance is a waiver of the literal provisions of a land use ordinance when it works a hardship on a landowner. It may relieve an owner of either use or area requirements of the ordinance.

12. A special exception, special use, or conditional use, is a use permitted in a land use ordinance, but only conditionally, subject to the satisfaction of criteria set out in the ordinance.

33

2. Contracting to Acquire Project Property

definition of a word or phrase found in an ordinance; they might concern an environmental regulation governing wetlands or property protected in its natural state; or a finding of consistency with state-wide land use plans. Approvals of all types take time to obtain and may lengthen the executory period to a point that the developer investigating approvals might well begin obtaining them during a contract's due diligence period—or else decide not to proceed with the contract.

Approvals are vital to a project. A developer may well decide not to proceed without them. However, the same government that gives out approvals may also provide incentives for a project that lowers the developer's capital costs (by providing utility and transportation infrastructure for a project), subsidizes its net operating income (by providing property tax abatements or low interest financing), or even provides adjacent public facilities (through the use of eminent domain). See State ex rel. Brown v. City Warr Acres, 946 P.2d 1140 (Okla. 1997) (finding a valid public purpose in a city's underwriting a long-term ground lease for a business), and Maready v. City of Winston Salem, 467 S.E.2d 615 (N.C. 1996) (holding that a multimillion dollar program of governmental incentives had a valid public purpose in encouraging developers to agree to relocate businesses in the city). These cases and similar ones involve the extent to which a government may use its police power to improve the health, safety, and general welfare of the public. They are informed by the very deferential attitude of courts toward the definition of a public use or purpose as used in the Fifth Amendment to the U.S. Constitution. (" . . . nor shall private property be taken for a public use, without just compensation") as made applicable to the states in the Fourteenth Amendment. See, e.g., Kelo v. City of New London, 545 U.S. 469 (2005) (holding that the city's use of eminent domain for economic development alone was a valid public purpose). In *Kelo*, the creation of jobs and increased tax revenues was the city's public purpose for its condemnation of private property not otherwise blighted or run-down.

Rezoning permissions are subject to a well-developed case, ordinance, and statutory law. Incentives are not: they are granted according to legislative criteria rewarding some development projects but not others, so long as some valid pubic purpose is served. The fact that some developers receive a private benefit from an incentive while others do not is far from saying that an incentive program does not have a valid public purpose.

MARKETABLE TITLE CLAUSES—EXPRESS AND IMPLIED

Implied in every contract of sale is a condition subsequent that at the closing of the transaction the seller will produce evidence that his title is merchantable or marketable. (The last two words are used interchangeably, depending

2. Contracting to Acquire Project Property

on the region of the country.) A marketable title is one that a reasonable and prudent buyer would accept, that is both free from reasonable doubt and reasonably free of the possibility of litigation. "A marketable title is one that may be freely made the subject of resale." See Trimboli v. Kinkel, 123 N.E. 205 (Cardozo, J., N.Y. 1919). Whether a title is marketable is a question of law.

The benefit of the marketable title doctrine can be waived by the buyer. (Some encumbrances may be of no concern to particular purchasers and the benefits to them of certain encumbrances, such as utility easements, must be considered as well.) The seller has the burden of proving a title marketable, although in many regions of the country the buyer may actually pay for the title search and examination.

The implied condition that a title will be marketable is likewise applied when the buyer's presents a quitclaim deed at closing. A contract of sale calling for the use of a quitclaim deed is not a waiver of an implied (by law) obligation that the seller produce a marketable title at the closing. A buyer should not be held to have waived such an important protection unless he does so clearly. By definition, a quitclaim affects the seller's warranties but need not affect the standard of marketability of the title that the seller must produce.[13] In some situations, quitclaim deeds are commonly used — for instance, by trustees conveying property from a trust.

Further, an "as is" provision in a contract of sale is typically only a reference to the physical and use characteristics of the land (for instance, to improvements on it), and not to its title. The law's strong implication that a requirement for a marketable title survives in this instance too.

A higher title standard is a title "marketable of record," meaning that each link in the chain of title leading to the seller is evidenced by a deed or other public document or recorded instrument. For example, a probate decree and a court judgment are public records, admissible and self-proving in court, but a title based on adverse possession, while marketable, is not "marketable of record" until embodied in a judicial decree. A developer's attorney often insists on this higher standard. For instance, a call for an attorney's approval of the title would in effect impose a higher title standard because disapproval would rescind the contract. Otherwise the seller would have the right to make the title marketable during the executory period, and here the attorney may advise against doing so.

An "insurable title" standard is generally taken to mean "marketable and insurable" — marketable, as that basic title call is incorporated by implication

---

13. Some title companies will not, however, issue a title insurance policy when the title is based on a quitclaim deed. Why? The deed will then limit the insurer's subrogation rights after paying a claim and many insurers regard its presence in the chain of title as a red flag indicating undisclosed title problems either created by the seller or existing in the chain of title.

2. Contracting to Acquire Project Property

into every contract of sale, as well as insurable with a title insurance policy customarily used in the jurisdiction. If the contract called for "a marketable and insurable title," the second adjective adds nothing. It does imply, however, that the title insurance policy called for will contain the usual coverage and the usual exclusions and exceptions, and be issued at regular premium rates. The title insurer may in some regions of the country provide coverage for the unmarketability of a title, but if the title is unmarketable to begin with, it will not provide title insurance.

A contract calling "a title insured by the XYZ Title Insurance Company" is also valid as a matter of law, but it is advisable for a party to test any preprinted insurer's name to make sure that another, equally reputable title insurer would be acceptable as well. If another is not, then the possibility of an illegal business tie-in with the named insurer should be considered — and avoided — by the party to whom the suggestion is made.

In some regions of the country, the mechanics of showing a title to be marketable work like this: first, the seller produces his evidence of title; second, the buyer examines the evidence. Elsewhere, the buyer assembles the title evidence from the public records and then examines it. No matter how the evidence is produced, it is the buyer's obligation to object to any defects in the title and to have the vendor cure them by the time of the closing. If a defect is not objected to and cured by then, it is deemed to be waived by the buyer.

Examples

Example 13

The abstract shows that the title is subject to an unsatisfied mortgage with a 20-year term and a $20,000 principal amount. The mortgage was executed a decade ago, but the holder of the mortgage lien cannot be located. Is V's title marketable?

Explanation

No. The mortgage lien could be foreclosed anytime within its term, plus whatever time the applicable statute of limitations for mortgages provides. When the term of the mortgage is 20 years, the mortgage is still enforceable, and the title is thus not reasonably free of the possibility of litigation, the mortgagee having ample time to show up, demand the payments due, and bring an action to foreclose the lien. If the mortgage were executed 60 years ago, the answer would change. The probabilities then are that the mortgage is now unenforceable by an action in foreclosure. The mortgagee has probably abandoned or waived enforcement of the lien and the statute of limitations has run on its enforcement. A finding of marketability requires no more than a reasonable degree of freedom from litigation; it

2. Contracting to Acquire Project Property

is not a guarantee to the purchaser that no litigation will occur or that no encumbrance exists.

Example 14

The abstract shows that a mechanic's lien for $5,000[14] has been filed against the project property. Is the seller's title marketable? If not, what is the buyer's remedy?

Explanation

No. The title is unmarketable, but the remedy is a simple escrow established before or at the closing in an amount sufficient to prevent the lien from being foreclosed.[15]

Example 15

A brief but enforceable contract of sale for project property calls for the seller to deliver a fee simple absolute to buyer "subject to easements of record." During the executory period the adverse user of an undocumented easement over the property ripens into adverse possession. Is the title marketable?

---

14. Mechanics lien laws vary from jurisdiction to jurisdiction. Unpaid contractors and material suppliers on construction sites may file such a lien on property that has benefitted from their work or materials; they are given a definite period of time—usually weeks or months—to file after payment is due. The priority of such liens relates back to an earlier date, often the date on which work commenced or materials were delivered. Other than these points, generalities about these statutory liens are hazardous for an attorney not familiar with the applicable law. One generality is possible, however, and that is when filed, such a lien must state the amount sought. Standard form American Land Title Association (ALTA) title insurance policies contain an exception for mechanics liens.

15. The attorneys involved in a transaction should not serve as escrow agents in this situation. An attorney represents one party; an escrow agent is the mutual agent of both parties and has a duty to be impartial in carrying out the escrow. This role conflict will prevent the attorney from continuing to represent both buyer and seller in the event of any dispute over the escrow. A third party, often the title company, is a better choice as escrow agent. It will likely have a clear escrow agreement at hand for this situation or any other involving encumbrance or lien that can be monetized.

37

2. Contracting to Acquire Project Property

Explanation

Title by adverse possession is generally a marketable title if the proof required to establish it is available to the buyer. However, this rule is for the benefit of the holder of the dominant estate benefitting from the easement. It does not apply here. The buyer of the servient estate should not be forced to buy a lawsuit. Marketability is shown at the closing and here the title will then be burdened with the easement. The title is unmarketable and the buyer need not accept it, absent an agreement to the contrary. Whether the "subject to easements of record" language is an agreement to the contrary is a matter of contract interpretation. The language means "subject to easements existing on the record as of the closing date." An easement arising by adverse possession is not one evidenced on the public records; rather it arises through the actions of the adverse possessor. The buyer has not agreed to accept it. If the suit to establish the easement were reduced to judgment by the closing date, the judgment will be "of record." A title need not be shown to be marketable until the closing. The vendor is given the executory period to get the title into a marketable condition.

Example 16

A contract calls for a fee "subject to leases" and "marketable of record." During the executory period a tenant's lease expires and the seller renews it for another term. Is the seller's title marketable?

Explanation

No. Here the seller is actively creating an encumbrance on the title. This is a slander[16] of the buyer's equitable interest in the title. Buyer need not accept a title subject to the lawsuit he would have to bring, for slander of title, against the seller. In a commercial transaction, the contract should permit a buyer during the due diligence period to review all leases affecting the property, request estoppel letters from all tenants, and then ask the seller

---

16. Slander of title is a tort action requiring the plaintiff to prove that the defendant "uttered a false statement" about the plaintiff's title to real property, which statement resulted in actual loss by the plaintiff. Likewise, anyone recording a contract of sale with the knowledge that it is unenforceable for any reason is liable in an action for slander of title. Recording the contract is the utterance and when the recording is made with knowledge that the recording party does not have an enforceable interest in the property, malice is sometimes presumed by the fact of the recording itself, although in some jurisdictions, actual malice must also be shown. See Rogers Carl Corp. v. Moran, 246 A.2d 750 (N.J. Super. 1968). Finally, the necessary element of an actual loss might be indicated by a lost sale.

2. Contracting to Acquire Project Property

for a representation that they are valid and that there are no other leases. The representation should be true and accurate when made and continuous during the executory period.

"TIME IS OF THE ESSENCE" CLAUSE

Time is seldom "of the essence" in a commercial transaction involving project real estate. When the parties execute the contract of sale, they seldom know all of the problems that arise during the executory period to prevent a scheduled closing: for instance, the buyer's satisfying the conditions of a loan commitment may take longer than anticipated. The longer the list of closing conditions in the contract, the less essential a closing date is likely to be. Thus the closing date is seldom an essential term of the contract. In some jurisdictions, e.g., New York, "time of the essence" clauses are not even customary.

Seldom doesn't mean never. A seller's health may be in decline, he needs to book a gain or loss before the end of his tax year, or the transaction is part of an IRC §1031 like-kind exchange of properties requiring meeting strict time deadlines. In such situations time may be made of the essence in the contract.

Traditionally, in an action for damages for breach of contract, a call for a closing on a certain date (e.g., "Settlement shall occur by [a date certain]") is sufficient to make damages available from the party not ready to close on that date when the party seeking damages tenders whatever performance is due at the closing, unless that performance is excused, e.g., by the nonperforming party's anticipatory repudiation. See Cohen v. Kranz, 189 N.E.2d 473 (N.Y. 1963). The use of the phrase like "time is of the essence in this contract" means that each closing condition in the contract shall be performed promptly at the time or date specified. A failure to perform is taken as a waiver of the other party's performance. See Marioni v. 94 Broadway, Inc., 866 A.2d 208, 220 (N.J. Super. Ct.), cert. denied, 874 A.2d 1109 (N.J. 2005).

However, in equity, time is not of the essence unless expressly made so in the contract or implied from circumstances available to interpret the contract. Time not being essential in equity, a standard of due diligence is substituted; so specific performance is available to a buyer, even after a date fixed for performance or closing and remains available for a reasonable time after that date.

Today, in both legal and equitable actions, fixing a specific date for closing in a contract does not make time of the essence. See Parker v. Byrne, 996 A.2d 627 (R.I. 2010), and Kalalik v. Bernardo, 439 A.2d 1016, 1019 (Conn. 1991). Thus a failure to perform or close on a stipulated date is not *per se* a

39

2. Contracting to Acquire Project Property

breach of the contract actionable by the nonbreaching party; a later performance might well be found to be substantial performance.

If no time is set for a closing, a reasonable amount of time is implied. See Bryan v. Moore, 863 A.2d 258 (Del. Ch. 2004) (finding a 30-day delay not unreasonable as a matter of law). But a contract lacking a time is of the essence clause is no excuse for a party's not closing on the day, time, and place named in the contract. See Mouat v. Wolfe, 556 A.2d 99, 101 (Vt. 1989) ("Where time is *not* of the essence, the buyer who tenders payment late *may* bring a suit in equity, depending on the reasonableness of the delay, to compel delivery"), and The Winterton, LLC v. Winterton Inves., LLC, 900 N.E.2d 754 (Ind. App. 2009).

A contract may set a date for closing, but when a reasonable time after that date is past, either of the parties can make time of the essence, in both law and equity, by a clear notice setting a future closing date, reasonably distant from the time of the notice. Thus, even when the parties to a contract postpone a closing twice but thereafter agree to make time "of the essence" for a third closing, the mere use of those words may persuade a court to make it so, refusing to examine extrinsic evidence of the parties' intent to determine whether both parties knew the words' impact. See Arnhold v. Ocean Atlantic Woodland Corp., 284 F.3d 693 (7th Cir. 2001) (holding that substantial, though late, performance is then insufficient). Further, when the contract is silent on a closing date, either party during the executory period may call for a closing within a reasonable time

Making performance an essential term; coupled with a forfeiture can easily make a contract into an option, as in "time is of the essence of this contract: If the purchaser does not make full settlement within 90 days, the deposit is forfeit as the vendor's sole remedy and purchaser relieved of all further liability hereunder." See Dixon v. Haft, 253 A.2d 715 (Md. 1969), discussed in Green Manor Corp. v. Tomares, 295 A.2d 212 (1972). That time is an essential term may be implied from the forfeiture alone.

No matter how long it may take a party to meet the contract's closing conditions, the contract should set an outside closing date. In some jurisdictions, moreover, failing to include this may make the whole contract void under the Rule Against Perpetuities. For instance, setting the closing for a date "when the buyer's loan commitment is funded"—an indefinite date in the future—is neither prudent nor without legal risk.

Examples

Example 17

In a land market in which prices are falling, a farmer agrees to sell his farm to a developer. The contract of sale calls for a closing "within three months." After three months and one week, the developer has not closed the deal. Is time of the essence in this contract?

2. Contracting to Acquire Project Property

Explanation

Here the essentiality of the time of the closing can be implied from the market circumstances surrounding the contracts. Making time an essential term prevents the developer from waiting to make a better deal with the farmer. See Kasten Constr. Co. v. Maple Ridge Constr. Co., 226 A.2d 341 (Md. 1967), and Doering v. Fields, 50 A.2d 553 (Md. 1947).

Example 18

A contract provision states that a failure to make any one of two executory period deposits on the date named "is essential to the performance of this contract" and when buyer fails to make any one of these, the sums so far on deposit are forfeited to the seller. The buyer makes the first but not the second deposit. Thereafter the buyer brings an action for specific performance of the contract. May the buyer have a decree in specific performance?

Explanation

Yes, but only if the buyer is willing to put all of the purchase price in readiness, even in escrow with the court, to fulfill his contract obligations. Specific performance requires a full tender of performance by the plaintiff. The buyer must pay the full purchase price, without any credit for the first deposit. After all, the first deposit is forfeited under the terms of the contract. No closing date has been set; therefore the equitable rule of due diligence controls and the decree of specific performance can set a reasonable closing date.

ANTI-ASSIGNMENT CLAUSE

During the negotiations for a contract, a landowner and a developer have an opportunity to size each other up. The seller has decided to sell to the buyer—and in some cases, may have dealt with several prospective buyers before making this decision—and should realize that the general rule is that unless the assignment of the contract is expressly restricted, the buyer will, immediately upon executing it, have the right to assign it. As with other types of contracts, free assignability is the rule. This may lead the seller to conclude that if other prospects are waiting in the wings to buy, this assignability should be restricted. Or the seller may wish to propose

41

some restriction in order to see if the buyer is the agent of an undisclosed principal. (There is nothing fraudulent about being such an agent if no misrepresentations are made.)

When the buyer resists a blanket prohibition on an assignment, one alternative might be: "This contract shall not be assigned unless the seller consents in writing, such consent not to be unreasonably withheld." This gives the seller an opportunity to determine if the proposed assignee is just as (say) honest or creditworthy as the buyer. Another alternative is for the seller to permit assignability more freely but insist on the right to capture some or all of the profit the buyer makes "flipping" the contract.

Like the contract itself, its assignment is subject to the Statute of Frauds and must be in writing. The buyer/assignor does not warrant the marketability of the seller's title or the contract's performance; he only warrants its existence. If the title is unmarketable, this is not a failure of consideration for the assignment: the assignee may not thereafter recover the money paid for it. (This means that the assignee will likely insist that the money he paid be put into an escrow pending the closing.) Likewise, the assignee takes subject to any defenses based on the contract and available to the seller. An assignment in violation of any anti-assignment clause is nonetheless a valid contract between the assignor and the assignee for purposes of the latter's suit for damages.

REMEDIES FOR A BREACH

Buyers and sellers typically want to walk away liability-free from a contract gone sour—or at least walk away with their liabilities set within clearly defined limits. The template for remedies in a development contract is, for the seller, damages with a cap or maximum amount, and for a buyer, specific performance. This template isn't far from the bargained-for result in many situations, but requires some explanation and further detail.

As to the seller's damages remedy, the rationale is that, after the buyer's breach of contract, the seller will still have the property and can resell it, thus the seller is often limited to nominal or out-of-pocket damages (what he or she could have recovered at common law before the advent of specific performance in the early nineteenth century). Many buyers will bargain further for a provision that such nominal damages also be liquidated damages, knowing that in many jurisdictions courts will infer that such a statement means that the provision for damages is a seller's exclusive remedy. See, e.g., Seabaugh v. Keele, 775 S.W.2d 205 (Mo. Ct. App. 1989). If the land is in a neighborhood subject to development, moreover, the resale should be quick as developers compete for land "ripe" for development. Further, a seller's suit for damages will only encourage a counterclaim by the buyer

2. Contracting to Acquire Project Property

for specific performance, tying up the property and preventing its resale: As a result, sellers are given an incentive to settle for nominal damages.

When sellers insist on more than nominal amounts of damages in a falling market, buyers sometimes bargain to have the seller's damages measured, not at the time of the breach, but at the time of the seller's resale of the property. This in effect limits the seller's damages remedy.

Thus, in a commercial transaction, seller landowners typically insist that the seller either not be subject to a damage remedy, or be subject to only a nominal amount of damages, thus leaving the developer buyer either to rescind the contract unilaterally or sue for specific performance of it when the seller is in breach. See Jones v. White Sulphur Springs Farm, Inc., 605 S.W.2d 38 (Ky. App. 1980) (holding that a breach must be "grave" to justify unilateral rescission). This limitation is important when the seller is a trust or a legal entity such as a limited liability company or limited partnership. Since rescission requires the parties to return to their position *status quo ante*, the buyer may also recover its transaction costs, that is, the amount spent in the due diligence study period and during the binding executory period thereafter. (The contract should expressly either permit or negate such a recovery.)

As to the buyer's specific performance remedy, it rests on the rationale that real property is not fungible like money—the common law word was that real property was "unique" and so damages as a remedy was inadequate, hence a preference for specific performance as the most efficient method of giving the buyer what he expected. That rationale functions uneasily in a commercial real estate transaction because of the developer's desire to turn the project property into an income producing asset with rents and profits of various types. Moreover, as to the damages remedy being inadequate, developers often can predict what the rent roll will be when marketing and *pro forma* analyses are available at the time of the seller's breach—these are sometimes called collateral lost profits, deriving from contracts in the offing when development occurs. That is, the more the value of the property is to be monetized, the less applicable is the usual rationale for giving the buyer the remedy of specific performance. Further, since a suit for specific performance will become a cloud on the seller's title when a *lis pendens*[17] is filed in connection with the suit, sellers often bargain for a time-limit on the buyer's filing such a suit—typically within three months of the breach.[18]

---

17. A *lis pendens* (law Latin for "suit pending") is a recorded notice that a lawsuit has been filed involving the title to real property. Recording this notice alerts a potential purchaser or lender that the property's title is disputed; this renders its title unmarketable and subject to the outcome of the lawsuit.

18. The outside limit on the time for filing should be well within the due diligence period for any back-up prospective buyer's contract for the property.

2. Contracting to Acquire Project Property

Why then is even the severely limited remedy of specific performance allowed the developer buyer? If nominal and compensatory damages are computable, why force the breaching seller to yield up the project property pursuant to a decree of specific performance. The answer may be that those damages, even when available and computable, are inadequate. They are inadequate in the sense that after expending time and money in doing due diligence, hiring expert appraisers, engineers, architects, city planners, environmental consultants, all working over a span of time sufficient to arrange construction and permanent financing and to rezone the project property to a use suitable for development, the developer has undertaken risks that the development won't materialize and has meanwhile invested indebted funds and has built equity in the property. These investments have occurred over a span of perhaps a year or more and the developer can't retrieve them any more than he can get the time back.

In a commercial real estate transaction, there is also an asymmetry of effort: the developer buyer's efforts are extreme when compared to the seller's.[19] So specific performance remains his go-to remedy, even when it is severely limited in time and even if damages might recoup lost profits.[20] It is moreover the remedy that least changes the developer's costs in negotiating the contract.

This rationale for the developer's specific performance action leaves the seller hoping that the developer buyer will not pursue specific performance because, to do so, he will still have to show that (1) damages are inadequate and (2) the costs of his due diligence efforts, risks, and investments of time and effort are not speculative.

When limiting a seller's liability to a legal entity, buyers a should be concerned that sellers (if an entity) will immediately take the purchase price tendered at closing and disburse it to the members or partners in the selling entity, leaving the entity an asset-less shell unable to satisfy a judgment against it. Thus any damage remedy against the seller will likely be backstopped by a third-party guarantee or letter of credit covering both any post-closing contractual or tort liability. Likewise, a seller should investigate the financial adequacy of any entity used by the buyer to take title.

Buyers may bargain for both nominal and consequential damages, but will often agree to the former or to damages capped by the amount(s) paid as earnest money or down payment during the executory period. So limited, damages may then be described as the exclusive damage remedy, forfeited

---

19. Recall that the asymmetric situation is reversed in the case of warranties and representations: there the seller strains to meet the buyer's expectations while the buyer makes many fewer representations to the seller.

20. An exception might be made for property bought for flipping and speculation; in this instance, the property has no business-value for a buyer. Such a buyer might well agree to damages as an exclusive remedy. Such a buyer might be a developer "warehousing land" either for future use or to keep it out of the hands of competitors.

2. Contracting to Acquire Project Property

as liquidated damages. When the developer is taking title at closing with an entity such as a limited liability company or partnership, the contract will limit its liability in damages to the assets of the entity so as to protect the members or partners involved from personal liability.

Remedies of whatever type—damages, specific performance or rescission—should be expressly labeled as being either alternative or exclusive. For instance, the forfeiture of a deposit as liquidated damages will typically be an alternative to a seller's suit for specific performance. See Palmer v. Hayes, 892 P.2d 1059 (Utah Ct. App. 1995), and Perroncello v. Donahue, 859 N.E.2d 827 (Mass. 2007). In some jurisdictions, just permitting the retention of the deposit as liquidated damages does not waive other remedies. See Margaret H. Wayne Tr. v. Lipsky, 846 P.2d 904 (Idaho 1993). Moreover, remedies of all three types should be named and labeled as either available or not. Keeping in mind that negotiating the availability of each remedy in the contract is cheaper than litigating about its availability later, both buyers and sellers should have ample incentive to reach an agreement on this matter.

When agreeing on which remedy which party has, the parties should also, in a separate section of the contract, define which closing conditions are subject to waiver, and by whom. For instance, typically a buyer may waive a financing condition, but the seller may not. Likewise, the seller's delivery of tenant estoppel certificates assuring the buyer that existing leases are valid and binding, and an irrevocable commitment of a title insurer to issue the buyer a policy of title insurance, are generally a buyer's preconditions to a closing. Unmet conditions exceeding a defined value may also entitle the buyer to terminate the contract or turn some conditions into post-closing obligations of the seller. Unmet conditions or representations may also be subject to a right to cure. See Weintraub v. Stankovic, 840 N.Y.S.2d 487 (N.Y. App. Div. 2007) (not extending seller a right to cure when express in a contract was itself a breach of contract). Thus a failure to meet a closing condition, which normally excuses non-performance by the opposite party, need not become a breach of the contract.

CHAPTER 3

Environmental Concerns

Matters involving environmental laws and regulations arise early and often in real property transactions these days—as early as when the broker shows a listed property. In commercial transactions, they are likely to arise during the due diligence period provided for in the contract of sale. This is a period during which the purchaser investigates the property, its financial position, its marketing potential, and its physical characteristics. At this point, environmental risks often prove a deal-breaker. Common law theories of negligent misrepresentation, fraud, and infliction of emotional distress sometimes involve environmental statements, reports, risks, and even phobias. In addition, when a broker uses amenities in the off-site environment as a selling point for property, he or she should be careful to investigate and disclose to the developer those problems in that environment as well.

CONTRACT OF SALE DISPUTES

Environmental problems give rise to several types of legal disputes involving the transfer of real property. Here is a survey of three of them, all based on the documents involved in such transactions that set out the parameters of an environmental dispute.

3. Environmental Concerns

Marketable Title

Marketable property means land and improvements that have value, but a marketable title is one that is reasonably free of the possibility of litigation. Thus, marketable property and marketable title are not the same.

Contamination or pollution with a hazardous waste does not render the title to land unmarketable. The contamination refers to the physical nature of the land, not the title to it. A buyer's remedy when contamination by pollutants is found would have to be an environmental contingency clause in the contract or representations and warranties against such conditions. Nevertheless, since marketable title is a common law doctrine, an environmental law, statute, or regulation mandating the clean up of a property may result in the levy of a fine or penalty, or a lien or judgment that, on being levied or docketed, becomes a matter of public record, and so affects marketability of title.

Deed Warranties

The conveyance of contaminated land is not a breach of the warranty of title. See United States v. Allied Chemical Corp., 587 F. Supp. 1205 (N.D. Cal. 1984). Following this lead, every court litigating the same issue has refused to expand both the marketable title doctrine or the type of encumbrances included in a deed warranty to make the presence of hazardous waste an encumbrance on title. See HM Holdings v. Rankin, 70 F.3d 933, 936 (7th Cir. 1995); and see generally Comment, Toxic Clouds on Titles, 19 B.C. Envtl. Aff. L. Rev. 355, 378-382 (1991). Thus again, a buyer's remedy must lie in environmental contingencies or representations and warranties in the contract of sale.

Title Insurance

The contamination of land whose title is insured does not by itself create a claim that there is an encumbrance or title defect under a title insurance policy. Some courts hold that a standard exclusion in the policies for environmental laws applies. Others hold that there is no coverage for land use matters as opposed to title matters. See South Shore Bank v. Stewart Title Guar. Co., 688 F. Supp. 803 (D. Mass. 1988), and Chicago Title Ins. Co. v. Kumar, 506 N.E.2d 154 (Mass. App. 1987). Only when a lien for cleanup costs has been filed, and not disclosed and excepted by the title insurer searching the title, does the insured have a claim under a policy. Policies otherwise specifically exclude state and federal "superliens" for the recovery of environmental cleanup costs. Policy endorsements for environmental cleanup liens are available in many states. They will generally cover only

3. Environmental Concerns

liens arising under the authority of specifically named federal or state statutes. Likewise, the insurance afforded by the endorsement will be effective only for specifically named land uses.

MORTGAGE DISPUTES

Most mortgages, residential or commercial, contain covenants providing (in paraphrase) that the mortgagor/borrower shall not cause or permit the presence, use, disposal, storage, or release of any hazardous substance[1] on or in the secured property, nor violate or permit the violation of any applicable environmental law, except for the presence, use, or storage of small quantities of hazardous substances generally recognized as appropriate for the property's normal use and maintenance; Likewise, once a violation is noted or noticed to the mortgagor that any removal or other remediation of any such substance is necessary, borrower shall promptly clean up the property.

In a commercial mortgage, specific references to particular environmental statutes appear in similar covenants. State and federal governmental liens to recover governmental costs incurred for cleaning up a hazardous substance typically will take priority over the lender's mortgage lien. Under such covenants the lender typically acquires no right to step in and perform any compliance cleanups. Actually, that's the last thing a lender would want to do, because a right to clean the secured property might later become the basis of finding a duty to do so.

The presence of hazardous substances on real property is of great concern to both sellers, buyers, and mortgage lenders, particularly when the latter are about to foreclose their liens.

When only a portion of a commercial, multi-parcel, mortgaged real property is affected by hazardous substances, a foreclosing mortgagee may elect a partial foreclosure, foreclosing only on the uncontaminated portions of the secured property. See Pownal Dev. Corp. v. Pownal Tanning Co., 765 A.2d 489 (Vt. 2000). Such an election frees the remainder of the property of the foreclosed lien. It is an abandonment of the lien as to the unforeclosed portion. This process is a variant of the doctrine of marshalling.[2] Were it otherwise, more than necessary amounts of land would be rendered

---

1. Here "hazardous substances" means those substances defined as toxic or hazardous substances by statute as well as gasoline, kerosene, other flammable or toxic petroleum products, toxic pesticides and herbicides, volatile solvents, materials containing asbestos or formaldehyde, and radioactive materials.

2. The doctrine of marshalling provides that where two or more lien holders seek foreclosure on the same property, where one lien applies to part of the property and the other applies to the whole property, the lien applying to the whole may be required to seek satisfaction from only so much of the whole as satisfies its lien.

3. Environmental Concerns

unusable, and so partial foreclosure promotes the free alienability of land and the equitable nature of foreclosure.

In addition, mortgage lenders engaged in workout negotiations with mortgagors must review environmental indemnity and insurance policies to determine the effect of the workout on these agreements.

When a commercial mortgage is to be pooled with other mortgages, securitized, and sold to investors in the secondary market, the major rating agencies for these securities require a Phase I environmental audit of the secured property. The audit is performed according to the widely accepted ASTM International (formerly the American Society for Testing and Materials) (ASTM) standards. When environmental problems are found, the agencies require an indemnity agreement, environmental insurance, a government-approved remediation plan, an escrow of estimated remediation costs, and/or a no further action letter with a covenant not to sue from the government before the loan is put in the pool. See Edmund Greene, Environmental Best Practices for Commercial Real Estate Financing, Prac. Real Est. Law. (Sept. 2006), at 41. These requirements, imposed on commercial mortgages destined for the secondary market, mean that when a Phase I audit finds environmental problems with a property a developer contracts to buy, the prospective purchase is unlikely to proceed past the due diligence stage of the developer's contract's executory period.

HAZARDOUS SUBSTANCES

Hazardous substances being released into the ground is a nationwide problem that is strictly regulated. Federal regulation came about in response to incidents like one involving the disposal of poisons into groundwater around Buffalo, New York (the so-called Love Canal incident); congressional legislation to address this problem was introduced for six years in the House, and three years in the Senate, before Congress enacted the Comprehensive Emergency Response, Compensation, and Liability Act (CERCLA) in 1980.

CERCLA

CERCLA's legislative history found that over 2,000 sites in the country had been used for the disposal of hazardous substances,[3] that many more were

---

3. The act created a so-called Superfund site list, a/k/a National Priorities List (NPL). As of the end of 2018, some 46,000 sites had been investigated for hazardous substances, and about 220,000 were cleaned up and ready for re-use. See Walter Mugdan, Superfund Update, 35 Prac. Real Est. Law. 45 (Mar. 2019).

3. Environmental Concerns

contaminated in other ways, and that the costs of cleaning them all up would be immense.[4] Moreover, many sites were abandoned — and no one appeared responsible for cleaning them up. Thus, in addition to the liability of present owners for cleanups, past owners had to be made liable as well.

CERCLA has three principal objectives: (1) to find an effective device for protecting the public from the health and safety hazards posed by the land parcel's contamination, (2) to place the burden and the costs of cleaning up upon those responsible for the contamination, and (3) to deter future similar disposals of hazardous substances. Many courts have found the purpose of the statute to be "overwhelmingly remedial," meaning that the statute's purpose is to restore a site's environmental quality and that courts therefore interpret its provisions liberally and with an eye to imposing liability for a site's remediation. See United States v. Fleet Factors Corp, 819 F. Supp. 1079, 1083-1084 (S.D. Ga. 1993) (citing cases).

CERCLA creates private causes of action, as well as an action by the government, to recover cleanup costs. To incur liability under CERCLA, a waste or hazardous substance site must be a "facility" at which a "release" or "threatened release" of any "hazardous substance" has occurred or may occur and which causes the public or private plaintiff to incur response costs in cleaning up the substances.

As to the identity of the defendant, CERCLA makes the current owner or operator of a regulated site strictly liable for the costs of cleaning it up, regardless of whether that person or entity owned or operated the property at the time of its contamination. See Tanglewood East Homeowners v. Charles-Thomas, Inc., 849 F.2d 1568, 1572 (5th Cir. 1988). It makes four categories of persons (potentially responsible persons or PRPs) responsible for the disposal and cleanup. No developer wants to become a PRP.

As to the four categories of PRPs, see 42 U.S.C. §9607(a) (CERCLA §107(a):

(1) the *owner and operator* of . . . a facility,
(2) any person who at the time of *disposal* of any hazardous substance owned or operated any facility at which such . . . substances were disposed of,
(3) any person who by contract, agreement, or otherwise *arranged* for disposal or treatment, or arranged . . . for disposal or treatment, of hazardous substances owned or possessed by such person . . . , and
(4) any person who accepts or accepted any hazardous substances for transport to disposal or treatment facilities . . . .

---

4. Mugdan, op. cit., reports nearly $65 billion has been incurred in clean-up expenses — $25 billion by the government and nearly $40 billion by private parties liable under CERCLA. With such amounts involved, the government has ample incentive to sue landowners and others for recovery of its costs and enforcement of its injunctions and orders.

3. Environmental Concerns

Subsections (1) and (2), taken together, make plain that Congress intended that this statute be retroactive in its reach: it applies to present and past owners of contaminated property. See Carson Harbor Vill., Ltd. v. Unocal Corp., 270 F.3d 863, 870-871 (9th Cir. 2001), cert. denied, 535 U.S. 971 (2002). Moreover, all of the foregoing PRPs "shall be liable for—"

(A) all costs of removal or remedial action incurred by the United States Government or a State . . . ;

(B) any other necessary costs of response incurred by any other person; and

(C) damages for injury to, destruction of, or loss of natural resources, including the reasonable costs of assessing such injury, destruction, or loss resulting from such a release.

The retroactive effect of §107(a) was challenged as a matter of constitutional law, as a violation of the *ex post facto* clause. However, that clause is generally taken to prohibit and limit penal, but not civil, liability; civil liability may be imposed *ex post facto*.

The reach of this statute is broad indeed, as is apparent in a discussion of the highlighted terms. First, the phrase *owner and operator* means the present owner(s) holding a legal interest in the property. Similarly, an operator is a lessee, a licensee, or the holder of a possessory interest in the tainted property.

This three-word phrase—*owner and operator*—in §107(a)(1) is written in the conjunctive in the statute, but many courts have read it in the disjunctive in order to broaden the reach of the statute. So §(a)(1) is taken to apply to present owners while §(a)(2), immediately following, expressly applies the statute to past owners. Thus, a developer as the landlord of a project property is just as liable as one of his tenants who violates CERCLA.

A *facility* is defined in §9601(9) as "any building . . . or any site where a hazardous substance has been deposited, stored, disposed of, or placed, or otherwise came to be located." And a *disposal* includes the "discharge, deposit, injection, dumping, spilling, leaking or placing" of any hazardous waste so that it "may enter the environment or be emitted into the air or discharged into any waters, including groundwater." A disposal can be either an active or a passive action. Thus, a developer who uncovers or disturbs a hazardous substance on land he owns may have, in the course of a project's construction, "disposed" of it and violated CERCLA: more precisely, uncovering or disturbing hazardous substances and causing them to mix with clean soil is a "disposal" and violates CERCLA.

Similarly, *arranged* means liability for an "arranger" for disposal or treatment of a hazardous substance, not just the person who actually treats or disposes of it. "Arranged" implies intentional action directed toward a specific purpose—e.g., a developer's cleanup of contaminated land. Thus,

3. Environmental Concerns

arranging for cleaning up a hazardous substance, when the cleanup is not done properly, may subject a developer to CERCLA liability. Only when the "disposal" occurs after the hazardous substance has left the site is the developer free of "arranger" liability under CERCLA. See Burlington N. & Santa Fe Ry. Co. v. United States, 556 U.S. 599 (2009) (narrowing arranger liability and holding that a developer's knowledge that a lessee might discharge a pollutant is insufficient to establish arranger liability).

In tandem, then, the current or past "owner(s)" who "disposed" of a hazardous substance or on whose land such a disposed substance leaked, is liable for "all costs of removal or remedial action" in cleaning it up. This liability once found could easily soak up a developer's portfolio! Not only is the owner at the time of the initial disposal liable, but also liable is the owner at the time any containers in which the hazardous substance was stored start to leak. The leak is in effect a separate "disposal" of the substance. By analogy, also liable is a developer who grades contaminated soil, even though the grading does not add any prohibited substance to the site.

The liability of all these owners is strict as well as joint and several. The government is interested in recovering its costs first, leaving the owners to sort out their respective liabilities among themselves. Strict liability and retroactivity are the twin doctrines on which courts have relied to assign the costs of cleanup among those with an interest in a chain of title. Thus, litigation over CERCLA liabilities is multi-party litigation — and more time-consuming on that account.

Moreover, CERCLA reaches more than owners in the sense of those in the chain of title who hold or have held the fee simple. In addition, homeowners associations, construction lenders with a security lien, residential and commercial developers, and brokers who have shown the property to prospective purchasers may be liable for cleaning up toxic properties as well. See Kaiser Aluminum & Chemical Corp. v. Catellus Dev. Corp., 976 F.2d 1338 (9th Cir. 1992) (dispersing and excavating contaminated soil in the grading and preparation of land for a residential development is a "disposal" by an "operator" under the Act) and Tanglewood East Homeowners v. Charles-Thomas, Inc., 849 F.2d 1568 (5th Cir. 1988) (recognizing a private cause of action in a residential setting for a homeowners association against a developer).[5]

CERCLA is all about the government's authority to hold PRPs responsible for the government's costs incurred in cleaning up hazardous substances contaminating real property. There are CERCLA provisions permitting suits by citizens, but such suits may not be brought while federal CERCLA remediation is on-going. See 42 U.S.C. §9659(a) and (h).

---

5. Importantly, CERCLA does not cover contamination by petroleum or its by-products. State statutes sometimes fill this gap.

3. Environmental Concerns

Because CERCLA litigation is multi-party, expensive and complex, most such actions result in a settlement with the government. Not settling will leave a defendant with joint and several liability for the government's costs incurred in cleaning up property. In contrast, a settlement will typically result in the defendant contributing a set amount to those costs. See Cooper Industries, Inc. v. Aviaill Serv., Inc., 543 U.S. 157 (2004).

Examples

Example 1

A developer purchases an easement over land that contains a "hazardous waste facility" in order to provide access to a project that he has just completed. Is he liable under CERCLA as an owner or operator?

Explanation

No. The common law does not regard the holder of an easement as an owner; an easement holder is a user. To extend the statute this far would upset numerous easement transactions and still permit the disposer or polluter to escape paying for the cleanup. See Long Beach Unified Sch. Dist. v. Godwin, 32 F.3d 1364 (9th Cir. 1994). Nor are easement holders operators, in the sense that they are limited users; as such, they would make inefficient monitors of disposals. See Grand Trunk Western R.R. Co. v. Acme Belt Recoating, Inc., 859 F. Supp. 1125 (W.D. Mich. 1995).

Example 2

A developer builds a "build to suit" project for a prearranged tenant. The developer then leases the project to the tenant under a net lease.[6] The tenant's premises then became contaminated from leakage of a hazardous substance on adjacent land. Is the developer still an "owner" within the definition of CERCLA?

---

6. A "build to suit" lease is a lease including and providing for a construction agreement for a building built for a predetermined tenant, with prearranged specifications, on land at a predetermined location. Once built, the building is leased to the tenant for a longer term than is usually in commercial leases — often 10 years or more, with renewal rights. It produces a stream of income for its landlord sufficient to pay for the land purchase and carry the building's construction mortgage. This type of lease is used by big box stores, and companies doing business at many locations, like fast food chains, Walmart, and Amazon. See George P. Bernhardt & James E. Goodrich, Build-to-Suit Lease: A Construction Contract and a Lease Merged into One, 29 Prob. & Prop. 32 (May/June 2015). For a discussion of net leases, see Chapter 12, infra.

3. Environmental Concerns

Explanation

Yes. In this situation, it may be difficult to impose "operator" liability on the landlord. A long-term, net lease that a landlord may not terminate, that may be subleased or assigned without the landlord's consent, and imposing all maintenance costs, taxes, and insurance premiums on the tenant, may be grounds for imposing "owner" liability on a tenant, but that does not relieve the landlord of liability as an owner. Owner and operator liability are to be separately considered, and only tenants who are *de facto* owners are considered as such under the statute.

Example 3

A developer is boring and drilling on land to investigate its geologic ability to support the foundation of a project he intends to construct on the site. The drilling disturbs water that (when tested) contains methyl tertiary butyl ether (MTBE). MTBE is widely used to oxygenate gasoline, is highly soluble in water, and is attracted to water molecules, while not attracted to soil—thus it travels easily into and with groundwater. The developer notifies federal environmental regulatory agencies; they conclude that the MTBEs comes from a nearby gas station, owned by Motley Oil Co., a subsidiary of Magna Oil. He comes to you for advice, and asks whether he is liable under CERCLA. What do you advise?

Explanation

You might give four pieces of advice. (1) MBTE is a petroleum product, not a CERCLA-controlled "hazardous substance" or waste.[7] (2) As a private citizen, he cannot sue Motley Oil under CERCLA until and unless the government has first initiated a cleanup or has failed to carry out its authorized powers under the Act. See 42 U.S.C. §9659(a)(1).[8] Challenging on-going CERCLA investigations is barred and federal courts have been stripped of jurisdiction over such suit "challenges." See, e.g., Anacostia Riverkeeper v. Wash. Gas Light Co., 892 F. Supp. 2d 161, 171-172 (D.D.C. 2012). In addition, no CERCLA recovery would include a citizen's expenses incurred due

---

7. Some other federal statutes are no help either. The Clean Water Act (CWA) does not protect groundwater. It applies only to the discharge of a pollutant into navigable waters from a point source. CWA §502(12), 33 U.S.C. §1251 et seq. Groundwater is not navigable, and so the CWA does not apply. In the same vein, the Safe Drinking Water Act (SDWA) does apply to underground sources of water, but it protects only public water supplies. 42 U.S.C. §§1421 et seq. So the SDWA is not helpful either.

8. The Resource Conservation and Recovery Act (RCRA) may in theory provide some grounds for suit, but most courts have held that CERCLA's provisions control this Act too. See Margot J. Pollans, A "Blunt Withdrawal "? Bars on Citizen Suits for Toxic Site Cleanup, 37 Harv. Envtl. L. Rev. 441 (2013).

3. Environmental Concerns

to the contamination. CERCLA will not help the developer. (3) The developer might consider state nuisance or trespass law as the basis for a suit against Motley Oil. The cases are split on whether CERCLA preempts such suits in this situation, although some state environmental statutes regulate MBTEs. (4) Finally, a corporate parent, such as Magna Oil, may be derivatively liable for the "disposals" of its subsidiary if it actively participated in and controlled the subsidiary's operations. Being an "operator" of the "facility" (rather than a focus on the parent/subsidiary relationship) is the key to its derivative "operator" liability. See United States v. Bestfoods, 524 U.S. 51 (1998).

Indemnification Agreements

PRPs liable for the response costs of a cleanup cannot avoid liability through making any type of private agreement or arrangement among themselves. CERCLA is focused on the government's ability to recover its response and cleanup costs. However, private risk shifting of the costs of compliance with the statute is possible. Thus, when dealing with §9607(e)(1) and (2), courts have held that indemnification agreements—agreements to hold a person harmless—are not enforceable against the government, but are enforceable against the private parties to such agreements. See Smith Land & Improvement Corp. v. Celotex Corp., 851 F.2d 86 (3th Cir. 1988).

However, from the perspective of a developer negotiating to buy real estate, an indemnification agreement should include, first, a warranty by the seller that the property is in compliance with all applicable environmental statutes (state and federal), codes, ordinances, as well as rules and regulations—and that the property will be conveyed free of all pending violations and noncompliance notices. Second, it should include an indemnity against all damage, loss, and injury, direct or consequential, occasioned by any noncompliance and/or violation. Finally, it should require that the response to any discovery of contamination should include the most technologically effective, though not necessarily the most cost-effective, method of treatment and cleanup.

The seller will typically negotiate to limit the warranty and indemnity given to the buyer to (1) specific, named statutes and regulations or (2) contamination limited to specific substances, and by (3) contractual provisions requiring the buyer to mitigate damages and act reasonably upon the discovery of the offending substance, in order to prevent further leaks and spills.

A seller wishing to shift liability for response costs to a buyer must clearly do so. An "as is" clause, and even an acknowledgment or statement that the purchaser has inspected the property, is unlikely to shift the response costs. A buyer should expressly assume responsibility for these costs. See Niecko

3. Environmental Concerns

v. Emro Marketing Co., 769 F. Supp. 793 (E.D. Mich. 1991), aff'd, 973 F.2d 1296 (6th Cir. 1992). Furthermore, if the hazardous substance becomes known to the parties during the executory period, the price of the property should be negotiated, or renegotiated, to account for the risks and costs of compliance. If only one portion of the property is contaminated, then the acreage subject to the contract can be renegotiated as well.

Insurance

Environmental damage to property is generally not "property damage" and so is not compensable under general liability insurance policies. See Towns v. Northern Security Ins. Co., 964 A.2d 1150 (Vt. 2008). Thus there are special types of insurance policies to cover environmental cleanup costs. Policies are available for site owners, mortgage lenders, and persons who want to insure against the risk of remediation cost overruns. For site developers and owners, policy claims are triggered by the presence of a covered pollutant. For mortgage lenders, policy claims are triggered by not only the presence of a pollutant, but also by a mortgagor's default under the mortgage loan documents. Since environmental cleanup claims are generally very large, only a few major insurance companies offer some type of pollution insurance at any one time. These insurance policies offer an indemnity for cleanup costs for any pollution discovered (and not a guarantee against the existence of hazardous substances) during the period covered by the premiums. The indemnity provided in these policies covers the reasonable and necessary costs for investigation, removal, and treatment, plus civil fines and penalties. It does not cover criminal fines, loss of use, or lost profits. Such indemnity policies require, as a precondition to issuing them, an ASTM environmental audit (Phase 1) of the insured property. The person or firm performing this audit should be certified by the insurer, as well as named in the contract of sale by the parties. Thus, the policies provide an indemnity from the auditor (a professional environmental engineer or other qualified inspector) who has made an environmental assessment of the property but failed to uncover contamination violating specified environmental statutes and requiring a cleanup.

Insurance Policy Terms

This insurance covers only an "allowed use" of the audited property; a change in the use of the property will void the policy. Its term is typically a three-year period. It does not include an automatic right to renew, although some insurers promise reissue rates 20 to 25% lower than those charged for the initial term. Premiums are set as a percentage (say, 2%) of the amount of the insurance, going down as the amount of coverage rises over $1 million,

3. Environmental Concerns

to (say) 1.5% of the amount of insurance. Coverage amounts are typically capped at a set amount per discovery, often with a high deductible. Statutory coverage is spelled out, statute by statute. Those covered are typically CERCLA, its amending acts, and the Clean Water Amendments. State statutes are covered by endorsement. Common law causes of action are generally not covered, or if they are, then only for third-party property liability. Statutory coverage is given as of the date the policy is issued. This means that policies typically do not cover amendments to the statutes named that are enacted after the effective date of the policy.

The "insured" is the named insured, but this may be a legal entity. The pre-policy discovery and failure to disclose contamination on the property, by any officer, employee, or partner in the entity, is likely to be imputed to all other parties to the entity — and this imputation too avoids coverage for the undisclosed pollution. When this defense is available against the borrower, a lender will usually take out its own policy because there is in these policies no standard clause freeing a lender of the defenses an insurer might have to a borrower's claim. Some carriers may, however, include such language. Typical exclusions are pre-policy discoveries, fraud, willful or fraudulent acts, coverage under other types of insurance, contract liability, post-sale liability, contamination by asbestos, radon, and PCBs, or nuclear-related liabilities; also excluded are the results of war, terrorist attacks, natural resource damages claims, fire, earth movement, or discoveries made during a change in use. Mold and other microbial matter may also be excluded in some policies. Gas station and heavily industrialized sites may not be insurable at all.

Examples

Example 4

A contract called for an insurable environmental audit. The audit is performed, and after issuance of a policy, covered contamination is discovered migrating from neighboring property. Is this contamination covered by the policy once the covered property used for its "allowed use" is contaminated?

Explanation

Yes, but often (not always) such migrating pollution is excluded from coverage. Thus, when the neighborhood is an industrial area, the attorney for a developer/buyer should be alert for any such exclusion. Migrating pollution may still, however, create CERCLA liability as a passive "disposal" of a hazardous substance when the "safe harbor" requirements of 42 U.S.C. §9607q (providing a safe harbor for buyers performing due diligence on environmental issues and imposing compliance, inquiry, reporting, and cooperative duties on owners) are not met. So insurance protection may be worth negotiating.

3. Environmental Concerns

Example 5

What if the migrating pollution was caused by a spill of hazardous materials being transported in a truck that overturned in front of the insured property on a public highway?

Explanation

The answer is even less clear here than in the prior Example. The environmental auditor can inspect the neighboring properties and assess the risk of pollution migrating from them; however, an assessment of the risk of contamination brought by trucks traveling along a highway is more difficult. So the presence of a nearby or abutting highway is a reason for discussing this problem with the insurer.

Example 6

Environmental regulators suspect that insured property is contaminated by a covered substance. They order an investigation of the property and the insured incurs costs in monitoring the course of this investigation. The investigation does not disclose any contamination. Are the insured's investigatory costs covered?

Explanation

These policies typically provide only an indemnity against cleanup costs. They are not concerned with whether there is pollution on the property; were it otherwise, these policies would then provide a guarantee that the property is not contaminated. So investigation alone (not leading to remediation or cleanup) is typically not covered, and should be specially negotiated. When the government requires investigation, but nothing is discovered, some policies will not pay a claim for investigation costs.

ENVIRONMENTAL AUDITS

Phase I

A potential buyer of property, with CERCLA liability in mind, should first examine the chain of title presented by the seller to determine if there are any names in it indicating that a prior use of the property might have involved hazardous substances. For example, the name of a dry cleaning store, a gas station, or a chemical company might indicate that the premises should be physically inspected for such substances.

Second, a governmental records search — for notices of violations of environmental laws — should also be conducted. This involves a search of federal records, typically those in the possession of the Environmental Protection Agency and the Securities and Exchange Commission. State regulatory records about the location of storage facilities, landfills, pollution discharges, and so on should be checked as well. If the property was ever used by an interstate trucking company or other common carrier, then the U.S. Department of Transportation may also have relevant records.

Third, a review of loan applications is conducted (if the audit is being performed for a mortgagee). Finally, interviews with various parties to follow up leads disclosed on the title and governmental records, and a site inspection, round out a Phase I audit.

Phase II

Depending on the results of the Phase I audit, further inquiries may be necessary. These involve sampling the groundwater and soil and analyzing the samples for the presence of hazardous substances. A Phase II audit is necessary to resolve and refute any suspicions raised in Phase I. The results of a Phase II audit, unless governed by an agreement to keep them confidential, should be reported to the appropriate regulatory agencies.

The practice of conducting environmental audits is routine in commercial property transactions. The American Society for Testing and Materials, now ASTM International, promotes the most widely used standards for conducting these audits. While a Phase I audit might take several weeks, a Phase II will take several months. See Joseph Forte, Environmental Due Diligence: A Guide to Liability Risk Management in Commercial Real Estate Transactions, 42 Real Prop. Prob. & Tr. J. 443 (2007).

Environmental Consultants

Two types of consulting firms have emerged to facilitate environmental due diligence in real estate transactions. The first is capable of doing a Phase I audit. The second generally grew out of industrial engineering firms, adding environmental audits to their services as clients requested it. They perform both Phase I and II audits; they often have their own

3. Environmental Concerns

laboratories for testing soil and water samples (while the first type does not and relies instead on independent labs) and can do cleanups as well. Choosing a firm is often the product of competitive bidding, as well as a check of references and coverage. Sometimes a search for the fewest exclusions from a proposed Phase I audit certificate provides a good way of selecting a consultant. Some exclusions might be for asbestos, drinking water, electronic fields, flooding, geologic faults, landslides/mudslides, indoor and outdoor air quality, lead paint, radon, wetlands, and land use restrictions.

Examples

Example 7

An environmental consultant conducting a Phase II audit drills a well (to test groundwater quality) that inadvertently punches through the land's subsurface to an aquifer below, contaminating it with a toxic waste covered by CERCLA. Is the consultant a PRP under that statute?

Explanation

Maybe. Engaging in a cleanup isn't generally a basis for CERCLA liability. However, one case stated that such testing is a "disposal." See United States v. CDMG Realty Co., 96 F.3d 706 (3d Cir. 1996) (stating so without deciding whether the tester was a particular type of PRP, such as an operator, but finding that negligent testing was disposal), discussed and noted at 103 Mich. L. Rev. 1930 (2005). Other courts have said that engaging in cleanups cannot be a disposal unless wastes are moved to an uncontaminated part of the property. See Blasland, Bouck & Lee v. City of North Miami, 96 F. Supp. 2d 1375 (S.D. Fla. 2000). A consultant is no "operator": it has no management authority — only access to the property. But when the consultant's punching through to the aquifer was negligent, liability might follow on that account.

ENFORCEMENT

When the government seeks to enforce joint and several liability for response costs, the first task it undertakes is a title search. With an abstract of title in hand, it can readily learn the names of all persons or entities in the chain of title, and thus whose title to the property places them on the list of potential defendants as either owners, operators, or PRPs.

3. Environmental Concerns

CERCLA DEFENSES

Persons or entities who would otherwise be responsible as owners and operators, and so on, are not responsible for acts of God, war, or the acts or omissions of third parties with whom the defendant has or had no contractual relationship. CERCLA §107(b).

Congress has amended CERCLA several times to create "safe harbor" defenses—for an innocent owner, the bona fide purchaser, and the bona fide prospective purchaser. Their successful assertion requires many things, generally including due diligence in environmental audits, reporting, and remediation of any hazardous substances found, as well as compliance with existing regulations and land use restrictions.

Lender Defenses

CERCLA also excludes from the §107(a) definition of an "owner or operator" any "person, who, without participating in the management of a . . . facility, holds indicia of ownership primarily to protect his security interest in the . . . facility." Like other CERCLA defenses, when this lender's exemption is invoked, a court imposes on the person seeking it the burden of establishing entitlement to it. See United States v. Fleet Factors Corp., 901 F.2d 1550 (11th Cir. 1990), cert. denied, 111 S. Ct. 752 (1991). Merely providing loans does not step beyond the bounds of this exemption, even if the lender is the sole source of financing. *Fleet Factors* held that a secured creditor's participation in the management of its debtor precluded summary judgment for the creditor on the issue of the applicability of a CERCLAsecured creditor exemption. This made mortgage lenders very nervous about lending on property with environmental problems. In response to *Fleet Factors*, Congress enacted several amendments to CERCLA in 1996. These amendments state that the "term 'security interest' includes a right under a mortgage, deed of trust, assignment, judgment lien, pledge, security agreement, factoring agreement, or lease and any other right accruing to a person to secure the repayment of money, the performance of a duty, or any other obligation by a nonaffiliated person." Courts have recognized that Congress meant to provide lenders with a safe harbor in the exemption's definition of a security interest. See Monarch Tile, Inc. v. The City of Florence, 212 F.3d 1219, 1222-1223 (11th Cir. 2000). "While much of *Fleet Factors* reasoning and holding remain intact, Congress has abrogated the part of *Fleet Factors* holding that deals with the liability of lenders who participate in the management of properties operated by polluting firms. *Fleet Factors* held that lenders and other parties who participated 'in the financial management of a facility

62

3. Environmental Concerns

to a degree indicating a *capacity to influence* the corporation's treatment of hazardous wastes' could be liable for cleaning up pollution created by an operator's activities. Largely in response to the perceived over breadth of the *Fleet Factors* rule, Congress amended CERCLA in 1996, narrowing somewhat the sweep of lender liability under CERCLA." Id. at 1222, n.2. These amendments thus supersede *Fleet Factors'* management-participation liability. A lender's capability to influence the decision making of the borrower's financial management is an insufficient ground for CERCLA liability, and to get beyond the bounds of the exemption, a lender must actually participate in management of a borrower's hazardous wastes.

The lenders' exemption was available to any person or entity found to be a lender as the result of a recharacterization claim asserted in bankruptcy, foreclosure, or other forum. See Waterville Indust., Inc. v. Finance Auth. of Maine, 984 F.2d 549, 552 (1st Cir. 1993) (applying it to a sale-leaseback transaction) and Kemp Indust., Inc. v. Safety Light Corp., 857 F. Supp. 373 (D.N.J. 1994) (collecting the cases).

Another amendment is 42 U.S.C. §9601(20)E–F(iv) (enacted in 1997), providing that a lender is not a §107 owner or operator when it forecloses on a tainted property and then, having undertaken a cleanup, sells it within a commercially reasonable time. However, lenders should be wary in any event and not actually participate in management before foreclosure — the exemption is lost if they do.

Examples

Example 8

A developer leases a "built-to-suit" project to a tenant for use as an automobile repair facility. The tenant places a small gasoline underground storage tank on the premises. The lease is terminable at the developer's option when there is any violation of any applicable environmental law. It allocates to the tenant the obligation to repair the premises and further provides that the developer has the right to inspect the property at any time during business hours. The tenant's tank leaks into the groundwater under the premises. The developer learns of the leak, but the tenant suggests that it is fixed. The developer's mortgage on the premises is held by M. The mortgage covenants give M a right to appear and settle any proceeding to adjudicate the violation of any applicable environmental law, charging the costs of the appearance and settlement to the developer as a future advance of mortgage loan proceeds. The jurisdiction in which the project is located has a statute regulating underground storage tanks patterned closely on federal CERCLA. Are the developer and M liable for cleanup costs caused by the leaking gas tank?

63

3. Environmental Concerns

Explanation

Liability for the cleanup from a leaking underground storage tank containing petroleum or petroleum products is not covered by federal CERCLA and so cases decided under its banner are only authority by analogy. See Zands v. Nelson, 779 F. Supp. 1254 (S.D. Cal. 1991). As to the developer, liability does not arise from ownership alone, but in *Fleet Factors* ownership, coupled with some form of control over the operation of the business on the premises, may give rise to such liability. See Struve v. Payvandi, 740 N.W.2d 436 (Iowa Ct. App. 2007) and Resolution Trust Corp. v. Rossmoor Corp., 40 Cal. Rptr. 2d 328 (Cal. App. 1995). Thus, when the landlord plays an active role in the tenant's business and when the lease gives the landlord the authority to play that role, the landlord has a duty to control the environmental hazards involved in operating the tenant's business. However, a right to control is not a duty to do so; moreover, every tenant has an implied duty (of good faith and fair dealing) that requires the tenant to avoid exposing the landlord to liability for environmental hazards, even when the lease is silent about them. See Dominick's Finer Foods v. Amoco Oil Co., 1993 U.S. Dist. LEXIS 17668 (N.D. Ill. Dec. 7, 1993) and Sachs v. Exxon Co., U.S.A., 12 Cal. Rptr. 2d 237 (Cal. App. 1992). In addition, viewing the lease as a contract, the tenant has a contract duty to mitigate the landlord's liability. Finally, the lease here—giving the landlord a right to terminate the lease for any environmental problems—shows an intent to disassociate the landlord from environmental liability.

As to M, the mortgagee, *Fleet Factors* is more squarely on point. The mortgagee lacks the "ownership" interest present in the landlord's situation. The active participation of the daily management of a faltering business, present in *Fleet Factors*, is not present here. So there is no *Fleet Factors* liability. Moreover, the mortgagee's right to appear and settle any environmental problem is a method of protecting its security and minimizing its liability, not an indication of the mortgagee's active control over the developer and tenant's management of toxic substances.

Site Owner Defenses

A defense for an innocent owner (a bona fide purchaser who had no knowledge of the presence of prohibited pollutants when purchasing a site) was provided by Congress in its 1986 CERCLA amendments. See 42 U.S.C. §9610(35). This proved problematic because if ignorance of the pollution was sufficient, then every purchaser would profess ignorance. Thus, this defense was modified to an "all appropriate inquires" defense. To assert this defense, a purchaser has to show not only ignorance (using an "I don't know, and had no reason to know" approach), but also that he made "all

3. Environmental Concerns

appropriate inquiries." See 42 U.S.C. §9601(35)(B)(3) (enacted in 2002 and providing 10 criteria to determine if an inquiry is appropriate). This defense was feasible because of the development of industry standards using ASTM guidelines. In practice, "appropriateness" requires an environmental audit sufficient to meet ASTM standards for the site. See Larry Schnapf, The New "Appropriate Inquiries" Rule, 24 Prac. Real Est. Law. 7 (Jan. 2007). Finally, disclosure of a post-purchase discovery of a hazardous substance must be made when the property is re-sold, so while there is a defense for liability as to governmental cleanup costs, cleaning up before the next transaction is still required. Thus, here the innocent buyer avoids liability as an owner or operator, but the nondisclosing seller is strictly and fully liable.

THE TAX STATUS OF CLEANUP COSTS

Must cleanup costs be capitalized—that is, added to basis—or depreciated, or may they be deducted in the tax year incurred?[9]

The cost of environmental studies is not deductible. See IIRS Tech. Adv. Memo. 95-41-005 (1995). If cleanup costs incurred in the operation of a project are treated as repairs and maintenance, they are deductible as business expenses under IRC §162. When they (1) are incurred in preparing property for a developer's project, they are treated as permanent improvements under IRC §263, or (2) are incurred as part of a plan for rehabilitation or restoration of business property, they are capital expenditures and so must be capitalized. See IRC §263A. If the property after the cleaning is used for a different purpose or increases in value, then capitalization is all the more likely tax result. See Priv. Ltr. Rul. 94-11-002 (1994). Capitalization typically requires the taxpayer's creation of a tangible asset with future benefits and a useful life beyond the tax year at issue.

BROWNFIELDS

The high cost of CERCLA cleanups, the administrative delays in governmental cleanups, and the lack of uniform cleanup standards have combined with CERCLA's comprehensive liability scheme and narrow exemptions to ensure that some already contaminated lands are not redeveled. In older, urban,

---

9. Deductibility produces an immediate savings in tax liability, whereas capitalization defers the tax benefit until the property is sold. Likewise, depreciation allows deduction of the costs over time, a certain percentage per year; so this issue is a matter of immediate importance to the taxpayer incurring the costs.

3. Environmental Concerns

industrial areas, such lands are known as brownfields—and developers seek greenfields instead. There are several million acres of brownfields in the United States. CERCLA provides that new buyers of brownfields, designated as such by state statute, will not be liable under CERCLA for the disposal of hazardous substances by prior owners or operators, so long as the buyers comply with state cleanup statutes. See 42 U.S.C. §9601(40), §9607(r). Neither will the passive migration of substances from cleaned-up sites be a basis for imposing CERCLA liability on adjacent owners. Id., §9607(q). The Environmental Protection Agency (EPA) authorizes state brownfield cleanup programs and delegates the certification of cleanups to the participating states. States have approached brownfield cleanups in many ways, mandating either flexible background, health-based, or site-specific standards. Site-specific standards may vary with the neighborhood and the proposed use for the site. Oversight of a cleanup by certified environmental consulting firms is also required in some states.

State programs apply to any land where there is no pending enforcement action. First, a cleanup plan is formulated, sometimes in a negotiated agreement with the state, submitted, reviewed, and approved by the state agency in charge of environmental matters. The plan describes the parcel, the nature of the problem, and cleanup methods to be undertaken; in addition, it involves cost estimates, time schedules, and dispute resolution procedures. Second, the plan is executed as approved, and its execution is then reviewed, either by a certified professional or the agency. Third, if the review is successful, the state will issue a completion certificate or "no further cleanup" letter, which serves either as a waiver of future enforcement rights or a covenant not to sue an owner or purchaser—who then records it in the chain of title or with the parcel's deed. Either or all of these three steps can be the subject of a statute or administrative regulation.

OTHER HAZARDS

Asbestos

Asbestos is a carcinogen that produces lung cancers. In the past, this substance was used in pipe and furnace insulation. When it dries out and deteriorates, it often enters the ventilation system of a building. Asbestos is also found in older plaster, drywall, and flooring and roofing materials. It is now regulated by both the Environmental Protection Agency (EPA) and the Occupational Safety and Health Administration (OSHA) in the Department of Labor as an air pollutant. The EPA regulations apply to new construction, as well as any activity in a private building that might cause exposure to asbestos—demolition, alteration, repair, maintenance, installation, cleanup,

3. Environmental Concerns

transportation, disposal, and storage. OSHA regulations require identification and notice of the presence of asbestos, as well as the regulation of employment activities generating contact with it.

Lead

Lead has often been used as solder in plumbing fixtures and pipes, where it can enter the drinking water and then build up gradually in the body. Lead was typically used in paints until 1978, when its use as a paint additive was banned. Numerous physiological studies have shown that lead causes brain and neurological disorders when ingested or inhaled. In the courts, property owners and managers have been found negligent in maintaining lead in rental properties. The federal Residential Lead-Based Paint Hazard Reduction Act, 42 U.S.C. §§4851 et seq., requires sellers and landlords owning housing built before 1978 to disclose lead hazards before selling or renting.

Endangered Species

Every developer's proverbial nightmare is the discovery on his project's land of a species of animal or plant listed as endangered by either federal or state wildlife regulators. See 16 U.S.C. §§1531 et seq. (the federal Endangered Species Act, or ESA). The Act's §7 prohibits the "taking" of endangered wildlife. A "taking" is any action that would kill, harm, or harass the species—including just one member of it. ESA's §9 prohibits the government from authorizing activities that jeopardize the species' continued existence or adversely affect its habitat—designated as critical to it beforehand. On designated habitat, such jeopardy is far more likely to be found and so far more likely to stall a developer's project. With a developer's critics sometimes searching for affected endangered species, their discovery becomes more likely, and, once discovered, a process of consultation with regulators begins. The likely result of this process is the developer's having to survey the property for endangered species, modify his plans and project, or obtain an exemption, an "incidental take" permit, or a "no jeopardy" opinion. Often the last will require that voluntary restrictions be imposed on the property in the form of conservation easements and covenants.

Radon

This is a natural radioactive gas found trapped in homes and buildings in certain regions, or "hot spots," around the country, where it leaks from

67

3. Environmental Concerns

the subsurface. Its presence is thought to be connected to the increased incidence of certain types of cancers. Newer, energy-efficient homes with a tighter fit and finish serve to trap more gas than older, "leaky" ones. Statutes and local ordinances sometimes mandate testing for this substance at the time of a sale, and brokers, sellers, and others may be liable when failing to disclose the presence of the gas on the property.

CHAPTER 4

Acquisition Techniques Other than Executory Contracts

This chapter explains four land acquisition and financing methods not involving a straight executory contract of purchase and sale. One involves an alternative form of contract known as an installment land sale contract, also known in some jurisdictions as a contract for deed. Another is a ground lease for an undeveloped project site. Yet another involves a seller/landowner's take-back or purchase money mortgage financing, accompanied by an agreement with the landowner to subordinate the lien of his mortgage to the developer's later construction financing. And a final one is a wraparound mortgage that preserves a seller's existing financing. All are aimed at minimizing the initial amount of cash the developer has to devote to the acquisition of land for his project.

INSTALLMENT LAND SALE CONTRACTS

An installment land sale contract (ILSC) is an installment purchase device. It is a contract for the sale of real property whose executory period is stretched out over a period of years. The buyer goes into possession immediately, however, paying little or nothing down, avoiding the payment of closing and settlement costs and not having to deal with most of the requirements of mortgage lenders — instead financing the purchase of the land through a series of periodic payments. In the residential market, an ILSC extends credit to some who may not qualify for a conventional mortgage. In a commercial

69

4. Acquisition Techniques Other than Executory Contracts

real estate transaction, a developer might use an ILSC to warehouse land for later development.

In such an arrangement, the seller does not convey the title to the property until the purchaser makes the final installment payment or makes an agreed-upon amount of payments. The seller enjoys the financial advantage of ultimately selling the property at an installment, or higher, price and the tax advantages of selling on the installment method (that is, she will, if complying with the provisions of Internal Revenue Code §453, realize the income from the sale only as she receives it).

The seller retains title to the property, but possession and the obligation to pay taxes and other carrying charges pass to the buyer. In a majority of jurisdictions and absent a contract provision otherwise, the contract buyer has the risk of loss of improvements due to fire or casualty.

During the extended executory period of ILSCs, both the buyer and seller have an interest in the property—the seller the legal title (alienable, mortgageable, subject to levy and sale by her creditors in a majority of jurisdictions, etc.) and the buyer an equitable interest (alienable, mortgageable, and, in most jurisdictions, subject to levy and sale by her creditors too). A majority of jurisdictions treat both parties' interests as subject to lien creditors, so when used in a commercial transaction, the contract should provide that both landowner and developer cross-indemnify each other for any liens placed on the property. Otherwise the buyer runs the risk that when it is time for the seller's to convey title, that title will be clouded and unmarketable. Traditionally, the seller's duty to convey at the end of the executory period is independent of the buyer's duty to make installment payments, although there is some authority limiting this rule. Most jurisdictions permit ILSCs to be recorded, although some sellers would rather they were not.

ILSCs often contain draconian provisions that have three features: (1) automatic forfeiture of all amounts paid toward the price, upon default; (2) retention by the seller of those amounts as liquidated damages; and (3) termination of the contract upon forfeiture. In addition, many will contain provisions permitting the seller to foreclose the buyer's interest as a mortgagee would a mortgage. In a commercial, transaction, each of these features should be modified as follows, to the effect that

(1) forfeiture of payments will not be automatic, but subject to a right to cure and reinstatement—some courts have found that the seller has waived the right to a forfeiture by accepting late payments. See Kirkpatrick v. Petreikis, 358 N.E.2d 679, 680 (Ill. App. Ct. 1976);

(2) only those portions of the installments representing rent of the property will be forfeited, and once the unpaid installments are reinstated, the nonrental portions are regarded as the buyer's equity in the property, recoverable by the buyer choosing to terminate the contract—California, Connecticut, and Utah cases have taken

4. Acquisition Techniques Other than Executory Contracts

this approach. See, e.g., Engstrom v. Bushnell, 436 P.2d 806 (Utah 1968); and

(3) termination of the contract will require mutual agreement.

Other judicial responses have treated the ILSC as the functional equivalent of a mortgage. Viewing the ILSC buyer as a mortgagee, these courts reason that the ILSC's draconian installment payment forfeiture provision in effect eliminates a mortgagee's much-protected equity of redemption.[1] These courts restore the equity by treating the ILSC as a mortgage *de facto*. See Anderson v. Anderson, 697 N.E.2d 25, 31 (S.D. 2005), and Fraser v. Fraser, 702 N.W.2d 283 (Minn. Ct. App. 2005). Likewise, when the buyer has paid a considerable portion of the price or the property has increased in value since the execution of the contract (particularly if the buyer's improvements to the property caused the increase), some courts have used their inherent equitable powers to decree that the property be sold at judicial sale, with the surplus over the debt distributed to the buyer. See Ward v. Union Bond & Trust Co., 243 F.2d 476 (9th Cir. 1957), Myers v. Leedy, 915 N.E.2d 133 (Ind. 2009), and Skendzel v. Marshall, 301 N.E.2d 641 (Ind.), cert. denied, 415 U.S. 921 (1973).

By no means do a majority of jurisdictions reach these results, but where they are the law, it means that a total, automatic, damage-liquidating, forfeiture provision will be enforceable only through foreclosure. The most valuable right gained by the buyer-mortgagor in foreclosure is (again) the equitable right of redemption, which permits the buyer first to seek refinancing and then, with the proceeds of the loan, to redeem the property under contract. Because of the pro-buyer results of these cases, the developer using an ILSC in the commercial setting has a valuable advantage over his seller providing the contract interest in a project site.

Most of the courts that have applied this functional equivalency doctrine to turn the contract into a mortgage have done so in factual situations in which the buyer (1) goes into possession immediately upon executing the contract, and (2) thereafter pays a substantial portion of the contract's purchase price, thus building up equity in the property. In *Marshall*, for example, 71% of the purchase price was paid. See also Goff v. Graham, 306 N.E.2d 758 (Ind. App. 1974) (forfeiture permitted with only 40% paid).

---

1. Long recognized by the common law, the equity or right of redemption is the right to redeem legal title from a mortgagee by paying off the mortgage, thus giving the mortgagor both legal and equitable title and ending the mortgagee's interest in the secured real property. It applies even when a mortgage is in default and until the equity is foreclosed by the mortgagee, generally at the foreclosure sale. The equity is a distinct estate in land that is descendible, devisable, and alienable. It passes automatically and directly to a decedent's heirs or devisees upon the holder's death. It may also be assigned and conveyed by deed, the assignee acquiring the equity without assuming the mortgage. It buys time for a mortgagor to pay the outstanding contract price (in cash or through a refinancing with a third party lender).

4. Acquisition Techniques Other than Executory Contracts

Some of these opinions converting the ILSC into a mortgage do so with a general holding to that effect. See Sebastian v. Floyd, 585 S.W.2d 381 (Ky. 1979). That leaves many issues unresolved. If a mortgage is established, then:

- is it a lien or title mortgage?
- what type of foreclosure will be used (strict, judicial or power of sale)?
- are all the formalities of a foreclosure (notices, rights to reinstate the debt, defenses, etc.) available to the parties?
- is the "mortgagee" entitled to rents pending foreclosure?
- or to a deficiency judgment?
- is the mortgagor entitled to any applicable statutory redemption right?

Each one of these questions raises technical legal issues regarding foreclosure. Even if foreclosure is pruned of the attributes unfavorable to the buyer, it would be inequitable to return all of the money paid by the buyer. The latter would then have received interim possession rent-free, so the buyer should receive back all payments, minus the property's fair rental value.

In jurisdictions with these cases, when a buyer mortgages her equitable interest in an ILSC and there is a forfeiture of that interest, the mortgagee is accorded the rights of a junior mortgagee or lienor upon a senior foreclosure.

Thus where a jurisdiction's case law recharacterizes an ILSC as a mortgage, the recharacterization need not be automatic. Moreover, the developer/buyer with a good attorney can draft fair forfeiture provisions that can then enforced as written. Provisions for notice of an impending forfeiture, with a time for the buyer to cure the default working the forfeiture, or provisions for the seller's retention of part of the payments as rent and for giving back the excess, would make the forfeiture less harsh.

Creditors' Rights to Reach Contract Interests

When an unsecured creditor of either the seller or the buyer obtains a judgment, by statute the judgment typically creates a lien on real, but not personal, property of the debtor. The lien attaches when the court clerk in the county where the property is located, dockets the judgment in the appropriate public record or docket book. In a majority of jurisdictions, the buyer's interest in an ILSC is real property for purposes of the judgment lien statute. This result is reached as a matter of statutory interpretation or as a recognition of the effects of the doctrine of equitable conversion.

Under these statutes, the seller's interest is also real property in a slight majority of jurisdictions. To reach this result, courts have to ignore the equitable conversion doctrine and concentrate instead on the seller's retention

4. Acquisition Techniques Other than Executory Contracts

of the legal title until all installment payments are made by the buyer. The creditor's judgment lien attaches, more particularly, to the equitable vendor's lien, itself an interest in real property,[2] for the amount of the due and unpaid installments. Moreover, the vendor's lien is regarded as taking its priority from the time of the execution of the contract.

The minority rule is (as you might imagine) that the seller's interest is personal property. See Cannefax v. Clement, 818 P.2d 546 (Utah 1991) (adopting the minority rule). This is just another way of saying that the creditor seeking to attach the seller's interest will have to bring a second action to execute or foreclose the lien, thus assigning it to a priority attaching at the time of the execution or foreclosure decree.

The minority rule is consistent with the doctrine of equitable conversion and, in jurisdictions in which contracts are not recordable, protects the installment buyer from having to search the title for judgment liens before making each payment due under the contract. Indeed, this search burden might make installment contracts impractical for many buyers. Moreover, under the minority rule, any buyer at the sale of the seller's interest dare not pay more than the total of existing senior mortgages. The other result under the minority rule is that classifying the seller's interest as personalty may subject it to the provisions of the Uniform Commercial Code; under such provisions, a financing statement must be filed in order to assert a lien. But this requirement may turn into a procedural blessing when the requirements of foreclosing a Code security interest and foreclosing a mortgage lien are compared. The Code action is much simpler.

Mortgaging the Buyer's Interest

There is no technical reason why a buyer's interest in an installment contract cannot be mortgaged. There may also be some question about the business prudence of the mortgagee in this situation because the security for the loan is only the purchaser's equitable interest in the contract. See Gilbert Builders v. Community Bank of DePere, 407 N.W.2d 706 (Minn. Ct. App. 1987). The mortgage based on the contract would end with the contract. This result would be the same if the buyer executed a lease, created an easement, or abandoned his interest—termination of the buyer's interest extinguishes all interests dependent on it. See Fincher v. Miles Homes, Inc., 549 S.W.2d

---

2. In equity and at common law, during the executory period and after the closing, the seller has an equitable lien—a vendor's lien—for any unpaid amount of the contract's purchase price. It can be foreclosed. Likewise, the buyer has a lien—a vendee's lien—on the property subject to the contract for any amount of the purchase price paid during the executory period.

4. Acquisition Techniques Other than Executory Contracts

848 (Mo. 1977), noted in 43 Mo. L. Rev. 371 (1978).[3] There was, however, little question about a developer being able to acquire a project site with an ILSC and then mortgaging his interest to reduce his land acquisition costs, regarding the mortgage loan proceeds as a bridge loan.

How would the developer's mortgagee modify the usual covenants in the note and the mortgage to protect herself? Probably first and foremost by charging a higher rate of interest on the proceeds of the mortgage loan. Probably, too, by insertion of a provision for notice to the seller of the mortgage and by a further covenant that the mortgagor-buyer will notify the mortgagee of any default in the contract in a timely manner, in order to give the mortgagee time to exercise a right to cure that default. Otherwise a forfeiture might occur that would wipe out the mortgagee's security for its loan; or, in a jurisdiction treating an installment contract like a mortgage, the seller might foreclose his interest and, at the seller's foreclosure, the mortgagee, if not joined in that action, would assume the status of an omitted junior mortgagee, with the two remedies traditional for such parties: reforeclosure or redemption.

Bankruptcy

Upon the seller's bankruptcy, the trustee in bankruptcy may reject the ILSC. See 11 U.S.C.A. §365 (1990). The buyer in possession must "perfect" her interest and tender all of the future, unpaid installment payments to avoid trustee's rejection of the contract. U.S.C.A. §365(i). The buyer ousted by the trustee obtains a lien for any payments of the purchase price paid. Id., §365(j). This means that when the contract is otherwise silent, it is up to the trustee to determine what portions of the installments are to be treated as a payment for possession and what treated as a purchase price payment. Only with the delivery of a deed by the seller does the trustee lose the power to reject the contract.

The rules stated in the preceding paragraph would require a developer buying and using an ILSC expressly to provide in the contract that the seller's filing for bankruptcy triggers an automatic conveyance by the seller of legal title to the buyer/developer. Such a provision denies the trustee of the

---

3. In *Miles*, the mortgagee contended that before the buyer executed a deed of release of her contract interest, she had to give notice to the mortgagee, and without that notice, the mortgagee was entitled to assert her lien against the seller's title. In *Miles*, the seller had actual notice of the mortgage and, because the mortgagee had recorded its interest, the mortgagee argued that the seller knew that the title had its equity attached to it. By analogy, then, the mortgagee is an omitted junior, and the seller receiving the deed of release is analogous to the buyer at the foreclosure sale that the deed avoided.

4. Acquisition Techniques Other than Executory Contracts

power to reject the contract. See Boone Coal & Timber Co. v. Polan, 787 F.2d 1056 (6th Cir. 1986).

Remedies

Upon default of the buyer, the nondefaulting seller has (1) any contract action outlined in the ILSC and all contract remedies generally, (2) an action to recover possession of the property, such as ejectment, (3) an action to quiet title, and (4) a foreclosure action. The nondefaulting buyer's remedies are those typically associated with a contract: (1) an action for rescission — the recovery of payments made by rescinding the contract and restoring the consideration received under it, (2) a damage action for breach, and (3) an action for specific performance. See Robert Isham, The Default Clause in the Installment Land Contract, 42 Mont. L. Rev. 110, 127 (1981). Some authorities that support an action for specific performance require that the seller's breach be an anticipatory repudiation of the contract.

Closing an Installment Contract

Absent a contractual provision to the contrary, the seller under an ILSC has a duty to convey a marketable title to the buyer at the closing, but when the seller's title is unmarketable at the time of the contract's execution, there is as yet no breach of this duty. The traditional rule is that the seller's title must be marketable only on the date of the payment of the last installment or the closing, but need not be marketable beforehand. If the buyer wants an assurance of a marketable title sooner, she must bargain for it. So, absent some provision for assuring the buyer as to the quality of the title during the long executory period, the seller is not in breach if the title is meanwhile unmarketable. (Holding the seller in breach would normally relieve the buyer of any further performance of the contract.) Many courts have responded to this traditional rule by holding that, even though the seller is not in breach, the buyer does not have to keep making payments without further assurance from the seller that a marketable title will ultimately be conveyed. Meanwhile neither party is in breach. Proper drafting by the developer's attorney should ensure that a procedure for providing such assurance is written into the contract.

While the contract is outstanding, the seller has a cause of action for waste — so a seller's exercising the forfeiture provision in a contract may be unwise so long as this cause of action, often with multiple damages allowed by statute, is provable. Conversely, the buyer has a cause of action for unjust enrichment when, having improved the property, the seller exercises a contract's forfeiture provision and derives a benefit from the improvements thereby.

4. Acquisition Techniques Other than Executory Contracts

The Measure of Damages

A seller's filing a cause of action to forfeit the contract and clear the title of the cloud created by it is traditionally viewed as incompatible with a cause of action for damages on it. Implicitly the seller agrees to accept the property back as compensation for the buyer's default. (In contrast, California limits the seller seeking forfeiture to actual damages.)

However, a seller's seeking forfeiture is not necessarily incompatible with a waste action based upon the buyer's actions committed while the contract was outstanding. A seller's decision to seek forfeiture of the contract is a decision to rescind it, and by operation of law converts the buyer's interest in the property into either a periodic tenancy or a tenancy at will.

Following a theory that the contract is recharacterized as a tenancy when the seller exercises a forfeiture provision, some courts have permitted the seller to retain only the fair rental value of the premises, thus forcing her to return that portion of the payments that the court finds is in excess of the rental value. Similarly, after the seller declares a forfeiture improperly or in bad faith, some courts have permitted buyers to recover the equity built up in the property during the executory period. Thus, a buyer's damages are either measured by difference money — the difference between the fair rental value and the contract price — or the benefit of the bargain to the party seeking forfeiture. Both measures are applied as of the time of the breach. Whichever measure applies, it is the buyer's burden to show that a forfeiture provides the seller with more than actual damages and so results in an unjust enrichment.

ILSCs are traditionally used in agricultural areas by farmers expecting to retire and use the installment payments as they would an annuity. In the latter situation, they are a financing device that developers might use to warehouse land and when purchasing land outright and then selling it to investors, a method of reducing land acquisition costs while at the same time attracting investors as ILSC buyers.

Examples

Example 1

Suppose that, in a rapidly appreciating market for land, an ILSC developer/buyer sells her interest by means of another ILSC, and the new vendee under this second ILSC goes into possession. The vendee thereafter makes payments directly to the seller. (1) The vendee goes into default on the payments. Is the developer/buyer entitled to notice from the seller of the default before the seller cancels the ILSC under its forfeiture provision? (2) Would your answer change if the original ILSC were assigned and the buyer and the vendee had not executed a separate ILSC? (3) Would your answer to the

76

4. Acquisition Techniques Other than Executory Contracts

first question in this Example change if the vendee paid the amount of the buyer's equity as down payment on the second ILSC?

Explanation

Yes to the first question. See Roberts v. Morin, 645 P.2d 423 (Mont. 1982). This case held that the buyer is entitled to notice and has a right to redeem. As to the second and third questions, the answers are also yes; the fact that the buyer had been paid her equity would make a difference. The failure to execute a second contract is here an implied assignment of all buyer's rights under the first contract, and when the developer/buyer has received compensation for the totality of her interest, so that its remaining worth is at or near zero, strict foreclosure might be an appropriate remedy against the buyer.

Example 2

When a developer buys land outright and then sells it to an investor using an ILSC, pledging the right to contract payments to another investor, is that a pledge of personal property?

Explanation

Yes. A pledge is a bailment (the transfer of possession, without a transfer of title, to the payments). After distinguishing between the right to transfer the right to the payments from the title to the property, the right to receive the payments is personal property, and the judgment lien statutes of many (though a minority of) jurisdictions should not automatically reach the land. Another action will have to be brought to attach the seller's interest.

As previously discussed, a consequence of classifying the developer's interest as personalty is to bring the right within the scope of the Uniform Commercial Code, §9-102(1). If a UCC security interest is not perfected by filing a financing statement, the assignee of the right to the payments is an unsecured creditor under the Code. Once the distinction between the right to receive the payment and the title to it is accepted, when the seller suffers a judgment, then his interest in the title can be levied and sold to satisfy the judgment because the real property is bound over to satisfy the judgment to the extent that the purchase price under the contract is unpaid. To the extent that the seller could assign the right to payment, she can be forced to do so by levy and sale, as to future payments.

Following is a fairly typical ILSC, taken and adapted from Minn. Stat. §507.14, Uniform Conveyancing Blanks, Contract for Deed (2004).

4. Acquisition Techniques Other than Executory Contracts

INSTALLMENT LAND SALE CONTRACT

This agreement, made this _____ day of _____ (month), _____ (year), is between, _____ Seller, and, _____ Buyer.

    Witnesseth that the Seller, in consideration of the payments to be made by the Buyer and the conditions and covenants to be kept and performed by him, agrees to sell, and the Buyer agrees to buy, the real property, situated in the _____County of _____, State of _____described as follows:

_____

_____

_____ for the sum of _____ (U.S.) dollars, and the Buyer, in consideration of the premises, promises and agrees to pay the Seller the aforesaid sum of money, for all said real property, as follows, to wit: _____ dollars upon the execution and delivery hereof, the receipt whereof is hereby acknowledged, and the balance of _____ dollars in installments, including interest on all unpaid principal from date hereof until date of payment at the rate of _____ per centum per annum. The first installment of _____ dollars to be paid _____, _____, and a like amount shall be paid on the same day of each _____ thereafter until the balance of principal and interest has been paid in full. The amount of the final payment, however, shall be the total of the principal and interest then due.

IN ADDITION IT IS AGREED AS FOLLOWS:

1. Possession. Possession shall be delivered to the Buyer upon the execution and delivery of this agreement, unless otherwise provided herein.
2. Taxes and Assessments. The Buyer shall pay all taxes and assessments from date hereof and assessed and levied against said property hereafter, unless otherwise specified herein. Taxes for the fiscal year ending June 30th following the date of this agreement shall be prorated, unless otherwise specified.
3. Deed, Title. The Seller on receiving payment of all amounts of money mentioned herein shall execute a grant deed for said property in favor of said Buyer and shall deliver said deed to said Buyer. As of the date of delivery of deed, the Seller shall supply the Buyer with a Policy of Title Insurance or Certificate of Title, issued by a reliable title company, that shows the title to said property to be merchantable and free from taxes, assessments, liens and encumbrances, except those set forth herein and those that may be suffered or created hereafter by Buyer. The Seller shall pay for this policy.
4. Default by Buyer. Should the Buyer default in the payment of said purchase price or any of the covenants and/or conditions herein provided, and if such default shall continue for 30 days, then, after the lapse of said 30 days, all moneys and payments previously paid shall, at the option of the Seller without notice or demand, be and become forfeited and be taken and retained by the Seller as liquidated damages and thereupon this contract shall terminate and be of no further force or effect and thereupon the Seller shall be released from all obligations in law or equity to convey said property and any occupancy of said property thereafter by Buyer shall be a tenancy at sufferance and Buyer shall never acquire and expressly waives any and all rights or claims of title because of such possession.

4. Acquisition Techniques Other than Executory Contracts

> 5. Legal Expenses. Should the Seller sue the Buyer to enforce this agreement or any of its terms, the Buyer shall pay a reasonable attorney fee and all expenses in connection with Seller's enforcement.
>
> 6. Seller's Option to Deliver Deed in Exchange for Note Secured by a Mortgage. The Seller reserves the right to deliver the deed, at any time during the term thereof, and the Buyer, in lieu of this agreement, shall execute and deliver to said Seller or his assignee a note for all amounts of money then unpaid and said notes shall be secured by a Mortgage on said property, Buyer executing and delivering this Note and Mortgage at the same time.
>
> 7. Effect of Waiver. The waiver by the Seller of any covenant, condition or agreement herein contained shall not vitiate the same or any other covenant, condition or agreement contained herein, and the terms, conditions, covenants and agreements herein shall bind the heirs, successors, and assigns of each of the parties hereto. Time is the essence of this agreement.
>
> 8. Fire Insurance. The Buyer shall insure the buildings now on said property, if any, or such buildings as may be placed thereon, against fire, for not less than 75% of the value thereof, with an insurer approved by the Seller and any loss thereunder shall be paid to the Buyer and Seller as their interests may appear. Should said property be not insured by the Buyer, the Seller may insure it and the cost thereof shall be paid by the Buyer upon demand. All insurance policies to be issued shall be delivered to and held by the Seller until all amounts of money to be paid by the Buyer have been paid in full.
>
> In Witness Whereof, said parties have executed this agreement as of the day and year first above written. [Signatures and acknowledgments follow.]

Example 3

Numbered paragraph 3, "Deed, Title," in the foregoing contract gives the buyer a right to have a title insurance policy "supplied" to her. How does this right fit prior law?

Explanation

Recall the traditional rule about proving the title marketable, and you will realize that this is more generous to the buyer than prior law generally was. Because the rules applicable to executory contracts of sale have been applied to ILSCs without much thought about the differences between the two types of contracts, the ILSC seller has no duty to prove that her title is marketable until the last installment payment is made. A lack of marketable title in the seller in the meantime does not give the buyer the right to rescind the contract. See Luette v. Bank of Italy Nat'l Tr. & Sav. Ass'n, 42 P.2d 9 (9th Cir.), cert. denied, 282 U.S. 884 (1930). In regions where title insurance is the only form of title assurance available, there is scant difference between this

79

4. Acquisition Techniques Other than Executory Contracts

provision and prior law, but there are many unanswered issues arising under ¶3. For example, is the buyer to be the insured party? If not, may the buyer become a third-party beneficiary of the seller as an insured party? Probably. Is the policy to show that the title is marketable—or "merchantable" here, meaning the same thing—or once the other "defects" are noted, is it enough that the title is merely insurable? No. An insurable title is never enough.

Example 4

A seller executes the foregoing ILSC. The buyer damages the property and defaults. The seller, realizing that the forfeiture clause will end the buyer's interest in the property, calls you for advice on whether to proceed with a forfeiture. What questions would you ask before advising the seller to proceed?

Explanation

What might the seller give up by using the forfeiture provision? In general, you might research the question of whether forfeiture is the seller's exclusive remedy under this contract. See Matter of Witte, 841 F.2d 804, 808 (7th Cir. 1988). Paragraphs 4 and 7 of the contract are silent on this point, but the drastic nature of a forfeiture would encourage a court to find that its use was an exclusive remedy. This conclusion might be based either on the idea of preventing a double recovery by the seller when payments are also retained, or on the premise that the retention of payments is the equivalent of a liquidated damages clause. If the buyer has damaged the property or committed waste thereon, the seller might not want to end the contract relationship before suing for damages or in waste. Using the forfeiture provision might also be found to be a waiver of other remedies. See Rudnitski v. Seely, 452 N.W.2d 664, 666 (Minn. 1990). Moreover, in a jurisdiction in which an ILSC must be foreclosed like a mortgage, may the seller accelerate the unpaid contract debt after a default? In some jurisdictions, accelerating the debt is possible as an exercise of a court's equitable powers, even though there is no express acceleration provision in the contract; if the court implies a right to accelerate, the seller should foreclose the contract and provide for a period of time in which the buyer has a right to redeem the property for the amount accelerated.

Example 5

A seller using the foregoing contract wishes to have the buyer execute a note and mortgage as provided in ¶6. Does the buyer have the right to respond by prepaying the unpaid contract debt?

4. Acquisition Techniques Other than Executory Contracts

Explanation

On a principal of mutuality, when the seller has rights under ¶6, the buyer should have the privilege of prepayment where permitted by state law. A buyer should not be forced into a new, long-term relationship against her will, particularly when the seller/mortgagee has the right to assign the mortgage to a third party, as provided in ¶6.

Example 6

Mortgages often contain a union or standard mortgage clause, permitting a mortgagee to deal directly with any insurer as an insured and not be subject to any defenses that an insurer would have against the insured. Is ¶8 of the contract such a clause?

Explanation

No. Giving the seller the right to be insured and to hold the policy is not the same thing as giving him rights under the standard mortgage clause. When a contract is transformed into a mortgage, its express provisions should control and trump the importation of other standard mortgage covenants into the contract.

State Legislation

Many jurisdictions have legislated on some of the problems discussed here. An Oklahoma statute, for example, provides that an ILSC "shall be deemed and held to be mortgages, and shall be subject to the same rules of foreclosure and to the same regulations, restraints, and forms as are proscribed in relation to mortgages." See 16 Okla. Stat. §11A (2004, enacted 1978), discussed in Note, The Decline of the Contract for Deed in Oklahoma, 14 Tulsa L.J. 557 (1979). The Oklahoma statute makes no distinction between residential and commercial transactions.[4]

---

4. In contrast, Ohio Code Ann. §5313.07 (2013) requires foreclosure when an ILSC is used for property improved with a "dwelling" when its residential purchaser has made payments

4. Acquisition Techniques Other than Executory Contracts

Florida has a similar statute. See Fla. Stat. Ann. §697.01 (2005). It too makes no distinction between residential and commercial buyers. With such a statute in its code, a jurisdiction is returned to the questions raised by a general holding that a ILSC may be re-characterized as a mortgage: If the contract is to be treated as a mortgage, what type of mortgage? Title or lien? Because the statute is probably intended to avoid the drastic effects of its forfeiture provision, the best guess is that the legislature intends an ILSC to be treated as a lien mortgage. Unless the buyer has little or no equity in the property, the courts are also unlikely to grant her the traditional remedy for a title mortgage default (strict foreclosure). See Vandenberg v. Wells, 721 So. 2d 453 (Fla. Dist. Ct. App. 1998).

When after default will the mortgagee be able to take possession of the secured property? Only if the recharacterized contract is treated as a title mortgage does the "mortgagee" have the right to possession upon default. Probably not. The intent of the statute is to make the forfeiture provision less, not more, self-executing. Moreover, if the contract is subjected to all the rules relating to mortgages, and not just foreclosure, then the right to possession will be postponed until sometime after foreclosure is complete.

When an ILSC is subject to foreclosure, it is typically also subject to the ancillary actions, such as an action for a deficiency judgment, which usually accompanies foreclosure, except where anti-deficiency judgment statutes apply; there the mortgagee might not obtain a deficiency judgment when arising from the foreclosure of the recharacterized contract.

Other generally worded state statutes provide a redemption period — 30 days to a year. See, e.g., Ariz. Rev. Stat. §§33-702 and 33-472(D) and In re Kelland Invs., LLC, 2013 Bankr. LEXIS 4130 (Bankr. D. Ariz. Sept. 30, 2013). The Arizona statute provides for a variable redemption period, depending on the amount of payments made. Typically, the period starts to run when the seller provides a notice of her intent to terminate or cancel the contract. These redemptive periods have been used by courts nonetheless to imply a right to refinance and to assign the redemption right. Harder to imply are a buyer's right to any, even a partial, refund of payments. See Wayzata Enters., Inc. v. Herman, 128 N.W.2d 156, 158 (Minn. 1964) (denying such a right). During the redemption period, the buyer usually has the right to cure the default, and if cured, the contract is reinstated.

GROUND LEASES

Consider the developer who purchases the land (here meaning the sub-surface, soil, the surface, and the air space above the surface — the common

---

of more than 20% of the purchase price or has made payments for five years. If the ILSC is otherwise silent, qualifying payments must be those allocated to principal, not interest.

law version of real property) on which a project will be located, then immediately sells it, and simultaneously leases it back. Or, the same developer can lease the ground (meaning the land defined previously). Leasing the ground means splitting the title to it into a term for years and a reversion (the latter including the contractual right to receive ground rents). See Elda Corp. v. Holliday, LLC, 171 N.E.3d 124 (Ind. Ct. App. 2021), and Rockledge Assocs. LLC v. Transamerica Life Ins. Co., 2017 U.S. Dist. LEXIS 16039 (D. Md., Feb. 3, 2017), aff'd, 717 Fed. Appx. 222 (4th Cir. 2018).

A lease of the ground will also provide a lease of the air space, in which the building can be constructed. As an income tax matter, the ground is not depreciable, but the ground lease rental is a business expense for a developer, and depreciation deductions can be taken on any building or improvement once constructed — thus a ground lease often maximizes the tax advantages offered the developer by the Internal Revenue Code.

Ground Lease Negotiations

What sort of motives are involved when parties negotiate the terms of a ground lease? The holder of the fee simple title to the ground, the landlord, may wish to receive income from land that has appreciated, or that she believes will appreciate, greatly in value, but is not yet willing to pay the taxable gain that would be recognized upon a sale of the property. (She may, for example, be near retirement and want a less labor-intensive involvement in the real estate market; she may even be thinking of the lease as an estate planning device, planning to use it as a way of passing the property to her heirs, who can receive it with a stepped-up basis; or she may have no immediate need for liquidity.) The lease preserves her capital asset.

The prospective developer and tenant, on the other hand, want to own enough property rights to permit her to exercise her managerial and organizational skills. She will also want to limit the recourse of the landlord to the business she organizes on the leased premises and steer clear of putting her personal assets at risk. She wants the lease to be "nonrecourse" except as to the business conducted on the leased premises. This means that in the event of default by the tenant, the landlord may seize the building or assets of the business conducted on the leased premises, but may not seize any of the tenant's other assets. Landlords looking to the cash that will likely flow to the tenant from the project, rather than to the personal credit and assets of the tenant as the basis for making the lease, are likely to agree to a nonrecourse lease. The landlord, however, may well resist this, arguing that if any later mortgagee will want recourse to the personal assets of the tenant, why shouldn't the landlord be on a par with that mortgagee?

The tenant will bargain hard for freedom to arrange for financing, including the right to subordinate the lease to later mortgage liens, and for

4. Acquisition Techniques Other than Executory Contracts

the right to assign the lease. Will the landlord want to restrict such rights and bargain just as hard the other way? The landlord wouldn't push too hard for such restrictions. Often she doesn't have much incentive to do so, but even if she did, the landlord who involves herself in project decisions runs into the rule in a majority of states that when a tenant acts as an agent for the landlord who requires or authorizes improvements on the leased premises, a mechanic's lien will attach to the landlord's reversion and fee simple title; without some such affirmative action on the landlord's part, however, a mechanic's lien that is filed because of the actions of the tenant will not attach to the fee.

This lease must be drawn up, however, with an eye to making it possible to finance with a construction, and later a permanent mortgage, lender. Those lenders may even be in on the negotiations, insisting that they have the right to step in to cure lease defaults and to prevent the lease from being forfeited. Like the landlord, the lenders will look primarily to the project's cash flow to repay their loans.

Let's use the office building developer for some further elaboration of a "buy only what he needs" rule. After you have divided the surface and the air space into different "parcels," think about how the developer might deal with each parcel. Each can be bought outright; bought, then mortgaged; sold and leased back; or leased outright.

Consider the air rights as one parcel. It can be physically subdivided; the condominium regime is an example of such a subdivision. But that can't happen until the building is up; meanwhile, the developer will need to have capital sufficient to carry her to the point of sale of the condominium units.

Meanwhile, it can also be "subdivided" along a time line—split into present and future interests. The present interest is the right to possession, given in leases to occupants. One future right is the right to manage the possession of the property. A third right is the landlord's reversion. (This split is the invention not of a lawyer, but of a developer, William Zeckendorf, short on cash for one of his early New York projects.) For example, in any office building lease, the tenant pays for two things of value: (1) the present right to occupy and (2) the cost to the landlord of postponing the latter's own possession to a future date. These things can be separated—that is, the income stream from the property can be divided into two parts, depending on the aims of investors. Once separated, they can be used as collateral for two separate mortgages, in advance of receipt of the income from the building.

Consider two identical office buildings, each with a single tenant of equal creditworthiness. In Building 1, the lease has 3 years to run, but was negotiated 12 years ago and brings in $100,000 in rent annually. Building 2 fetches $200,000 in rent from a lease negotiated last year but with 14 years to run. If the reversion is mortgaged, Building 2 will fetch relatively little, while Building 1 will fetch a lot more; if the present right to occupy is mortgaged, the reverse is true.

4. Acquisition Techniques Other than Executory Contracts

Different investors have different aims. One may be interested in the long term; her money will be "patient" since she can accept the benefits of the ground lease. (Pension funds and insurance companies are examples.) She will become the lessor of the ground lease. An investor with less patience will become the holder of the reversion in the air rights. And an investor with even less patience (defined here as interested in shorter-term investments) will become the recipient of that portion of the income stream representing the present right to occupy, which can fluctuate as individual leases in the building are negotiated.

How does the building stay legally attached to the land if the mortgagee of the ground lease could foreclose and wipe out inferior (junior) interests, such as the construction mortgagee's lien? One method is a subordination agreement. Another answer lies in exploring the components of the ground lease. It transfers a right to possession to the lessee for a term; that right might include the nonpossessory right to create an interest that attaches the building to the land — an easement of access, or a covenant that attaches to the lease and runs with it, to bind the successors of the ground landlord.

The seller/landlord willing to execute a ground lease is often another developer with land inventory to spare, or a developer's family that wishes a long-term, secure, passive investment for family members no longer interested in the real estate development business themselves. Sometimes a developer uses a ground lease to permit the tenant to operate an interim business until the developer needs the premises for his own development. See Triple J Parking, Inc. v. SCSB LLC, 436 P.3d 185 (Utah. Ct. App. 2018) (involving a nine year ground lease for a parking lot). Governmental agencies also favor ground leases as a way of giving them leverage over projects developed on their land. Finally a private lessor might be interested in deferring capital gains tax which would be payable on a sale when in contrast, the rent the seller receives is taxed at ordinary income rates.

The ground lease thus permits a developer to take possession of the ground for long periods of time, typically for decades and sometimes for terms as long as 99 years, without paying its full purchase price. A developer pays ground rent instead, thus increasing his cash-on-cash return while permitting him to improve the ground with whatever commercial real estate development project he has in mind. For federal income tax purposes, the ground rent is fully deductible in the year paid and, when the improvement project is complete, repair and maintenance expenses are likewise fully deductible, plus the improvements can be depreciated (while the land beneath it cannot). In turn, those improvements typically provide security for the payment of the ground rent. (At the end of the ground lease's term, the ground landlord will of course own the improvements, but by then the developer/tenant will have recouped his investment.)

Both the landlord's and the tenant's interests are assignable and mortgageable. Typically the tenant warrants and represents that it will maintain

85

4. Acquisition Techniques Other than Executory Contracts

the project property "in good order and condition" and not mortgage it if the ground lease is in default. See 58 Swansea Mall LLC v. Gator Swansea Prop., LLC, 981 F.3d 117 (1st Cir. 2020). When the tenant contemplates improving the project property, however, his mortgagee will also insist the landlord not mortgage its interest until after the tenant's mortgage is executed and recorded; otherwise any foreclosure of the landlord's mortgage will wipe out the then junior tenant's mortgage. The tenant's mortgagee will underwrite a loan based on the completed and present value of the project improvements amortized over their expected life. Conversely, the longer the term of the ground lease, the less the landlord's interest will be worth to a mortgage lender when the improvements (valued at the end of the lease's term) are discounted to their present value.

The ground lease is typically a "bond lease" or a "net lease" — and usually a "triple-net lease" — that is, the developer as a tenant has the duty to pay three types of obligations imposed on any commercial development owner: (1) the real estate taxes, (2) the insurance premiums, and (3) operating costs, not just for the ground itself, but also for the maintenance and repair of the improvements on it. In addition, the ground tenant agrees to indemnify the landlord for any tort and environmental claims. In these ways, the ground landlord attempts to escape the liabilities of ownership. To emphasize this fact, the ground landlord requires the ground lessee to warrant and represent that the tenant and any sub-tenant of the improvements on the ground will not use or dispose of hazardous or toxic wastes on site, and will in addition properly and safely maintain the improvements on site.

The ground lease, viewed as a financing device, is akin to the owner of the ground conveying the fee simple to the ground and accepting a take-back, purchase money mortgage instead of the purchase price. See State v. Goldberg, 85 A.3d 231 (Md. 2014). Indeed, often the ground rent looks like an unamortized mortgage payment in amount. See In re Kelland Invs., LLC, 2013 Bankr. LEXIS 4130 (D. Ariz., Sept. 20, 2013) (discussing factors considered to avoid re-characterizing the ground lease as a mortgage). To distinguish the ground lease from a take-back mortgage, the term of the ground lease is typically longer than the term of the developer's mortgage. See Randall Ford, Inc. v. Randall, 2021 Ark. App. LEXIS 386 (Ark. Ct. App., Sept 29, 2021). The reason why the ground lease has a longer term than the leasehold mortgage is lender-driven: toward the end of the lease term, a lender will find it more difficult (if not impossible) to sell the loan and exit the deal, as the assignee of the mortgage will lose the security for the mortgage when the leasehold term ends. No rational mortgage lender would extend a loan for 10 years if the ground lease was going to end in 5 years — just as no rational buyer would buy the improvements just before the ground landlord's reversion and right of reentry becomes a present interest. By the same token, it may become difficult to renovate or modernize an improvement sited on a ground lease as the lease nears its expiration. These

4. Acquisition Techniques Other than Executory Contracts

financing problems may be mitigated by the landlord giving the tenant an option to purchase the fee simple, but landlord will bargain hard before extending such an option when it is about the receive the improvements, tax-free, at the end of the lease. Better, from the tenant's perspective, to bargain for such an option at the beginning of the ground lease.

Absent the need for special rules, the same rules of construction and interpretation governing leases generally also govern ground leases

The following document is a bare bones one — with provisions asking you to think about timing its execution and putting its provisions in sync with leasehold construction and permanent mortgages. Some further provisions are explored in the Examples following it.

GROUND LEASE

Lessor by this document, grants, lets, and demises to the *Lessee* Development Corporation (Lessee), *for a term of 40 years* commencing on the date of execution of this lease, *without contingencies*, with *an option to renew* for an additional term of _____, all those premises known as _____, and described as follows:
[insert legal description, habendum, and warranties]
The consideration for this lease shall be

A *Deposit* of ___, paid at the execution of this lease, and a *Base Rent* of _____ annually, paid monthly, with an *abatement [or prepayment]* of _____ and . . . .

Lessee warrants and represents that it has performed its due diligence during the 90 days prior to the execution of this lease, found the premises suitable for the development of _____(the project, comprising at least 80% of the ground subject to this lease), and further warrants that will indemnify Lessor if that the project is not completed within 3 years of the commencement of this lease.

Lessee further warrants and represents that it will start the project identified in the prior paragraph within ___ months of the commencement date of this lease and pursue its development diligently and in good faith, *completing the project within 3 years of the start date, with extensions* for force majeure events and for satisfying the requirements and demands of leasehold lenders and mortgagees.

Lessee further warrants and represents that it will deposit in an *escrow account satisfactory to any future leasehold mortgagee*, monthly deposits to pay real estate taxes, assessments, and insurance, the escrow being.

Lessee further warrants and represents that it has delivered to the Lessor in a form satisfactory to any future leasehold mortgagee (1) *guarantees of payment and completion* to indemnify Lessor for the construction and completion of the project, (2) evidence that all *pre-construction permits* have been obtained, (3) evidence that a *fixed price or guaranteed maximum price contract* with a general contractor satisfactory to Lessor, (4) evidence that the lessee has met *all equity requirements* for starting construction of the project, (3) evidence that the lessee has *closed a construction loan for the project*, along with any guarantees required by the leasehold mortgagee closing that loan, and is entitled to the first advance of construction loan proceeds.

87

4. Acquisition Techniques Other than Executory Contracts

The *Lessee shall not sublease or assign* this lease without the prior, written approval and consent of the lessor; such consent shall not be unreasonably withheld; provided that (i) nothing in this paragraph shall prevent the Lessee from mortgaging this lease and (ii) the approval provisions of this paragraph shall not apply to transfers made to any leasehold mortgagee or to third parties by reason of a default of the leasehold mortgagor and the foreclosure of such mortgage. Assignees of this lease shall assume, and not take subject to, all obligations of the Lessee hereunder.

Lessor shall provide Lessee with a certificate stating the rents paid hereunder to any leasehold mortgagee designated by Lessee.

This lease *shall not be terminated or amended* without securing the prior written consent of any leasehold mortgagee and before it may be terminated by the Lessor for any default, notice on any existing default shall be provided to such mortgagee; such mortgagee shall, upon notice, have the right to cure the default or take any remedial action necessary to cure and prevent termination, including rights of entry on the premises.

This lease is *not terminated by the bankruptcy of the Lessee* [or may be so terminated if first an opportunity to foreclose the interest of the leasehold mortgagee is provided].

Given and acknowledged this day of, 20__, by our signatures below.

Lessor

Lessee

Here is some commentary on the italicized words and phrases used in this form.

—*Lessor* may or may not be a special purpose entity (SPE). The developer's attorney will point out the advantages of using a separate SPE to the lessor leasing premises. Thus both the lessor and lessee will likely be an SPE. An SPE is typically a separate limited liability company to hold the lessor or lessee's interests in the ground even if either party enters bankruptcy. (This can be important when the completed project is securitized.) A provision to this effect appears later in the lease. As long as certain accounting criteria are met, neither party has to record the entity in its accounting records. SPEs make both parties look less risky and more profitable than they otherwise might appear.

—*Lessee* will undoubtedly be an SPE.

—*for a term of 40 years?* How is the term determined? Any mortgage lender will want it to be longer than the mortgage, and since that is unlikely to be more than 30 years, 40 years is long enough from the lender's perspective. But the lessee as the owner of the building will want the term to last as long as the useful life of the building constructed on the leasehold—and although 40 years exceeds the depreciable life of the property for income tax purposes, the actual useful life will likely be longer. If the lessor resists a longer term, the lessee can offer to increase the rent periodically, according to some predetermined index. The term could be longer. Ground lease

4. Acquisition Techniques Other than Executory Contracts

terms of 99 years are not uncommon, particularly in downtown areas of cities. See Fay Corp. v. Frederick and Nelson Seattle, Inc., 896 F.2d 1227 (9th Cir. 1990) (involving a 99 year lease of a department store). However, the term must have an immediate commencement date; a term starting "upon the completion of a building now under construction upon the promises" creates a future interest — a springing executory interest—in violation of the common law Rule against Perpetuities and so is void *ab initio*. Most jurisdictions have modified the Rule by statute, and some jurisdictions—e.g., California and Louisiana—have limited the terms of various types of leases to a fixed number of years.

—*an option to renew*. Typically such renewal options have a deadline by which the lessee must notify the Lessor of its intention to renew. The deadline is just that—the lessee could renew sooner. The lessee wants the exercise of any option to coincide with dates resetting the rent. Why? Just to give the lessee some leverage in the reset. This leverage becomes all the stronger if the parties agree on a 99-year lease with cancellation rights instead of renewal rights during the term. From the developer's point of view, a single term with periodic rent adjustments might be preferable, but some lessors might resist. What if the neighborhood changes around the leasehold, or the developer does not renovate the building to the lessor's satisfaction? Any lender at the time that the right to renew may be exercised will want the right to step in and exercise the right if the lessee does not exercise it in a timely manner.

—*without contingencies*. If the parties have had prior successful dealings, perhaps in implementing an agreement or letter of intent to lease, with this form attached as an exhibit, or when the market is lessor-friendly, the ground lessee will have completed its due diligence during a set period of time during the term of the agreement; when this agreement precedes the lease, a lessor might be obligated to tender the exhibited lease at the end of the lessee's due diligence period. As with most letters of intent, the agreement to lease should contain exclusivity, confidentiality, and nonbinding provisions. See Landan v. Wal-Mart Real Estate Bus. Tr., 2016 U.S. Dist. LEXIS 129481 (W.D. Pa. Sept. 22, 2016). Otherwise the lessee's due diligence will be performed during the lease's term and after its commencement date. In a lease that provides the lessee with a due diligence period, the lessee's estate or interest should be a future one—i.e., the date of execution and the date of commencement should be different, with the latter following the former; between those two dates, the lease will provide that it will commence only when the lessee gives a so-called notice to proceed, with the commencement date following within a certain number of days after the notice.

—*Deposit*. It might also be characterized as interim rent, paid between the execution and the commencement date of the lease when those two dates are defined separately in the lease. In general, lessees often resist merging the two dates. Why? Because any transfer taxes applicable to the lease

4. Acquisition Techniques Other than Executory Contracts

will be due and payable on the lease's commencement date. So putting that date off, into the future, will save the lessee the tax due for the interim.

— *Base Rent.* For a ground lease of vacant land, the Base Rent is the appraised fair market value of what the lessor demises and delivers to the lessee. Thus the value of the vacant land delivered to the Lessee, unencumbered by the lease and available for any permitted land use and with all development rights not brought to the land from other land parcels, provides the basis for the initial appraisal. Thus the lessee does not want any reference in the definition of Base Rent to the project property or any improvements constructed by the lessee.

With a deposit paid at the lease's execution, the first payment of Base Rent is made after the commencement date of the lease. For leases with shorter terms, a Base Rent schedule for each succeeding year of the lease term might be set out as an Exhibit incorporated by reference into the lease. For longer leases, "bumps" up in the Base Rent are scheduled every 2 to 5 years, the bump referring back either to the original Base Rent or to the last prior Base Rent bump. The bump can be stated as a percentage increase in the Base Rent — somewhere in the minimum-maximum 3% to 8% range, depending on the predicted inflation built into the market — or as an increase measured at a minimum by the regional Consumer Price Index, or CPI, over the chosen adjustment period. See Howard Town Ctr. Developer, LLC v. Howard Univ., 278 F. Supp. 3d 333 (D. D.C. 2017). An alternative index for Base Rent bumps might be the current yield to maturity of United States Treasury bonds with a remaining term equal to that of the lease, plus a defined annual percentage yield. On every bump resetting the Base Rent, the reappraisal (if there is one — probably a process to be used only when the bumps are widely spaced in time) should be based on the fee interest of the lessor, now encumbered by the lease.

— *abatement [or prepayment]*, depending on whether the market favors lessees or lessors, respectively. If the market is pro-lessee, an abatement of several months is more likely, and if it is pro-lessor, prepayments are more likely.

— *completing the project within 3 years of the start date, with extensions.* Lessors often request a cap for any extension of a set number of months. For any extension, the lessee might provide some additional security (such as a letter of credit), pay an extension fee, and/or prepay the Base Rent for the extension period, the prepayment credited only against Base Rent after completion of the project. Leases often also require some showing of diligent pursuit of completion.

— *escrow account satisfactory to any future leasehold mortgagee.* In practice, this account will be controlled by the mortgagee. If the market for the lease is lessor-friendly, the lessor might in addition require an escrow for the transactional costs of the leasing transaction.

4. Acquisition Techniques Other than Executory Contracts

—guarantees of payment and completion typically cover the general contractor's performance of its contractual obligations to the developer, not the lessee's performance of its leasehold obligations. This warranty is insisted on by many lessors because the SPE-lessee typically has no credit history and, aside from the construction loan to follow, no prior extensions of credit. Bonds for this purpose are expensive, so the presence of a guarantor supplied by the lessee, plus letters of credit and cash deposited in escrow are often combined to satisfy this requirement. However, piling these types of completion assurances on top of each other may create completion assurances with "executory" features subject to rejection in a lessee's bankruptcy.

—pre-construction permits. This warranty provides back-up assurance to the lessor that construction can be started and finished within the time allotted in the prior warranty in the lease.

—fixed price or guaranteed maximum price contract. These two types of contracts are preferred by lessors who when they subordinate the lease to future construction and permanent lenders, know the maximum extent of the subordination.

—all equity requirements. Equity is required by lessor as assurance that the tenant/developer has skin in the game and, when the equity is in form of mezzanine financing[5] and comes from third-party investors, that the finances for the project have been given independent scrutiny by those investors.

—closed a construction loan for the project. The four warranties in this paragraph of the lease assume that the lease itself is one of the last documents bringing the project to the start of construction. When this is not the case, then each and every one of them can be re-worded and turned into a pre-closing condition precedent to the lease's execution.

—Lessee shall not sublease or assign. This paragraph and the following three paragraphs of the lease are for the benefit of a leasehold mortgagee, who will want its attorney to review the lease to assure itself that the basis for its mortgage lien may not be destroyed (thus destroying the mortgage lien itself in many jurisdictions). What are the alternatives to the anti-assignment clause as written? The lessor and the mortgagee may have difference levels of interest in preventing an assignment, but each will seek reassurance that any assignment is to an assignee with a credit rating equal to or better than the lessee's, or that any assignee have the same business expertise so as to be able to step quickly into the lessee's business, or that when the lessee's current entity structure is changed, the same or similarly qualified businessmen continue to control it. Each of these more limited assignments might replace what's in the lease now.

---

5. For a discussion of mezzanine financing, see infra, Chapter 9.

4. Acquisition Techniques Other than Executory Contracts

— *This lease shall not be terminated or amended.* The "no termination or amendment" clause may be a blanket protection for the leasehold mortgage lender. However, the latter's real concern may be that there be no renegotiation of the rental covenant in the lease, or that the mortgagee be included in any renegotiation. In the alternative, on termination, the lessor might agree to enter into a new lease with the leasehold mortgagee for the remaining term of the mortgage, perhaps paying the lessor's costs involved in entering into the new lease. Because rejection of the ground lease in a bankruptcy is possible, this "new lease" provision should be in a separate document.

— *not terminated by the bankruptcy of the Lessee.* This provision might be deleted if the leasehold mortgagee is given an opportunity to foreclose before any voluntary bankruptcy.

— *given and acknowledged.* This means that the lease will be recordable, and it or a memorandum of its contents should be recorded. The significance of this provision is that it gives successors in interest to the land and building notice of the agreement between the lessor and the lessee. It prevents any third party from becoming a bona fide purchaser under the applicable recording act.

What other provisions might be included? Obviously there are many more provisions possible, but several might include the following:

(1) An anti-merger provision, preventing the destruction of the lease when the ground and building come into the same hands, as when the developer buys the ground and does not wish to have to renegotiate the mortgage loan;

(2) A provision concerning the lessor's right to mortgage the ground. A mortgage lender for the building might be concerned if and when the lessor mortgages the ground in the future, using the ground lease rent as collateral—thus this right might be prohibited outright, or if not, then provision might be made either for the lessor's mortgage to be subordinate to the lessee's leasehold mortgage or for the lessor to pledge the rents and provide nondisturbance assurances from any future lender;

(3) A provision subordinating the lease to any future mortgage for improvements. Modernizing and renovating the building will benefit both lessor and lessee, but the lessor might have a concern that the building not be overimproved with improvements that the fair market value of the building will not reflect. So the lessor may want some right to review modernization plans, or else a lockbox for income and profits from the building insofar as they are necessary to guarantee payment of the ground rents;

(4) An option for the lessee to purchase the ground. If such an option is exercisable at so low a price, relative to the ground's fair market value, that the lessee is unlikely to let the option lapse, the Internal Revenue Service will likely deny a §162(a) business deduction for

4. Acquisition Techniques Other than Executory Contracts

the ground rents and instead treat the "lease" as a sale. To avoid this, (a) rental payments should be at fair rental levels, not be large over a short period of time, not be labeled anything other than rent (and particularly not labeled interest), and should not be applied to the purchase price; (b) an express appraisal procedure for setting the option price at its fair market level should be provided; and generally (c) the lease should satisfy the "economic factors" test in Frank Lyon Co. v. United States, 435 U.S. 561 (1978), discussed in Chapter 6.

Examples

Example 7

A prospective ground lessor proposes that the Base Rent for the lease be calculated as so many "dollars per buildable square foot." As the lessee's attorney, how would you respond?

Explanation

With caution. The project will be built according to the plans and specifications designed by the architect, but the "as built" plans and specs needed for the maintenance and repair of the project may not be identical to them. Thus a "buildable" square foot may not be a rentable or useable one that will be used to establish the cash flow of the project.

Example 8

A prospective ground lessee proposes that the Base Rent be defined in a schedule of payments for the first 10 years of the leasehold term. As the lessor's attorney, how would you respond?

Explanation

With caution. The proposal suggests fixed payments of Base Rent over time; that in turn suggests that the alternative investment for your client is a bond of some type. That is how the schedule should be evaluated by the client. The proposed payments should be discounted to present value and evaluated against the predictable increases in occupancy rents over time. Lessor and lessee may use different discount rates, thus valuing the lease differently. This difference may bring on disputes and litigation later, as there would be no meeting of the minds at the execution of the lease.

93

4. Acquisition Techniques Other than Executory Contracts

Example 9

A prospective ground lessee proposes to eliminate the definition of the lease's fair market value proposed by the lessor in the definition of Base Rent when used for any rent bump. The lessor proposes that the definition be "the value of the vacant land delivered to the Lessee, unencumbered by the lease and available for any legally permitted land use and with all development rights not brought to the land from other land parcels and reflecting all property tax incentives for which the site is qualified." As the lessee's attorney, how would you respond?

Explanation

A good idea, if the parties can agree. The more complicated this appraisal definition becomes, the more likely it is to breed disputes and litigation on any Base Rent bump. It may be better to agree to a percentage increase after the initial appraisal and upon any bump rather than continue to use the initial definition of the lease's fair market value; a fixed percentage will take the value of the project built on the site into account. In addition, the lessee may want to narrow the phrase "any legally permitted use" to the use "as built"; this will eliminate controversy if the site is up-zoned in the future. In general, the lessee will want to retain for itself any value it adds to the site: "qualifying for tax incentives" is value added to the site by the lessee, implicates local government decisions which are in themselves hard to anticipate and subject to no fixed criteria. Indeed, only existing, named, and known incentives should be part of the initial appraisal.

Example 10

Lessor proposes to include in the ground lease a provision that "upon default by lessee and termination of this lease before project completion, Lessee shall deposit with lessor the estimated cost to complete the project." As the lessee's attorney, how might you respond to this proposal?

Explanation

You might respond by resisting this guarantee with an offer to prepay the ground rent for the duration of the lease, or for a fixed period after termination while the site is returned to its pre-lease status by lessee's paying for (1) the demolition of the project and (2) the release of any liens attaching to the site.

4. Acquisition Techniques Other than Executory Contracts

Example 11

Lessor's attorney proposes that the ground lease include a "hell or high water" provision — to the effect that the lessee will continue to pay the ground rent even if the project improvements on the premises are destroyed or are unusable. How should the lessee's attorney respond?

Explanation

By checking with any contemplated leasehold mortgagee. The mortgagee will react favorably. Why? Because it will render its security for the mortgage (the improvements) more secure. In any event, the lessee might impose a similar provision on its creditworthy sub-tenants. More generally, wouldn't the provision drafted as a covenant in the lease be a real covenant and "run with the land," binding remote tenants? The requirements for a real covenant — evincing an intent to run, its subject touching and concerning the land, and horizontal and vertical privity — would be satisfied. The "hell or high water" provision referenced in the sub-leases, evinces the intent; the ground lease, involving the use and possession of the premises, certainly touches and concerns the land; and recording the ground lease and the sub-tenants taking possession of their premises, satisfies the third requirement of privity. But see Duenas v. George & Matilda Kallingal, PC, 2012 Guam LEXIS 4 (Guam 2012) (holding that a ground lease provision charging interest on delinquent rent does not run).

Example 12

The lessor's attorney proposes that if and when the land is ever condemned, the lessor receives the condemnation proceeds until it is paid in full, receiving the fair market value of the fee estate, as if no condemnation occurred; the remaining proceeds are the lessee's. As the lessee's attorney, how would you respond?

Explanation

This is not a subject with which the lessee should be overly concerned. Why? Because each claim on the proceeds will be subject to the leasehold mortgagee's rights in them. However, the higher the mortgage's loan to value ratio is, the more you might push for a pro rata sharing of the proceeds based (again) "on the value of each estate, as if no condemnation occurred." Likewise, the claim on and use of all insurance proceeds are likely governed by the covenants in the leasehold mortgage, which will typically contain a duty to restore the premises bottomed on a common law duty not to commit waste. Conforming the lease provision with the mortgage's provisions

4. Acquisition Techniques Other than Executory Contracts

in this regard will make the dispute over insurance proceeds more contentious than the dispute over condemnation proceeds.

Example 13

Lessor's attorney proposes that the lessee accept the delivery of the site "as is, without any representation or warranty as to its condition, and will indemnify the lessor against all conditions, past, present, and future." As the lessee's attorney, how would you respond?

Explanation

Your first thought will be, what about environmental conditions? Or conditions that require future compliance with laws and regulations applicable to the site? You might accept liability for anything occurring after your client takes possession, but not for anything occurring beforehand, without any consideration of fault in creating the condition. You might also agree not to seek indemnity from the lessor for anything occurring before your possessing the site as long as the lessor will agree not to seek indemnity from you for anything arising afterwards. This is a contentious subject.

* * *

The assignment of ground leases. When documenting several types of commercial transactions, a recurring issue is the assignment of the rights of each party. You've probably studied the assignment of residential leases and mortgages. Similar issues arise in transaction involving ground leases. From the perspective of the lessor, a prohibition or lock-out period on the assignment of the lease until the completion of the construction of the project is probably a starting point for negotiation. See Duenas v. George & Matilda Kallingal, PC, 2012 Guam LEXIS 4 (Guam 2012). After completion, lessor will want an assignment "subject to the lessor's consent, not to be unreasonably withheld." For residential leases, the case law that interprets this phrase is well-developed. Not so for ground leases. Thus objective criteria limiting the lessor's right to withhold consent are necessary. The following criteria are illustrative. An assignor's curing all defaults beforehand is one such. An assignee's recognizing the lessor's superior rights to rents over the rights of operating and occupancy lessee's is another. Limitations on assignments to creditworthy assignees is still another. In each instance, objectivity in the criteria is preferred over criteria involving the assignee's reputation or trade experience. Some lessors may want more—namely, upon notice of a proposed assignment, the lessor might want the right to buy out the lessee's interest by proposing a right to purchase the leasehold, along with

4. Acquisition Techniques Other than Executory Contracts

a contract doing so, effective for (say) 30 days or longer if due diligence requires. Some lessees might respond by asking for the same — namely, the right to buy out the lessor who wishes to assign the leasehold's reversion and rights. The typical lessor will resist this response. By stipulation, the parties might readily agree that a default in either contract is not a default in the ground lease.

Examples

Example 14

Why would a lessor resist giving the lessee a right to purchase the lessor's reversion?

Explanation

A lessee's purchase right flies in the face of the lessor's rationale for using a ground lease in the first instance: that is, the lessor's desire for a secure, long-term, passive investment and an alternative to active management of the project on the site. Thus a lessee's purchase rights are only rarely used in ground leases, save only for an individual lessor's very long standing interest that may have so increased in value such that a stepped-up basis can reduce federal capital gain income taxes when sold by the lessor's heirs to the lessee after the lessor's death. However, considering that both lessor and lessee are likely to be SPE-LLC entities with multiple members, such a situation is very infrequent.

Moreover, no matter which party is exercising a purchase right, the contract's implementation is fraught with potential disputes and perhaps not worth the effort; it might be rejected and then replaced by a sweeter deal for the eventual assignee, leaving the opposite party feeling cheated. See Randall Ford, Inc. v. Randall, 2021 Ark. App. LEXIS 386 (Ark. Ct. App. Sept 29, 2021), and Medical Plaza One, LLC v. Davis, 552 S.W.3d 143 (Mo. Ct. App. 2018).

TAKE-BACK FINANCING AND THE SUBORDINATION AGREEMENT

As the discussion of installment contracts and ground leases makes clear, few developers will want to have a substantial amount of money tied up in the purchase of the land for a project. The developer may either be thinly capitalized or else be carrying a large inventory of land parcels, using each

97

4. Acquisition Techniques Other than Executory Contracts

parcel only as needed. One solution to this problem is to finance the land acquisition with a mortgage. However, interest rates on raw land tend to be higher than for improved property, for loans with lower loan-to-value ratios and shorter terms. The developer's response to this situation is typically an attempt to obtain her financing from the seller, in the form of an option, installment contract, a ground lease, or a purchase money or take-back mortgage.

If the developer is successful in securing a take-back mortgage, a covenant in that mortgage will typically provide:

> Mortgagee covenants that he will subordinate this mortgage to a good faith construction loan mortgage (1) not exceeding the principal amount of . . . [blank for insertion of an amount] or (2) a larger amount if approved by the mortgagee in its sole and exclusive discretion, provided in either event that this mortgage is not in default at the time of the subordination or approval.

If an installment land sale contract (ILSC) is used, the contract will similarly contain an option to convert it into a deed when the construction loan is funded, when the proceeds of that loan are available to pay off the buyer's contract obligation. When an ILSC is used, a sidebar agreement might in the alternative provide that the contract will be recorded only after the recording of the construction mortgage.

Whichever method is used -- the installment contract or the take-back, purchase money mortgage -- there is either an express provision in the contract or a reference to a sidebar agreement in the mortgage, to the effect that the seller will subordinate her interest in the property—either the lien of the mortgage or her vendor's lien under the contract—to the later lien of the construction lender.

Strictly speaking, subordination is a status, not an agreement. A subordination agreement is then a contract to shift the priority of a senior lien to a less preferred status, junior to the lien of a later identified development or construction lender. It establishes the priority of different existing liens on the same parcel by some means other than "first in time or on record, first in right or priority." The subordination of a lien is a type of waiver of its priority. It can be either a provision of a contract of sale, the escrow instructions, a mortgage, or a separate agreement. The construction lender will require a first lien on the land, and the subordination agreement is a method of achieving that and, at the same time, permitting the developer to put as little cash as possible into land acquisition.

A majority of courts considering the issue have refused to enforce subordination agreements that they consider vague and indefinite. Only definitive agreements are subject to specific performance. If the subordination clause or agreement is sufficiently precise as to the type of lien that is to attain priority over the seller's, the later subordination—meaning now a reversal

98

4. Acquisition Techniques Other than Executory Contracts

of the priorities that would otherwise be established under the recording acts—can be automatic. Thus a subordination agreement should include a statement of the maximum amount of the construction loan, the purpose of the loan, its interest rate, its term, its monthly payment, as well as a warranty that the disbursal of the loan will be applied to the particular project. Incorporating a particular mortgage form by reference is also a good idea.

The following is a skeletal subordination agreement of this type.

SUBORDINATION AGREEMENT

This agreement, made this day *[date]* between *[developer]* and *[purchase money seller, mortgagee, or lienholder]*, recognizes that the developer is about to execute a *[construction agreement, note and mortgage, referenced herein]*, and that a condition precedent to obtain the proceeds of this construction loan is the lender's obtaining a lien on the real property superior to that of the seller, NOW THEREFORE the seller agrees that he consents to and approves all provisions of the construction note and mortgage securing this note, and all agreements governing the disbursal of the proceeds of this loan. Seller further unconditionally waives, relinquishes, and subordinates his lien in favor of the lien of the construction mortgagee.

A non-automatic subordination agreement would require that the seller take a second look at the construction loan note, mortgage, and agreement, reviewing each document for compliance with the earlier agreement. Such a subordination is known as an executory subordination.

If the seller does not have this opportunity to take a second look, a court asked to review the automatic agreement is asked an all-or-nothing question: Is the agreement enforceable? Or is it too vague, or does it lack a material term and fail for indefiniteness? Would you expect a court to look more closely at an automatic or at an executory subordination? Obviously a court is less likely to second-guess a seller who has had the opportunity to review and approve the construction loan documents, and so the executory subordination will receive less scrutiny on judicial review.

If a subordination agreement requires that the proceeds of the construction loan be applied to the seller's parcel, then the diversion of the funds intended to pay off the seller is a payment for land, not for construction. To the extent that loan funds are used that way, the seller can accept the payment, benefit, and still assert a breach of the subordination agreement. The result of such a breach reestablishes the original priorities, putting the parties' *status quo ante* the subordination agreement; not a complete reordering of the priorities, but only to the extent of the breach. That breach is the diversion of construction loan proceeds, even when used to pay for fees and commissions owed by the developer-borrower for the project on the seller's parcel. The lender's priority under the agreement extends only to loan amounts properly expended for construction. Thus, when a subordinated

99

construction loan lender has misused loan proceeds to the prejudice of the subordinating seller, courts protect the seller on the theory that the lender owed an implied good faith duty inherent in the subordination agreement.

Often a lender has been held to be a third-party beneficiary of anti-diversionary provisions inserted in the subordination agreement. To counter such a holding, the seller and the developer may agree that "the construction lender in making disbursements pursuant to the note, mortgage, and construction agreement does not represent that it will, and is under no obligation to, see that the disbursements are used for the purposes agreed to." Sometimes, too, language is inserted, in larger, boldface type, warning the seller that some of the loan proceeds may be expended "for purposes other than improvement of the secured property."

The subordination agreement must preexist any default on the subordinated lien. When the mortgagee preferred in the agreement takes advantage of the subordination, it must search the public records for documents that would prevent it from assuming the agreed-to priority.

Generally, a subordination agreement will be interpreted and enforced strictly according to its express terms, However, any such agreement to subordinate to an otherwise junior lien is also, by implication, an agreement to subordinate to any lien superior to the preferred one. For example, an agreement to subordinate to a third mortgage is also an agreement to subordinate to a second mortgage.

Because a subordination agreement is a reordering of the liens and recording act priorities of the mortgages involved, it must generally be in a writing satisfying the requirements of the Statute of Frauds. If the agreement is an automatic one, the real property section of the statute is immediately applicable. If the agreement is nonautomatic, the agreement is, at its execution, an executory contract subject also to that section of the statute; that is so if (say, under the terms of the English Statute of Frauds largely adopted in this country) the later subordination is to occur a year or more in the future.

The risks of subordinated lending. Subordinating a mortgage lien is a risky business for prior lenders because once their lien becomes a junior one they risk being washed out in the foreclosure of the then-superior construction loan lien. From the construction lenders' perspective, the subordination agreement may limit their ability to amend their mortgage, grant an easement over the developer's property, agree to covenants, dedicate streets, make future advances, or share insurance proceeds or condemnation awards. Such matters may be expressly provided for in the agreement. In addition, the construction lender may be concerned about any prepayment of the now-junior lien loan affecting the ability of the developer to repay the construction loan. It may also want the developer to escrow an amount sufficient to cure any defaults in the junior lien loan, or may wish to receive any default notices the junior lienor gives to the developer/mortgagor so that it can cure them. Most courts considering the issue have refused to find

4. Acquisition Techniques Other than Executory Contracts

that a construction lender as the beneficiary of the agreement has any duty to the subordinating party to supervise the disbursal of the construction loan for the latter's benefit.

Examples

Example 15

A seller taking back a mortgage agrees that she will record this mortgage just after the construction note and mortgage are recorded. The developer and the landowner/seller make no other agreement. What type of subordination agreement is this—automatic or executory?

Explanation

Automatic. These are the facts involved in Middlebrook-Anderson Co. v. Southwest Sav. & Loan Ass'n, 96 Cal. Rptr. 338 (Cal. App. 1971). See also Carolina Builders Corp. v. Howard-Veasey Homes, Inc., 324 S.E.2d 626 (N.C. App.), rev. denied, 330 S.E.2d 606 (N.C. 1985). Further, the case law is well developed on the minimum terms required for a subordination agreement capable of specific performance. For example, required are a maximum principal amount, interest rate, and term for the construction mortgage; a use to which the construction loan funds will be put; and maximum loan to value ratios (to provide the subordinating seller with an equity cushion). These are all terms and requirements that minimize the risk that later lenders will destroy the seller's security. See MCB Ltd. v. McGowan, 359 S.E.2d 50 (N.C. App. 1987) (holding a subordination that does not specify the interest rate or principal amount of later loan void for indefiniteness as a matter of law). Lack of material terms voids the automatic subordination. Additionally, a decision to imply a subordination agreement would have to infer its terms—a reason in itself not to imply an agreement—from the actual knowledge of the construction lender—a difficulty of proof giving rise to further difficulties. Finally, as a matter of policy, the lender is best able to bear the risk of construction; it is an expert in construction lending, and so best bears the duty to achieve a clear agreement. See Handy v. Gordon, 422 P.2d 329 (Cal. 1967). Automatic subordinations are not a prudent business practice for a lender.

Example 16

If a jurisdiction voids a subordination agreement for failure to include a material term, will it also deny specific performance of such an agreement?

4. Acquisition Techniques Other than Executory Contracts

Explanation

Yes. When the agreement has already been found indefinite or vague, it seems unfair to enforce it further, particularly if the party alleging the indefiniteness has already won litigation to that effect. See Roskamp Manley Assocs. v. Davin Dev. Inv. Corp., 229 Cal. Rptr. 186, 190 (Cal. App. 1986). There is, however, authority to the contrary. Note, Real Estate Finance-Subordination Clauses: North Carolina Subordinates Substance to Form — MCB Ltd. v. McGowen, 23 Wake Forest L. Rev. 575, 592-595 (1988).

Subordination Lien Circuity

Subordination agreements sometimes create situations that result in a circuity of liens. Developers of undeveloped farmland encounter this situation when the land is subject to crop and seed loans. See Co-Alliance, LLP v. Monticello Farm Serv., 7 N.E.3d 355 (Ind. Ct. App. 2014). In this situation, every lien is superior to one as well as inferior to another. For example, O conveys a mortgage lien to A, who agrees to subordinate the lien to a later construction loan lien. A records only her lien, not the agreement. O conveys a lien to B. B records. O then conveys a third lien to C, who is a qualifying construction lender under the subordination agreement and records.

Every grantee has promptly recorded. In this instance, under any type of recording act, there is a circuity of liens. In this instance, a circuity is created by the subordination agreement.[6]

Some courts have assigned priority to B, then to C, and last to A. An agreement to subordinate to a third lien is also an agreement to subordinate to the second. B, after all, knew nothing (at least through the records) of the A-C agreement and so should not suffer on account of it. C is assigned the next slot on the list of priorities because she bargained to step ahead of A, who is left to bring up the rear. See AmSouth Bank, N.A. v. J. & D. Fin. Corp., 679 So. 2d 695 (Ala. 1996). This is the so-called "complete subordination rule." Is this a good solution? Perhaps, but B is preferred in a situation in which she did not expect to go first and so is given a windfall priority. (In terms of legal doctrine, B is made an third-party beneficiary of the subordination agreement without being named as such in it.) C, on the other hand, expected to go before A, at least to the extent of A's lien. C's expectation can be put as a matter of subrogation: C expected to step into A's shoes.

Thus, the better solution is the "partial subordination rule," preferred by the weight of modern authority. See Pricewaterhouse Coopers, Inc. v. Decca Design Build, Inc., 46 P.3d 408 (Ariz. 2002). This majority rule proceeds

---

6. There is a surprisingly large case law on circuity. Later during the construction process, circuity might also occur when the intervening lien (B's lien) is a mechanic's lien. See, e.g., VCS Inc. v. Countrywide Home Loans, 349 P.3d 704 (Utah 2015).

4. Acquisition Techniques Other than Executory Contracts

as follows: first, to set aside the amount of A's lien, which C expected to precede; second, to pay out of the amount set aside in step 1 the amount of A's lien to (1) C, up to the amount of her claim, and then (2) to A, to the extent there is any remaining balance within the amount set aside; third, to pay out to B any amount remaining after A's claim is set aside and paid out as before; and fourth, to pay out any balance remaining after the first three steps are taken, to C, up to the amount of her claim, and then to A. The first step prevents B from realizing any windfall. It also first enforces the subordination agreement to the extent possible out of a claim of which B had constructive knowledge through the records. It enforces the agreement, to the extent possible, without violating B's expectations. Then B is paid. Then the agreement is enforced again, as to the remaining balance. See Futuri Real Estate v. Atlantic Trustee Servs., LLC, 835 S.E.2d 75 (Va. 2019) (collecting the cases). This method also carries the *sub rosa* message that for the agreement to be enforced fully, it should be promptly recorded.

Examples

Example 17

B in the foregoing text is often a provider of construction services claiming the protection of the mechanic's lien statutes. A is the purchase money lienor and the landowner from whom O buys the land. And C is a construction lender-lienor. A's lien is in the amount of $4 million, B's $1 million, and C's $4 million. At the foreclosure sale, O's property is sold for $5 million. Who gets paid what?

Explanation

C is paid $4 million, and B $1 million. But the steps are different in the two methods advanced here.

Example 18

If O diverted $1 million from the construction site on A's former parcel, would your answers change?

103

4. Acquisition Techniques Other than Executory Contracts

Explanation

There is authority that says yes and that to the extent of the diversion, C does not step into A's shoes and is not preferred over A. Thus, A would still have priority over C and B, to the extent of the $1 million. However, the weight of this authority is diminished when there is no express warranty that C will police O for A's benefit in the subordination agreement. Few cases imply such a warranty. It is something for which A could have bargained but did not and C, not being a party to the original O-A agreement, is not bound to it. Thus, in the view of the majority of courts considering the issue, C has no duty to police O for A's benefit. The majority view is bolstered by cases on other, related issues — for example, whether a lender has a duty to inspect a construction site to make sure of the quality of the construction for the benefit of its later purchaser. Quality in this context is often measured by the housing code or the implied warranty of habitability. Most cases answer that the lender has no such duty. Only when the lender clearly violates prudent lending practices is such a duty likely to be imposed.

Example 19

Your developer client finds a parcel of land on which small storekeepers rent space but toward which the financial district of a city is moving. O purchased the property with its improvements 2 years ago for $2 million, but the land, if improved with a 10-story office building "constructed to the limit of the zoning envelope" for the land, would be worth $10 million. Construction costs for the building are about $8 million dollars. C is willing to provide that $8 million. O purchased the land with $100,000 down and financed the balance with a mortgage for $1.9 million, at 9% interest for 20 years, with M. After 2 years, the mortgage has an outstanding balance of $1.875 million; it is, in the jargon, "paid down" only a little. O has a firm purchase price for the property of $2.5 million dollars. In the 2 years that O has owned the property, interest rates have risen to 12%. What should you advise your client to do?

Explanation

You might advise your client on two options. You can attempt to convince M to subordinate her mortgage lien to C's or convince C to provide you with a "wraparound mortgage," in which you agree (by covenant or in a sidebar contract) to continue to pay off M's loan. Either way you will be using both M's and C's money, not your own. Of awraparound mortgage, more later in this chapter.

104

4. Acquisition Techniques Other than Executory Contracts

Example 20

If your client takes one of the options in the prior Example, he will have to come up with cash to buy out O's equity in the property — to the tune of $625,000. How can your client avoid this?

Explanation

By renting the property with a ground lease. O will continue to own the property, but you can demolish the stores and construct your building with the proceeds of C's loan. This lease might contain an option to buy the lessor's property at some future date and following some specified procedure. However, C will need to know that you will continue to pay the rent to O and that if you don't, C can step into your shoes and cure any default in the lease.

THE WRAPAROUND MORTGAGE

When a project needs renovation or modernization, or the developer needs new financing for any other reason, the financing is often provided by a wraparound loan (commonly referred to a "wraparound," "wrap" or "all inclusive mortgage"). It is a mortgage that has a subordinate and subsequent lien on real property as to which a superior lien remains unsatisfied. See generally Annot., 36 A.L.R.4th 144 (1985). It is not, however, a standard form junior mortgage. It is different in three respects. First, in addition to the mortgage covenants and the note, a third document is executed between the borrower and the lender. This third document is often in the form of a sidebar agreement or a rider to the mortgage, providing that the borrower will continue to pay all installments and charges due the superior mortgagee as they become due and payable, in order to keep the superior mortgage from going into default. See Adams v. George, 812 P.2d 280 (Idaho 1991).

The other two distinctive features of the wraparound loan are found in the note. The first of these is the note's principal amount. It is the sum of the outstanding amounts due on the superior loan and the new funds advanced upon this refinancing. The principal of the wrapping, subordinate loan thus appears much greater than it is in fact, because only the funds actually disbursed are at risk; they are secured, meanwhile, by the equity in the property built up since the execution of the superior mortgage.

The third feature differentiating a wraparound mortgage is the note's interest rate. It will usually be higher than the first or superior mortgage,

105

4. Acquisition Techniques Other than Executory Contracts

but lower than the current market rate. Thus, the wraparound mortgage is used to preserve the prior extension of credit at lower rates than those currently available. (Of course, a due-on-sale or due-on-encumbrance clause in the superior mortgage may throw a crimp into the use of the wraparound loan.) This third feature explains the economic incentive to use such a loan.

The following is an example of a wraparound agreement.

WRAPAROUND MORTGAGE AGREEMENT OR RIDER

This agreement is made with reference to a mortgage [the wraparound note and mortgage] dated _____ between _____, the mortgagor, and _____, the mortgagee. The secured property is subject to a lien described as follows: [the senior mortgage(s)]. Mortgagor agrees to comply with all covenants, terms, and conditions of the senior mortgage, except the requirement to make all payments of principal and interest, which payments mortgagee agrees to pay when due, so long as the mortgagor shall not default on any other term.

Mortgagor agrees further that, to the extent mortgagee makes payment on the senior mortgage, mortgagee shall be entitled to a pro rata lien on the secured property and be subrogated to the rights of the senior mortgagee. Upon default by mortgagor under the senior mortgage, the mortgagee hereunder may pay, compromise, or settle the claims of the senior mortgage.

To the extent not previously assigned, all rents and profits from the secured property are hereby assigned to the mortgagee as further security for the debt to him. Any default in the senior mortgage is also a default hereunder.

Mortgagor shall notify the senior mortgagee of the right of mortgagee hereunder to make all payments directly to said senior mortgagee, and also request that said senior mortgagee notify the mortgagee herein of any default in the senior mortgage. Any amount found in violation of the applicable usury laws shall be applied in reduction of principal of the notes secured by this mortgage.

The wraparound mortgage also has other names: It is sometimes known as the hold-harmless, the all-inclusive, or the overriding mortgage.

Another use for the wraparound loan occurs upon a sale of the real property, as purchase money financing. Here the seller gives the buyer a deed to the property, and the buyer executes a wraparound note and mortgage, along with a third document, a mortgage rider or agreement in which the seller is obligated to continue to pay off the first mortgage, still outstanding and unsatisfied after the title is transferred. The buyer takes title subject to the outstanding, third-party mortgage lien and gives the seller, as a down payment, the value of her equity in the property, over and above the amount of the fair market value necessary to secure the outstanding lien. The principal amount of the wraparound loan is the market value of the property, and the buyer pays interest on the face amount of the wraparound

4. Acquisition Techniques Other than Executory Contracts

loan, often at current rates of interest (often higher than the rate on the wrapped, superior mortgage note). Here the seller, promising to continue to pay off the superior mortgage, receives the payment on the wraparound loan, passes along monies necessary to keep the superior loan from going into default, and pockets the difference.

In this second, purchase money use of the wraparound loan, the seller is functioning as a lender; the seller is essentially lending her creditworthiness to the buyer — which is why a developer/buyer might use this device. It is a means to avoid borrowing in one's own name or using one's own line of credit if that line is stretched thin.

Wraparound loans can be tiered, so that there are many subordinate, and wrapping, loans, each one used in connection with a refinancing of the property or with a transfer of its title.

Examples

Example 21

In a foreclosure, a foreclosing mortgagee holds a "credit bid." Such a bid refers to a mortgagee holding a judgment for the amount of its outstanding mortgage debt. When bidding at its own foreclosure sale, the mortgagee is permitted to bid up to the amount of the debt,[7] essentially bidding the judgment instead of cash. (This is known as a credit bid; all other bidders will typically be using a certified check.) Its bid is as effective as a cash payment would have been, and if the bid is successful, the judgment amount is reduced by the amount of the bid. In foreclosing a wraparound mortgage lien, what is the amount of the credit bid permitted the junior, wraparound lender? Is it the face amount of the wraparound loan or the amount actually disbursed by the junior mortgagee?

Explanation

The amount of the credit bid is but the tip of the iceberg of a larger problem, which probably can't be addressed until we know whether the wraparound lender, or a third-party buyer, is the successful bidder at the sale.

---

7. Wary mortgage lenders seldom do this if they want to also sue for a deficiency judgment — that is, using on the mortgage note to recover amounts of the debt that the foreclosure sale doesn't fetch. However, data shows that many lenders don't sue for a deficiency, even if entitled to; and some jurisdictions by statute don't permit such judgments for purchase money mortgages in any event.

4. Acquisition Techniques Other than Executory Contracts

Example 22

Suppose the wraparound lender is buyer at the sale. What then?

Explanation

Because the senior lien is not affected by this foreclosure, a credit bid of either the face amount of the loan or the amount of the "true loan" (the amount actually disbursed) will permit the wraparound lender to take the title subject to the senior lien; it in effect will free the title of any equitable interest created by the rider or agreement on the part of the developer and/or seller to continue to pay the wrapped, outstanding superior loan. No matter what the bid, the wraparound lender gets her bargain: the ability to take possession and the title subject to the senior lien, and hence the right to assume the mortgage payments on the senior lien herself.

However, because either the face amount or the true loan amount will have this effect, the lesser should probably be used. Consider that a credit bid of the face amount may wipe out the obligation of the wraparound borrower (to the wraparound lender) to repay the superior lien — so a wraparound lender is ill-advised to bid the face amount. Worse, doing so may result in a claim by the wraparound borrower on the "proceeds" of the foreclosure sale. If the lender is eventually required to back up her credit bid with cash, the borrower may claim the proceeds in excess of the amount actually disbursed or outstanding on the wraparound loan as her own. Indeed, this claim is stronger when a third-party buyer pays cash in excess of the true loan amount of the wraparound loan.

Example 23

Suppose a third party purchases at the foreclosure sale, paying cash at the sale. What then?

108

4. Acquisition Techniques Other than Executory Contracts

Explanation

The proceeds in excess of the true loan should go to repay the superior lien before being given to the borrower—that is, the person conducting the foreclosure should recognize that in the foreclosure of a wraparound loan, the mortgage rider or agreement to repay outstanding debts creates an implied obligation to distribute the proceeds of the sale to the superior mortgagee before giving any proceeds to the wraparound borrower. This implied term of the rider may be thought of as an implied agreement to repay the superior loan upon foreclosure of the wraparound lien. The weakness of this analysis is that it results in an early windfall repayment of the superior lienholder's debt. However, the alternative is to tempt the borrower to force a default and foreclosure on the wraparound mortgage in order to get at the proceeds, bid in cash by an unsuspecting third party purchaser. Subjecting the distribution of the proceeds to the implied term permits that purchaser to take the property as debt-free as possible, and uses each and every dollar bid to free the title of the superior lien. Depending on how much is bid, however, remember that the purchaser will still take the title subject to superior lien.

In foreclosure, the better view is that a wraparound mortgagee has a certified bid for the amount advanced, not the face amount or the outstanding balance of that mortgage, and any excess will go to the wraparound mortgagor. See Restatement of the Law (Property), Mortgages, §7.6, at 546. Notice of the foreclosure sale should include notice that a junior lien is being foreclosed, that the sale buyer has the obligation to make payment on the existing mortgage, and that the existing senior mortgage will be unaffected.

CHAPTER 5

Forming and Capitalizing an Entity for Acquiring Title

Commercial real estate developers typically find the bulk of the capital for their projects from mortgage lenders. However, there is often a need for more capital than the developer obtains from them. For example, many of the soft costs of a project — e.g., for land acquisition and planning — cannot be taken from funds in a construction loan. So the developer must share the income from the project as well as the tax benefits conferred by the Internal Revenue Code with high-income, equity investors.[1] The legal entity of choice for accomplishing this and for taking title to the project property is the limited liability company (LLC).[2] See ELF Atochem North American, Inc. v. Jaffari and Malek, LLC, 727 A.2d 286, 289-291 (Del. 1999) (discussing the origins of the LLC).

---

1. Since World War II, Tax Reform Acts (TRAs) underline the dependency of the real estate sector of our economy on the IRC's provisions. In the 1970s and 1980s, in intervals of two years or so after 1974, Congress enacted TRAs with major provisions affecting the federal income taxation of real property development. In particular, the tax rate levied on capital gains and losses was lowered, and the depreciation deduction was first shortened and then lengthened: the longer the period, the less the value of the deduction. The recovery period is now 27.5 years and 39 years for residential rental and nonresidential properties, respectively. For this purpose, "residential" means a structure deriving 80% or more of its rental income from dwelling units.

2. The Commissioners on Uniform State Laws promulgated its first Uniform Limited Liability Company Act in 1996, revised it in 2006, and amended the revised version in 2011. Most jurisdictions have adopted some version of the act(s); 18 states and the District of Colombia have adopted the revised Act. Each jurisdiction's Act should be reviewed by the developer's attorney for its variations from the uniform Act. The same prudent practice holds true for the (revised) uniform partnership and limited partnership Acts.

5. Forming and Capitalizing an Entity for Acquiring Title

The developer's entity choice is driven by several factors. First, real estate markets rise and fall with the changing needs of the economy. So the developer wants to limit his liability for the debts and obligations incurred in operating a project to the project itself. What he invested in the entity should be the extent of his liability for the project. He doesn't want to put his past projects at risk by developing his latest one.

Second, the developer wants to pay income taxes on the project only once. This means that the entity formed for a project should not itself incur any taxes. Entities that are taxed in themselves are to be avoided.[3] An LLC (or, for that matter, a partnership of any type) is not recognized as an entity for federal income tax purposes: no taxable events occur at the entity level.[4] Rather, taxes are paid by the LLC owners or partners individually. By the same token, the tax benefits of the partnership's activities pass through to the individual members or partners. Thus it is often said that the LLC or partnership is a conduit or pass-through device for tax benefits.

Third, because (again) real estate markets rise and fall, the developer wants his entity to be able to adapt to changing market conditions. The entity must be an adaptable one, freely changing management style and its ability to attract new capital. Developer's counsel must provide management documents that permit adaptability while at the same time providing the predictability that equity investors crave.

The LLC is currently the type of business entity most free of federal income tax restraints as well as many regulatory restrictions imposed on corporations. It is the entity of choice for real estate investment and development today. Because limited partnerships (LPs) have provided the entity structure for almost all the real estate investment activity in the past, LP law has provided precedent for issues arising in LLCs.[5] Moreover, the LLC builds

---

3. Contrast the limited liability company with the corporation. The latter is a legal entity in its own right for purposes of paying federal income taxes. As a result, the income it receives is taxable both at the corporate level and when it is distributed to shareholders as dividends. The partnership and the LLC avoid such double taxation. Neither can corporate shareholders deduct losses attributable to their shares; likewise, there is no pass-through of corporate tax benefits.

4. This is not to say that, in a partnership, no tax decisions are made at the entity level. In fact, many tax planning decisions are taken at that level. Decisions on choosing the tax year, electing the method of depreciation, and choosing accounting methods are made there. In addition, the characterization of the tax benefits associated with the entity, as a gain, loss, deduction, credit, or otherwise, is also made there. So when a business expense deduction is characterized as such at the entity level, its benefit is taken by the partners individually. Thus the partnership or an LLC is an aggregation of its partners insofar as tax benefits are concerned, and the benefits of the Internal Revenue Code's (IRC's) provisions accrue to the partners individually.

5. The modern partnership had its origins, first in the tenancy in common, and then in the Uniform Partnership Act—UPA, and RUPA (the revised UPA), adopted in most of our jurisdictions—and finally in the Uniform Limited Partnership Acts (ULPA, and RULPA, the Revised ULPA). The former applies to general partnerships, the latter to limited ones. The

5. Forming and Capitalizing an Entity for Acquiring Title

on the basics of partnership law, giving it a precedential foundation in the law governing what was the entity of choice for most developers.[6]

THE LIMITED LIABILITY COMPANY

A limited liability company (LLC) is a noncorporate legal entity that (1) will provide limited liability for its owners, regardless of the level of their participation in and control of management, and (2) will qualify as a partnership for purposes of federal income taxation. It is not subject to many comparable corporation code restrictions on management, operations, or capital. It may have perpetual life, may be formed for any lawful purpose, and is a separate legal entity distinct from its owners or "members."

A member may be a natural person or another legal entity, including another LLC. The doctrine of limited liability — i.e., that the personal liability of members is limited to their investments in the entity — as with LPs, applies to an LLC. Its members may not be sued in their own right by any third party dealing with the LLC. It need not subject managing members (akin to general partners) to more liability than any other member of the entity; they are generally subject to the business judgment rule used in corporate law, not to negligence rules or fiduciary duties.

The permissiveness of many LLC acts requires well-drafted operating agreements in order to be classified as partnerships for federal income tax purposes. See 1988 Rev. Rul. 88-76, 1988-2 C.B. 360 and Anderson v. Wilder, 2003 Tenn. App. LEXIS 819 (Tenn. Ct. App. 2003). In particular, the LLC's operating agreement must negate what otherwise would be a majority of the four corporate features of an entity.[7] Typically operating agreement do this in the following manner:

---

common law provided sufficient definition of either type. "A partnership is an association of two or more persons to carry out as co-owners a business for profit," states UPA §6.

6. RULPA and the UPA are "tiered." See RULPA §1105 (favoring interpreting RULPA first, before interpreting comparable RUPA provisions. Absent a controlling provision in a limited partnership agreement, then ULPA or RULPA controls, and if that does not resolve the problem, UPA controls. Again, absent a contrary provision in a general partnership agreement, UPA controls. This tiering reflects a preference for interpreting the acts as a series of default rules: unless the partners agree otherwise, by default or the silence of their agreement, the acts control. Further but non-precedential tiering is introduced by the advent of the limited liability company acts.

7. Some background: until 1997, the IRS took the position that, for federal income tax purposes, a legal entity was presumed to be taxable as a corporation unless its governing documents provided otherwise. So partnership agreements, drafted from 1960 through 1996, required restrictions on the dissolution of the entity or on transfers of partners' interests, on infusions of capital into a general partner, or on limited partners' decision-making powers — all as a way of negating at least two of the following four characteristics of a corporation: *continuity of life*, *free transferability of interests*, limited liability, and centralized management. The first two italicized characteristics were the ones most often and easily negated. See

5. Forming and Capitalizing an Entity for Acquiring Title

(1) At least one LLC member must be personally liable for the entity's debts and obligations, otherwise the Internal Revenue Service (IRS) would rule that it lacks the limited liability feature of a corporation, permitting double taxation.

(2) LLC memberships cannot be freely transferable (as would corporate shares) if the pass-through or conduit feature of the LLC is to be maintained.

(3) The LLC cannot have perpetual life (as would a corporation), so it must end and be re-established upon the withdrawal or death of a member.

(4) The LLC must not have centralized management distinct from its members. This fourth feature is the one least surrendered by drafters of an operating agreement. Thus two of the first three features of a corporation (liability limited to the investment made, free transferability of memberships, and limited life) must be negated by the provisions of the agreement.

In addition, many LLC authorizing Acts include three provisions important to the tax classification of these entities. First, they provide that members are not personally liable for the debts and obligations of the entity; second, that the death, bankruptcy, or withdrawal of a member will terminate the LLC unless the remaining members consent to its continuation in business; and third, that LLC membership interests may not be transferred without the consent of other members. These provisions provide default rules for an LLC's operating agreement: that is, they are subject to agreement otherwise. The Acts also provide easy-to-follow formation procedures.

All jurisdictions authorize LLCs by statute, often modeled on the Uniform or Revised Uniform Limited Liability Company Act (ULLCA or RULLCA). An LLC is thus everywhere a creature of statute and cannot be implied in law or exist by estoppel.

In about a dozen jurisdictions, including Delaware, an LLC may create distinct "series memberships." This means that an umbrella LLC may create a series of sub-LLCs, each of which has separate assets and investment objectives, with each having its separate limited liability, so that a series can deal with third parties who are limited to recourse against the assets of a particular sub-LLC. This way of organizing LLCs can be useful for multistage real estate developments—for example, when land acquisition, construction, and management of a property is contemplated. While the series LLC might

---

United States v. Kintner, 216 F.2d 418 (9th Cir. 1954), accepted by the IRS in the form of the so-called Kintner regulations in 1960, and Larson v. Comm'r, 66 Tax Ct. 159 (1976). After *Larson*, the real estate industry used the case as a blueprint: The industry treated the documents as controlling the practices of the entity and gave each characteristic equal weight. So the typical limited partnership agreement retained limited liability and centralized management as too important to its operations to give up, but placed restrictions on the continuity of life of the entity and restricted its interests' transferability. Events dissolving the entity were specified, and a maximum number of years defined its existence. Interests were transferable only with the consent of other partners, or transferable to other partners. Such provisions of the partnership agreement allowed the entity to achieve noncorporate, pass-through tax treatment.

5. Forming and Capitalizing an Entity for Acquiring Title

save administrative costs in forming and managing them, uncertainties about how the series would be treated in bankruptcy, or where no statute authorizes a series LLC, as well as the lack of title insurance endorsements for the series, has meant that the idea is not yet widely used.

An LLC Compared to a General Partnership

A general partnership is a collection of mutual agents — each partner is the agent of every other — for a specified business purpose. That is, at common law, it was not recognized as a separate legal entity, but is only an aggregation of individuals.[8] Absent an agreement to the contrary, no partner (such as a developer might be) is entitled to compensation for the conduct of ongoing partnership affairs. General partners have personal liability for partnership debts, absent some contractual limitation — such as the negotiation of a nonrecourse note[9] and mortgage. The LLC has no similar liability and is preferable.

An LLC Compared to a Limited Partnership

In most all jurisdictions, the limited partnership (LP)[10] shed the aggregate theory of partnership, replacing it with "the entity theory."[11] In order to

---

8. At common law, the traditional theory was that the partnership was the aggregate of its partners' actions. This aggregate theory of partnership leaves no room for defining behavior or actions that can be attributed to the partnership itself, regarded as an entity separate and distinct from the actions of the partners. Defining the partnership as a legal entity, with a life of its own, is the task of a second theory, a/k/a, the legal entity theory. The intent of the drafters of the partnership acts was to establish the legal entity theory of the partnership for situations in which the partners deal collectively with the outside world. So a "person" as used in the act was defined as including "individuals, partnerships, corporations, and other associations." UPA §2. Moreover, the nature of the partner's interest is a "share of the profits or surplus" and, as such, is personal property. UPA §26. That is, the partner's interest is distinct from partnership's assets.

9. A nonrecourse note is one enforceable only in foreclosure. See infra, Chapter 8.

10. Unlike a general partnership, the limited partnership (LP) is not a collection of mutual agents. It is a partnership in which some partners (the limited partners) delegate the management of partnership affairs to others (the general partners). General partners in an LP are personally responsible for the LP's debt and can contractually bind the LP. Limited partners, however, are not personally liable for debt so long as they do not participate in the control of the business, and do not have the ability to bind the entity to contracts. The general partner is often a legal entity set up specifically to control the business and deal with persons outside the partnership. It is often a general partnership or an LLC.

11. Consider, as an example of the legal entity theory, a conveyance to a partnership. The UPA enabled (but did not require) the acquisition of real property in partnership name, and once so acquired, required its transfer in that form. UPA §8(3). Upon neither acquisition nor transfer was the use of words of inheritance ("and its heirs") necessary. However, issues of apparent authority of a partner to bind the partnership, in UPA §§9(1) and 10, made

115

5. Forming and Capitalizing an Entity for Acquiring Title

achieve limited liability and tax pass-through status, it has traditionally been necessary to make the general partner in a limited partnership a separate entity, separately capitalized, so that the general partner contributed at least 1% or more of partnership's total capital and takes at least 1% of each item composing the entity's gain (or loss). See IRS Rev. Proc. 89-12 (1989). Thus the LP can provide 99% of the same benefits provided by an LLC, which can achieve limited liability and tax transparency without the two-tiered structure and its attendant legal fees. Although the corporate general partner might also be an S, rather than a C, corporation, that arrangement has its own, additional strictures—all of which make the LLC look even more appealing. Thus, it is much easier to organize and authorize a manager member in an LLC.[12]

An LLC Compared to a Subchapter S Corporation

Such corporations are small business corporations avoiding entity-level taxation on distributions to investors after electing a pass-through status. However, they are limited to two classes of shares, may have no more than 35 shareholders, and may not be a corporate subsidiary. In addition, they cannot pass through losses attributable to debt, and electing S-corp status does not prevent taxation of some undistributed profits. These are only the most prominent among other IRC restrictions imposed on this type of

---

transfers from a partnership problematic, and so for some time partnership conveyances often continued to be executed in the names of the partners. Requiring each partner to convey away partnership property estops each partner from denying the validity of the transfer. RUPA §302 has provided a solution by limiting the partnership's ability to recover property once transferred. §302(b) (giving recovery only from nonremote, for-value transferees with actual knowledge or notice of a lack of authority or with actual knowledge or notice of property's being transferred being partnership property).

12. The managing member of an LLC can in addition write its own version of the fiduciary duties attaching to its activities. Relevant here are provisions of the partnership act to which it is inappropriate to apply the tiering and default principles to the acts, UPA §21 imposes general fiduciary duties owed by partners to each other, while RUPA §404 limits fiduciary duties to more detailed and limited duties of good faith and fair dealing, loyalty, and due care. The first of these is not further defined. The second (the duty of loyalty) includes situations giving rise to a constructive trust, but is further limited to specific transactions in the life of the partnership, e.g., to self-dealing. The third duty of care is "limited to refraining from engaging in grossly negligent or reckless conduct, intentional misconduct, or a knowing violation of law." §404(c). Further, a partner may "further the partner's own interest" without violating these duties. §404(d). Finally, a partner is authorized to lend money to and transact other business with the partnership. §404(f). These provisions govern litigation between a partner and the entity over (say) the sale and acquisition of partnership real property. These fiduciary provisions in RUPA are mandatory. Partnership agreements may flesh them out—identifying activities—but may not waive, narrow, or eliminate them. The legal entity theory of partnership is available to enforce RUPA's fiduciary duties. RUPA §405.

5. Forming and Capitalizing an Entity for Acquiring Title

entity. In addition, only individuals (with some exceptions for trusts) may be shareholders, and foreigners are prohibited from holding shares.

When should an LLC be considered? For investors who think they might need to participate in management, for a landowner wishing to participate in the profits from development by his purchaser, and for S corporations undertaking a new project, an LLC should be considered. Interstate businesses might remain wary of LLCs because tax treatment might vary as business crosses state lines.

Forming an LLC

Two documents are necessary to start up an LLC.[13] The first is one containing the articles of organization. See ULLCA §203. Like articles of incorporation, they state the name (including a designation as an LLC), business purpose, the registered agent, and the principal office of the company. If the company is to be manager-led, not member-managed, the articles must state this. ULLCA §203(a)(6). The articles are filed with the state and become a public record.

The second document is an operating agreement, similar in function to the bylaws of a corporation. ULLCA §103(a) ("all members of a limited liability company may enter into an operating agreement, which need not be in writing, to regulate the affairs of the company and the conduct of its business. . . ."). Failure to execute an operating agreement is not a prerequisite to formation in some jurisdictions. See Advanced Orthopedics, L.L.C. v. Moon, 656 So. 2d 1103 (La. App. Ct. 1995). In others the agreement must be in writing. See D.C. Code §29-1301(21). This agreement does not need to be filed and so may address issues that should not be disclosed to the public, so long as the terms of the agreement are consistent with the articles. Unless the agreement states otherwise, management decisions are vested in the members as a group and made by a majority vote in about 30 jurisdictions; in 4 jurisdictions, a default rule assumes manager-managed LLCs in which only the manager/member votes.[14]

Most LLC acts permit operating agreements to vary but not to eliminate the fiduciary duties that members owe each other, including the duties of loyalty and care and the contractual obligation of good faith and fair dealing.

---

13. Two parallel documents are generally used to establish a limited partnership: (1) a certificate of partnership filed with the government, akin to a corporation's charter, and satisfying jurisdiction-specific requirements as to its contents; and (2) the partnership agreement, akin to the corporation's or partnership's bylaws and operating rules.

14. A model operating agreement was first drafted by a task force of the American Bar Association's Section on Business Law, whose report appears in Joint Task Force, Report: Model Operating Agreement with Commentary, 63 Bus. Law. 385 (2008).

5. Forming and Capitalizing an Entity for Acquiring Title

Jurisdictions vary on when the company comes into legal existence. The company is legally established either when the articles are filed or when a certificate of formation is issued by the state. Thereafter, a member's liability is limited to the amount of its capital contribution. The member's LLC interest is classified as personal property, similar to a partnership interest. The economic attributes of the interest are freely assignable, although the right to participate in the LLC's management is not — or at least not without the consent of the other members, or more commonly, some percentage of them.

Some LLC statutes typically require that the entity must have at least two members, but most jurisdictions now permit one-member entities. See ULLCA §201(d). A single member LLC is typically used by a developer to hold title to the real estate assets in a project. It is a subsidiary of another LLC, is disregarded for income tax purposes and does not have to file even an informational tax return, and is "bankruptcy remote" — that is, cannot be forced into bankruptcy for reasons not directly related to the project. (Mortgage lenders in particular insist on this last feature.)

Up to 1997 and as discussed previously, LPs and LLCs both had to negate their tax status as a corporation by drafting their operating agreements to negate at least two of the four attributes of a corporation. Thereafter, the IRS's 1997, self-classifying, so called "check-the-box" regulations,[15] make the tax classification of the LLC so much easier that tax-tailoring the entity becomes a matter of precaution rather than a tax-planning necessity. Some jurisdictions have responded to these regulations by repealing statutory restrictions on continuity of life, centralized management, and the free transferability of memberships. One state, California, has refused to adopt parallel check-the-box regulations. So some jurisdiction-specific research and tailoring is still necessary.

Examples

Example 1

The relevant LLC statute states that "members [of the LLC] are not liable for the acts or obligations [of the LLC] simply because of their membership."

---

15. Effective January 1, 1997, the rules based on the Kintner regulations and *Larson* were eliminated in favor of a simple — that is, check-the-box — election by a taxpayer. Except for some entities that must be treated as corporations (such as publicly traded partnerships), all subsequently created entities may elect their federal income tax status. This election applies to LPs and LLCs. "Check-the-box allows business entities with two or more members to have the choice of qualifying as a corporation or a partnership." Treas. Reg. §301.7701-1 (as amended by Treas. Dec. 8697, 1997-2 I.R.B. 11). One caveat: in an audit, the election to be taxed as a partnership may be challenged when the underlying and never repealed statutes and regulations are not observed.

5. Forming and Capitalizing an Entity for Acquiring Title

The state sues a member for environmental cleanup costs for toxic substances found on real property that is an entity asset. Does the statute limit the liability of a member to the LLC's assets, including the defendant's membership?

Explanation

Maybe not. This is typical limited liability language, but suggests that if there is any independent basis for the member's liability, other than membership status, then the liability is not limited. Environmental and other liability insurance are in order.

Example 2

An LLC is often in part a collection of real estate professionals — including an architect, broker, attorney, etc. Could the articles and operating agreement limit liability for a member's malpractice where the member's professional services are the contribution to the company and the member isn't otherwise conducting a professional practice?

Explanation

No. It is unethical by professional standards for attorneys, brokers, and architects to avoid liability for the professional's own acts. Some state LLC acts expressly permit use of the LLC by professionals, but some do not — and many more are silent on the subject. In any event, no statute should be taken as permission to authorize unprofessional conduct. A series LLC may be appropriate here.

Example 3

Could an LLC limit malpractice liability to the member actually committing the malpractice?

119

5. Forming and Capitalizing an Entity for Acquiring Title

Explanation

Yes, partially. Even when a member's acts are found to be company actions, so that the company becomes liable, members are liable only to the extent of their contributions, so that each member is not liable for any amount greater than the contribution.

Example 4

Could the general partner of a limited partnership use an LLC to conduct his activities?

Explanation

A one-person LLC is authorized by statute in many states. Such an LLC might affect the centralized management or free transferability of interests of the entity, so there is a possibility of corporate treatment and, unless this issue is clarified by statute in the state of formation, an LLC should plan to have two or more members.

A Developer's Use of These Entities

No matter whether the investment or title-holding entity is a LP or LLC, three criteria control its selection and formation. First, it is a device for sheltering and deferring taxes. Depreciation and the early losses of the project shelter the partner's other income and defer taxes on it until recapture upon a profitable resale. This device was validated by Comm'r of Internal Revenue v. Tufts, 461 U.S. 300 (1983).

Second, it is a device for exercising leverage. Leverage means a developer's power to control entity assets without paying cash for them, but also has a second definition: the addition of the amount of partnership mortgages, along with cash investments, to the partners' tax basis for partnership assets. This use of leverage was also validated in Tufts. To illustrate, a 20-member LP or LLC purchases a property worth $1 million. Each member or partner owns a 5% interest in this entity. It paid $200,000 down, financed the rest

5. Forming and Capitalizing an Entity for Acquiring Title

of the price in an $800,000 note and mortgage, and each LP or LLC member paid $10,000 for a 5% interest. To this cash investment each can add $40,000, for a $50,000 basis in the entity's property. Against this basis, he or she may depreciate a pro rata share of the depreciation taken as well as a share of any losses, until the basis is zero. See Treas. Reg. §1.752(e).

Third, the entity must be a device for converting ordinary income into capital gains when there is a disparity between (lower) capital gain and (higher) ordinary income tax rates.

These three principles have had different impacts over time. As to the first, for example, Congress has changed the rates of depreciation permitted by the IRC every two years or so and so the quality of the shelter has varied. The second principle, leverage, has been modified by the IRC's "passive losses" rules, as discussed in the next section of this chapter. The third principle is a topic of continuous congressional debate in response to various rising and falling real estate markets.

Partnership Taxation

When an entity elects to be taxed as a "partnership"—meaning a general or limited partnership or an LLC—that is, not as a taxable but rather as a pass-through entity filing an informational tax return—each partner or member reports income and losses on the members own tax return with that income and those losses determined at the entity level and based on the allocation provision of the entity's operating agreement using the entity's accounting procedures. Making partner or member's contributions, either in kind or of capital, is not a taxable event and the entity's distributions, either in kind or of capital, are likewise tax-free except to the extent that they exceed the person's basis in the entity.

After 1986, a member taxpayer's deduction for losses from a property was limited to the amount the taxpayer had at risk in the property. See IRC §465(c)(3)(D) (thus limiting a taxpayer's loss deductions to his cash contributions to an LLC, the adjusted basis of the property contributed, and mortgage amounts (prorated for his interest in the partnership) for which he is personally liable. This limitation required that LLC members be personally liable and required recourse mortgages, except that Congress provided an exception for "qualified nonrecourse financing" that may be included in a taxpayer's at-risk basis; this is financing given by a third-party mortgagee with three attributes: a mortgagee (1) regularly making real property loans, (2) unrelated to the taxpayer unless the loan is commercially reasonable and is made on terms that an unrelated individual would extend, and (3) not the recipient of a fee with regard to the loan transaction. See IRC §465 (b)(6).

Second, deductions for passive losses are limited. See IRC §469. A passive loss deduction may be taken only against other passive income—that

121

5. Forming and Capitalizing an Entity for Acquiring Title

is, not active or portfolio income, but rather income derived from a trade or business in which the taxpayer "materially participates." Passive income also includes investment income derived from the sale of property. All rental income is presumed passive (no matter how hard the taxpayer works to collect it and regardless of whether the taxpayer oversees the management of a property generating it) subject to (1) an exemption that allows the deduction of passive losses against active income up to $25,000 for an individual taxpayer and (2) a provision permitting deduction of a passive activity loss for real estate professionals who spend more than 750 hours during the tax year materially managing or overseeing a property. The intent of Congress in enacting this amendment was to deny a tax shelter for salary and portfolio income.

Third, mortgage interest incurred in a trade or business in which a taxpayer materially participates is fully deductible. However, when the taxpayer is an LLC member or limited partner or has any other interest stemming from business activity in which the taxpayer does not materially participate, related mortgage interest is deductible only to the extent that investment income exceeds investment expenses, although deductions lost in this manner may be carried forward. See IRC §163(d)(3).[16]

Drafting an LLC's Operating Agreement

Some Context for Three Major Issues. By the time a developer is forming the LLC that will take title to the real property that will become its major asset, the developer is seeking equity investors, either individuals or entities willing to be liable for planning and acquisition costs. This search is a form of reverse engineering for a project because institutional investors will likely be later sought for major financing — that is, for purchase money mortgage and construction loans.

Equity investors[17] who are not as risk averse as mortgage lending institutions are the developer's best prospects at this stage. For instance, if institutions will not agree to be liable for project costs in advance of construction, then equity investors who will assume this liability are sought; likewise,

---

16. One response to the three limitations on partnership entity tax benefits was to merge partnerships themselves into larger ones, so-called Master Limited Partnerships (MLPs), to provide a way of putting passive income and passive losses together into one entity whose assets included older, well-established, income-generating projects as well as just-established, loss-generating younger ones. In response, IRC §7704 was enacted to deny the MLPs traded on stock exchanges — the ability to shelter passive income with passive losses. It (1) provided that a person's income from such MLPs was portfolio, not passive, income and (2) generally denied such entities the benefits of the *Kintner* regulations. See n. 7, supra, this chapter. Their publicly traded interests meant automatic treatment as a corporation.

17. The positions of equity investors is further discussed infra, Chapter 9.

5. Forming and Capitalizing an Entity for Acquiring Title

investors who will personally guarantee later loans are sought. For a developer, this is like building a financial pyramid from the top down, in effect building the financial structure of a project in reverse.

1. Contributions Both the LP and the LLC are vehicles for a developer—meaning both a general partner in an LP and the organizing member of an LLC—to attract, as a borrower, investors to a project. Investments are known as "contributions" in both RULPA §501 and the Uniform Limited Liability Company Act (ULLCA) §401. Contributions of capital to an entity are often made in several cash payments according to a schedule set out in the provisions of a note given to the entity by the investor. See RULPA §§501, 502, and ULLCA §§401, 402. Remedies available to the entity upon an LLC member's default in payments are usually severe, often including forfeiture and sale of the defaulting investor's interest, either to other limited partners, members, or third parties. See ULLCA §402(a).

Contributions may also be in the form of a developer's services—putting the project together, acquiring the land, negotiating the contract of sale of it, obtaining rezoning and other land use permissions for the project. See ULLCA §401. For the nonmanaging partner or member, the services contributed may be consulting or bringing whatever professional skills are needed. They must be rendered without the person doing so being deemed to be in "control" of the entity: acting as a contractor, agent, or employee of the partnership, consulting or advising the general or managing partner or member, acting as a surety for the entity, and acting to amend the entity's operating agreement are permitted (safe-harbored) under this section. See also RULPA §303(b).

Capital contributions by the limited partners or LLC nonmanaging members are entered on the capital account of each such partner or member. A capital account starts with whatever contribution a person makes at the outset, is increased by any taxable income received, and is decreased to the extent of any tax benefit received and any distribution of cash made by the entity. It is maintained for each person at the entity level. See IRC §704(b). Its purpose is to determine whether the allocation of profits and benefits has, under the Treasury's Regulations, a "substantial economic effect"—a very complicated subject, but one that provides the justification for keeping these accounts. Suffice it to say, the purpose of the regulations is to insure that the tax benefits of the project are taken by those who bear its business risks (by contributing appropriately). When a person's account is negative upon a dissolution and winding up the entity, the person with the negative account will have either to pay those with positive accounts or take a reduced share in the final distribution of profits or bear an increased share of final losses, finally balancing the risks and the benefits of holding an interest or membership.

For an entity's accountant, the default procedure is to allocate the tax benefits *pro rata*, to the extent of each person's contribution; assigning all

123

5. Forming and Capitalizing an Entity for Acquiring Title

the tax benefits to the limited partners or nonmanaging members, with the developer being paid entirely on a fee basis (with good planning, a fee deductible by the other partners), is risky. Rather, the allocation of tax benefits should be made in the operating agreement, not in midstream as one limited partner or member needs the benefit, and not orally. If the IRS determines that the allocation is without substantial economic effect, the agreement's allocation will be overruled and the IRS will reallocate in accordance with each person's capital contribution.

2. *Waterfalls* In return for the equity investor's assuming a higher level of financial risk and a lower level of security as to remedy, the level of compensation demanded is concomitantly higher than what an institutional investor with greater security can demand. Sometimes compensation is pegged to the interest rate on a second or junior mortgage, sometimes to an equity multiple.[18] The analogy to a second mortgage is only a rough one, however, because the return of the equity investor is accompanied not by a lien on the LLC's real property, but by a right to dip into a project's cash flow.

Enter the investment waterfall.[19] Picture a pool or pools of funds flowing downward. It is a method of dividing the project's cash flow among partners/members that permits its uneven distribution of the project's cash flow. It permits equity investors to reward the sweat equity of the developer with an uneven, extra, disproportionate share of profits. This extra, uneven, and disproportionate share is in the industry called the "promote." The promote is the portion of the developer's split of the profits that exceeds her capital contribution. The promote is the product of two related and negotiated issues: (1) what is the percentage interest of the developer's promote? and (2) what is the amount of profits or cash flow against which the promote percentage is applied? The answers to both issues are the product of negotiations between the equity investor(s) and the developer.

The developer typically receives the promote only if the project's cash flow is higher than expected, higher than a return measured by either a discounted

---

18. An equity multiple is similar to the total cash-on-cash return of an investment. It is the ratio between total cash received and equity invested over the life of the investment. It is the sum of all equity invested + all profits divided by the total equity invested, or

$$\frac{\text{Total Equity} + \text{Total Profits}}{\text{Total Equity}}$$

measured from the perspective of the project (including that of both the developer and the investor(s), or the equity alone.

19. The waterfall is further discussed infra, Chapter 9.

5. Forming and Capitalizing an Entity for Acquiring Title

cash flow (DCF)[20] or internal rate of return (IRR)[21] analysis that protects the investments of others—hence the phrase "hurdle rate" or "return hurdle."[22] It is a subjective and difficult thing to set, in part because when setting it the developer must consider both the equity investors' rate of return as well as future (mortgage) financing costs. It is an amount of profit that once hurdled, allows the developer to receive the promote. In turn, the promote is the reason developers are willing to go forward with a project, (again) putting the project together, acquiring the land, obtaining proper zoning, and seeking capital funding. Typically the promote goes down in amount as the project proceeds and in some proportion to the amount that the investors return goes up.

A further word on the promote. It is an equity interest in the LLC given in return for services. It can be calculated either as a return on the value of the LLC's assets, or as a return on its project's profits. The former is of immediate value to the developer, the latter is initially an unknown.

Examples

Example 5

A developer is given a 25% interest in a LLC's project and the investors are given a 75% interest. The projects sole asset is Blackacre, the fair market value of which is $1,000,000. What is the value of the developer's promote?

---

20. DCF analysis is widely used in all phases of real estate development. It is perhaps the oldest method for valuing investments. The DCF's formula requires adding all the cash flows for each investment reporting period and each time dividing these sums by one plus the discount rate raised to the power equaling the number of all reporting periods. The discount rate is the rate of return used to discount future cash flows back to their present value; it is sometimes a required rate of return (set by investors comparing this project with rates possible if his money was invested in alternative investment vehicles), or a "hurdle rate." See infra, n. 22.

21. The IRR is that percentage rate of interest earned on each dollar invested for each period it is invested. Its use requires the developer to know what the cash inflows will be; otherwise its computation is not possible. So the IRR reports the percentage rate earned over each investment period, while the equity multiple in contract measures the rate over the life of the investment. So the IRR, best computed on a banker's calculator, not manually, is the rate at which the net present value of a project's cash inflows and outflows, measured over the project's life, equals zero. The IRR can be manipulated by timing the cash flows. The IRR considers the time value of money, and is independent of interest rate changes in the economy. It holds the level of investment opportunity constant over the life of the project. This constancy is magical thinking. An IRR ignores any economies of scale a project might achieve, its surroundings (its dependence or not on surrounding projects), or the possibility that later cash contributions by investors or others might be needed by the project. Further, the IRR cannot tell a developer with undeveloped land whether it is best to build a hotel or an office building on the site; it can give an IRR for each, but cannot tell which is the better investment.

22. The return hurdle is the rate of return that must be achieved before cash moves on to a different pool and to the next hurdle within that pool. It is an investor's minimum acceptable rate of return on its investment—a/k/a, the hurdle rate. It is the discount rate an investor uses to run a DCF model software for the project. That is, the higher the discount rate, the lower the value of the project. It is the rate that triggers the disproportionate profit splits. Often the IRR or equity multiple is the return hurdle.

5. Forming and Capitalizing an Entity for Acquiring Title

Explanation

$250,000 if the promote is a capital promote. If the promote was a profits promote, its value would be the fair rental value of Blackacre, when and if it is rented. If its assumed fair rental value is $100,000, the profits promote would be the developer $25,000 of that amount. A profits promote gives the developer either a share of profits attributable to either a share of future profits or the future appreciated value of the LLC's asset(s).

Example 6

A developer receives a profits interest in Blackacre LLC. Is this interest taxable in the tax year received?

Explanation

No. Since it is an interest in future profits, it is taxable only when a distribution on it is made. Were it otherwise, the developer would be given a tax liability before the interest was of any value to him. So receipt of a profits interest is not a taxable event. On the other hand, receipts of a capital interest is a taxable event because it has an immediate sales price or value. See IRS Rev. Proc. 93-27 (1993). Thus a developer's receipt of a capital interest is sure to give him the willys! Further IRS regulations provide that a profits interest be treated like a capital interest on which a tax was due, but not payable until it actually had a sales price. See IRS Notice 2005-43 (2005). Consequently, when a distribution is actually given to the developer, it is treated as a capital gain, currently taxable at a lower rate (20%) than the highest rate of taxation on ordinary income (39.6%).[23]

* * *

Like a waterfall in nature, the investment waterfall is a series of pools that fill up with the cash flow from a project and once full, cascade down its excess cash into additional, lower pools. The highest pool in the waterfall contains the "preferred return." It is the first claim on profits until a target return is achieved, and it is a first claim on profits before other project participants — the developer or other investors — are paid any distribution. It

---

23. This difference in tax rates for promotes is the subject of an on-going congressional debate and occasional proposals for congressional legislation.

5. Forming and Capitalizing an Entity for Acquiring Title

has a "preference" return hurdle that once met, allows excess profits to flow and be distributed as agreed in the operating agreement. Thus explained, the waterfall is a crucial, much negotiated, business provision of an LP or LLC's operating agreement — crucial to both developers and investors — and will be reviewed by future mortgage lenders financing construction of a project.

3. *Management Decisions* Equity investors control risk in part by voting on the major business decisions of the entity, such as leasing, mortgaging, or selling its property. Participating in such decisions is one method that investors have of controlling the predictability of return on their investments. Such participation in the past ran the risk that investors could be found to be in "control" of the entity and thus have general liability for all an entity's debts and other obligations. Most LP and LLC statutes today "safe harbor" such decisions. These statutory safe harbors were enacted after cases, such as Delaney v. Fidelity Lease Limited, 526 S.W.2d 543 (Tex. 1975), found limited partners liable as general partners for having taken control of the entity as officers of a corporation that served as the general partner. LPs and LLCs are designed to expand these safe harbors.

Examples

Example 7

What do you think are key issues in setting this preferred return hurdle?

Explanation

Some are obvious, some not: here are five of them. (1) What the overall rate of return? Historically it has been between 8 and 12%. (2) Is the preferred return collateralized? If so, any shortfall might be paid by either the developer or the LLC's operating funds on hand. If the developer is eager for the investor's money, personal guaranties are not unknown, but not typical, and not likely to be given when the developer and the investor have a successful track record of working together. (3) Do all equity investors or just some number of them receive the preferred return? Early investors are most likely to receive it. Some further issues relate to the situation in which the preferred rate is not attained. (4) Is the preferred return cumulative or noncumulative — that is, is it measured in each distribution period or over the life of the project? This measurement period is crucial when in a given distribution period, there is not enough profit to provide it. If the profit is insufficient, it might (if cumulative) be added to an investor's balance due for the next period until it is eventually paid. (5) The nonpaid cumulative return might be compounded at the preferred rate of return or accrue

5. Forming and Capitalizing an Entity for Acquiring Title

simple interest at a negotiated rate when not paid out? And if it is compounded, the frequency with which that occurs will have to be negotiated.

Example 8

A developer is taking its promote from the highest pool in the waterfall, and the equity investor is taking from the next lower pool, but the investor has not recouped its preferred rate of return by the time the project is sold.

Explanation

The investor might get to "look back" over the project's life and look at the amounts earlier given to the developer, forcing him to disgorge amounts that give the investor its promised preferred rate for the life of the project, distributed at the end of its life. In the alternative, investor might prefer and negotiate for a "catch up" provision might give 100% of profits to the investor until the return hurdle is achieved in every distribution period, with 100% of the excess going to the developer. The difference between a look back and a catch up provision is crucial, although both are "clawback" provisions and one is a variation on the other. The difference is who gets to hold the money over the project's life—with the look back, it's the developer, and with the catch up, it's the investor. Thus developers prefer the look back provision (because they get to use the money even if they might have to disgorge it later) while investors prefer the catch up provision (because she gets paid first and won't have to ask the developer to write the disgorgement check).

A Developer as a Fiduciary

A limited partner or LLC member's "obligation to contribute money, property, or other benefit to, or to perform services for" an LLC is not excused by death, disability, or "other inability to perform personally." See ULLCA §402. The partnership or LLC operating agreement will provide a schedule and detail the events triggering a contribution. One of the major differences between partnership or LLC operating agreements drafted from the limited partner's perspective and those drafted from the developer's has been that the former will contain many warranties about the property and the transaction that the latter will not contain. If and when the deal goes sour, the developer will want to argue that if the warranties do not cover precisely what went wrong and that any express warranty will replace any implied warranties or common law fiduciary duty to which the developer might

5. Forming and Capitalizing an Entity for Acquiring Title

be held. The UPA require that an accounting be made periodically, and it is unlikely that this right can be waived in the agreement and exculpate the nonaccounting general partner or developer. See UPA §19-22. A rule of periodic accounting has been dropped from later acts, so that today a rule of reasonable access to an accounting prevails. See ULLCA §408. A duty to account for the profits is the overriding principle, but, nonetheless, any general partner or managing member is entitled to reasonable compensation for her services, provided it is disclosed to other partners or members.

A general partner or managing member is a fiduciary. ULLCA §409. Nondisclosure of entity business by the general partner can also be a breach of fiduciary duty. For example, even if a resale price for entity property is reasonable in market terms, if a breach of fiduciary duty is involved—as where the general partner or managing member has sold to an entity in which she is interested—often no damages need be shown in an ensuing lawsuit. The breach is actionable regardless of the damages sustained. This example contains a breach of two such duties: first, the duty of loyalty, breached by the self-dealing, and second, the breach of the duty to disclose. See Dixon v. Trinity Joint Venture, Ltd., 431 A.2d 1364 (Md. App. 1981).

The same breaches occur if the general partner purchases a property in another name and then flips the property to the LP or LLC for a profit, undisclosed to the other partners or members. See Bassan v. Investment Exch. Corp., 524 P.2d 233 (Wash. 1974), noted in 50 Wash. L. Rev. 977 (1975). The situation here is often styled as the duty not to compete with the partnership. ULLCA §409(b)(3) makes this duty express. This duty not to compete may even survive the withdrawal of the breaching partner or member and the dissolution of the entity. See Leff v. Gunter, 658 P.2d 740 (Cal. 1983).

The general partner or LLC managing member is held to these fiduciary duties because she alone is able to evaluate the entity's projects. She will be able most easily to reconstruct the financial analysis done for the project. The duty to account and disclose arise (Securities Acts' liability aside for the moment) only after the limited partner makes the investment. Realistic assessment of the project can be made only when the project has a track record, however short. Thus, until some two years into the project's operation, the tax benefits of the project may blind equity investors to its economics. The general partner or LLC manager is in a unique position to take advantage, and fiduciary duties are the anodyne for that advantage.

In the ULLCA, its manager is "liable for loss or injury caused to a person, or for a penalty incurred, as a result of a wrongful act or omission, or other actionable conduct, of a member or manager acting in the ordinary course of business of the company or with authority of the company." ULLCA §302. ULLCA §409(b)-(f), and (h), imposes a duty of loyalty on a manager (and a member in a member-managed company) "to account to the company and to hold as trustee for it any property, profit, or benefit derived . . . in

5. Forming and Capitalizing an Entity for Acquiring Title

the *conduct* or winding up of the company's business or derived from a use . . . of the company's property, including the *appropriation* of a company's opportunity." ULLCA §409(b)(1) (applicable to a manager through §§(h)), discussed in Carter G. Bishop, The Uniform Limited Liability Company Act: Summary & Analysis, 51 Bus. Law. 51, 69-70 (1995).

Common law professional malpractice liability is also possible, in negligence, for misstatement of the investment potential of a partnership interest. See White v. Guarante, 372 N.E.2d 315 (N.Y. 1977) (where an accountant was held liable to a partnership for audit and tax services).

Examples

Example 9

In a jurisdiction adopting the foregoing provision of the ULLCA §409, when, for himself, a manager purchases real property suitable as company property and located in the course of his search for such property, is he liable under that provision?

Explanation

Yes. This would seem a breach of the fiduciary duty of loyalty owed by a general partner to an LP, so the issue is whether the law of such duties is applicable to the LLC manager as well. ULLCA §409(b)(1), supra (embracing a theory of constructive trust that seems to permit a broad definition of the "conduct" of company business as inclusive of acquiring property as "the appropriation of a company's opportunity"). A second issue is whether the operating agreement has limited the duty of loyalty owed by the manager. ULLCA §103(b)(2)(i) (stating that "this duty may not be eliminated, but that the operating agreement may identify specific types or categories of activities that do not violate the duty of loyalty, if not manifestly unreasonable . . . "). A further issue is the measure of damages when the property has no operating or track record. A final issue is, are there other possible sources of law for this situation? The answer is yes, that the law of corporations and its business judgment rule for directors and managers might provide another source. The ultimate issue is whether the law of partnerships or of corporations will be applied to the LLC in the state of formation.

Securities Acts' Liability

For larger partnerships, the registration of the partnership with the Securities and Exchange Commission is typical and gives rise to a duty of due diligence, imposed on a general partner participating in the preparation of the registration statement. See 15 U.S.C. §77k(a) (Securities and

5. Forming and Capitalizing an Entity for Acquiring Title

Exchange Act of 1933, §11). Thus, if the terminal value assigned partnership property is misleading, the general partner would have breached a duty to make a reasonable investigation of the appraisal method used to arrive at this value. Negligence is the ground for an investor's cause of action under this section. Section 11 can also snare any expert—attorney or accountant—participating in the preparation of the registration statement because it does not require that there be privity of contract between the expert and the investor or limited partner.

Another section of the Securities Acts creates liability not only for a registered partnership interest but also for offering to sell a security, registered or not. See 15 U.S.C. §77k(b)(3). Privity of contract is required with the investor, but some courts have extended this section to experts, as "participants" in the sale, when the data they prepare is relied on by the limited partner making an investment decision.

Section 10b and Rule 10b-5 of the Securities and Exchange Act of 1934 impose liability for reckless conduct in the preparation of data or reports, for any registered or exempt offering that results in any material misrepresentation of fact about the project. These are antifraud protections for investors. For liability based on fraud, a professional's errors and omissions policy may not provide coverage.

An issue similar to the one discussed in the last Explanation arises here as well: is a membership in an LLC a security for purposes of the federal securities laws? Some states have LLC acts that answer no for state law purposes, but that does not bind the federal Securities and Exchange Commission. Much rides on the answer, because registration of a security is an expensive and time-consuming piece of legal work. Because the advent of the LLC has brought partnership-like entities closer to corporate status, the result is in doubt. Investor participation, now possible without taking "control" as in an LP, may affect the outcome. When defined in the operating agreement, participation may make possible avoidance of the securities laws by making the entity more like a joint venture exempt from registration.

As the legal foundation for LLCs is broadened by state statutes and IRS rulings and revenue procedures, whether their memberships are securities is perhaps the most interesting residual issue for them. LLCs may more closely resemble general rather than limited partnerships, but they look like close corporations, too. The continuum of close corporations, general partnerships, and limited partnerships has blurred the definitions of each type of entity, with entities classified as one or the other overlapping in many of their features. So entity analogies only go so far. What's more relevant and important is the investment instrument. As long as LLC operating agreements are privately negotiated and have no ready secondary market when issued, LLC memberships should be classified as neither stocks nor investment contracts under the prevailing test for a security. See S.E.C. v. W.J. Howey, 328 U.S. 293 (1946). In short, the form of ownership for the

5. Forming and Capitalizing an Entity for Acquiring Title

membership is not as important as the instrument used to attract capital to it. Whatever the form of organization, a closely held entity conducts its search for capital outside of the securities markets. LLC investments may have some characteristics analogous to investments made in those markets, like limited liability. However, the incentives of the investors are very different; they are more involved in the operation of their entities for three reasons: their sophistication, their personal guaranties, and the securitization of virtually all of the entities' assets—and because their investments themselves are illiquid. Limited liability doesn't eliminate risk, and centralized management doesn't mean unsophisticated, information-less investing needing consumer safeguards. In short, LLCs are entitled to a presumption that their memberships are not securities; instead, the rights and duties they engender are adequately controlled outside of the securities laws by fraud, fiduciary duties, and contract law.

Investment Trusts

Real estate investment trusts (REITs) are business trusts formed for holding either mortgages or the fee simple to real property. They are tax-free intermediaries. See IRC §§856-860. They must (1) distribute a very high percentage (95%) of their net annual income to shareholders; (2) derive at least 75% of their gross income from real property, without engaging in short-term holdings of real property interests (no speculative, quick-turnover investments); and (3) have 100 or more shareholders. Most large REITs have their shares traded on major stock exchanges. Thus REITs are a specialized type of mutual funds for real property investments. Often they are formed by a bank or insurance company, but many are standalone entities.

Some ownership REITs have thrived over time, in part because they have specialized in holding title to one type of property. Developers form REITs to provide an influx of capital for many projects, with those projects forming the assets of the REITs, or to provide capital to stave off foreclosure or bankruptcy. They free developers of their former dependence on more traditional sources of mortgage capital.

CHAPTER 6

Taxes and Investments in Real Property

TAX EVENTS

The purchase of a project does not have immediate federal income tax consequences for a buyer/developer. The closing and transaction costs—for securing the mortgage loan, inspecting the property, securing title search and insurance, paying your attorney—are not deductible expenses. Rather, the closing costs must be added into your "tax basis" in the property. "Basis" is an Internal Revenue Code[1] (IRC) term for cost; thus, the tax basis in the property is the purchase price plus the costs of acquisition (closing costs, and so on). So the developer's acquisition, construction, or improvement costs are not deductible in the year she closes or thereafter. The IRC does not permit it. Instead, they are added to the purchase price and become the initial cost basis of the taxpayer and which later is used to compute the difference between that cost basis and the price realized when the taxpayer sells to another; that difference becomes the gain or loss recognized either as income or a capital loss deduction for the property.

Once the developer is in possession, the IRC provides various types of tax advantages. The receipt of mortgage loan proceeds, used to finance the purchase of a project—or, for that matter, a residence—is not a receipt of income and not taxable. Second, the Code permits the deduction of

---

1. The Code is contained in U.S.C. title 26. Citations to the IRC in this chapter are to sections of the Code.

133

6. Taxes and Investments in Real Property

mortgage interest. IRC §163(a).[2] However, there is no deduction for the repayment of mortgage loan principal, which makes sense. If the receipt of the loan principal is not income, no deduction should be permitted for its repayment. This is an example of what might be called "tax symmetry," a powerful argument used by tax lawyers in interpreting the Code. Third, the IRC also permits a further (but limited after the Tax Reform Act (TRA) of 2017) deduction for state and local real property tax payments. See IRC §164(a). Likewise, deductions for casualty losses for business and investment properties are also available on a limited basis, calculated by using the property's adjusted tax basis, minus its salvage value. Through these various deductions, real property owners enjoy tax benefits that are not provided to renters. Generally speaking, renters are prohibited from deducting rent payments.

After taking possession, the recognition of gain or loss in the fair market value of the property awaits its sale and is determined by calculating the difference between its tax basis and the sale price. The sale is the taxable event that triggers the Code's provisions as the gain goes untaxed until that time. Compare this practice with that of the local real property taxes, where unrealized gain in the fair market value of a property is taxed every year as the property is re-assessed, whether or not the taxpayer has realized any cash from the property with which to pay the tax.

A taxpayer's cost or tax basis may be increased during ownership not only by the acquisition costs, but also by the costs of any capital improvement and construction, but reduced by the depreciation deductions[3] previously taken. The depreciation deduction allows an owner to recover the cost of the property on an annual basis but must be also taken into account when figuring any taxable gain or loss upon sale. Tax symmetry again.

The IRC treats foreclosure of depreciated mortgaged property in the same way as a voluntary sale. See IRC §1001(a) (governing the "sale or other disposition" of property). "Other disposition" also includes the transfer of mortgaged property to the mortgagee. Even if the mortgagor defaulted on the loan, he doesn't avoid this same treatment. The general rule is that taxpayers are taxed on whatever mortgage debt is cancelled by the foreclosure or forgiven in the negotiations for a deed in lieu.[4] See Rev. Rul. 90-16, 1990-8 I.R.B. 5.

---

2. This deduction is permitted no matter the type of residence: for example, when the taxpayer is a tenant stockholder of a cooperative housing corporation through his ownership of a cooperative apartment, then the taxpayer may deduct his proportional share of the corporation's mortgage interest and real estate taxes. See IRC §216(a).

3. For more on depreciation, see infra, this chapter.

4. Since the 2007 real estate recession, mortgage debt cancellation has not resulted in taxable income for qualified residences: this qualified principal residence exemption has been extended through tax year 2020, and many be further extended. See IRC §§108(1)(e) and 108(h) (part of the Mortgage Forgiveness Debt Relief Act of 2007, as amended and extended), providing forgiveness of mortgage debt up to $2 million for a married couple

6. Taxes and Investments in Real Property

Examples

Example 1

Taxpayer purchased Blackacre with the proceeds of a $1.85 million nonrecourse[5] note and mortgage. Taxpayer owned the property for three years, and in each year took allowable deductions on it. After three years, the adjusted basis was $1.45 million. He then sold the property. Its purchaser paid nothing down but assumed the outstanding mortgage debt of $1.80 million. At the time of the sale, the property was worth $1.40 million. The taxpayer then claimed a $50,000 loss—the difference between $1.45 and $1.40 million. Will the claim succeed?

Explanation

No. The IRS will claim that the taxpayer had a gain of $350,000. This gain was the difference between the outstanding mortgage balance assumed by the purchaser and the adjusted basis of the partnership in the project. These are the facts of Comm'r v. Tufts, 461 U.S. 300 (1983). Taxpayer is deemed to realize a gain when the cancelled, foreclosed, or assumed debt is more than the basis, even (as here) if the secured property is worth less than the basis. Otherwise taxpayer would have the benefit of the receipt of mortgage proceeds without ever having to count them as income. The further question is whether the $350,000 is taxed as a capital gain or as ordinary income. Because the taxpayer's mortgage was nonrecourse, the tax is at the lower, capital gains rate. If the mortgage was a recourse (giving the mortgagee recourse to a deficiency judgment), the tax rate levied on this taxable event is split between ordinary income (on the amount of any deficiency) and capital gain (on the amount cancelled up to the amount of the value of the property at the time of the cancellation).

Example 2

A developer purchases Blackacre, with a fair market value of $1.4 million. It takes out a 90% note and nonrecourse mortgage for $1.26 million. It

---

filing jointly (and $1 million for a single taxpayer) of a qualified "principal residence" (not then for a second home). Thus for taxpayers having mortgage debt cancelled when the residence is "underwater" or is sold in a short sale, cancellation of indebtedness income is not recognized. A "principal residence" is defined as it is in IRC §121. This debt relief was given to aid taxpayers by encouraging alternatives to foreclosure in the economic downturn starting in 2007 and suspending the usual taxation on the difference between the lower value of a qualifying residence and any higher amount of mortgage debt forgiven.

5. Nonrecourse debt is secured by the real property: Should the borrower default on his loan obligation, the lender may foreclose on the property used as collateral for the loan but may not seize any of the borrower's other assets.

135

6. Taxes and Investments in Real Property

pays the loan down to $1.15 million and adjusts its basis in the property downward to $900,000. The fair market value of the property drops to $1 million. The developer defaults on the mortgage loan and the mortgagee forecloses. At the foreclosure sale, the property is sold for $1 million. What is the developer's tax liability? How is this case different from *Tufts*? Does the difference (if any) matter?

Explanation

It is $.25 million—that is, $1.15 minus $.9 million, or the amount of debt forgiven minus the adjusted basis, or $.25 million. Does the fact that the taxpayer's basis is below the fair market value matter? No, but it matters as to how the income is treated: the distinction is between what is capital gain ($1.0 - $0.9 = $0.1 million) and taxed at a lower rate, and what is ordinary income ($1.15 - $1.0 = $0.15 million) and taxed at a higher rate.

DEFERRING THE RECOGNITION OF GAIN

Upon sale, federal taxation can be deferred in several ways, one of which is the use of the IRC's installment sale section. See IRC §453. If at least one payment of the sales price is received by the taxpayer in a year after the year of sale, gain from that sale is prorated and income realized in the tax years in which the payment is actually received. Thus, if a seller takes back a mortgage securing a portion of the purchase price, the income from the mortgage payment is taxed as the payments are received and in the year in which they are received. The installment method is a way of deferring tax, not avoiding it; it is a specific illustration of the IRC's not taxing income until the income has been received.

BUSINESS OR INVESTMENT PROPERTY

An owner of business or investment property, like the owner of a residence, has available deductions for mortgage interest (see IRC §163(a)) and state and local real property taxes (IRC §164(a)(1)); however, the business or investment owner also can depreciate the property (IRC §167(a)(1)) and deduct repair and maintenance costs (IRC §212(2)) (expenses for the production of income).

6. Taxes and Investments in Real Property

Depreciation

Depreciation is the Code-conferred right to write off or recover the cost of a capital asset. Real property other than land qualifies as a capital asset. Thus, the purchase price of the property, adjusted to include closing and settlement costs, is allocated between land and improvements, and the amount allocated to improvements is then divided by the appropriate depreciable life (set out in the Code) in order to arrive at the annual depreciation deduction amount. IRC §167.

The IRC §167 depreciation deduction is perhaps the greatest incentive to investment in real property in the Code.[6] With its benefits, the investor can reap the benefit without the outlay of cash on a dollar-for-dollar basis. With deductions for repairs, mortgage interest, and local taxes, the taxpayer must actually foot the bill before taking the deduction. Not so here.

Consider: The depreciation deduction is a writing off of the cost of the depreciating asset—generally speaking, this asset is the improvements on the property, but not the land, even land underlying the improvement: land is not depreciable. The deduction permits writing the asset off, at an even rate of 3 to5% a year over a 27- to 31-year useful life, down to its salvage value.

Consider further:

1. The deduction will be computed on the basis of the down payment or cash investment in the property plus the mortgage loan amount used to acquire the property.
2. As with residential property, the receipt of the loan proceeds was not a taxable event.
3. The depreciation deduction is available even if the property is actually appreciating in fair market value.
4. For both commercial and residential property, the federal tax-man does not take an interest until there is a taxable event, such as a sale or other disposition of the property.

This means that the depreciation deduction can be large in comparison with the cash outlay needed to become entitled to it. Consider further that the only thing that will make this deduction less valuable is a cash outlay

---

6. Unlike business property, a residence—unless we are dealing with a portion of it used exclusively as a home office—cannot be depreciated. See IRC §262(a) (prohibiting depreciation for personal or family expenses) and §280A(c)(1) (allowing depreciation on home offices). Similarly, losses upon the resale of a residence are not deductible. Neither are the costs of repairs deductible, §262(a), although additions and improvements can be added, at cost, to the taxpayer's basis in the property.

6. Taxes and Investments in Real Property

that is uncompensated for by at least an equal deduction. The one thing that threatens its tax value is the repayment of the mortgage loan principal. Deductions are available for repaying mortgage interest, but not for repaying principal; therefore, when in any one tax year the amortization of principal in the mortgage payment is covered by the depreciation deduction, the depreciation deduction is "sheltering income" for the owner or investor.

The shelter ends when the repayment of principal exceeds the depreciation; thus in the early years of loan repayment, when the amortized payments are mostly principal, there is shelter; later there is no shelter, because then the principal repayment, which is actually money out of pocket, without an entitlement to a correlative deduction, is greater than the depreciation.

The time at which the shelter ends is often called the crossover point. After this point is reached, the investor owner in a tax-driven transaction is likely to sell, while the owner of property with real economic value will not sell. Upon the sale or other disposition of appreciated real property used as the basis for a depreciation deduction, the deductions taken over the course of the taxpayer's tenure will be recaptured. IRC §1245. No good thing lasts forever.

Congress can easily expand or contract the tax benefit of the depreciation deduction by extending and reducing the term over which the depreciation may be taken. The high-water mark, from the taxpayer's perspective, was reached in 1981; the TRA of that year had the shortest periods on which to base calculations, so the tax benefit was then the greatest. Terms were then 15 years for some properties; now they are sometimes double that.

Passive Losses

The IRC also has rules limiting the deductions resulting in passive losses to deductions taken from income derived from business or investment properties in which the taxpayer has a similar, passive interest. IRC §469. Such deductions had previously been available to offset income from other activities, even to the extent that tax losses were produced. Deductions or credits from passive business or investment activities will be disallowed to the extent that they in toto exceed income from all passive activities (exclusive of portfolio income), and so losses from passive activities will not be generally available to offset salary, interest, dividend, and active business income. For example, no matter how hard the taxpayer works at collecting rent, it remains classified as passive income, and only passive losses can offset it. To the extent that passive losses cannot be deducted in any one tax year, however, they may be carried forward into future years, when they are again available to offset passive income. IRC §469(b).

6. Taxes and Investments in Real Property

INVESTMENTS IN REAL ESTATE

What a developer's attorney calls a complex transaction involving an office building, a shopping center, or an industrial facility is in fact a series of somewhat simpler transactions. Financing for these types of projects requires lenders with different investment objectives —some interested in long-term investments, some short-term. Long-term capital is provided by hedge funds, pension funds, and insurance companies; short-term capital, including construction financing, is provided by commercial banks. This capital must be put into the hands of those with the managerial skills to construct the project and into a combination of entities — typically LLCs) — or persons including developers, investors, managers, and professionals with the skills necessary to complete the project.

Mortgage lenders have a keen interest in the structure of the entity seeking funding. For instance, a mortgage lender may take a look at the form of foreclosure available in a jurisdiction and decide that foreclosure would be too cumbersome, costly, and time-consuming should trouble develop with the project. Being able to seize an LLC's membership shares, in which the lender has a security interest under Article 9 of the Uniform Commercial Code, may be an attractive alternative to foreclosure.

In a commercial transaction, the larger the loan principal, the smaller the number of lenders available. Once familiar with the world of commercial lending, a lender may tend to seek larger loans within this universe of transactions because the administrative costs are relatively constant no matter the size of a loan. Moreover, there is a panache to making the largest loans; being the mortgagee of the Willis Tower (formerly called the Sears Tower) or the TransAmerica Building has a value to the lender involved. There is also a certain panache in making certain types of loans: shopping malls, Texas office buildings, and Los Angeles shopping centers have all had their time basking in the sun of lender approvals.

Considering mortgage debt and equity investments together, a higher percentage of debt to fair market value is available in real property investments than is available elsewhere, in other forms of investments. This percentage is sometimes called leverage (although this term is used in a slightly different way when talking about "leveraged depreciation," a term explained later in this chapter). Leverage is valuable because it permits a developer to control large properties with small amounts of cash investments. At the same time, nonrecourse mortgages reduce the risk that the developer will lose past investments. Such mortgages are common in commercial lending, both for business and tax reasons. High leverage also increases the developer's pretax return on the cash she does invest, as well as providing her with noncash tax benefits, such as depreciation, resulting in a post-tax "shelter" for her cash flow.

6. Taxes and Investments in Real Property

Examining the Setup for a Project

Every setup (sometimes also called a *pro forma*) is a statement of income and expenses for an operating project. Today the use of personal computers and their attendant software enable any user to produce elaborate and professional-looking setups. This is all the more reason to look closely at this document. A setup may be just that.

A setup may be seen as a series of graphs with two axes. It has a vertical x-axis, which provides details of income and expenses in any one year. It also has a horizontal y-axis, which provides a series of annual statements and predictions for each item of income and expenses, year by year, until the property is scheduled for sale. Thus, analysis of any one year moves down one of the x-axes with the setup, while moving along one of the y-axes provides a comparison of the same income or expense item over several years.

Some signs of a good deal—defined here as one that is not just tax-driven, but rather one that makes economic sense too—are outlined next. The developer's attorney's task is not necessarily to warn his client off—leave the business decisions to the client—but to prepare him to encounter risks and to formulate methods of dealing with them.

Much has been written on this topic. See, e.g., Thomas F. Kaufman, Real Estate Metrics: Numbers Never Lie—Or Do They?, 32 Prac. Real Est. Law. 31 (Sept. 2015); Ibid., Understanding Real Estate Economics, 30 Prac. Real Est. Law. 35 (Jan. 2014), and Marvin Kelner, Real Estate Tax Shelters: How to Tell a Good Deal from a Bad Deal, 25 Clev. St. L. Rev. 44, 57-69 (1976).

Consider the following 11 factors. They are not arranged in any particular order of importance.

1. The type of project. Is it one that is often offered investors, funded through the pooling of investor funds? If so, a close examination of the project prospectus and backgrounds of the investors is warranted, comparing it to similar projects' prospectuses and other investments. The capitalization rates[7] for particular types of projects have historically varied over time, becoming more or less profitable with demographic and market shifts. Some projects hit the market just at the right time, meeting a demand, but some do not.

a. Garden apartments. These are the type of project most often syndicated. They have a short life. Real depreciation, not just tax-related depreciation, occurs. They are built for a short life, and so maintenance expenses can often rise faster than rents. They are occupied by short-term tenants, and the high turnover requires an on-site manager. If rising mortgage interest rates make home ownership impractical for tenants, however, they may be a good

---

7. "Cap rates" are discussed infra, Chapter 8.

6. Taxes and Investments in Real Property

subject for syndication. In a review of the performance of six large public limited partnerships, 67% of the cash invested went into the purchase of apartment house properties, but the investment units were found to be worth less than 100% of unit cost and no partnership studied had increased the value of its units. Of course, in the meanwhile, tax benefits had been distributed as well, but the signs of a risky investment are still present because in this age of two-year cycles for tax reform, no tax benefit can be counted on forever. See Thompson & Williams, What Is My Partnership Investment Worth?, 20 Real Est. Rev. 26, 29 (1990) (using an 8% capitalization rate appraisal to value the partnership's assets).

b. Office buildings. Except in very competitive markets, these are built for a longer life (30 to 50 years) but often need new fixtures within 10 years or so of construction. Their leases tend to be for longer terms than those for garden apartments and are often "net leases"— meaning that any increases in the costs of taxes, insurance, and utilities are passed along to the tenants. (A lease that passes increases in all three items is called a "triple net lease.") The tenants themselves are businesses whose major expenses are for personnel; rent is a relatively minor line item on their ledgers. Moreover, the best property managers tend to be attracted to office buildings—the work is easier. However, the leasing period may be lengthy in overbuilt markets. Recently, in some markets, the vacancy rate for new construction has topped 20%, but that may indicate that bargains can be had just as well as indicating a danger sign. In such markets, front-end "rent holidays" may be offered as an inducement to lease; in some markets, rent concessions for the first year are customary. Check the local situation on this. Moreover, a 5% to 7% vacancy rate in a building rented to one, or even a few, major tenants represents less lost value than it would be in a building not dominated by a few tenants. A landlord may even be tempted to renew a lease at a lower rent rather than have a major tenant move out.

c. Shopping centers. Here land (a nondepreciable asset) is a major component of the project's fair market value. Thus few centers are funded by pooled investor capital. Net leases make the deductions smaller too. But, once again and until recently, the tenants have been stable and long term. The property is often preleased, too—that is, major anchor tenants, such as department stores and larger retailers, are committed to the center in advance of construction. They will want to install the fixtures in their space themselves, and many both improve and maintain it. Appreciation in value is computed with income multipliers or capitalization rates and so will be slow. This is an investment for patient money—all the more, since competition from e-shopping is reshaping the tenant pool.

Moreover, for any type of property, there may be a real estate investment trust, or REIT, which specializes in holding any one of the foregoing types of projects. (REITs are discussed at the end of Chapter 5.) Comparing their success with the project under review is likely to prove informative.

141

6. Taxes and Investments in Real Property

2. In studying a setup, look first for automatic increases in (say) rental income. If it increases at 5% a year, that is a good indication that a lease-by-lease analysis has not been done. If the leases are too long, they will limit income growth; if too short, they make income flow uncertain. A lease-by-lease analysis may not show rent concessions, as, for example, when a lessee has rent abated for the first four months after moving in or has rent abated every January. Further inquiry of the tenants will show these concessions, and an "estoppel letter" from them will be necessary to make sure that the inquiries produce the truth. Among other matters, this letter may certify that a tenant's lease is in effect, is not in breach or default, and is not subject to an agreement to prepay rent or any other sidebar agreements.

No lease-by-lease analysis will show the credit rating of the tenant. A high rent may be charged a tenant whose credit rating is low, thus making the setup look good, when in fact the income flow is unstable. On the other hand, a lower rent may be appropriate when the tenant's credit rating is higher.

3. Do not look just at a property's debt service coverage ratio (or DSCR, comparing income to debt) and ignore the credit ratings of tenants. A lender might justify a higher loan principal by the blind use of the ratio, but the possibility of a loan default might be greater too.

Consider another example. If the building is a small one, the usual rules of thumb on vacancy rates for rental real property investors may not apply. A large apartment building may properly be assigned a vacancy rate of 5%—that is, 5 out of every 100 units will likely be vacant at any one time. However, if the building has only four units in it, the rate will be 75, 50, or 25%, depending on the number of vacant units. At any rate, applying a 5% rate to such a building is a meaningless gesture. And, in a single-tenanted or build-to-suit building, a vacancy rate is meaningless.

4. A constant income-expense ratio over time. If income can be expected to rise over time, so can expenses. The conservative prospectus will estimate both as rising over time, particularly if the real depreciation rate of the project is steep. Moreover, expenses may exceed income in the long term. That is, expenses rise in older buildings as they age. Building codes change and older buildings are not necessarily grand-fathered and immune from the changes. Spending 40 cents of expenses for each dollar over the first 10 years, a prudent owner can count on double that if the building is over 30-40 years old. For example, if you know that the ratio of expenses to net operating income (before mortgage payments are made) is 0.396 for the first 10 years, and 0.571 for the second 10 years, then if expenses are estimated to grow at 5% a year, what should the expected income growth look like?

$$[0.396 \times 1.05^{10}] = 0.677$$

6. Taxes and Investments in Real Property

If 0.677 has to be 0.571 of income in 10 years, then 0.677/0.571 = $1.19. Or a dollar of expenses in 10 years will produce $1.19 of income. So income of $1.00 today must grow at a 2 to 3% annual rate to keep pace with rising expenses.

5. Collection losses, brokerage leasing commissions, and the value of tenant improvements should be computed into the setup. Any noncash, imputed income should be deducted as well. (Remember, however, that imputed income can be added in later, when the tax benefits are computed.)

6. The longer the y-axis for any item, the less reliable it is likely to be, because it is more prediction than fact. However, the longer the y-axis in general, the greater the resale value (sometimes called the recapitalization rate) will be, because the property will have time to appreciate. If the investment requires the recapitalization to be profitable, then particular attention must be paid to the method used to compute the resale value. An internal rate of return or IRR is particularly suspect on this account. How tied to known market facts is it?

7. A re-syndicated project. This is a warning sign, not an absolute bar to investing. Before investing, further research into the resale value of the project is warranted. If the resale or terminal value is computed with an income multiplier or a capitalization rate, it may not reflect the fair market value of the project and need to be checked by comparison with a market data appraisal using comparable properties.

8. Heavy loading of front-end fees. Syndicators live by fees, but a project can die by them. One recent study of public limited partnerships that performed poorly shows that such fees represented 21 to 27% of the price of an investment unit. See Thompson & Williams, What Is My Partnership Investment Worth?, 20 Real Est. Rev. 26, 31 (1990). One way to short-circuit an examination of each and every fee is to divide the paid-in capital (the sum of all cash investments) for the project by its net operating income (NOI), defined as gross income reduced by all expenses, but not by debt service — that is, mortgage carrying and servicing costs. The result is a type of price-earnings ratio for the LLC or partnership.

9. A long pay-in, contribution, or investment period for limited partners or nonmanaging LLC members. If the investors are given too long a time to invest, their investment objectives might change, and the investment might not fit their needs. This would mean they might not invest as promised, and the entity's collection costs in enforcing the notes the investors give will rise. The shorter the pay-in period, the better.

10. The resale or reversionary value. If a capitalization rate is used to value the project, the longer the period before the project is resold, the less likely it is the project will prove to be a good investment. See Michael J. McMahon, Applied Tax Finance Analysis of Real Estate Tax Shelter Investments, 27 B.C. L. Rev. 721 (1986).

6. Taxes and Investments in Real Property

11. The track record of the developer. Does he have experience with similar types of property? Does he have a track record with lenders? Successful first deals tend to lead to the successful second ones. Information on the background of the syndicator is usually found in an attachment or addendum to the syndication prospectus, but remember that only projects deemed similar by the developer are included. A computerized search of periodicals, using the name of the developer, may be helpful in discovering what the background portions of the prospectus do not disclose. In particular, an examination of the length of time the investments are held is worthwhile. If the holding periods are long, this may be an indication that it takes a long time to justify the terminal or resale value of the project. On the other hand, it may be that the property is a particularly good one and valuable in generating "passive" income with which to offset passive losses.

Examples

Example 3

The owner of about 50,000 acres of rural timberland asks your advice about whether it is a good idea to establish an LP or LLC to hold and manage this land and the logging operations on it. The predominant type of timber on the land is thingagummy pine, which can be used for both building supplies and wood pulp. When the building trades slack off, the price of pulp tends to rise, so the venture would be a stable business. If clear cut, the land would be timbered over in about 15 years. Would such land make a good investment property? What criteria would you use to make this decision?

Explanation

This is not the type of property offered to investors very often. The value of the property is largely land, which is not subject to depreciation; thus that tax benefit is not available for transfer between investors and developers. Second, the logging operation that brings in the profits is likely to require personal rather than real property. Even sawmills are portable today. Thus, the large startup losses present in real estate development are not likely to be available here. Third, the increase in land values is not likely to be great, so the asset of the entity is not likely to appreciate to the point that makes investment attractive to those interested in more than the logging. Fourth, logging is labor-intensive, and the liabilities that therefore might flow from the operation indicate that a corporate structure that offers limited liability might better suit it. Overall, this is not a good prospect for a shelter entity, but if the logging is the precursor of a change in land use so that some of the traditional tax benefits accorded real property apply, a closer look might be warranted.

6. Taxes and Investments in Real Property

The Difference Between Income and Cash Flow

After you have skeptically examined all the components of the income flow that a property will generate, you may well find that in the early years of a project, there will be negative income, or losses. The IRC recognizes this fact and provides a way of generating a "cash flow" when the income stream is negative. So after analyzing the income stream depicted in the setup, your next task is to find out whether the benefits conferred by the Code provide enough benefits to turn the negative income into a positive cash flow.

These benefits typically will be three: (1) the deduction for mortgage interest payments (see IRC §163), (2) the deduction for state and local taxes on the property (IRC §164), and (3) the deduction for depreciation (IRC §§167-168). Together, these provide an amount of deduction that "shelter" a taxpayer's income to the extent the deductions reduce the tax liability of the developer. If the deductions add up to "D," then the tax savings will be $D \times b$%, where b is the tax bracket in which the taxpayer finds herself. Thus if federal income tax is computed at the 28% rate, $D \times 0.28$ is the amount of the tax benefit that may change the negative income or loss into a positive cash flow.

Of these three types of deductions, as previously discussed, the depreciation deduction is particularly important. It is true shelter for income because, unlike the other deductions mentioned, it involves no cash outlay by the taxpayer. The others do: A taxpayer has to pay the mortgage interest to the lender before she can take the deduction, and she has to pay the tax man before she can deduct the amount of the taxes. In contrast, she does not have to pay anybody money before she can take the depreciation deduction. Moreover, the amount of the deduction is computed as a percentage of her investment in the property plus the amount of her mortgage on it. This is leveraged depreciation.

Thus it is often said that as long as the depreciation deduction is more than the mortgage and tax deduction, the sheltering of income continues, and the taxpayer should retain the property. Once it is less, the shelter is over, and the taxpayer should sell the property — all this assumes, of course, that the deal is a tax-driven one and that the property is not valuable for some other reason.

Some types of development are deemed particularly worthy of a tax subsidy. For example, if the property is a certified historic structure being rehabilitated, or low- or moderate-income housing, tax benefits in the form of tax credits are available in the Code as well. These credits are given in addition to the ones already described. IRC §469.

A credit is better than a deduction. The latter is an amount subtracted from income to determine the amount of taxable income; the credit is a percentage of taxable income subtracted from the tax liability once computed.

145

6. Taxes and Investments in Real Property

Why is the resulting number labeled the "cash flow" and not income? Because it is money saved, not money given to the taxpayer. It is not cash in hand; rather, it is a subsidy within the Code, but not a direct payment to the taxpayer. Thus the income generated by a project is the measure of the amount of money in the investor's pocket before federal income taxes are paid; cash flow is the measure of the amount of money in an investor's pocket after taxes.

This distinction between income and cash flow is a vital one because the real property development that breaks even or goes into the black only after taxes is said to be tax-driven. The best deals are the ones that make economic sense: Their profit levels are positive to begin with and are only enhanced by the tax benefits. The developer's attorney's task is to look for them.

CHAPTER 7

Preparing for Construction

AN OVERVIEW OF THE CONSTRUCTION PROCESS

The construction process involves three essential parties: an owner or developer (hereafter the developer) of the property to be developed, an architect, and a general contractor. This chapter discusses their roles in the process through their contractual rights. The developer traditionally performs three distinct and separate steps prior to construction. He or she first conceives the project, then hires an architect who designs it, and finally (with or without the architect) hires a general contractor to build the project. The contractor may be selected by competitive bidding, by negotiation, or by selection (or some combination of these three processes). Generally, contractors are selected through competitive bids, and the project delivery method is commonly referred to as design-bid-build. Under this model, the developer enters into separate contracts with the architect and the contractor for the project's design and construction.

However selected, the general contractor receives the completed construction drawings from the architect. Because the project developer has a significant interest in ensuring that the project is constructed according to the construction drawings, he or she will designate an individual to serve as the construction manager charged with overseeing construction activities. This person may be an architect, a member of the construction management firm, or the representative of the owner or construction lender. One or more of these parties will appoint a person or firm to inspect the construction as it proceeds.

147

7. Preparing for Construction

Key inspections include those conducted when the foundation is complete, when the first floor is laid, when the framing is done, and so on. These are times at which the owner and lender accept the work of the contractor. These are likely to be times when the work can be inspected by code enforcement officials of the local government. These are also the times at which the construction loan will be serially disbursed by the lender. That is, this type of loan is not disbursed at closing, but later, as the work progresses and is inspected for the lender's benefit; meanwhile, the developer/mortgagor pays interest only, and only on the disbursements actually made. Interest owing is taken, up front, out of the next disbursement. This traditional procedure requires the completion of distinct steps in the construction process, completing the preceding one before undertaking the next. From the developer's perspective, it has the advantage of permitting a precise determination of what the project will look like and what it will cost, made in advance of any construction on the project.

If the architect as an inspector becomes a project overseer, she is still not its supervisor. If anyone supervises, it's the general contractor on a day-to-day basis. See Emanuel Halper, Negotiating Architectural Contracts, 17 Real Est. Rev. 65 (Summer 1987). Thus, absent a contractual duty, an architect is not required to supervise construction.

This chapter describes in more detail the roles of the architect and the general contractor—two actors with which a developer must deal in planning the construction process for a project, be it an office building, a shopping center or mall, or apartments—and the documents the developer must negotiate in order to start that process.

DOCUMENTING THE PROCESS

The process of preparing for construction is a process dominated by standard forms, modified to suit the project underway. Each of the forms is biased in favor of the trade group promulgating it. None of the forms are written from the point of view of the developer. Thus the developer's attorney must review them carefully. All are available by subscription.

This chapter is not designed to track any of these forms in detail. The forms are constantly evolving and particular forms require close study. Close analysis here would be outdated when written.

The most prevalent forms are those maintained by the American Institute of Architects (AIA). The AIA, established in 1887, revises its forms every decade or so. The most recent revisions were in 2007 and 2017. AIA forms consist of two main types of documents—one governing the relationship between the owner and architect, and one governing the relationship

7. Preparing for Construction

between the owner and the general contractor. The American College of Real Estate Lawyers (ACREL) has published commentary on the AIA forms, and because the AIA forms are architect-oriented, its commentary is useful when representing an owner or developer. The AIA also publishes canons of construction for the construction process, referred to in AIA documents as "general conditions."[1]

The Associated General Contractors of America (AGC) and the Engineers Joint Contract Documents Committee (EJCDC) each publish a set of forms, representing yet other points of view.

Yet another set of documents has been published by a consortium of construction industry trade associations and groups (adding the points of view of sureties, subcontractors, and construction lenders to the mix). See Consensus DOCS Construction Contracts (2007).[2]

PROJECT PLANNING AND DESIGN

The developer who has already executed but not closed on a contract of sale to acquire project property has the project's size, type, and location in mind. Next he needs to acquire architectural services. Such services will be set out in an agreement between the architect and the developer; that is the architect's employment agreement. It will describe the scope of the architect's work, the compensation the developer will pay, its work product, and its duration.

An architect is a professional who is state licensed. Most architects hold either an undergraduate or a two or four year graduate degree in architecture (and sometimes both), studying the structural components, the envelope, and the interior of an enclosed space. He or she will be in charge not only the aesthetics of the form for the project — how it looks from both its exterior and interior, how it fits into its neighborhood or environment — but also the function of the project — most basically, the physics of the form and

---

1. See, e.g., David Eligator, The AIA's Revisions to Form A 201 General Conditions, Real Est. Fin. (Oct. 2008), at 18 (emphasizing 2007 changes giving the developer more project control over inspections, requiring a contractor to report defects, giving a developer a streamlined right to carry out the construction when the contractor does not perform, and by limiting a contractor's right to ask for or audit a developer's financial data once construction starts) and Hugh D. Brown, Kristine Kroenke, & Dean Thomson, The New 2017 AIA General Conditions (2017) (providing limitations on an architect's liability for contract interpretations "made in good faith," limiting the types of notice that must be sent in writing, expanding the contractor's right to additional time and money when the project is suspended and to have the developer demonstrate that the financing for the project is adequate, available at http//www.fwhtlaw.com/briefing-papers).
2. Available at http//www.consensusdocs.org/catalogue.

149

7. Preparing for Construction

structure—does it stand up? and, does it serve the needs of the developer's tenants and customers? The standard of care for an architect is that of "a professional skilled architect under the same or similar circumstances in carrying out his technical duties in relation to his services undertaken by his agreement." See Aetna Ins. Co. v. Hellmuth, Obata & Kassabaum, Inc., 392 F.2d 472 (8th Cir. 1968). This duty is to assure that the project is built in substantial conformity with plans and specifications and ties the architect to plans that she has already presented to the owner. See Schreiner v. Miller, 24 N.W. 738 (Iowa 1885) (a leading case). The developer may have an architect in mind too, someone with whom he has worked successfully in the past and who can deliver constructible/buildable, commercially feasible plans and specifications for the project.

Programmatic design requirements soon follow:

— the specific property location
— its acreage
— the dimensions of the building (e.g., an eight-story Class A office building)
— a construction budget
— time-line for the construction to serve as an envelope within which the architect is to work
— the major features of the project (e.g., a lobby atrium, a landscaped, bricked entry way, etc.), as well as
— performance requirements for infrastructure (e.g., communications, electrical, plumbing, and HVAC performance standards)

As for the scope of the architect's work, typically the developer/architect agreement calls for schematic building and site plans; floor plans; sectional plans; and elevation drawings. These are prepared for the developer's review. After all reviews are complete, they are followed by architectural, blue-line design drawings incorporating all designs approved previously. At the end of the construction process, the architect will prepare as-built drawings, reflecting the completed project and incorporating any revisions made during the process. As-built drawings will guide the maintenance, repair, and operation of the project. A schedule for the delivery of each type of drawing should be set—say, thirty (30) days after the execution of the agreement for schematic drawings, and sixty (60) days after the developer's review and approval of blue-line design drawings. The tighter this schedule, the less delay in commencing construction.

In smaller construction projects, specifications may be included on the approved blue-line drawings. Typically, however, they are a written narrative establishing requirements for materials, equipment, building infrastructure, performance standards, and workmanship.

7. Preparing for Construction

The architect's fee consists first of a retainer, typically regarded as and often stated to be the minimum payment to the architect under the agreement if the agreement is terminated early. Often the retainer is paid and then credited against (or recouped when) one or more of the final payments to be made to the architect. Thereafter, the fee is either a fixed fee, or is computed at an hourly rate with a cap or as a percentage of total construction costs. The fixed fee is most useful for a developer when the architect's scope of services is precisely defined. An hourly rate with a cap is perhaps the most used in these agreements because developer's fear that the third type of fee—set as a percentage of the total construction costs—gives the architect too much incentive to design a more costly project than the market for it warrants.

Termination of the agreement may be either for cause (generally nonperformance) or "for convenience" (when the developer loses confidence in the architect's professional quality of work). Terminations for convenience typically require that a break-up fee be paid the architect. This payment is to avoid the argument that the termination for convenience provision is illusory. See Questar Builders, Inc. v. CB Flooring, LLC, 978 A.2d 651 (Md. 2009), and SAK & Assocs. v. Ferguson Constr., Inc., 357 P.3d 671 (Wash. Ct. App. 2015). The break-up fee is compensation for partial performance. It must be, as a matter of law, proportionate to the work done. Litigation over terminations for convenience is more litigated in public construction projects than in private sector construction. See generally Ryan P. Adair, Limitations Imposed by the Covenant of Good Faith and Fair Dealing upon Termination for Convenience Rights in Private Construction Contracts, 7 J. Am. C. Constr. L. 127 (2013).

The architect is the lead designer of a project, but he or she will typically delegate many portions of the design work to civil, electrical, and mechanical engineers, also licensed by the state. These are utility, plumbing, HVAC (heating, ventilation, and air conditioning) components of the project, as well as its structural components. These specialized components of the project may either be performed the architect's in-house professionals or by independent engineering firms working as subcontractors. The architectural plans must comply with state and municipal building codes and municipal zoning ordinances and regulations in order to receive building and occupancy permits at the end of the construction process.

Examples

Example 1

A developer is unwilling to wait to credit the retainer until the last payment made to the architect. What alternatives would you suggest?

7. Preparing for Construction

Explanation

You might suggest either recouping the credit over the deadlines for each of the many drawings the architect is obligated to produce, or, on the idea that the retainer is actually a mobilization fee, allowing for recoupment of the costs of proposal preparation, etc., a credit given the developer when schematic or blue-line drawings are delivered.

AN ARCHITECT'S DUTY TO PREPARE PLANS AND SPECIFICATIONS

Because of liability exposure and rising costs, architects have been narrowing their roles to that of designers. Their agreements with developers have also evolved to take account of redesigning a project, detailing when and if the architect is entitled to extra compensation for the redesign. When the redesign was made because of the developer's changing requirements for the project, an extra fee is typically appropriate. When already set requirements are not met, the architect typically bears the responsibility to redesign at no extra cost to the developer.

State codes sometimes provide special statutes of limitations for suits on architectural design defects. See Minn. Stat. Ann. §541.250 (10-year statute of limitations). The majority of courts considering the issue have decided not to impose implied warranties of fitness or suitability for design services rendered to owners. See Union College v. Kennerly, Slomanson & Smith, 400 A.2d 850, 853 (N.J. Law Div. 1979). Unlike other professionals such as attorneys and doctors, the architect is hired to produce an exact result—that is, a building that fits within the zoning envelope and is a certain size with a certain access and elevation, and so forth. (In the context of a residential subdivision project, however, a warranty of habitability for the benefit of the owner may be appropriate.) For a minority rule case finding an implied warranty, see Tamarac Dev. Co. v. Delamater, Freund & Assocs., P.A., 675 P.2d 361 (Kan. 1984).

Thus, any liability of the architect must ordinarily be based on an express contract duty or, on the contract as a whole, in tort. In a few states, like Michigan, the architect has been characterized as owing a fiduciary duty to her employer. When a duty is imposed in a contract, the injured party can either bring a cause of action for breach of the contract, in contract, or for breach of the duty, in tort. Compare Bernard Johnson, Inc. v. Continental Constructors, Inc., 630 S.W.2d 365 (Tex. App. 1982) (recognizing a cause of action for negligent performance of a contract duty),

7. Preparing for Construction

with Lesmeister v. Dilly, 330 N.W.2d 95 (Minn. 1983) (refusing to recognize this cause of action).

Accidents causing bodily injury and property damage happen during construction. These risks can be insured against. Design defects, however, are often found by courts to be the result of mistakes, not accidents, and so are uninsured risks. In some jurisdictions, the cost of remedying a defective design is deemed an economic loss unrecognized in a negligence suit against an architect. Thus, an otherwise negligent architect is shielded from liability for such economic losses. Therefore, an express provision in an architect's contract must contain an agreement promising, warranting, or guaranteeing standards of design quality.

The design defect that is also a violation of a building or a housing code is sometimes identified as architectural negligence per se. See Roy v. Poquette, 515 A.2d 1072 (Vt. 1986). An architect has also been found liable in negligence for a failure to install a guardrail on the project site, Geer v. Bennett, 237 So. 2d 311 (Fla. Dist. App. 1970), and for the collapse of sheeting and shoring work in an excavation for a project. See Erhart v. Hummonds, 334 S.W.2d 869 (Ark. 1960). Thus in a redrafting of standard owner-architect's agreements, the word "supervise" might be eliminated so that the courts would not be called on to construe it.

Examples

Example 2

An architect may be called upon to meet with the developer and general contractor as construction proceeds. Typical contracts set out a schedule for such meetings. In large projects, should the architect be required to attend public meetings before municipal zoning and subdivision boards and officials in order to help the developer obtain necessary approvals and permits for the project?

Explanation

Yes. In large projects, obtaining public approvals may require several meetings with several boards and commissions. Particularly when the project encounters public opposition or raises issues of public concern, the timing of these meetings may stretch over a time period longer than anticipated; thus the architect's obligation to appear may outlast the duration of the architect's initial agreement with the developer. This obligation to appear and participate should be express in the agreement. It should set a maximum number of appearances and expressly name the boards and commissions thought to be involved, along with visits to their staffs to explain the architecture of the project. When key members of the architect's staff are particularly adept at such public appearances, they should be named as well.

153

7. Preparing for Construction

Example 3

When an owner-architect agreement provides that the architect "will not be required to make exhaustive or continuous on-site inspections to check the quality or quantity of work" (the phrasing of AIA Document B-141, §1.5.4), does the architect have a duty to supervise a roofing subcontractor constructing a roof?

Explanation

Maybe. The generalized language quoted here is architect-friendly. It is intended to prevent a shift in compliance to the construction drawings from the contractor to the architect. However, this contractual language does not preclude a court finding that the architect has a limited duty to supervise, so a contract cause of action by the owner is possible. Depending on the applicable case law, the case might be pled either in contract, in tort for negligence, or in tort for the negligent performance of a contractual duty. Note, Architectural Malpractice: A Contract Based Approach, 92 Harv. L. Rev. 1975 (1979). The determination sometimes depends on the probability of a successful assertion of a defense or on the measure of damages available. The architect's duty is to render the supervisory service with the care reasonable under the circumstances. If the design is in some sense novel or untried, closer but not exhaustive supervision may be required—for example, to find out whether the windows specified in the drawing have a two-inch gap at the top and will cause leaks and consequent damage if left that way—but no duty to inspect the construction.

Example 4

What suggestions might you advise when the language in the prior Example remains so general?

Explanation

You might propose an exclusion, adding a clause providing that "the architect will not be responsible for construction means and methods" or more elaborately, "construction means, methods, sequences, techniques, or processes." After all, the architect is making site visits and is not in a position to continuously observe the construction process—that is clearly the work of the general contractor.

7. Preparing for Construction

Example 5

What if in Example 3 the architect had no notice of the roofing contractor's deviation from the plan and specifications for the roof?

Explanation

In and of itself, the lack of notice may not matter in a cause of action for negligent supervision. See Lotholz v. Fiedler, 59 Ill. App. 379 (1895) (holding the architect liable for hidden deviations from plans and specifications), and Paxton v. Alameda County, 259 P.2d 934 (Cal. App. 1953) (architect with notice liable). Both the architect and the developer may wish to avoid the lack of notice issue by requiring the contractor to submit samples of the roofing materials to be used—known in the construction trades as a "submittal." An approved "submittal" is often a contractual precondition to for the contractor's doing the roofing work.

Example 6

The ultimate control over job progress is the right to reject or stop work. What if the architect has that right?

Explanation

The right to reject or stop work has provided the basis for imposing a duty to supervise. Compare Miller v. DeWitt, 226 N.E.2d 630, 633 (Ill. 1967) (architect's failure to advise shoring up a renovation project roof, which collapsed on contractor's employees and injured them, was negligence when the right to stop work was express in the owner-architect agreement), distinguished in McGovern v. Standish, 357 N.E.2d 1134 (Ill. 1976) (architect's right to reject or correct materials is not a right to stop work and does not result in negligent failure to supervise), with Reber v. Chandler High School Dist. No. 202, 474 P.2d 852, 853-854 (Ariz. App. Ct. 1970) (rejecting Miller). In Miller, an express duty in the owner-architect agreement was extended to the separate agreement between the owner and the general contractor as well, something the parties probably did not intend—why use separate agreements, after all?— and so should be expressly handled in each.

7. Preparing for Construction

Example 7

In lieu of contract language that might imply a duty to supervise, an architect proposes that the architect "will recommend to the developer the rejection of work not in compliance with the construction plans and specifications." If you were the attorney for the developer, how would you respond the this proposal?

Explanation

When you check with the developer, he or she might ask the architect whether the noncompliant work is still in conformance with applicable building codes and regulations. If it is, the developer might readily adopt such proposed language. Why? The experienced developer might prefer to have the option of not accepting the architect's recommendation. Accepting noncompliant work might keep the project on schedule, and the developer might then bargain for a credit on the contract price with the contractor. On the other hand, a developer who is inexperienced or who is unfamiliar with the type of construction the project requires, will likely want to leave the power of rejection with the architect.

Example 8

Once the general contractor has received the plans and specifications for the project, drawings and diagrams will be produced by the contractor or subcontractor showing how work will be performed with regard to a particular section or design detail of the construction. These drawings and diagrams are known as "shop drawings." An architect proposes that such a subcontractor's drawing first be submitted to the general contractor for conformance with the plans and specifications for the project before submission to the architect for review. Should the developer pay for this double review?

Explanation

Almost certainly: two eyes on the drawings are better than one, so the money for the review is well spent. Architects are also likely to insist on this double review, as well as the right to summarily reject drawings not previously reviewed by the general contractor. Duplicate provisions in both the architect's contract with the developer and the general contractor's agreement with the developer are typical. Developer's counsel needs to check that these provisions are working in tandem and are cross-referenced. Recall that the developer/architect contract will be the first executed, so the architect has the upper hand in this matter.

156

7. Preparing for Construction

Example 9

If the architect cannot be held liable under a duty to supervise, then what other, later acts, performed by an architect in the course of the construction process, might render her liable?

Explanation

Two examples are a negligent issuance of an inspection certificate and a negligent disbursal of an amount under a construction agreement.

Example 10

If an architect has a limited duty to inspect a project for design defects, should she also serve as a construction lender's inspector at the same time?

Explanation

No, not without some expansion of her contractual duties, unless gross negligence or bad faith is involved. A prudent lender will require a direct contractual link with an inspecting architect.

Example 11

An agreement for architectural services provides that the architect "will visit the construction site on eight (8) occasions," naming the phase of construction when each visit will occur, and "on such other occasions as are authorized or confirmed by" the developer. The developer requests an additional visit to confirm that a change in roofing material has been made. How should the architect respond?

7. Preparing for Construction

Explanation

By checking the agreement. Typically, it will define the basic services provided,[3] including the number of site visits. What those additional occasions and services are, is difficult to predict. "Authorization" should be obtained before performance, but often this ideal sequence isn't followed—as in this Example, in which the architect is asked to respond to a change order in the specification of construction materials. The "confirmation" language quoted here permits the architect to obtain an after-the-fact basis for compensation. Visiting the site, the architect should make clear whether the materials are in technical compliance with the change order, not whether the materials are called for in the construction contract. More generally, the architectural services agreement should limit the architect to interpreting only technical documents, not contractual documents, and to making recommendations based on those documents alone. The developer's attorney needs to make sure that the architect isn't practicing law!

Under the typical contractual agreement for an architectural services, architects seldom inspect and never supervise the work of the general contractor or its subcontractors—rather, they observe that work. They may also review an application for payment by the contractor, even vetting the application before it is formally submitted to the owner, then certifying that the application included the work performed in the most recent schedule of payments. That certification will trigger a developer's obligation to make the payment.

Reviewing an architect's agreement with a developer, an attorney for either party will examine whether the architectural services are delineated from that of the general contractor; whether a duty to inspect the construction might be implied from the agreement; whether, when more than typical services are to be rendered, they are compensated; whether the architect or the developer may reject work not in compliance with the plans and specifications, as opposed to just recommending to the developer that work be rejected; and whether upon substantial and final completion of work, the architect is (upon being notified by the contractor that the work is substantially complete) to prepare a punch list of work remaining, and (upon final completion) to certify that the final payment of the construction loan proceeds may be made by the developer/borrower. The last is not a final certification of completion, but rather a final certification of payment.

---

3. Ideally, the scope, fees, and scheduling of additional services that the architect might perform should be set out in the architect's agreement with the developer. Additional services might include revisions to the plans and specifications, including those required to meet green building regulations, or services required after the period during which basic services were initially contemplated, due to construction delays.

7. Preparing for Construction

Examples

Example 12

An AIA document provision states that the architectural drawings remain the property of the architect. General Conditions A-201 (attached to AIA owner-architect agreement A-101 or A-111 (1987)). ACREL recommends that all drawings be the property of the owner. How should an attorney facing a negotiation over this question respond?

Explanation

By sorting out the interests involved. The owner has an interest in seeing that the same building, or a building with the same architectural detail, isn't erected next door. Moreover, the owner is paying for the services of the architect. "Ah ha!" says the architect. Services are what the owner gets, not the drawings (which are only the product of the service). Further, the architect knows that there is no such thing as a completely original building and that she will use some of the features included in the owner's building again. Moreover, she is proud of her design and does not want the owner copying it in locations and sites for which it is not appropriate. That design, moreover, may be the subject of copyright, but it also may be deposited with local building permit officials as a condition of the permit and so become a public record. Finally, the architect is responsible for the design and liable for any defects in it; its reuse, under circumstances over which she has no control, extends that liability.

Example 13

Taking each of the interests described in the prior Example into account, what middle course between the *meum* and *tuum* (mine and thine) of the AIA and ACREL provisions can you suggest?

Explanation

The extreme view of a developer's rights is that the owner can assign the right to use, or reuse, the architectural plans to some third party for her own use. To this the architect might object that the proposed reuse of the plans in another location might be unsuitable for any of several reasons having to do with the site, the type of use proposed for the building, and so forth. The architect, however, might be given a right to refuse reuse of the plans through procedures established to obtain the architect's consent to reuse. The right to refuse cannot be exercised unreasonably, however. A less extreme view of the owner's rights is that the owner has an interest

159

7. Preparing for Construction

in using the plans on a continuing basis in connection with her own use and with the occupancy of the premises; she does not wish to go back to the architect each time maintenance or renovation of the premises is undertaken. The owner may also wish to use the plans for any planned addition to the project. The more the project is likely to be altered in design by later changes or the more likely the plans are to be put into unskilled hands, the more likely the architect is to insist on retaining some rights in the plans.

Resolving this ownership dispute may also turn on the uniqueness of the design. A developer won't appreciate seeing a unique design appearing in the project of competitors. The architect might fear that if the developer owns the plans, they will be used again without consultation with or extra compensation for the architect and perhaps used in a way that increases the exposure of the architect to liability for the design.

Generally standard form AIA and other documents in this area give the architect ownership of the plans, along with the right to copyright them. When assigned initial ownership rights in the plans, the architect might be willing to negotiate over her rights in the plans when (1) the plans are used to complete the project after the termination of the architect's agreement; (2) an indemnity for the use of the plans in other projects or on other projects or sites is involved; (3) a mortgage lender insists on the right to use the plans to complete the project or to undertake activities necessary to protect its rights under the covenants of the mortgage; all the while, the architect may insist on retention of the right to use the plans—or more likely, its components—on other projects; (4) the architect is in default on the design contract; and (5) the developer is operating, maintaining, repairing, or renovating the project.

THE GENERAL CONTRACTOR

A general contractor (the GC) has at least three main jobs. The GC is the person or firm primarily responsible for constructing the project using the plans and specifications provided by the architect. The specifications include performance standards for the project. Second, the GC also is responsible for scheduling the construction work, coordinating all the materials delivered to the construction site, their use and installation by construction workers, and the workers' arrival and departure from the site. Third, the GC is responsible for compliance with standards set by the federal and state governments for worker health and safety under the Occupational Safety and Health Act (OSHA), 29 U.S.C. §651 et seq.

7. Preparing for Construction

Selecting the General Contractor

The general contractor may be selected by competitive bidding, by negotiation, or by selection (or some combination of these three processes). Generally, general contractors are selected through competitive bids, and the project delivery method is commonly referred to as design-bid-build. Under this model, the developer enters into separate contracts with the architect and the contractor for the project's design and construction.

Once selected, the general contractor receives the completed and final construction drawings from the architect. (He will have examined interim plans while bidding.) With those in hand, he can proceed to hire subcontractors for previously-mentioned specialized components of the project.

Project Inspections

Because the developer has a significant interest in ensuring that the project is constructed according to the plans and specifications, he will designate an individual to serve as the construction manager charged with overseeing construction activities. This person may be an architect, a member of the construction management firm, or the representative of the developer or construction lender. One or more of these parties will appoint a person or firm to inspect the construction as it proceeds.

Key inspections include those conducted when the foundation is complete, when the first floor is laid, when the framing is done, and so on. These are times at which the owner and lender accepts the work of the contractor. These are likely to be times when the work can be inspected by code enforcement officials of the local government. These are also the times at which the construction loan will be serially disbursed by the lender. That is, this type of loan is not disbursed at closing, but later, as the work progresses and is inspected for the lender's benefit; meanwhile, the owner/developer/mortgagor pays interest only, and only on the disbursements actually made. Interest owing is taken, up front, out of the next disbursement. This traditional procedure requires the completion of distinct steps in the construction process, completing the preceding one before undertaking the next. From the owner's perspective, it has the advantage of permitting a precise determination of what the project will look like and what it will cost, made in advance of any construction on the project.

If the architect as an inspector becomes a project overseer, she is still not its supervisor. As architects have stepped back from a supervisory role, the general contractor has stepped up into it. So recently if anyone supervises, it's the general contractor on a day-to-day basis or someone specially

161

7. Preparing for Construction

employed for and on the job as needed. See Emanuel Halper, Negotiating Architectural Contracts, 17 Real Est. Rev. 65 (Summer 1987).

CONSTRUCTION CONTRACT AGREEMENTS

Owner/developers and general contractors and major subcontractors[4] typically agree on one of three types of payment contracts for construction of a project. The three types are (1) a fixed-price agreement, (2) a cost-plus agreement, and (3) a guaranteed maximum price agreement.

(1) A **fixed price agreement**. The first is an agreement providing for delivery of the building for a fixed price, inclusive of the contractor's profit. See American Institute of Architects, AIA Document A201 (2017) (Construction Contract General Conditions). The price is paid regardless of the actual cost of the construction.

Developers such as federal, state, or municipal agencies typically use a *fixed price agreement* for their projects; often their authorizing statutes require competitive bidding and this type of agreement.

Private sector developers that use a standard design for which contractors can readily estimate construction costs (a warehouse or distribution center might be examples), projects without environmental or geological issues, and housing developments that use standardized building components, may also use this type of agreement.

In a fixed-price agreement, the contract names a stipulated sum that a developer will pay for performance of the work (1) identified in the plans and specification provided the contractor and (2) performed by a stipulated date. The contractor keeps any savings it is able to achieve during the construction process and runs the risk that the price will prove inadequate due to cost overruns during the process. In effect, the contractor's price will have to be high enough to compensate for this risk. This type of agreement is often used when the bidding for subcontractors has been conducted on a competitive basis and when few changes in plans are anticipated. Conversely, when the plans and specification are incomplete and thus many changes can be anticipated, few contractors would agree to a fixed price agreement. (Thus this type of agreement is seldom used for a fast-track[5] project.)

In the alternative, a fixed price agreement might also be used for additional work for which a price has been "fixed" — defined, established and agreed to — for example, a provision for a change order in the materials used for the "skin" of a building or in the "fits and finishes" in its interior.

---

4. In this section a reference to a "contractor" refers both to general contractors and major subcontractors on a project.
5. For an explanation of a fast-track project, see infra, this chapter.

7. Preparing for Construction

Another variation in a fixed price agreement is a fixed "allowance" for some incomplete portion of the plans and specifications which the contractor cannot obtain a cost estimate at the time the agreement is executed—for example, some component of the electrical or communications systems for a building.

Like all construction agreements, a fixed price agreement requires a schedule of payments to be disbursed as construction progresses. These progress payments are made on a schedule assigning to each payment the completion of a percentage of the total work required and as a percentage of the fixed price. This schedule is typically required by the construction agreement for general contractors and major subcontractors. It is agreed to when that agreement is negotiated. It is known as a "schedule of values."[6] The schedule of values apportions the fixed price among all components of the construction. (There is no construction industry standard naming each component, nor is there a standard cost threshold requiring that a line item be assigned to a component.) The price of each component is based on the general and/or subcontractors' approved budget. Thus each component has its own line item schedule. Considered as a whole, the schedule of values is used for submitting applications for progress payments. The party submitting an application bills on a percentage basis, so the amount requested (typically monthly) is a percentage of the overall line item. As a spreadsheet, the x-axis lists the components of construction, the y-axis the frequency of payment. The application for payment is reviewed[7] by the developer or the architect. The amount due is then disbursed.

(2) A **cost plus agreement**. Here the developer is reimbursed for its actual construction costs, usually measured by the amounts it owes its subcontractors, plus the contractor's overhead and profit, usually either a lump sum, fixed fee, or measured as 5 to 15% of the costs. Cost plus agreements are often used for negotiated, as opposed to competitively bid, contracts. One advantage of negotiated bidding is that the contractor can be involved in the pre-construction planning process, allowing early use of his expertise. This expertise is most often useful in budgeting a project, particularly in estimating the cost of labor and materials. Such involvement is called "value engineering"; in this situation, when the developer lacks planning experience, the contractor supplies it. From the developer's perspective, this

---

6. A schedule of values may be used as an auditing device for any type of construction contract. It does not vary with the location or type of project.

7. When the payment applied for is a percentage of the total fixed price assigned to that component, the developer or architect will add this percentage to the total amount previously billed to determine the total work completed to date, then subtract that amount from the total cost or value assigned that component. These calculations tell the developer, contractor, or lender whether the project is "on time" (the developer and the contractor will be particularly concerned about this) and whether the balance is "on budget" (the developer and the lender will be particularly concerned about this).

163

7. Preparing for Construction

sometimes enables construction of the project to start before its plans and specifications are complete; this in turn allows the developer to respond to market changes as the project's design is completed.

For the developer, this advantage is often outweighed by the disadvantages of this type of agreement. It gives the contractor little incentive to hold down the costs of construction unless it is accompanied by a developer's right to review the results of the bidding process or by a requirement that all subcontractors competitively bid their work, or both. For a general contractor, it eliminates the risk that the actual construction will cost more than anticipated in the construction budget, while for the developer, it creates the concomitant disadvantage that it does not provide the developer with the certainty of knowing a final cost of construction—and this uncertainly ripples down into his ignorance of the project's financing costs and the ultimate profitability of the project. It also puts the focus of both the developer and the general contractor on negotiating a list of reimbursable costs and is typically accompanied by a reduction in reimbursable costs included in the contractor's general conditions—or in some instances by the elimination of those conditions.

(3) A **guaranteed maximum price (GMP) agreement**. Such an agreement is often preferred for large or complex projects and often used when the design of a project is incomplete when construction begins. Both the profit potential and financing costs for a project determine when some construction precedes full design. It provides that the contractor's total cost for the building will not exceed a stipulated price. It further provides that the developer agrees to pay on a cost plus basis up to the GMP, and that the parties will split any savings below the guaranteed price. The savings split is weighted—often 25/75—in favor of the contractor in order to give him an incentive to achieve cost savings. The more local construction is booming regionally, the more favorable the savings split is likely to be. When the cost of construction is greater than the GMP, the contractor bears the excess cost alone, sometimes with some carve-out costs which the developer will share on an agreed basis with the contractor.

A GMP might either be an overall cap or ceiling on the total cost of construction or a series of GMPs on individual line items of the work. A series of GMPs makes it impossible for a contractor to transfer costs savings from one line item to another, so contractors generally resist line item GMPs.

The right to an MGP is often built into a cost plus agreement—that is, the contractor may be required to generate an MGP when (say) 75 percent of the building is completed, or when all major subcontractors have agreed to work on it, or when a mortgage lender insists on it—all provided that no previous cost estimate is exceeded. If the general contractor and the developer cannot agree on a GMP at this point, a method for dealing with the disagreement will have to be built into the contract, or else the developer have the right to terminate the contract or the contractor have the obligation to accept the lowest bid from all future subcontractors.

7. Preparing for Construction

Examples

Example 14

While advising the general contractor (your client) negotiating a schedule of values for a fixed price agreement, the client asks that you front load the percentage values assigned to some components of the schedule. How should you respond?

Explanation

You should resist this request. Although cash flow is crucial to every contractor, this type of over-billing may, when a dispute over an application for a progress payment arises, front-load the amount of mechanic's liens[8] as well. Further, third party eyes will be on the schedule if there are payment and performance bonds on the construction. Finally, a contractor does not want to take the hit to its reputation which it will acquire as an over-biller.

Example 15

A contractor agreeing to a cost-plus agreement is able to obtain building materials at a substantial discount because it is working multiple jobs in the locality. The contractor bills the full price for the materials. How should the developer respond?

Explanation

Courts interpreting this type of agreement have taken it to require the actual costs, less all discounts, rebates, etc. Thus the contractor's savings should be passed on to the developer. Today standard developer/contractor construction agreements stipulate this, but negotiation over the matter is also typical.

Example 16

Standardized cost-plus agreements have language suggesting what type of labor costs are properly reimbursed, but developers and contractors

---

8. Mechanic's liens are discussed infra, this chapter.

165

7. Preparing for Construction

often modify such language. What modifications would you suggest for a developer?

Explanation

Although most developers would agree to including on-site supervisory personnel wages, developers balk at including those of off-site supervisors and other administrative personnel, as well as those expediting the production or transportation of materials or construction equipment to the site. Although wages for construction workers are routinely included, fringe benefits and other incentives are sometimes disputed.

Analogous disputes relating to materials might include distinguishing materials incorporated into the project and those lost to waste and spoilage and allocating a portion of the contractor's general liability insurance premium to the project.

Example 17

Contractor resists inclusion of a "time of the essence" provision in its construction agreement with your client. How should you respond?

Explanation

By insisting on it again. Time is money, and the provision makes the contractor's on-time performance of the agreement a material one. At common law, in contrast, insubstantial, untimely performance was not a material breach of the agreement. The developer wants the contractor to oversee the construction closely. Including this provision provides incentive to do so, unless truly heavy penalties are occasioned by the project not being on time or on schedule. Thus a "time of the essence" provision is included in most construction agreements.

Example 18

After the developer insists on a "time of the essence" provision in the construction agreement, the contractor insists in a right to suspend work on the project. How should the developer's attorney respond?

166

7. Preparing for Construction

Explanation

By explaining that typically the developer is given the right to suspend and the contractor needs no such corresponding right. The developer after all is in touch with the construction lender and problems arising in the administration of the construction loan may require suspension of the work, but the contractor has no such need. Without agreeing to a mutual right to suspend, the developer's attorney might agree to limit the developer's right to suspend for a certain number of days, paying the contractor the direct costs of the suspension, and entitling the contractor to an extension of time caused by the developer's suspension of work.

Example 19

Advising a developer, you notice that the general contractor negotiating a construction agreement is insisting on detailed negotiations over the provision sharing savings with regard the difference between the actual construction costs and a GMP. What advice would you give your client on this point?

Explanation

Your advice might be that the developer should employ an independent, professional cost estimator at this point. Why? Because the general contractor might be looking to augment its fee. The GMP should be set at a realistic amount and your client now has been given some indication that the general contractor has set it above that amount.

Example 20

A developer suspends work on a project, giving the contractor an extension of time proportionate to the ensuring delay but invoking a provision in the agreement that there will be no damages for the delay. The delay lasts three months. The contractor sues the developer for damages. What result?

167

7. Preparing for Construction

Explanation

Some courts would uphold the damages suit, finding that the delay lasted an unreasonably long time, it being in bad faith and not contemplated by the parties to the agreement. See Law Co. v. Mohawk Constr. & Supply Co., 702 F. Supp. 2d 1304 (D. Kan. 2010), and Corinno Civetta Constr. Corp. v. New York, 493 N.E.2d 905 (N.Y. 1986). In a few jurisdictions (Ohio, Minnesota, and New Jersey are examples), a statute either limits or voids "no damage for delay" provisions.

WARRANTIES

Construction agreements of any type will contain express warranties and representations given by the contractor to the developer that the work will be performed with new materials, in a workmanlike manner, and in compliance with the plans and specifications given to the contractor by the developer. Exclusions from this warranty include warranties for equipment when the manufacturer's warranty is assigned to the developer and defective work caused by a defective design of the project. Such warranties typically commence upon substantial completion[9] of the project. In exchange for such warranties, contractors will bargain that performance of warranty work is the developer's exclusive remedy with regard to it "in contract, tort or otherwise, including causes of action, legal or equitable, in negligence or strict liability." The contractor may also ask for similar waivers from the developer, thus back-stopping the exclusivity of the warranty. Each party might also waive consequential damages to bolster this exclusivity.

Examples

Example 21

A developer requests an "evergreen warranty"—that is, an automatic extension and a re-warranty of work required by the initial warranty of work and running for the same period as the initial warranty. Why will the general contractor resist?

---

9. Substantial completion occurs when the developer can take possession or make beneficial use and occupancy of the project.

7. Preparing for Construction

Explanation

Contractors resist evergreen warranties because of the difficulty of getting subcontractors to re-warrant their work, leaving the contractor in a warranty gap requiring that it absorb the cost of evergreen work.

Example 22

A general contractor builds a project in compliance with the plans and specification supplied by the developer. The resulting building fails to meet the developer's expectations. What is the developer's recourse?

Explanation

In general, the developer implicitly warrants that the plans and specifications will be adequate once the developer delivers them and the contractor complies with them. The developer's "warranty of constructability" is implied into every construction agreement, absent language to the contrary. See United States v. Spearin, 248 U.S. 132 (1918). *Spearin* supplies the contractor with a defense against the developer's suit for defective work or breach of warranty, absent the contractor's express warranty or negligence: the contractor is not responsible for defects in the developer's plans and specifications. See, e.g., Ruthrauff, Inc. v. Ravin, Inc., 914 A.2d 880 (Pa. Super. Ct. 2006). *Spearin* also supplies the contractor with a counterclaim for the costs of remedying defective work or extending the schedule of work. The contractor's contractual obligation to check the plans and specifications does not negate this implied warranty from the developer. See Coghlin Elec. Contractors, Inc. v. Gilbane Bldg. Co., 36 N.E. 3d 505, 515 (Mass. 2015)

Likewise, the *Spearin* doctrine also provides that a contractor, once agreeing to build according to the plans and specifications supplied by the developer, though not responsible for unforeseen difficulties caused by the project site itself, will not be entitled to additional compensation because unforeseen difficulties are encountered. See Costello Constr. Co. v. City of Charlottesville, 97 F. Supp. 3d 819, 826 (W.D. Va. 2015).

7. Preparing for Construction

OTHER PROVISIONS IN CONSTRUCTION AGREEMENTS

Retainage. These agreements typically contain a provision giving the developer the right to retain and withhold a percentage of each progress payment made to the general contractor; that contractor in turn may have a similar right in its agreements with subcontractors. The percentage is usually about 10% of the payment. All amounts withheld will be disbursed upon (substantial) completion of the work or the satisfaction or expiration of liens. In many jurisdictions, there are statutes governing retainage amounts. Some require that retained funds be escrowed and held in trust for eventual payment. See Snake Steel, Inc. v. Holladay Constr. Grp., LLC, 625 S.W.3d 830 (Tenn. 2021). Others put deadlines on payment, stipulating that they be paid (say) 30 days after completion or release of liens; this type of statute is known as a "pay-when-paid" statute.[10] A subcontractor's claim on retainage is both assignable and lienable. See Kenco Constr., Inc. v. Porter Bros. Constr., Inc., 2020 Wash. App. LEXIS 2769 (Wash. Ct. App. Oct. 26, 2020). Typically it is the developer who retains the funds, but lenders have also bargained for the right to do so.

Early notice of delays. Delays are the bane of the construction schedule. Though not often in a position to discover impending delays, developers can impose notice requirements on general contractors (1) to "say what they know" of impending delays and (2) to meet date-certain deadlines for completion of crucial components of the construction, paying a *per diem* penalty when those deadlines are not met, with carve-outs for excusable delays. Excusable delays include delays caused by the developer and *force majeure* delays (those caused, e.g., by unforeseen and unforeseeable site conditions, labor disputes, weather, natural disasters, or acts of God). The tighter and shorter the construction schedule, the more the developer and the contractor will negotiate the list of *force majeure* events.

Examples

Example 23

The *force majeure* delay provision in a construction agreement states that such delays "occur when construction is delayed for circumstances beyond the parties reasonable control, including without limitation, as a result of

---

10. As opposed to a "pay-if-paid" provision in a general contractor's construction agreement, providing that the contractor is not obliged to pay a sub until it is paid by the developer, creating a condition precedent to payment and putting the risk of nonpayment when the general contractor is unpaid squarely on the subcontractors. See Lemoine Co. of Ala., LLC v. HLH Constructors, Inc., 62 So. 3d 1020, 1026 (Ala. 2010). For more on "pay-if-paid" provisions in construction agreements, see infra, this chapter, at Example 31.

7. Preparing for Construction

natural disaster, fire, flood, strikes, war, armed conflict, terrorist attack or nuclear or chemical or biological contamination affecting the construction site." As the developer's attorney, would you object to this language?

Explanation

Yes. Developers generally want shorter, specific lists of events, while contractors want longer ones. The "without limitation" clause might, from the developer's perspective, be deleted. The broad scope of a "natural disaster" might be rendered more specific: "hurricanes, tornados, typhoons" might be substituted. Likewise, "strikes" might become "general strikes," lest a strike against one subcontractor shut down the whole site.

Change orders. They are the order of the day. No construction is likely to be completed without some modification in the scope of work required. Such change orders may be issued by either the developer or the general contractor, but universally they are ineffective unless in writing and until executed by both of these parties.

A second type of change order occurs when the developer (often one using in a fast-track delivery method for a project) bargains for a unilateral right to direct a change in the general contractor's scope of work even before the appropriate schedule and cost adjustments are made and in advance of a formal change order. This is an "order to follow" directive.

A third type of change is a constructive change. This occurs when a developer informally directs that extra work be performed, when the contractor is required to do extra work because the plans and specification prove defective, when the developer mistakenly rejects work that complies with those plans, or denies an otherwise justifiable extension of time. Thus, constructive changes are not formal change orders, but are instead those that could have been recognized under the agreement had they been recognized under it. If finally recognized, they permit the contractor either an extension of time or money damages, or both.

When a delay is excused (1) by the developer, (2) by the occurrence of unforeseen site problems, or (3) by a *force majeure* event, the contractor will typically be entitled to a schedule extension. Realizing that mid-project delays must be quickly and conclusively resolved, developers often try to limit the contractor to this remedy, making it an exclusive one in the construction agreement and augmenting this exclusivity with a "no-damage-for-delay" provision.

No-Damage-for-Delay Provision. Such a (NDFD) provision is customarily used in construction agreements and is routinely upheld but strictly construed. Thus a construction agreement may excuse a developer from paying delay damages, even if the developer is negligent. See Zachry Constr. Corp. v. Port of Houston Auth., 449 S.W.3d 98, 117-118 (Tex. 2014) (reporting that this so in 28 American jurisdictions); J.A. Jones Constr. Co. v. Lehrer McGovern

171

7. Preparing for Construction

Bovis, Inc., 89 P.3d 1009, 1014-1016 (Nev. 2004); and Corinno Civetta Constr. Corp. v. New York, 493 N.E.2d 905 (N.Y. 1986). Under an NDFD provision, the contractor assumes the risk of delays from an owner's change in the plans and specifications, the parties realizing that some changes are likely to occur during construction and that the contractor can protect itself from delays by adjusting the price bid for the agreement.

However, several exceptions to this exculpatory provision have been developed by the courts. The provision does not shield the developer from liability for deliberately and wrongfully interfering with the contractor's work. Nor from liability for the developer's gross negligence, fraud, misrepresentation, bad faith, willful and malicious conduct; nor for un-contemplated delays, delays so unreasonable in length that they are a fundamental breach of contract or its intentional abandonment. In general, these exceptions are a back-stop to the implied covenant of good faith and fair dealing. The "heavy" burden of proving the applicability of an exception is on the party asserting it.

As previously mentioned, agreements with an NDFD provision typically limit the contractor's remedy to an extension of time for performance of the work.

A typical provision might read that "the contractor shall have no claim for money damages or any additional compensation for delay no matter how caused, but for any delay in performance not caused by contractor, contractor shall be entitled only to an extension of time for performance of contractor's work."

Liquidated damage provision. Such a provision gives a monetary award of a predetermined amount for a specific breach of the construction agreement. The amount must be agreed to in advance of the execution of the agreement, fixing damages in advance of its breach. It requires no proof of actual damages on the date of the breach. It serves to simplify the resolution of a dispute over a breach of the agreement without resorting to litigation. It is appropriately used when damages are uncertain in amount. See R.W. Farmer Constr. Co. v. Carter, 454 S.W.2d 30, 32 (Mo. 1970). When appearing in a construction agreement, it is scrutinized in court using the same criteria that would apply in any contract: it must be not unreasonable in amount, fairly bargained for, and represent a reasonable approximation of actual damages so as not to be found to be a penalty. There is a trend in the case law on the subject to enforce such provisions because of the blurry line between such damages and a penalty. See Proulx v. 1400 Pa. Ave, SE, LLC, 199 A.3d 667, 673 (D.C. 2019).

In the context of the construction process, its reasonableness is scrutinized so that it gives the contractor incentive to complete the work on time. It is routinely stated as a *per diem* amount—that is, say, $400 for each day the work is performed beyond the deadline for its completion. The imposition of liquidated damages is sometimes delayed for a short period (say, 15 days) after the deadline.

7. Preparing for Construction

A typical provision might read that "contractor agrees to pay the developer (say) $400.00 for each calendar day completion of work is delayed beyond the scheduled completion date for such work."

GENERAL CONDITIONS IN CONSTRUCTION AGREEMENTS

"General Conditions" are services a contractor provides that are not directly incorporated into a project, but they give value to the contractor's efforts to complete the project. They typically include such line items in a schedule of values as management and supervisory costs, permit fees, site safety costs, trash and garbage disposal costs, temporary on-site offices, and site security costs.

Examples

Example 24

When examining the general conditions in a construction agreement, what should a developer's attorney look for?

Explanation

Duplication and over-laps with reimbursable costs. Supervision by off-site employees of the contractor may appear both as a reimbursable cost and as part of the agreement's general conditions. When an item appears as a general condition, it should be removed from the lists of reimbursable costs. Otherwise the contractor is double-dipping, perhaps in an attempt to recoup lost costs, and the developer is paying twice for the same service.

THE ROLE OF THE SUBCONTRACTOR

Once the developer has executed a construction agreement with the general contractor, the latter, in turn, will enter into agreements with the various subcontractors needed to construct the project. These agreements with the subs are the backbone of the general contractor's estimates for completing the project. Having these bids gives the general contractor, and in turn the

7. Preparing for Construction

lender, confidence that the project can indeed be built for the amount stated in the general contractor's agreement with the owner.

Typically there are separate subcontractors for site clearance, demolition, sheeting and shoring the site's subsurface, concrete foundations, structural components, skinning the structure, as well as electrical, plumbing, and heating and air conditioning (HVAC).

In general, the sub knows that her bid, if accepted, will become the basis of the construction agreement. When the sub's cost estimates are wrong and services cannot be delivered for the price stated, there will be economic loss up the line — from the sub, who will have to absorb the mistake or pass it along, to the general contractor, who will have insufficient loan funds to call on, to the lender, whose loan may become insecure as a result. Mistakes in a sub's cost estimates also cause delays on the job site. As a result, the general contractor may become liable to the owner under liquidated or other damage provisions in the construction agreement. As before, liquidated damages are often computed on a *per diem* basis. Both the general and the subcontractor suffer damages as a result of having to pay for labor and equipment for longer than anticipated.

Every construction project is subject to numerous "change orders." The onus of such changes in the work typically falls on the subs. Thus, suits for breach of contract and damages incurred in carrying out change orders generate litigation risks and problems in drafting agreements. On a large construction site, subs have considerable difficulty in showing that their contract losses were caused by a change order and, faced with suits involving many change orders, some courts have permitted the sub to claim that its original agreement was "abandoned" and sue for the total cost of doing the agreed-to work. See Prichard Bros. Inc. v. Grady Co., 436 N.W.2d 460, 468-468 (Minn. App. 1989). Similarly, subs' claims for consequential damages have included an increasingly long list of damages — for lost profits, office overhead, wage increases, lost opportunities, nonavailability of labor and materials, and so forth. As a result, the AIA General Conditions of the Contract for Construction include a blanket waiver of consequential damages.

In collecting its subcontracts, the general contractor collects warranties for the subs' work that are "back to back" — that is, without gaps in scope, effective dates, and duration — between what the general contractor has warranted to the developer and what it has received from its sub.

If the subcontractor cannot recover her damages through her agreement but has added uncompensated value to the project, it may file a mechanic's lien. The presence of such a lien in the public records may cause the lender not to issue the next disbursement of the loan, and further delays and damages can result from that. Usually any disbursed payment to the mechanic made by check has a waiver of lien rights on the check, above the space on the back for an endorsement.

7. Preparing for Construction

Examples

Example 25

A general contractor, seeking to patch a gap in the construction schedule for a project, calls an old and reliable subcontractor to the construction. The sub arrives and immediately deploys his employees to work on the site. An employee is injured just as the sub enters the construction site office of the general contractor to sign the subcontracting agreement. What are the legal consequences of this sequence of events?

Explanation

First, a denial of an insurance claim for the accident by the subcontractor's comprehensive liability insurance carrier. See Liberty Ins. Co. v. Ferguson Steel Co., 812 N.E.2d 228 (Ind. Ct. App. 2004) (finding that the injured employee was not to an "additional insured"). Second, having created this situation, the general contractor will have to rely on its own insurance in this instance.

MECHANIC'S LIENS

Mechanic's liens are statutory creatures. Their purpose is to provide payment for work performed or materials supplied in construction, repair, or improvement of real property and so to encourage that improvement and to protect those "mechanics" (the general contractor's subcontractors, and perhaps even sub-subs) who add value to property but who do not deal directly with the developer/owner/titleholder for whom the improvement is made. For those who deal directly, their remedy is to sue for breach of their employment contract. The person who benefits from an improvement will thus be unable to convey free of the lien after accepting the services or materials of the protected mechanic. These liens were unknown to the common law, although it is easy to regard them as an equitable remedy for unjust enrichment.

Generalizations about these statutes are hazardous. There is no such thing as a uniform, simple mechanic's lien statute. However, in general the lien is established by a recording of the lien by the mechanic. The description of the property to which the lien is to apply must be specific. Upon filing, the lien applies to both land and the improvements on it. Sometimes the lien is effective upon recording, but sometimes its effectiveness relates back to the "commencement of the work"— a term often defined as the commencement of any work on a project, not just of a particular mechanic's work on the improvement.

175

7. Preparing for Construction

Where this relation-back principle is used, a lender making the first disbursement for a construction loan will check the construction site to ascertain two things: first, that no materials have been delivered to it, and second, that no signs of work are visible on it. Either event might give rise to a mechanic's lien with priority over the lender's lien. The lender won't want the soil disturbed if its excavator can claim the benefit of a prior lien. The lender may even take pictures of the site on the closing or first disbursal date. Sometimes, as in Florida, the relation-back principle is used only when a notice of a lien is filed in advance of its recordation, and then only against intervening parties with constructive notice of this filing.

Although construction mortgage lenders attempt to protect themselves against a loss of priority to mechanics, the mechanic's lien laws of many states go further and provide expressly that when the mortgage is recorded prior to the commencement of construction, it is assigned a priority over any mechanic's lien arising during construction. Many state statutes give the construction lender's loan priority over the mechanics paid with its proceeds. This is often referred to as the majority or "priority" rule. With such a statutory provision in effect, one might better refer to the mechanic's lien law as the construction lender's law and dispense with mechanic's lien waivers (although the latter seldom happens). The rationale for such a provision is that no mechanic would be working on the construction site unless the lender were willing to provide the loan, so why not encourage such loans with just this type of provision?.

Eleven states do not accord this priority and follow a different rule.[11] In Missouri, for example, a construction mortgagee by definition is deemed to have subordinated its mortgage to mechanic's liens on the same project. Sometimes the mortgagee's control over the disbursement of the loan, or over a direct disbursement to the mechanic, is given as the reason for such a (minority) rule. See H. B. Deal Constr. Co. v. Labor Discount Center, Inc., 418 S.W.2d 940 (Mo. 1967).

There have been numerous attacks on the constitutionality of these statutes, most of which have been rebuffed. In the last several decades, however, several states have redrafted their statutes in response to Sniadach v. Family Fin. Corp., 395 U.S. 337 (1969) (imposing notice and hearing requirements on garnishments founded on the due process clause) and its progeny involving mechanic's liens.

---

11. These 11 states are Alaska, Colorado, Illinois, Indiana, Iowa, Maine, Missouri, Montana, Oregon, Virginia, and Wyoming.

7. Preparing for Construction

Scope and Inclusiveness of Mechanic's Lien Statutes

The definition of mechanics protected by these lien statutes has tended to become more inclusive over the years. Today, in some jurisdictions, an architect, surveyor, landscape architect, engineer, or urban planner may be covered as well. As a result, many statutes cover both those with direct contracts with the owner and those without such contracts. Thus, one method of delineating the scope of a lien statute is to include specific occupations and trades.

Another method of assessing a lien statute's scope is to examine the number of contractual links between the person claiming the lien and the owner. About half the states use the degree of removal from contractual privity with the owner as the measure of coverage. In these states, the general contractor and her subcontractor are covered, or the subs of the subs are covered, or (even) the sub-subs of the subs are covered. In the other half of the states, the lien covers any mechanic who adds value to an improvement.

If the applicable statute reaches the third tier of subcontractors mentioned, so generally will a construction lender's system of direct disbursement by check, with an endorsement line on the back under a waiver of lien.

Stop Notices

In some jurisdictions giving the construction lender's lien priority over mechanics, mechanics have the option of filing a stop notice with the lender, indicating that they are unpaid for work done or materials supplied. After this filing, the lender pays the person meant to pay the filing mechanic at its peril. This stop notice procedure recognizes that if the mechanic is to be paid once the construction deal goes sour, it is to the loan proceeds that the mechanic must look. The action to foreclose the lien asserted in this way must be brought within a certain time of the filing, or else the lien is lost. California and Washington have stop notice procedures in their statutes.

Enforcement

Mechanic's liens are enforced or perfected by judicial foreclosure. If several mechanics each obtain a judgment and the funds for satisfying all of them are insufficient, there are two main methods for resolving the problem. In some states, each takes equally; in others, a reverse order of contractual privity with the owner is used. In many states, if one mechanic gains priority over the construction lender, all mechanics on the same project do too. So the filing of any one mechanic's lien is a serious matter for a lender.

7. Preparing for Construction

Examples

Example 26

Is title insurance adequate to protect against mechanic's liens?

Explanation

Not in its standard form policies. Special endorsements are needed. Title insurers will often insist on site pictures and complicated escrow procedures handled by the title insurer itself. Because many title insurers found in the mid-1970s that their escrow procedures were insufficient protection, they will also insist on bring-down title searches before each disbursement. Such searches update a prior search, presumably made just before the last disbursement. After the search, the insurer is willing to change the "Date of Policy" to the search date.

Example 27

An excavator deposits topsoil at a construction site. The soil has been taken from elsewhere and transported to the site. Upon noticing the pile of topsoil, what should a lender considering a construction loan application do?

Explanation

Obtain a lien waiver from whoever delivered the soil. See Rupp v. Earl H. Cline & Sons, Inc., 188 A.2d 146 (Md. 1963).

Example 28

May a demolition company have a mechanics lien on a building constructed on the site where demolition occurred? Is a lien available for demolition work necessary to make way for the building?

178

7. Preparing for Construction

Explanation

Probably not. When the statute reaches only so far, the courts are unlikely to extend it without statutory authority. They are used to mechanics grasping at any theory to receive payment and are only too likely to send them to the legislature instead. The demolition company thus cannot "lien" the improvement.

Example 29

How about a swimming pool contractor who files a lien obtainable by any person "improving a building"?

Explanation

No lien. While a mechanic's lien statute is remedial and so should be liberally construed, its reach should not be extended beyond its plain meaning. A "building" is a structure intended for occupancy and shelter. Moreover, the legislative history of many mechanic's lien statutes includes a series of broadening amendments to add new lienable structures and services; perhaps the matter is best left to future legislative action. If swimming pools are to be lienable, the legislature should say so. See Freeform Pools, Inc. v. Strawbridge Home for Boys, Inc., 179 A.2d 683 (Md. 1962). In like manner, some similarly worded statutes might distinguish between "repairing" and "improving" a building. However an improvement is defined, most jurisdictions require that the mechanic fully perform his contract before awarding a mechanic's lien. Recall also that a lien may depend on whether the mechanic's contract derives from another contractual link to the owner, or whether it is regarded as independent of its derivation. Don't forget, these liens are solely the creatures of the statutes authorizing them.

Example 30

If the mechanic's work violates applicable setback or other land use control laws, can the cost of rendering the improvement legal be set off against the amount of the lien?

179

7. Preparing for Construction

Explanation

Yes. If the mechanic resorts to the law, she is bound to have done her work in conformance to applicable law, unless misled by the owner into installing a noncomplying improvement.

Example 30

If a material supplier files a security interest on a fixture, may she also have a mechanic's lien?

Explanation

Not in California. When a lien is uncertain, an Article 9 UCC filing is the backup protection, as it might be for demolition work or the construction of temporary work necessary for use on the job site.

Example 31

Many construction agreements (and some statutes) provide that if a general contractor has not been paid a progress or final payment, it has no obligation to pay its subs. Such a "pay if paid" provision may be invoked by a sub against a general contractor withholding a sub's payment in a dispute over the sub's work; this in turn may result in an unpaid sub filing a mechanic's lien against a project. In this situation, particularly if a final payment is involved, the developer may wish to pay the sub directly in order to lift the lien. May the developer's do this?

7. **Preparing for Construction**

Explanation

Some construction agreements provide for a developer's right to make a direct payment; others don't provide for such a right. See Envt'l Energy Partners, Inc. v. Siemens Bldg. Techs., Inc., 178 S.W.3d 691 (S.D. Mo. Oct. 25, 2005).

SURETY BONDS

A surety is a person who agrees, often in a document structured to look like a deed, to satisfy the debt or obligation of another (usually known as the "principal"). The person who is assured that the debt or obligation will be paid is the "obligee" of the bond. In the context of a construction loan and agreement, a surety is typically a bonding company specializing in such agreements, and the principal typically is the general contractor.

A surety offers three types of bonds to guarantee the completion of a construction project (only in the loosest sense can a bond of this type be labeled as insurance):

1. *Bid bond.* It guarantees protection for an owner whose low bidder fails to perform in accordance with the bid submitted and accepted. There is little use made of such bonds and little litigation, because the project bonded in this way is likely to be bonded in two other, more common ways as well.

2. *Payment bond.* Its function is to guarantee that the payments owed by a general contractor to subcontractors will actually reach the hands of the subs. This type of bond is akin to the surety's lending credit to the contractor: sureties issue bonds only to the creditworthy. If the general contractor does not pay subcontractors and suppliers, for example, the surety is obligated to pay them to avoid liens against the project property or claims on the loan proceeds still undisbursed. The surety is not liable on the bond unless the contractor is. Bonds often provide for direct payment by the surety on claims made by a subcontractor or supplier, but restrictions on such direct rights and payments in bond language have been upheld. The owner, after all, may wish to be certain that money paid on the bond goes to clear himself of further liability to the sub or supplier. Even when a subcontractor has no direct or express right to file a claim on a bond, courts have found one

181

7. Preparing for Construction

implied on the basis of a common law, third-party beneficiary status of the subcontractor.

The payment bond is usually drafted to protect payments to a certain group of subs and suppliers — say, first-tier subcontractors and suppliers providing materials directly to the construction site. The protected class defined by the bond is a matter for contract interpretation and may or may not be coterminous with the ability of the mechanic's lien laws to reach the project property. See American Institute Architects, AIA Document A311, Labor and Material Payment Bond. The surety is not bound to pay for the services or materials of others not named in the bond; in this respect, a surety is not bound beyond the terms of its bond. Bank loans made to a contractor whose payments are covered by the bond are not covered, and the surety cannot be held liable to the lender.

3. *Performance bond.* Its function is to guarantee that the construction contract will be performed, if not by the original general contractor and subcontractors, then by someone capable of finishing the project according to the original architectural and engineering plans and specifications. Under such a bond, a surety may be called upon to do anything called for in the original construction agreement. See American Institute Architects, AIA Document A311, Performance Bond.

A performance bond is often combined with a payment bond in a "performance and payment bond," although when combined, the surety still has two distinct obligations. The surety may meet its bond obligation in several ways: by providing new financing sufficient to complete the project, by finding a new contractor and paying the owner the extra costs associated with the contract between the owner and the new contractor, or by entering into a construction contract itself with a new contractor and performing that contract.

Direct rights for subs — the right to file a claim, receive payment, and sue on the bond — are more controversial for performance bonds. Compare Byram Lumber & Supply Co. v. Page, 146 A. 293 (Conn. 1929) (finding a direct right), with Fosmire v. National Surety Co., 127 N.E. 472 (N.Y. 1920) (denying such a right). The New York court indicated that finding such a right is less difficult with a payment bond. Do you see why? Likewise, some courts find a direct right easier to find when a public facility construction project is involved. Why should this be? See AIA Document A311, Performance Bond, for language negating a direct right.

A fourth product often offered by sureties is a bondability letter, showing that a contractor is bondable. Here, although no bond is actually issued for the project, the surety represents that it conducted its usual and customary investigation of the contractor and finds the latter of sufficient financial and business capacity to be bondable.

7. Preparing for Construction

Examples

Example 32

After a project is 75% complete, its general contractor abandons work and files for bankruptcy. The general contractor carries a performance bond. A reliable cost estimator states that the total construction costs associated with the project will be 125% of the total price of the construction agreement. The construction loan disbursement schedule calls for five additional progress payments. After obtaining a new construction agreement for completion of the project satisfactory to the lender, and after proper notice to the bonding company, how should the surety, the owner, and the construction lender proceed?

Explanation

Assuming that the project is sound as an economic matter, both the surety and the owner have reason to proceed. The surety will surely bring the construction lender into the discussions because a lender may be reluctant to make further disbursements without assurances that the surety is good for the extra 25%. "Why should we throw our money into a black hole," the lender might argue, "when we don't see where the extra money is coming from?" The surety might provide some assurance without spending any money, for example, by putting the money necessary for completion into escrow, by arranging for a new loan for the extra 25 percent, or by guaranteeing the extra if the original construction lender will advance it. The possibilities are numerous. And, once the extra is guaranteed, the next issue for the negotiations is the payout rate. Should the five remaining progress payments be disbursed from the funds of the original lender, up to 100% of the original loan agreement, or should each payment be 5% from surety funds and 5% from the original lender's, or should the surety go first, and the lender complete the payments? Again, the possibilities are numerous, and no one of them is likely to be mandated by the provisions of the bond.

In general, the surety's flexibility in performing on its bond obligation means that it picks up several types of rights along the road to performance by way of subrogation: a right to reimbursement and a right of contribution (from other sureties and, if there are undisclosed and unexcepted liens on the property, from title insurers as well). As it pays material men and suppliers on the payment bond, it steps into their shoes under the doctrine of equitable subrogation. As an example of reimbursement, consider that when the general contractor abandons the site, it was owed money, supplies, or labor, those are now due the surety stepping into the shoes of the general. Thus, to protect itself, the surety will proceed slowly and cautiously, attempting to tie up as many loose ends as possible; on a construction

183

7. Preparing for Construction

contract on which work has been paid for, for example, actions that would seem to abandon that contract will not be taken without first attempting to obtain agreements to perform.

Sureties are aggressive in their attempts to recoup their out-of-pocket costs fulfilling their bond obligations. The courts have limited their remedies in several respects. See International Paper Co. v. Grossman, 541 F. Supp. 1236 (N.D. Ill. 1982) (holding that a guarantor of a loan was not liable to a surety).

The subrogation rights of a surety are said to arise by operation of law, not by contract; this means, for example, that no Uniform Commercial Code financing statements need be filed by the surety to protect its subrogation rights. Subrogation is just too hardy a doctrine to be defeated, even by the UCC, which does not expressly reject it.

Examples

Example 33

The general contractor invokes its performance bond rights and then assigns the right to progress payments under its contract to a lender who, on the basis of the assigned contract rights, makes a loan to the contractor. The lender promptly files a UCC financing statement. Who has the superior claim on earned, but unpaid, progress payments — the performance bond surety or the assignee of the contractor?

Explanation

The surety. The assignee can take no more than the lender's right to the funds. See National Shawmut Bank of Boston v. New Amsterdam Cas. Co., 411 F.2d 843 (1st Cir. 1969) (holding that the surety has the prior claim on earned, but unpaid, loan disbursements as against the assignee of the contract rights of the general contractor), noted in 64 Nw. U. L. Rev. 582 (1969). The answer would be the same when, in the course of meeting its obligations on the bond, the surety makes a claim on retainages — those amounts withheld from payment pending a final inspection of the project. The theory is that the surety is more than a subrogee of the contractor but is also a subrogee of the owner and entitled to any rights that the owner has to the retained funds. While meeting the obligations on the bond, the surety may also have a right to have the retained funds escrowed on its behalf, but the surety actually only acquires its subrogation rights as it fulfills its bond obligations. (When the assigning contractor satisfactorily performed the work, and a check, intended as payment and made payable to the contractor, is deposited with the assignee, the assignee of the contractor prevails over the surety.)

7. Preparing for Construction

Example 34

Are consequential damages available from a performance and payment bond surety?

Explanation

Yes, although it seemingly violates the rule that the bond's principal is entitled to recover only the cost of completion stipulated in the construction plans and specifications incorporated into the bond by reference. When nonpayment of consequential damages stands in the way of completion, it is covered by the bond (though not by its literal provisions).

BUILDER'S RISK INSURANCE

Many unforeseen things happen on a construction site. Steel will be in place well before beams and joists give it stability. Welding can set the site ablaze. Wet concrete is heavier than dry. Construction equipment can damage work already done. General comprehensive liability policies typically exclude such events from coverage, but builder's risk insurance covers such hazards. It is a type of property loss policy for loss or damage to an insured builder's interest in a building or improvement under construction. Such a policy covers not only damage to the structure itself, but also damage to construction supplies and materials after work has commenced. This type of policy is typically purchased either by the owner or the general contractor, who along with prime subcontractors become its beneficiaries; a construction lender may become a loss payee or an assignee of the policy. It may be location or project specific, or cover more than one project or location. Typical exclusions are for a contractor's tools, equipment, and vehicles; poor workmanship, design defects, or wear and tear, and removal or replacement caused by either; and flood, earthquake, and landslides except those caused by nonnatural causes, such as excavation or a broken water or utility line. The measure of damages is either the actual cost of replacement or the cash value of the lost property. See Dan Millea, Jennifer Green, & Iman Ali, Questions and Answers About Builder's Risk Policies, 24 Prac. Real Est. Law. (Mar. 2008), at 21.

The availability of such insurance does not limit the liability of a surety issuing a payment or performance bond. The policy merely controls

185

7. Preparing for Construction

who—the surety or the insurer—performs first. In some cases the insurer has successfully defended a claim based on the negligence of the insured on the site, but other cases have rejected this defense

Examples

Example 35

A general contractor, with a builder's risk policy, experiences a good deal of theft of materials from a construction site. He then stores materials needed for a construction agreement off-site, for transit to the site as needed. Materials are stolen from storage. Is the contractor covered by the policy?

Explanation

Yes. The theft of materials that will ultimately be incorporated into the project at the site is covered. Site specific insurance means project specific. Materials may be in transit to storage, from the store house to the construction site, stockpiled on-site, or in place during construction, and be covered. See Village of Kiryas Joel Local Dev. Corp. v. Ins. Comp. of N.A., 996 F.2d 1390 (2d Cir. 1993). Coverage ends only with the completion of the construction, when comprehensive liability insurance becomes available, but coverage may still be limited by the express language of the policy. If the contractor uses the store house for future projects, he should make sure that the commencement date for the policy is inclusive enough to include delivery to the site before construction begins on-site.

Example 36

Materials for the erection of scaffolding are stolen from a construction site. Does an otherwise applicable builder's risk policy cover the loss?

Explanation

It may, but language in the policy on this matter should be checked and negotiated by an owner or contractor.

7. Preparing for Construction

GREEN BUILDINGS

Large buildings account for much of our energy consumption and production of greenhouse gases. Making them proof against climate change, weather related problems, and energy efficient when energy costs soar is the goal of "green architecture." Perhaps also in reaction to the "sick building" syndrome involving unhealthy indoor air, green buildings have been a focus of the environmental movement. Using natural light and recycled materials, installing coated glass, computer-controlled blinds, and solar cells are examples of what makes a building green, but their higher costs still make such buildings the exception, not the rule. Nonetheless, the use of tax credits, local zoning incentives, and good press are increasingly making developers consider building green. Starting in the 1990s, amendments to housing and building codes encouraged but did not require compliance with green standards.

Many jurisdictions, both state and municipal, today mandate such standards for all buildings open to the public and provide tax incentives for constructing a green building. In addition, some municipal governments require compliance with green building standards for all new commercial buildings, public or private; provide faster permitting for such green buildings; and reduce or waive fees involving in obtaining local permits.

In 2000, the nonprofit United States Green Building Council (USGBC) introduced a certification process called Leadership in Energy and Environmental Design (LEED) Green Building Rating System. Four versions of its rating system have been issued—first in 2000, then updated by LEED-NC (New Construction) Versions 2.1 and 2.2, again updated in 2009 as Version 3.0, replaced in 2016 by Version v4. The ratings deal with new design and construction, interior design and construction, building operation and maintenance, and single family residences.

The ratings focus on water and energy efficiency, site sustainability, construction materials, indoor environmental quality, and design innovation. A rating system is designed for a particular type of structure—e.g., commercial buildings, schools, and homes. It assigns points for meeting the standards and awards different levels of certification, depending on the number of points a building earned. The Green Building Council awards these certifications. See Keither Hirokawa, At Home with Nature: Early Reflections on Green Building Laws and the Transformation of the Built Environment, 39 Am. L. Rev. 507 (2009).

In 2017, the AIA promulgated a nonbinding Sustainable Projects Exhibit to attach to either its architectural and contractor agreements. These exhibits contain exculpatory language waiving consequential damages for either an architect or contractor's failure to obtain a desired LEED rating. A developer's attorneys might consider limiting the scope and breadth of this language.

187

7. Preparing for Construction

AN UPDATED CONSTRUCTION PROCESS

Time is money. The traditional construction process for an office building or shopping center is complicated and time-consuming and is often lengthened still further when things go badly by accusations and counteraccusations between the developer, the architect, and the general contractor, all leaving the developer without speedy relief. Shortening the process is worth money, if only in less interest paid on the construction loan.

Thus, nontraditional processes, used singly or in combination, are often tried, particularly for large and complex projects. One such is the "fast track" or "flash track" process. Here construction of parts of the building begins before other parts are completely designed. The architect (or sometimes the general contractor) breaks the process down into phases or "design packages"—for example, excavation, soil retention (sheeting and shoring), foundations, and structural steel—and a schedule of values is devised to support a smooth construction process. There are risks involved, but what's accomplished is that the pre-construction process is overlaid on the construction process itself, so that the building is designed and constructed in less time overall. This process is known as "design–build." It can be either architect-led design–build or general contractor-led.

Just as an architect can fast track the design, the use of multiple prime or general contractors may speed up the process by the execution of a construction agreement for the early parts of a building before the remainder is ready for agreement. Thus, construction agreements can be fast tracked in the same way a building's design can. This might save on the traditional general contractor's markup.

Another nontraditional process involves construction managers. This may mean that the general contractor is brought on board earlier in the process in order to oversee budgeting and design. In the alternative, the developer may hire an agent to oversee this planning. Either way, an inexperienced developer hires experienced people to identify problems before they get to the construction site, to package the work into tasks easily performed by the construction trades, to use materials that are cheap and readily available, and to provide early estimates of costs. Competitive bidding (at least for the manager's services) must be forgone in this process, but the cost savings are usually worth it, and the resulting construction agreements are more likely to be for a fixed price or a guaranteed maximum price.

A third nontraditional process involves making the general contractor also the designer of the project—a so-called design-build project. Here the developer turns the design and the construction over to a single entity or joint venture responsible for delivery of a fully operational building delivered for a fixed or guaranteed maximum price (GMP). The developer gives up some or all control of the design at an early stage, in return for shifting

7. Preparing for Construction

some or all of the budget overrun risks associated with construction to the design-build entity. Some of the risks thus shifted are delay costs due to failures of communication, vague or defective design documents, and faulty scheduling.

Examples

Example 37

Your developer client is considering making the general contractor the designer of an upcoming project. The contractor explains that the single entity/joint venture will make sure that developer-architect-contractor disputes over payment will not arise. Why? Because the developer will not be a party to such disputes. Likewise, if the developer's intent is clearly expressed in the plans and specifications, design disputes are less likely. Your client regards that "if" as a big one and is reluctant to lose full control over the design of the project, while the architect he has used for drawing up the plans and specifications resists. Why?

Explanation

Architects most often prefer developers as clients The contractor will insist that (1) the architect warrant its services free of errors or gaps in design, as an architect would to a developer, and (2) pay the additional costs of construction due to any such error. Traditionally architects work under a negligence standard of care that assumes that some errors and omissions in the design may occur.[12] The result of this difference in liability standards has meant that some of the best architects will not participate in general contractor design-build projects. In addition, the architect may be concerned that he or she will lose control of design revision necessary to keep the project on budget and on time.

Example 38

As a construction lender, what types of lending procedures will have to be modified for projects on a fast track? What if an architect and contractor are joint venturers in providing fast track services to owners? What advice should developers faced with such arrangements be given?

---

12. Recall that the architect's standard of care is that of "a professional skilled architect under the same or similar circumstances in carrying out his technical duties in relation to his services undertaken by his agreement." This duty ties the architect to plans already presented to the developer and the general contractor.

7. Preparing for Construction

Explanation

When on the fast track, the architect likely will become more than usually concerned about liability for her construction cost estimates. More generally, the allocation of the risk of cost overruns is also likely to become a hot topic for negotiations between the parties. Scheduling the various subcontractors is another concern. Much more attention will be paid to such scheduling, as well as to devising shorter timetables for handling change orders and disputes. Generally, the role of the architect and the construction manager will be increased, giving them a greater role in approving change orders and resolving disputes. For the lender, budget concerns are magnified more quickly: more items can get out of balance faster, and the lender will seek to retain more funds from all loan disbursements. With scheduling tighter, the concern for material stored on-site will increase; finding storage space, and builder's risk insurance against damage or theft, will reflect this concern. The earlier the involvement of the joint venture, the more likely that the general contractor will be responsible for the negligence of subcontractors, so insurance and indemnity provisions in the construction agreement will be adapted accordingly. The Design Build Institute of American (DBIA) has published yet another series of contract forms for design-build projects. See also Lewis Constr. Co. v. Harrison, 70 S.W.3d 778 (Tex. 2001).

A FINAL NOTE

In all that has been discussed in this chapter, a developer's attorney should not just act as an advocate in negotiations with architects and general contractors. He or she is such an advocate, of course, zealously guarding his client's interests. But the good attorney will go beyond this role; he will also attempt to educate himself on the role that these other professionals play in the construction process; this means getting to know them, attending meetings with them even when negotiations are not called for—in short, trying to understand their professional interests, attitudes, and roles in the broadest sense.

CHAPTER 8

Construction Lending Agreements

THE CONSTRUCTION LENDING PROCESS

Construction involves a developer as the owner of the property to be developed, an architect, a general contractor and subcontractors, and a construction mortgage lender. The focus of this chapter is on the lender.

Having first conceived of the project, the developer hires an architect who designs it in a preliminary way, uses those designs to interest a lender in funding the project, hires various design professionals (including and primarily an architect to draw up detailed plans and specifications for the project), and finally (with or without the lender or the architect) hires a general contractor to build it.

All of these parties, along with the documents that define the scope of their work, are presented to the lender for review. This review is known as the process of underwriting the loan — in this case, a construction loan note and mortgage.

CONSTRUCTION LENDING

Over time and depending on the economy, construction lenders have provided approximately 70 to 90% of the funds used for a construction project. The lower percentage is flexible and for the risk-averse, but the upper percentage is a ceiling that only the most daring lender would exceed.

191

8. Construction Lending Agreements

Developers are not bankers; they do not keep on hand amounts of capital sufficient to build even one of their projects—and if their business is large enough, their firms may work on multiple projects at the same time. Working multiple projects is a method of spreading the risk that one of their projects will fail or underperform for a time.

Construction funds reduce the developer's capital costs to between 10 to 30% of total development costs, and most developers seek to attract equity investors to reduce those percentages further. The more other people bare these costs, the less risk for the developer, but more important is that the greater the leverage, the higher the return on the developer's capital. In the trade, this reduction is known as seeking "leverage" or more precisely greater leverage—increasing the ratio of debt to lenders and investors to the developer's equity in a project. In part leverage is made possible by the different levels of return demanded by lenders and investors; construction lenders require a lower interest rate on their funds than do equity investors. The different levels are made possible by the different levels of security each demands. Construction lenders have a mortgage lien on the project as security, equity investors have a pledge of its cash flow.

Most developers build to hold; after all of the work construction entails, the holding period is measured in decades, typically at least two decades. In the course of construction, developers change roles, becoming more like managers until they have an income producing project that, if well managed, produces not only sustaining income but a profit as well.

Types of Construction Lenders

By the time the developer receives preliminary architectural drawings and perhaps during the selection of a general contractor, the owner-developer is discussing financing the project with three major, and very different, types of lenders.

The largest developers doing business on a regional or national scale may use lines of credit, modeled as a line of credit used by homeowners to fund family expenses—college tuition, uninsured health care costs, and home improvement and remodeling projects. Often more than one lender participates in extending such a line of credit.

Some large developers use such lines of credit to fund land acquisition as well as construction costs for multiple projects. Some use it to fund only the earliest, "soft" development costs. Whatever the range of uses for such funds, the extension of funds is knit together by cross-default and business covenants.[1]

---

1. These covenants are discussed infra, this chapter.

8. Construction Lending Agreements

Since the mid-twentieth century, construction lending reflects a blend of the investment objectives of two traditional types of mortgage lenders.

The first type is the construction lender, the lender who makes short-term loans for the money used in the construction process. These loans are for a period of one or three years—whatever time construction takes. They are given mostly by commercial banks familiar with the local real estate market. These lenders will review the developer's plans and specifications, architects' and construction agreements, the project budget, site inspection reports, site utilities' and access agreements, and land use permits and land use counsel opinions—as well as warranties and representations by the developer-borrower as to all of these—in the course of underwriting their loans. The difference between these loans and the residential mortgage loan is that the loan is not disbursed all at once. The residential mortgage and construction loan transaction have a mortgage lien in common, but in most other respects, the construction loan transaction differs from its residential cousin, as follows:

(1) First, the loan is disbursed in stages, not all at once: typically first to the owner, who pays the general contractor, who in turn pays the sub-contractors, for work already performed and certified done by the "clerk of the works" or other authorized inspector (sometimes the architect). This sequential disbursement is to compensate for the greater risk that a construction lender undertakes in comparison to a residential lender and to give the construction lender continuing assurance that the funds are properly applied to the construction project. It makes the construction loan akin to a future advance mortgage whose pay-out is obligatory according to the schedule of disbursements in the loan documents. See Bank v. Epic Solutions, Inc., 18 Wash. App. 2d 150 (Wash. App. Ct. 2022).

The construction lender's heightened risk is that the project will be completed over budget, not completed on time, not be worth its previously appraised value, and will be incomplete when the loan funds run out.[2] While the creation of the lien and its priority is also established in much the same manner as for a residential mortgage, the funds for a construction loan are typically set aside in some manner, often in a designated checking account for the loan or to a subsidiary entity acting as a disbursement agent for them.

(2) Second, the underwriting of a construction loan occurs without any historical data on an income-producing asset. The lender only has the

---

2. There are two major contingent risks as well: that the developer will "convert" (referring here to the common law cause of action for conversion, or trover and conversion) disbursements, putting them to some unauthorized use, and that a mechanic's lien will be filed and take priority over the lender's mortgage lien. These are risks arising due to lapses in underwriting the loan or poor administration of it. Mechanic's liens might arise and take priority over the construction lien when the lender makes discretionary disbursements of funds uncalled for in the construction loan agreement discussed infra.

8. Construction Lending Agreements

developer's market projections and studies and estimates of the costs of construction to consider.[3] Unlike a residential mortgage, the disbursement of a construction loan builds security or collateral in the project. Thus the construction lender's underwriting has two aspects—it investigates the soundness of the developer's plan for an income producing project[4] and it investigates the developer past experience and creditworthiness. As the second aspect, it is based on the realization that the loan is in part a line of credit similar to the lines extended to large national developers, but based on one not multiple projects, thus heightening the lender's risk.

(3) Third, the construction loan's fees and agreed rate of interest are collected from the lender's own reserved funds. This gives the construction lender an assured return for the period of time that the project will not be making any money or generating any cash flow. Its fees and interest are then added to the principal amount due the lender when it "sells the loan" to the takeout or permanent lender.

The Permanent Lender

This permanent lender has a longer-term investment objective: it provides the long-term financing for the project in the form of a note and mortgage on the by-then improved property. This financing may be for a term of 5 to 15 years. Thus a permanent loan may be provided by a large commercial bank or a pension fund or insurance company—institutions with large reserves of capital and a long view for its investment of those reserves.

In order to close the permanent loan, the developer must deliver the project on time, on budget, and complete—that is, appreciating in value and capable of producing income. Whereas the construction lender is, with each disbursement of funds, creating a project capable of having value

---

3. The construction costs under review are broadly defined. They include not only the costs of the actual construction—so-called "hard costs." Hard costs are the costs of actual construction, the aggregate of all costs for labor, construction materials, equipment, fixtures, and furnishings necessary to complete construction of the project. In contrast, "soft costs" include all land acquisition costs, any ground lease rents and fees, architects, city planners, engineers, and attorney's fees, loan interest costs, survey costs, estimator and appraisal fees, title, builder's risk, and casualty insurance premiums, as well as the costs of obtaining all regulatory approvals for the construction—that is, all other costs not hard costs necessary for completion of the project. Hard plus soft costs equal the total cost of construction. The total must be within the appraised fair market value of the building.

4. This process has two steps. A review of the completed building's rentable space will yield a square footage from which can be projected a rental income. That income is then capitalized to determine the fair market value of the building. That fair market value is then compared with the values of similar buildings around it—a rough reality check for the appraisal process. Then the construction budget is reviewed to determine if the cost of the building is within its market value—well within. Construction lenders generally expect to make $1.25 for every dollar that they lend.

8. Construction Lending Agreements

and producing income, the permanent lender relies on a built project that already has value and produces or will shortly produce income. The permanent lender thus has more collateral security than a construction lender.

In recent years, this heightened security has permitted the development of a secondary market for permanent loans on commercial real estate. It may be obvious, but no such market has developed for construction loans because the loan cannot easily be standardized or evaluated with other loans in order to bundle it into a mortgage loan pool for sale to investors.

Both construction and permanent lenders will be necessary to "do the deal" that involves the improvement and construction of commercial real estate, whether it is an office building or a shopping center. In those commercial real estate markets considered very "hot" or popular with permanent lenders, it may be possible to close a construction loan transaction, knowing with certainty that a takeout lender will materialize. But most lenders, being of a conservative or risk-averse bent of mind, would rather not proceed that way. Most, if not all, short-term construction lenders will want to know that a committed permanent lender is lined up to buy them out or "take them out" at the completion of the construction process.

Tying the construction note, mortgage and loan to the presence of a permanent lender makes good sense for the following reason: the construction mortgage creates a mortgage lien, which secures the debt and can be foreclosed upon default. The purchaser at its foreclosure sale obtains only the dubious privilege of completing the construction process. Moreover, the security for the construction loan mortgage lien is a half-built building. What's that worth? Commercial real property is valued for its income stream—the rents and profits from tenants—and without that stream on line, the building is valueless. Unless partial occupancy permits can be secured from the appropriate local government, a 40% completed construction process is just as worthless as one that is 90% completed. Thus, a commitment for the takeout loan, in the hands of the construction lender and the developer, is the best security for the construction loan—not security in the technical sense, to be sure, but the best assurance of repayment.

The buy-sell agreement. The takeout lender's commitment is accompanied by another document, negotiated between the developer and the two lenders. This is the buy-sell agreement: its subject is the transfer of the lien of the construction lender to the permanent one, in exchange for the permanent lender's funding of the loan—in effect, repaying the construction lender the proceeds of the latter's loan. When shown to a construction lender, it provides assurance that the appraisal of the project when built is worth the principal amount of the construction loan. Its representations and warranties will mimic those in preceding documents—the developer's acquisition contract of sale for the project property, the construction lender's loan commitment letter, and the construction loan agreement between the developer and the lender. (The last two are discussed infra,

195

8. Construction Lending Agreements

this chapter.) It provides a description of the permanent loan closing and details any preconditions that the permanent lender thinks must be met before the transfer of the lien. See Parke Bancorp, Inc. v. 659 Chestnut LLC, 217 A.3d 701 (Del. 2019).

APPRAISALS OF COMMERCIAL REAL ESTATE

For construction loans, appraisals are crucial to the underwriting and application process. The fair market values assigned to the project, and on which the principal amount of the loan must be based, are of course, at this stage, estimates. So the income or cash flow from the project must be estimated, and then capitalized. Two methods are typically used to do this, with a third used as a check on either. The first is based on applying a capitalization rate to a net income estimate. The second is called discounted cash flow (DCF), and is based on projecting income and expenses over several future years, usually five to ten years, then discounting the resulting annual amounts, giving them a present value.

The second, so-called DCF, method is based on many assumptions, each of which might turn into guesswork, and methods so complex that it becomes difficult to explain or defend. If the project is a multi-lease building, then the rates of change in rents, expenses, tenant improvements, and lease commissions; the probability of lease renewals, even for tenants who haven't yet signed leases; and re-leasing costs will all have to be estimated for the full number of years involved in the appraisal, plus one year more, at the end of the term, when it is assumed that the resale of the property occurs. Lack of historic data is often a further problem with this method. Being off by as little as 10% of what actually happens is the difference between a healthy and a failed project. Finally, the use of the method is often dependent on the use of computer software. Expertise in its use is really the best guarantee of the appraisal's validity, and glitches in using it are the most common reason for failure.

Thus, the first method — direct capitalization of the income stream from the project — is often regarded as less subjective and easier to explain and defend. It derives a net present value of the project (V) from its net operating income (NOI) or gross income reduced by operating expenses before debt service, divided by the capitalization rate (R). So V = NOI divided by R. For a new project, NOI is based on actual gross income at the time of the sales of similar properties or on market rents achieved by similar properties, reduced by estimates of expenses, often published in trade group expense guides. These last publications are as useful as the surveys behind them are representative. Expenses include (for example) repairs, maintenance costs,

8. Construction Lending Agreements

the cost of vacancies, management fees, and sometimes a replacement reserve for capital repairs.

If the actual gross income from a project is $100 and expenses add up to $50, NOI will be the $50 remaining before debt service is paid. Thus, the net present value will be $50 divided by R. So what is R? It's the rate of return that an investor would consider, knowing that the range of possible investments can vary between the safest (in terms of returning principal—say, a 10-year U.S. Treasury bond) and the riskiest (say, a junk bond) available in the bond market. Real estate markets are not as safe as Treasury bonds, but not as risky as junk bonds; they present investment opportunities lying somewhere between these two extremes and yield a return somewhere between the 2% a Treasury bond would pay and the 10% a junk bond would have to pay to attract investors. Deciding on a capitalization rate—the "cap rate" R—is thus a matter of experience and market expertise.

Thus, if R equals a 10% rate of return, then V will be the $50 NOI divided by .10, equally just over $500 (the capital value of the project); if R equals a 7% rate of return, then V will be the $50 NOI divided by 0.07, equaling just over $714—the value of a project whose NOI is 7% of $714. In a riskier market, closer to junk bond status, R might be 13%, so the value of a project whose NOI is $50 will be about $385. The higher the capitalization rate, the lower the value necessary to achieve the same NOI. Conversely, lower cap rates yield higher values.

Cap rates vary by market, nationally and locally. Markets for hotel properties have been, over the last several decades, much more volatile than ones for downtown office buildings. Likewise, garden apartment markets are more volatile than long-term residential rental markets.

Sales comparison appraisals (though less frequently used) are yet a third method of appraisal. For construction loans, such appraisals are most useful when reduced to fair market value per square foot. Such a number can be compared to construction costs per square foot. But comparable sales must be adjusted to reflect (say) the superior location of one property over another. It is difficult to make such adjustments objective by (say) including buildings along the same highway.

NONRECOURSE MORTGAGES

Much commercial mortgage lending today is conducted through the use of documents in which the mortgagor has no personal liability on the loan; the property alone is security for the loan. Thus, it is said that the mortgage loan is "nonrecourse" and the mortgage *in rem*. This is usually accomplished with a covenant in the note. This covenant is to the effect that the note

8. Construction Lending Agreements

holder covenants not to sue the maker, waives any rights to a deficiency judgment after foreclosure, and generally waives her rights against the mortgagor personally.[5]

The covenant is also accompanied by statements to the effect that the mortgagor expressly only secures the loan with the property and does not incur personal liability. The objective of the covenant is to limit the mortgagee to foreclosure as the exclusive remedy for defaults in payment[6] The covenant also usually states that the intention of the parties is not to release or discharge the debt.

The last statement is necessary because in some jurisdictions, there may be a question as to the validity of such a "mortgage." Remember that a mortgage is usually regarded as an agreement ancillary to the debt, so that if there is no personal liability, and hence in some sense no debt, there is nothing to which the mortgage can attach. But this is not a very sensible argument. If the lack of any personal liability were to mean the lack of in rem liability, why use a mortgage? The parties should not be presumed to have used a superfluous document. If both types of liabilities are removed, no mortgagee would do the deal. Indeed, the mortgagor has then been unjustly enriched and the mortgagee unreasonably impoverished. Would a court turn away a mortgagee's suit (against a mortgagor denying liability of the property in foreclosure) for unjust enrichment on a theory of quasi-contract? No. At this late date, too much commercial convention supports the use of nonrecourse mortgages.

Regardless of the presence of a nonrecourse covenant, mortgage lenders are continually searching for ways to feel secure and be assured of repayment of the loan. First, such a covenant may be used in a transaction also using guarantees by the borrower — that is, in transactions in which the borrower personally guarantees the repayment of the mortgage interest or guarantees to make up operating deficits (excluding debt principal) for the business to be conducted on the secured property. Often such guarantees "burn off" or expire when the project reaches a certain level of cash flow or

---

5. Typical language for a basic nonrecourse provision might be: "Except as otherwise provided in this provision, neither the borrower or any partner or member of the borrower's entity holding title to the secured property shall be personally liable for payment of any principal, interest, or other fee or sum evidenced by this note or for any deficiency judgment lender may obtain following foreclosure of the accompanying mortgage and lender's only recourse against borrower for any default under the note shall be limited to the secured property encumbered by said mortgage."

6. That is, a nonrecourse provision limits the lender to the collateral or security for the loan — that is, to the developer's project. The collateral is typically an illiquid asset: real estate is a prime example. By granting the developer a nonrecourse loan, the lender won't have the ability to have the loan repaid when a foreclosure sale doesn't recoup the full amount of the outstanding debt. This makes nonrecourse loans riskier.

8. Construction Lending Agreements

when the top portion of the loan is repaid. Second, a mortgage lender might require the placement of private mortgage insurance to insure repayment of the loan, so that the status of the debt is still secure. Third, a general partner, an LLC's managing member, or other syndicator will often offer a personal guarantee, offering to be treated as personally liable, for the nonrecourse debt of the partnership. Thus a detailed nonrecourse covenant in a mortgage might read:

> Except as provided in this clause, Borrower shall not be personally liable and Lender shall not commence or prosecute any action for payment or performance of the Note or other personal obligation associated with this mortgage. Lender shall not seek, obtain, or otherwise enforce any deficiency judgment associated with the foreclosure of this mortgage. Lender's sole recourse for the loan obligation associated with this mortgage shall be limited to the secured property, and Lender shall not seek specific performance or any relief or remedy requiring Borrower to expend funds of any type, nor will the Lender exercise any right to set off any funds of Borrower's in the Lender's custody, control or possession, except when . . .

And at this point in the covenant, the so-called carve-outs are listed, to the effect that the mortgage loan becomes recourse when and if, for example, the borrower commits fraud against the lender, diverts loan funds from their intended use, commits waste on the property, files for bankruptcy, or has misrepresented his credit or the security of the property on the loan application. Carve-outs are discussed in more detail in the following Examples.

Examples

Example 1

What if a title insurer misses a mechanic's lien in the course of its title search, pays off the lien to satisfy a claim under its policy, and then sues the nonrecourse mortgagor for the lien amount?

Explanation

Judgment for the mortgagor. The prohibition on the deficiency judgment in the insured mortgage precludes suit by the title company, as the subrogee of the rights of the insured mortgagee, from suing to recoup the amount of the claim based on the mechanic's lien. See Berks Title Ins. Co. v. Haendiges, 772 F.2d 278 (6th Cir. 1985).

8. Construction Lending Agreements

Example 2

Nonrecourse mortgages have several types of business uses. Can you identify situations in which they are likely to be used?

Explanation

Nonrecourse mortgages are likely to be used in speculative markets, particularly markets in danger of a downturn. In the 1930s, for example, when the banks and the government acquired many properties in foreclosure, nonrecourse covenants in a mortgage note were used to encourage potential purchasers to assume ownership, which many would do only if the risk of a further downturn in the economy was assumed by the mortgagor. Another speculative market in which such covenants are used is oil and gas drilling; financing documents contain such covenants to encourage the wildcatter to develop such properties.

Nonrecourse covenants are often used in three other situations: (1) when the parties to a mortgage transaction have had no prior dealings with each other, (2) when the value of the real property taken as security for a loan is in dispute, and (3) when a nonrecourse covenant is traded in exchange for an equity participation by the lender.

In the context of a loan to a limited partnership or LLC, the nonrecourse nature of the mortgage has been necessary if the limited partners or LLC members are to be able to attain a tax basis in the secured property that includes a prorated amount of the mortgage. The explanation goes something like this: limited partners are not typically liable for partnership losses, so when personally liable for mortgage loans, the increased basis is unavailable. However, if no partner, general or limited, is liable personally, all are eligible for the increase in basis. The lack of a risk of loss adds to the certainty of their interest, against which depreciation and deductions may be taken by each partner pro rata. See IRC §752(a)(2) and regulations issued under authority of this section.

THE CONSTRUCTION LOAN COMMITMENT LETTER

In times past, a construction lender would issue a commitment to lend. Today typically, the first step in a developer's obtaining a construction loan is the issuance by the lender of a "commitment" letter that in form more resembles a letter of intent or a term sheet for a commercial lease. That is, it is no commitment at all.

8. Construction Lending Agreements

Some lenders use an application format for such a letter. However the format, it states that it is not binding on the lender and that a loan agreement, note, and mortgage will be executed at the loan's closing. It is prepared by the lender's attorney at the developer's expense and reviewed by the developer's attorney, the latter realizing that the lender holds the cards with the stronger hand.

The letter sets out the basic triad of loan terms—the principal amount of the loan, its term or duration, and the rate of interest, often a floating rate. Its principal is typically not amortized, the loan being an interest only one. Its focus is often on time-lines, naming the dates on which loan disbursements will be made; the dates and amounts when the developer's equity investments, along with a schedule of capital calls for equity investors and/or mezzanine financiers,[7] must be made; and dates for the reimbursement by the developer of the lender's origination fees, legal fees, title insurance premiums, and other closing and settlement costs.

Pre-closing conditions are also listed: lease-up conditions, environmental and soil testing reports, a loan title insurance policy, and delivery of all architectural agreements, general contractors, major sub-contractors, and construction material agreements, all assignable to the lender, an agreement for disbursement of the loan and inspection of the work in progress, the forms required for certifying progress payments and disbursements, and the leasing agreements with major tenants. Finally, in a belt-and-suspenders move, the lender requires payment and completion bonds and guarantees.

Even if both the developer/borrower and the lender execute the letter, both reserve some discretion to walk away from the loan. The developer may want the discretion to accept a more favorable commitment letter, usually paying the costs incurred by the lender. The lender will reserve the discretion to walk away based on the loan's disapproval by the lender's loan committee, on regulatory changes on loan limits and risk, changes in environmental reports or risks, or on major adverse changes in the economy.

In some jurisdictions, litigation in the late 1980s resulted in the application of the jurisdiction's statute of frauds to "creditor agreements," including loan commitment letters. See, e.g., Colo. Rev. Stat. §38-10-124.

Once all the conditions outlined in the letter have been satisfied, the loan agreement will memorialize them in a loan agreement at the closing of the loan.

---

7. Equity investors and mezzanine financing is discussed infra, Chapter 9.

8. Construction Lending Agreements

Examples

Example 3

A construction lender underwriting a developer's loan discovers that the developer will not hold the title to the project site when the loan is supposed to be closed. Instead, a limited liability company or LLC will hold the title. How should the lender respond to this discovery?

Explanation

By asking for the list of the LLC's members and its operating agreement. The LLC's presence is an indication that the developer is seeking to minimize the amount of equity he has in the project: the less he puts into it, the greater his cash-on-cash return will be. So the lender is interested in the amount of equity that members, including the developer, have invested in the project. It is interested in the equity holders' "skin in the game" in order to encourage due diligence on their part. It is also interested in the timing of those investments and in particular, whether they are made before or after the lender starts to disburse the loan proceeds. From the lender's perspective, "before" is better. After this review, the lender will write equity requirements into the commitment letter. It may also review the developer's fees and reimbursable costs in order to prevent the developer from recovering them at too early a stage in construction; the lender will want the developer "working for his wages" throughout the construction process.

Example 4

A developer asks a potential construction lender whether the loan he seeks is to have a nonrecourse provision in the note or mortgage. If the developer is inexperienced in construction of the type of project he proposes, the lender might respond negatively. How might the developer respond to such negativity?

Explanation

If there is no call for a nonrecourse provision in the loan commitment, the loan will be fully recourse. For such a provision, it's often now or never. By proposing that the parties negotiate for the provision in advance of executing the loan commitment, or even dispense with a commitment altogether and negotiate all the loan documents now, the developer is pressing his advantage when he has it. Once the developer realizes that the lender's commitment is not really binding and is not likely to be treated as an executory

202

8. Construction Lending Agreements

contract[8] in litigation, the developer has little to lose by making this proposal at this stage. See, e.g., Renaissance North, LLC v. Fifth Third Bank, 2011 U.S. Dist. LEXIS 117732 (S.D. Ohio Oct. 12, 2011). What might the developer gain? In a word, leverage. The developer might realize that what slight leverage he has arises before the execution of the loan commitment when the lender is still looking to build an ongoing relationship with the developer and may still competing be for the developer's business.

A nonrecourse provision is often heavily negotiated. (And, once the lender agrees to the basic covenant, negotiations over the carve-outs to it will be even heavier.) Negotiating its language before executing the commitment takes time, but it makes later preparation for the loan closing easier and gets what might be a contentious negotiation out of the way, letting the parties assess each other in the meantime. Thus, instead of the commitment stating that the mortgage note "shall contain a nonrecourse provision acceptable to the lender," it might say that the developer "will execute a note not materially different from the note attached to this commitment as Exhibit 1." This approach takes time and energy up front, but prevents squabbles later.

Why do lenders even agree to negotiate a nonrecourse provision? True, it limits their remedy to foreclosure if the loan goes into default, but nonrecourse borrowers are also more likely to permit foreclosure once they realize that their equity in the property has substantially diminished in value. Lenders also realize that developers have legitimate concerns about the personal liability of equity investors like partners and LLC members, that there are tax advantages for the use of such provisions, and that developers do not want to put past projects in danger. Moreover, lenders can factor the increased risk and loss of remedies into the terms of the construction loan, increase their due diligence before closing such a loan, and use other forms of credit enhancements such as completion bonds, personal guarantees, and letters of credit.

Likewise, the developer's proposal to "negotiate now" might be used for any loan document the parties consider crucial to closing the loan. It merely accelerates a negotiation process normally occurring after the execution of the commitment. One reason to accelerate the process is the alternative: in

---

8. Specific performance of a loan commitment is unlikely. After all, the developer would be asking to receive the loan proceeds—i.e., money—not a unique commodity except in the situation in which the lender has the last dollar in the capital market and the economy is tending sharply against the developer's project. However, once executed, even the spongiest commitment would be subject to an implied covenant of good faith and fair dealing, however, meaning that the lender is subject to an obligation to negotiate in advance of the loan closing. See Teacher's Inc. & Annuity Ass'n v. Butler, 626 F. Supp. 1229 (S.D. N.Y. 1986) (holding that developer refused to negotiate in good faith after the interest rate in the commitment letter fell and granting loss of bargain damages to put the lender in *status quo ante* as if the loan had been closed).

203

8. Construction Lending Agreements

the worst case, from the developer's perspective, the lender will attach its own "killer" documents to the commitment letter, calling for their use at closing, and the developer will have to negotiate from there.

Example 5

Absent a nonrecourse provision, the developer executing a note and mortgage will be personally liable for repayment of the loan in full, and in jurisdictions permitting a deficiency judgment after foreclosure and when the property secured by the mortgage and sold in foreclosure does not provide funds for that full repayment, the developer will be liable for the deficiency. Once the lender agrees to a nonrecourse provision, its language should precisely define the extent to which the personal-liability, full-recourse rule is reversed. If the commitment is to provide crucial language to this effect, what should the commitment provide?

Explanation

A cross-referenced and identically worded provision in both the note or the mortgage is a start. When a lender's note or mortgage states that it will look only to the secured property collateralizing the mortgage and have no recourse beyond that, the lender might think about the incentives that provision creates for the developer. What incentive will the developer have then to maintain the project? In a full-recourse loan, that incentive will be higher than it will be when the loan is nonrecourse: the developer will maintain the property subject to a full-recourse loan so that it fetches a higher foreclosure sale price and a lower deficiency amount. When the loan is nonrecourse, however, a lower foreclosure sale price and a higher deficiency won't matter as much to the developer.

Thus, the lender using a nonrecourse loan pays particular attention to repair and maintenance provisions in the mortgage. In the nonrecourse provision itself, the lender encourages the borrower's attentiveness to repair and maintenance by providing for several exceptions to the nonrecourse language. These exceptions or "carve-outs" state that some actions by the borrower/developer will result in the restoration of full-recourse liability. One carve-out relevant here is "the commission of waste and a failure to maintain the project, causing its value as security for the loan to deteriorate." Another is a carve-out for "liability for environmental contamination due to the presence of hazardous or toxic substances on the site as defined in federal and state statutes." A further related carve-out is for "the nonpayment of real estate and other taxes and assessments that might result in a lien on the project superior to the lender's mortgage lien" because the lender's loss of its first lien status will certainly cause deterioration in the secured

204

8. Construction Lending Agreements

value of the project. Likewise, a carve-out for "the failure to pay insurance premiums" might cause the value of the lender's security to deteriorate if and when a claim is paid.

Taken together, the scope of all carve-outs can be extensive.[9] See generally Gregory M. Stein, The Scope of the Borrower's Liability in a Non-Recourse Real Estate Loan, 55 Wash. & Lee L. Rev. 1207 (1998). Relevant to the nonrecourse language are carve-outs for the borrower's actions that hinder or prevent the use of the one remedy left to the lender agreeing to a nonrecourse provision: foreclosure. Thus a law suit by the borrower to enjoin a foreclosure, or the filing of a bankruptcy proceeding that will stay a foreclosure action, will be carved out. Such carve-outs are more important to the construction lender than to a lender dealing with other types of commercial real estate financing. Why? When (again) foreclosing a construction note and mortgage and buying at the foreclosure sale, the lender stands to receive, not a completed project, but a partially built one—one without a cash flow; thus the lender really receives only the right to complete construction.

Example 6

A construction lender agrees that (1) the developer/borrower will take and hold title to the project property in the name of a limited liability company (LLC) and (2) the loan will be nonrecourse. What difference does the presence of both a nonrecourse provision and an LLC make to the lender?

Explanation

The lender, realizing that his remedy is limited to foreclosure and that the capitalization of the entity is limited to the project property, will further realize that the carve-outs have little value unless they are back-stopped by a "springing completion guarantee"—a guarantee becoming effective when a carve-out is invoked by the lender. The guarantee will then provide the funds that the entity may not have. It will also provide the funds to complete the project if and when the lender has to foreclose and buy it at the foreclosure sale. (After all, competing bidders at such a sale will be few if any.)

---

9. Other carve-outs often sought by lenders might be for "the commission of fraud or misrepresentation in the loan application" and "the conversion of insurance proceeds due the lender."

REVERSE-ENGINEERING: DOING THE DEAL BACKWARDS

This describes the pattern among risk-averse construction lenders. The developer collects a buy-sell agreement and a conditional commitment to lend from the permanent lender and then shows it to a construction lender as an inducement to extend the construction loan. This agreement is attached to a commitment letter or any application to the construction lender. Also attached are the many documents necessary to close the takeout loan: the note and mortgage that will be used, the type of title insurance policy required by the takeout lender, and so forth.

Thus, all the documentation for the construction lending process, from its beginnings with the construction lender to its end in the closing a permanent loan, is agreed on beforehand. The parties don't just agree to act reasonably and adjust their differences as they go along. That would be an invitation to litigation. No documentary surprises here—avoiding them is the major purpose of the whole process. Thus, a construction lending transaction is completed by assembling all the documents necessary to it, starting with the documents needed in the future and working back to those needed in the present to close the construction loan.

THE CONSTRUCTION LOAN AGREEMENT

The construction loan agreement is a management document: it governs the relationship between the developer/borrower and the lender. The agreement changes the role of the developer from loan applicant to that of a manager of the construction and so of the loan. In this respect, the agreement sets the construction loan further apart from its residential loan counterpart, in that it envisions in detail a post-closing relationship between lender and borrower. It is thus also a checklist for the loan closing. Whereas the residential loan borrower has only to repay the loan and observe its covenants, the construction borrower has an affirmative obligation to supervise its administration.

The agreement will set out the amount of the commitment fee (due, payable and nonrefundable upon execution of the agreement), a completion date for construction, a maximum amount for change orders, the names of guarantors for the loan, the names of person(s) authorized to request (monthly) disbursements of the loan, the percentage amount of retainage[10]

---

10. Retainage is a percentage of each draw withheld from either a general or a subcontractor to assure the lender and the developer that subcontractors will be paid and the project will be completed.

8. Construction Lending Agreements

held back with each disbursement, and a reference to the construction loan checking account established by the lender to be drawn upon only to pay authorized disbursements of loan proceeds. Conditions precedent for the initial draw upon on the loan proceeds, subsequent draws, and a final draw are also set out. Major provisions of the loan's note and mortgage are defined: the loan amount "to be used only for the payment of hard and soft construction costs," with all disbursements "not to exceed the actual costs of construction"; a maturity date for the mortgage, when full repayment is due, but with an option to extend the maturity date for known-unknowns to a set date.

Attached to the agreement as exhibits incorporated by reference will be a legal description of the project property, a loan title insurance policy, a project budget, land surveys, and the general contractor's contract, and major leases if the project is being built for such lessees.

The agreement must anticipate and mitigate the risks that construction typically faces — the project coming in over-budget, under-valued, incompletely built once all proceeds have been disbursed, subject to intervening liens, and with funds converted to an unauthorized use. It must take account of the fact that projects are routinely subject to cost overruns, changes in design and materials, difficulties in scheduling sub-contracted work, labor disruptions and strikes, weather delays, etc.

So far as possible, the agreement must anticipate these known-unknowns of the construction world. These risks are all related to one another. For instance, cost overruns not funded by the lender can sometimes turn into an uncompleted project. A change in the economy can be reflected in slower rentals and thus in a project with a value lower than its initial appraised value, forcing the developer to sell the project instead of being "taken out" by a permanent lender.

Drafting and reviewing the agreement is a daunting challenge for the developer's attorney. The agreement must be in sync with the note, the mortgage, and the agreements with the architect and the general contractor.

A professional cost estimator might be employed to put third-party eyes on the developer's construction cost estimates. Additional third-party reports on title,[11] surveys, appraisals,[12] and other settlement cost providers might have previously been done during the developer's due diligence study

---

11. For example, the loan title insurance policy called for in the agreement may, at the lender's insistence, provide for full coverage of mechanic's liens and matters about which the developer/borrower had prior knowledge, and containing no survey exception, as well as endorsements for access, contiguity, zoning, etc.

12. Although a lender might begin by accepting an appraisal conducted for the developer during the due diligence study period (or, for an already built improvement, the developer's purchase price in the acquisition contract of sale), the agreement should specify that an independent appraiser place a value on the project property as built. The agreement should specify the appraisal method to be used (because different methods can produce different

8. Construction Lending Agreements

period, and the lender might (or might not) accept these,[13] adopting them as its own once the credentials of the reporting firms have been investigated and the reports have been separately certified to the lender by the firms producing them (the latter re-certification of reports, make the reporting firms directly responsible to the lender and allowing the lender to stand in the developer's shoes).

The agreement will also provide for representations and warranties about the project. In many cases they will track those in the developer's contract of sale. The lender will use these as a way of learning about the project property, much as would a buyer. Asking for a warranty and seeing hesitancy or push-back about giving it is in effect a red flag for the lender; such hesitancy is sure to make the accuracy of the warranty a closing condition for the loan transaction. Generally, however, the representations and warranties given the developer as a buyer acquiring the project property should closely mirror the closing conditions for the construction loan. In the same way, the note, the mortgage, and the construction documents will track the construction loan agreement.

Typically the list of representations and warranties given by the developer to the lender is the longest section of any construction loan agreement. The developer as a borrower/mortgagor warrants, among other matters, that any legal entity participating in the loan transaction has been legally created, duly organized and existing, and able to do business in the jurisdiction of its creation; that the project plans are satisfactory to the developer and all versions delivered to all concerned are the same or in sync; that true and correct financial statements and *pro forma* financial analyses have been delivered to the lender; that no litigation or transaction is pending that might result in a judgment lien on the project property; that there exists no transaction that might constitute a default in the note or mortgage; that all utilities and roads needed for construction are available to the construction site; and that the developer has procured all permits necessary to start construction.

And those are just the present warranties! Continuing warranties involve, among others, complying with all laws and statutes applicable to the construction; a diligent pursuing of construction, in a workmanlike manner and in good faith; indemnifying the lender against all claims arising from the loan transaction (including brokerage claims) and construction; depositing all disbursements of loan proceeds in the construction loan checking

---

results) and that the appraised value equal or exceed the developer's value based on his financial projections. A closing condition in the agreement will track this appraisal, giving the lender the option to (1) terminate the agreement when the appraisal is too low or (2) reduce the loan principal pro rata.

13. Recall that these agreements, particularly those with architects and contractors, are or should be expressly assignable.

8. Construction Lending Agreements

account; permitting the lender to inspect the works; paying all hard and soft costs required for completion of the project; delivering to the lender all bills of sale, receipts, contracts, etc., for materials involved in construction; correcting any construction defects as the lender demands; and delivering to the lender for review any change orders before work is performed to satisfy them.

Breach of any of the agreement's warranties, present or future, is typically a default in the note, the mortgage, as well as the construction loan agreement itself.

Prime candidates in the agreement for negotiation as a loan closing condition will involve leasing, equity requirements, and construction conditions.

As to leasing conditions, 60 to 80% lease-up requirements are common; that is, the (office building) developer "will have executed leases, at commercially reasonable terms, with rents comparable to local market rents, for a term of no less than five years and no more than ten years, with a priority subordinate to the lien of the lender's mortgage, and in such form as lender approves, for 60% of the of the usable and/or rentable square footage of the [office building] project, in hand and delivered to the lender by the date the project's construction is" either complete or on the date of the closing for the takeout loan. Similar requirements will be imposed on developers of retail space projects.

As to equity requirement conditions, developers typically want to delay their deadlines for entity capitalization and equity investments because that delay gives the developer more time to use the generally cheaper dollars disbursed from the construction loan proceeds. Lenders push back for early deadlines on these items in an attempt to give the developer and other investors more "skin in the game," requiring that the deadlines be met before any disbursement of the loan proceeds. Lenders might also insist that the equity raised be used only to fund the hard costs of construction. The earlier in the construction process the equity requirements bite, the more a lender may be assured that the developer will focus—and continue to focus—on the project.

As to a construction condition, the developer "will begin construction of the project no later than 45 days after the loan closing, pursue construction with due diligence and in good faith, in a workmanlike manner according the plans and specifications previously approved by the lender, and completing construction on the date named in the attached schedule."

To mitigate the risk of cost overruns and an incomplete project build-out, the lender might require the developer's personal guarantee, the guarantee of a creditworthy participant in the legal entity holding title to pay all or part of the loan balance if not repaid in foreclosure, a letter of credit, payment and completion bonds, and other guarantees. See Robl Constr., Inc. v. Homoly, 781 F.3d 1029 (2015) (a dispute over the preconditions

8. Construction Lending Agreements

for enforcement of a personal guarantee given by an equity investor). Guarantees may cover all or part of the debt—the first part, the last part, or any fraction of the whole. Some guarantees may "burn off" or expire after some defined amount of time (a "shifting guarantee") or spring into existence upon some default defined in the agreement (a "springing guarantee"). Further, some guarantees may be limited in scope, as when they cover only environmental liabilities or a nonrecourse "carve-out" is invoked by the lender. Guarantees can put pressure on the developer to focus continually on the project.

Finally, the agreement will set out the details of the closing—its time, place, etc., in this respect and other details tracking a standard loan commitment.

Examples

Example 7

A construction lender client of your firm, in reviewing the developer's mark-up of a proposed construction loan agreement, discovers that one precondition to the lender's initial disbursal of loan proceeds calls for a "loan policy of title insurance in customary and standard form." Advise your client as to the adequacy of this call.

Explanation

The call is inadequate. It should provide for a policy insuring against both filed and inchoate mechanic's liens, mistakes in the survey submitted to the insurer and deleting any survey exception in the policy, and a pending disbursements clause.[14]

Example 8

A proposed construction loan agreement calls for conditions precedent to any loan disbursal made subsequent to an initial disbursement, including among other matters, representations and warranties that all such prior assurances are "true and correct as of the date of the disbursal effective

---

14. A pending disbursement clause in a loan title policy typically provides as follows: "Pending disbursement of the full amount of proceeds of the loan secured by the insured mortgage, this policy insures only to the extent of amounts actually disbursed, but increases as each disbursement is made, up to but not exceeding the face amount of the policy."

8. Construction Lending Agreements

as if made on that date," and an endorsement of the title policy as of the date of the disbursal. The disbursal to be made is one immediately after the completion of the foundation of the project building. What further, related precondition should be included in the agreement?

Explanation

At this phase of construction, a surveyor's certification that the foundation lies within the bounds of the initial survey submitted to the developer and lender with the commitment letter, assures both, as well as the title insurer, that the foundation is located so as to not create title and other problems for all these parties. They might all now require a further certification of the actual location of the foundation, submitted shortly prior (say, 10 days prior) to the disbursal request. All parties should readily agree to receive this further surveyor's certificate.

Example 9

Each disbursal request will routinely ask for mechanic's lien waivers. The endorsement line of each check disbursed will normally appear after an express waiver of liens. (If wire transfers are used, then the receipt of the lien waivers will precede the receipt of the wired funds.) How will these endorsements differ for checks issued to the general contractor as opposed to any subcontractor?

Explanation

When a subcontractor is paid out of funds disbursed to the general contractor, the general contractor is asked to waive for "all work performed to the date of the present disbursal," while a subcontractor waives for "all work performed through the date of the immediately preceding" disbursement. In some instances, major subcontractors may be paid directly by the lender, in which case their waivers will be identical.

Example 10

In addition to all other preconditions for a disbursal of loan proceeds, what further conditions should be placed in the final, hard costs, disbursal of proceeds?

211

8. Construction Lending Agreements

Explanation

Among other conditions, a final disbursal should be preceded by the receipt of approvals noting inspections by all governmental entities, land use counsel's opinion that the completed project is available for its intended and lawful use, certificates of completion from the architect or other inspector of the works, certificates of occupancy from local government, and evidence satisfactory to the lender and developer that all necessary utilities are available onsite and all abutting public roadways provide access to the project.

THE CONSTRUCTION NOTE AND MORTGAGE

Together, these two document provide evidence of debt and security for its repayment.

The Note

A mortgage note by itself creates an unsecured debt. It is the borrower's IOU. It can be enforced in any jurisdiction.

The note outlines the debt. It states the name of the developer/ borrower, the principal amount of the loan to be repaid, the term of the loan with the maturity date of the debt (for construction loans, typically one to three years), its interest rate (floating at 1 to 2 percentage points above the lender's prime rate, as measured by some specific financial index), and the frequency of disbursals and the date for repayment of principal and interest. The "prime rate" might either be one publically announced by the lender, or by a large national bank making construction loans, or published by a national publication such as the *Wall Street Journal*. If the interest rate is floating, the frequency of adjustment and any cap applicable to them will be stated as well. Sometimes the note's provisions for repayment are also set out in the construction loan agreement.

The note also sets out the events that will constitute a default (upon, for example, the loan's being "out of balance" (that is, lacking sufficient funds to complete the project with the remaining disbursals) or the lender's "insecurity"[15])— and the remedies available upon a default. In this regard, it might provide that "when this loan is out of balance for (say) 10 days and the mortgagor has not supplied funds necessary to complete the project, the

---

15. Similar mortgage loan and business covenants creating a default are discussed *infra*, this Chapter.

212

8. Construction Lending Agreements

interest rate shall increase to a 'default interest rate'"—sometimes 30% or more for the period of time that the default lasts.

A developer's attorney should identify the source of funds for a construction loan as that may impact the list of events constituting a default on the note. See Baybank Middlesex v. 1200 Beacon Props., Inc., 760 F. Supp. 957 (D. Mass. 1991) (where a default in the lender's funds agreement created a default under a construction loan note).

The commercial real estate lender may want the note to be negotiable—that is, in compliance with Article 3 of the UCC. However, because of the construction loan note's short term, its negotiability is not as necessary as it is for other types of commercial real estate loans that might more readily be assigned and sold into the secondary mortgage market.

As previously discussed, the mortgage note frequently contains a non-recourse provision. Construction lenders agree to such a provision when they are confident of their appraisal and underwriting process for the loan. When the debtor is a legal entity (typically a limited partnership or LLC) the nonrecourse language might apply to all partners or members, or to all except the general partner or managing member.

The Construction Loan Mortgage

A mortgage (of any type, residential or commercial) grants a lien to the lender holding the note. It reads like a deed doing just that. It can only be enforced in the jurisdiction in which the secured property is located. By itself, unaccompanied by a note, it is meaningless. Why? Because a mortgage lives and dies with the note—once the debt is repaid, the effectiveness of the lender's lien ends and the mortgage is a nullity.

In every jurisdiction, the mortgage is a conveyance; that is to say, in it the developer/borrower conveys a lien on the project property sufficient to enable foreclosure on that property upon a default in repayment and other events that reduce the value of the lender's security. That security is defined as the expected value of the project property at any foreclosure sale. The lien lasts only as long as the debt is not repaid; this is usually written into the granting clause of the mortgage, but it always appears somewhere in the document.

Because the disbursement of a construction loan proceeds is not made all at once, but is instead made as construction progresses, a construction loan is akin to a future advance mortgage. See Kim v. Lee, 31 P.3d 665 (Wash. 2001) (holding that the priority of future advances or disbursements relates back to the date of the original mortgage). A future advance mortgage provides for additional disbursements of funds so that the borrower can rely on obtaining funds from the lender without being required to obtain another loan for them. Future disbursements are subject to the progress of the work

213

8. Construction Lending Agreements

and the developer's title being lien-free at the time of each advance. It is the latter condition on future advances with which the case law relating to construction mortgages is most concerned. See, e.g., Midland Savings Bank FSB v. Stewart Group, 533 N.W.2d 191 (Iowa 1995).

Examples

Example 11

A future advance covenant in a construction mortgage does not specify the amount of funds to be disbursed after the execution of the mortgage. An intervening lien (one arising after the execution but before a disbursal) claims priority over the next disbursal of loan proceeds. Is the intervening lienor correct?

Explanation

No. In the context of a construction loan, the future advance covenant need not specify the amount of the future advance. Were it otherwise, the construction lender would have the obligation to check the land records before each disbursal. See Restatement (Third), Mortgages, §7.3 (comment b) (1997). A notice in the future advance covenant that there will be future disbursement of the loan is sufficient to defeat the intervening lienor's claim of priority. It is the lender's notice of the right to modify the principal amount of the loan.

Example 12

A developer's attorney proposes that the construction mortgage's *habendum* clause include a special warranty of title. The construction lender rejects this proposal. Why?

Explanation

Because a special warranty does not warrant title defects that pre-date the developer's taking title to the project property. Even if the developer acquired the property using a special warranty deed, such a deed is unacceptable to many lenders. They insist that the deed warrant title defects that preexist the developer's acquiring title, i.e., that the developer give a general warranty in the mortgage. In this regard, they insist that the developer grant more than he or she got.

214

8. Construction Lending Agreements

Example 13

A developer's attorney, knowing that public access to the project site will be to a public right of way fronting the site, notes also that the granting clause in the construction mortgage omits an easement granting access to a back lot. Should the developer's attorney disclose the omission to the lender?

Explanation

Yes. With a construction site, who knows whether the back-lot easement will or will not become important to the project? Construction is a risky business. The granting clause or the legal description following it should include all easements, appurtenances, rights to curb-cuts and public rights of way, and any other rights the lender or a purchaser at foreclosure would require to operate the project on the site. The developer is not a fiduciary for the lender, but the developer's attorney has a good faith duty of disclosure here.

Example 14

A statute in the jurisdiction in which you practice gives a "construction mortgage" priority over mechanic's liens recorded after the mortgage's date and time of its recording. Similarly, mechanic's lien statutes give the mechanic priority over all liens except liens of record recorded prior to the time of the mechanic's commencement of work. The construction lender sends one of its employees out to take pictures of the construction site just after the construction mortgage is recorded and just before the first disbursal of loan proceeds. The pictures fail to show lumber delivered to the site, located behind a rise in the ground, and to be used by the developer's general contractor in framing the foundation of the project. Does the lumberman have priority over the lien of the construction mortgage?

Explanation

Yes. The statutes in this Example are not unusual and in some jurisdictions restate the common law. It is not necessary that the funds disbursed by the lender be disbursed directly to the general contractor or any other provider of construction services to preserve the priority of the construction mortgage. It is sufficient that the disbursed funds are paid on account of construction activity. Nor is it unusual for the lender to photograph the site just before the construction mortgage is recorded. What the photographer missed in this situation is the "commencement of work" by the lumberman in delivering the lumber to the site. The lumberman's mechanic's lien relates back to the commencement of work — a time before the construction

215

8. Construction Lending Agreements

mortgage is recorded—and thus has priority over the mortgage. In this instance, the specific language of the mechanic's lien statute trumps the more general language of the construction mortgage statute. See Midland Savings Bank FSB v. Stewart Group, 533 N.W.2d 191 (Iowa 1995). Prompt recording of a construction mortgage is crucial to its operation.

Some jurisdictions by statute give the construction mortgage lien's priority over all mechanic's liens, even those whose work commenced before the recording of the construction loan mortgage. In these jurisdictions, the commencement of work is deemed to occur the moment the mortgage is recorded, but not sooner. The rationale for such statutes is that the construction loan is the energizer of all work by mechanics. But for it, no mechanic would get paid for work.

In this regard, some construction loan agreements and mortgages provide for a warranty by the developer/borrower that "no soil tests, surveying, or project site work, or other work related to construction of the project was begun or performed before the mortgage accompanying this agreement was recorded." As to such work, it is easy to imagine that a photographer might miss the signs of a soil test or a surveyor's marker.

Example 15

The statute regarding "construction mortgages" in the prior Example does not define further the term. A developer acquired the deed to the project site in part by conveying a purchase money mortgage back to the site's seller. A construction mortgage later negotiated with a lender does not contain a provision requiring the developer to build on the mortgaged site and permits the disbursal of the loan in two installments when (1) the project building is enclosed and (2) the construction is complete. Is this mortgage entitled to the priority assigned in the statute?

Explanation

Probably, but the result is uncertain enough that this mortgage should be re-reviewed either by both the developer's and the lender's attorney. The review is all the more important because in this Example, the purchase money mortgage for the site is not subordinated to the mortgage. See Juszak v. Lily & Don Holding Corp., 639 N.Y.S.2d 403 (N.Y. Sup. Ct. App. Div. 1995). The two-installment feature probably is not a killer, but the failure to provide that the mortgagor will construct a building on the site is. In this situation, the purchase money mortgagee/seller would be willing to subordinate her mortgage only because she expects that the construction on the site will enhance her own security, even when given a subordinated priority.

216

8. Construction Lending Agreements

Whether a mortgage is classified as a construction mortgage matters in the context of whether the anti-deficiency judgment statute of a jurisdiction protects a borrower from such a judgment after a foreclosure. Typically there is no such protection in an anti-deficiency statute itself. See Helvetica Servicing, Inc. v. Pasquan, 470 P.3d 155 (Ariz. 2020).

Example 16

A construction lender proposes that a due-on-sale-or-transfer provision be in the mortgage. The lender sees the transfer of the mortgage lien as a "transfer" under this provision and wants to accelerate the loan at that point, charging a fee for permission to transfer the lien. After a lender has underwritten a loan to one developer, it does not want to deal with another mid-way through construction. From the developer's perspective, such a provision requires attention. How?

Explanation

The "transfer" of the construction mortgage lien to a permanent lender should be an exception to the "due on" provision the lender proposes. A transfer of the construction mortgage lien to the permanent lender benefits the latter by giving it a priority dated from the beginning of construction. Even though the permanent lender may require a new title search in the buy-sell agreement, it still benefits from the earlier priority because it trumps mechanic's liens that may still be filed. Thus the assignment of the lien is a customary practice and is expected by the parties. At the time of the transfer and assignment, the construction loan will be paid off—so the construction lender is hardly less secure on that account. Thus the construction lender should readily agree to this transfer and assignment as an one-time exception to the due on transfer covenant. In some other types of commercial mortgages, the lender might ask for the assignee to assume the loan, rather than take subject to it, but when the loan is nonrecourse, that is impractical. Once the lien is assigned, of course, a full-blown, traditional due on sale clause will be needed—and so should be negotiated at this earlier stage with both the construction and the permanent lender.

Example 17

Some modifications might be required in any prepayment provision for the construction mortgage assignable to a permanent lender. What are they?

217

8. Construction Lending Agreements

Explanation

Since most construction loan notes use a floating or adjustable rate of interest, it is not usually a concern, except when fixed interest rates have decreased in the interval while construction occurred. When the transfer of the lien under the buy-sell agreement occurs on or before the maturity date of the loan, the construction lender and the developer should readily agree that the transfer of the lien is not a "prepayment" of the construction loan. Instead, it is an expected and excepted acceleration of the maturity date of the loan. Or, they might agree that no prepayment of the loan may be made during construction and before the transfer of the lien—a so-called "lock-out period" on prepayment, with a traditional prepayment penalty (either yield maintenance[16] or defeasance[17]) applicable afterwards. Which type of prepayment is preferred is for the permanent lender to decide.

Example 18

A proposed construction loan agreement, note, and mortgage all need a termination date, all three dates in sync with one another. A lender proposes that the termination date is the date on which construction is "complete." What alternative dates exist? List them.

Explanation

This is lender's problem, not a borrower's—but the borrower runs that risk that the commitment will be void for indefiniteness and so even the borrower needs to be concerned. The term of the loan must be defined, in either the note, the mortgage or the loan agreement in order to avoid violating the Rule Against Perpetuities and to give notice to persons who might otherwise become bona fide purchasers under the applicable recording act. Because the construction mortgage is a variant on a future advance mortgage, the termination date must

---

16. This is a one time, prepayment that allows the lender to attain the same yield to maturity as if the borrower had not prepaid. When the contract rate on the loan is higher than rates current when the prepayment is made, the difference between the contract rate and current rate is applied to the outstanding balance—that is, applied to the remaining payments, and then this stream of payments is added up and discounted to its present value. If the current rate is lower than the contract rate, no prepayment is due.

17. Defeasance is a process than substitutes escrowed bonds (usually U.S. Treasury bonds) for the property collateralized and securing the loan. The bonds have coupons valued at the amount of the repayments scheduled out to the loan maturity. It compensates the lender for what it would have received had the loan not been repaid. No prepayment occurs, the note is still outstanding, and the bonds are substituted collateral for its repayment. Often lenders selling their mortgages in the secondary market prefer defeasance to yield maintenance. It is difficult to classify either yield maintenance or defeasance as a penalty since both give the lender the return for which it contracted at the loan's inception.

8. Construction Lending Agreements

be linked to a definitive, certain, maximum amount of the debt, the secured amount for the mortgage, as well as a date related to the closing of the "takeout" loan. With a requirement for closing a takeout loan 30 days after the "completion of construction," completion might be defined as (1) a date certain, (2) the date of substantial completion, (3) the date the borrower takes occupancy of the project, (4) the date all occupancy permits have been issued (or at least some crucial permits), (4) the date of either the last loan disbursement or the disbursement of the retainage, (5) the date of completion of the punch list, (6) the date of completion of the major tenants' work letters, (7) the date major tenants occupy their premises, (8) all or some of the above.

Business and Financial Covenants

These are numerous and common in commercial mortgage documents, including those used for construction loans. Why? They have long been found in corporate finance transactions that are neither asset based nor secured by real property. The shift in the 1990s to mezzanine financing and to real estate being viewed as an operating business with more dependence on non-asset secured financing, has meant the inclusion of these covenants in construction mortgage lending loan commitments, and mortgage documents. See Andrew R. Berman, Risks and Realities of Mezzanine Loans, 72 Mo. L. Rev. 993 (2007). Their inclusion is most acceptable to developers with the best credit ratings, and in negotiating mortgage documents, their inclusion can be off-set by, for instance, a partial releases of liens, substitutions of security and collateral, and loan term extensions.

Such covenants are:

(1) material adverse change covenants (MACs) — referring to changes in the local economy or market for the project and giving the lender the most discretion of any business covenant: the broader this discretion, the more the construction borrower will push back with a request to identify the economic indicators that will be used to determine materiality and adversity;

(2) net worth maintenance covenants for the entity, requiring periodic reporting by the developer, managing member or partner of the project entity;

(3) loan to value ratio covenants, requiring a formula for either determining the fair market value of the asset, or capitalizing the net operating income (NOI) of the entity, with the borrower given the option of reducing the principal amount of the loan and with this cure, keeping the commitment alive or the mortgage default-free;

(4) geographic distribution covenants, requiring a representation that a borrower is not unreasonably exposed to risk in any one market or region;

8. Construction Lending Agreements

    (5) financial reporting covenants;

    (6) covenants restricting entity distributions;

    (7) covenants prohibiting mergers and consolidation of the entity, as well as perhaps the most common covenants of all,

    (8) debt service coverage ratio (DSCR)[18] covenants.

Example 19

The senior partner in your firm ask you as a new associate to review the impact of business covenants using the terms NOI and DSCR. You look puzzled but agree. What impact might you discover?

Explanation

DSCR is a widely used indicator of whether the projected NOI is sufficient to cover the debt service. This is akin to what the loan-to-value ratio indicates for a residential mortgage. That sufficiency is important because the rent roll or other income stream is the only asset that repays the commercial mortgage. Thus it is a widely used benchmark ratio for a lender making a loan to a project under construction (when its income is only prospective) because a projected DSCR and NOI provide a closing condition for a permanent lender's loan commitment. Financial ratios of various types are used by corporation and stock brokerage analysts all the time—DSCR is just one version. It is equal to

$$= \frac{\text{net operating income}\left(\text{NOI}\right)}{\text{total debt service}} = \text{DSCR}$$

where NOI = gross rents, minus the vacancy rate (the number of unrented units out of the total number of rentable units in a project), minus collection costs, minus operating expenses. Thus the NOI is calculated on pre-tax income streams. That means that for a construction lender negotiating a buy-sell agreement with a permanent lender, the DSCR ratio is some indication of the profitability of a just built project that hasn't yet been taxed. In this formula, operating expenses = taxes + insurance premiums + repair and

---

18. A debt service coverage ratio (DSCR), a/k/a "debt coverage ratio" (DCR), compares a project's net operating income with the money needed to service its mortgage debt as repayments fall due. It measures a project entity's (or any person holding title) ability to produce a cash flow sufficient to repay its debt. The higher this ratio is, the more comfortable a lender will be in making a loan.

8. Construction Lending Agreements

maintenance costs + utilities + management fees[19] + reserves.[20] *Note*: loan payments are not an operating expense.

A DSCR of one is a break-even cash flow — just enough to cover the debt service. A less than 1 ratio indicates that the NOI is insufficient to cover the debt service. For a lender, the ratio should be well over 1. The higher the better. Why? Because a 1 or more means that the property is generating enough income to repay its debts.[21] The longer the permanent mortgage term, the higher the DSCR is likely to be: life insurance companies require .10 more than other permanent lenders. Finally, the DSCR is used in lieu of profitability ratios (comparing (say) net or gross profits to rents or the net worth of the project), or solvency ratios (debt/equity ratios) because those alternatives are not good indicators when the operation isn't up and running yet.

Example 20

A permanent lender is considering taking-out of an already constructed apartment project with an NOI of $24,000 requiring a debt service of $20,000. What is the DSCR?

Explanation

$$\frac{\text{NOI} = \$24,000}{\text{Total Debt Service} = \$20,000} \text{ or } 24/20 = 1.2 \text{ DSCR}$$

A minimally acceptable DSCR for a lender! On the other hand, a .95 DSCR means that the mortgagor will have to come up with 0.5 of the loan balance in cash to repay the loan, i.e., there is only enough cash flow to cover 95% of the debt service the loan requires. It is not out of the question for a lender to make a loan when the ratio is less than 1.0 if the loan to value ratio is less than 60% or when the business on the site has strong outside income (e.g., an e-business not dependent on the bricks-and-mortar of a construction loan), but with the size of the loan, lenders grow cautious quickly. So a 1.2 DSCR

---

19. Management fees (typically of 3-6% of gross income) are included on the assumption that if the mortgagee had to take the project over, there would be a management fee to replace the developer or owner's management of it.

20. A construction lender will not always be concerned about establishing a replacement reserve account for a loan, but a permanent lender will be very concerned. The funds on the account are typically taken out of NOI. The developer/mortgagor will generally insist on owning these escrowed funds and earning interest on them.

21. Total debt service = principal + interest payments of all loans covering the property, not just the first lien or senior mortgage.

8. Construction Lending Agreements

indicates that the project has an NOI that is 20% more than is needed to carry its mortgage debt. When the lender thinks that the property is otherwise a good investment, what happens to the DSCR over the term of its loan? It goes up as (1) as the rents increase, (2) as the loan is repaid and its loan balance decreases and, finally, (3) as the taxes (federal, state, and municipal) vary year to year. The lender knows that the DSCR is only a snapshot in time. The first two factors are favorable to the investment, but the third is less predictably favorable. All this said, a construction loan is riskier than a permanent loan, and a construction lender will look for a DCSR higher than 1.2 with an eye to reviewing and perhaps negotiating the permanent lender's loan commitment.

Protecting the Construction Lender

Construction loan proceeds must cover acquisition, construction, and carried interest costs. Because the principal amount of a construction loan is advanced or disbursed in partial payments as inspections of the project's progress is made, a lender needs assurance that future payments will be sufficient to pay for the remaining costs of the project. When they are not, the loan is said to be "out of balance." To avoid cost overruns, the lending documents provide (as one of its business covenants) that if the loan is "out of balance," the mortgagor is required to invest additional funds prior to the next advance or to provide additional assurances that the project will be completed—perhaps a letter of credit from a bank or an infusion of funds from additional equity investors.

Examples

Example 21

How might a developer/mortgagor respond to a mortgagee alleging that the loan is "out of balance" while providing only some of the additional assurances requested?

Explanation

He might argue that the project's costs are less than at the start because of lower material and labor costs, or that project revenues are higher than expected because of (say) higher than expected rents or sales prices, or that tighter construction budget controls will bring the project "in balance," or (a rarity) that the takeout commitment has only one condition—that is, completion of the project.

With each advance that might be out of balance, the construction mortgagee will be torn between not wanting to become insecure and wanting to keep the project on schedule (one not on schedule will only make the

8. Construction Lending Agreements

insecurity greater). Moreover, if the mortgage has the right to withhold an advance if the conditions of the loan documents are not satisfied, then that advance is "optional" and the mortgage loses its priority as to that advance. So advances are seldom "obligatory." The optional/obligatory distinction is important when third parties (such as mechanics lienholders or junior mortgagees) enter the picture.

As a result of these considerations, conditions in a construction mortgage should be objectively defined and not subject to the mortgagee's control. They should not provide that an advance is subject to "satisfactory progress." The mortgage might instead provide that no default exists before the mortgagee sends notice of it to the mortgagor, or that advances made to protect the lender's security and collateral are obligatory. In the alternative, the proceeds of the loan might disburse all at once, but into an escrow account for disbursal; however, a mortgagor might object to the last option if interest runs from the date of the disbursal into the account.

At the execution of the loan commitment, the mortgagee traditionally retains the right not to disburse a certain percentage—a/k/a retainage—often 10% of the proceeds due to the general contractors and all the tradesmen that he hired as subcontractors. The percentage may vary, higher (say, 15%) in earlier advances than in later ones or in early advances for some trades (say, sheeting and shoring in which the subsurface geology is uncertain), but not others; or less retainage for early completion of any stage in the construction process. In retainage provisions, mortgagees retain the right to withhold some or all of the amounts retained until a final inspection, undertaken upon completion, with an exception for "punch list" work.

Example 22

A construction loan is out of balance at the last disbursement of loan proceeds. Unpaid mechanics file and record liens on the project. The construction lender turns to its title insurer, whose loan policy was just updated and files a claim on the policy in the amount of the recorded liens. Should the title insurer pay these claim?

Explanation

The insurer will probably not pay the claim. Although the cases are split on the issue, insurers have resisted such claims with the argument that the covenant invoked is a business covenant and that the amount of the loan, and its sufficiency to complete the construction, is a business and not a title matter. Thus it is matter for the developer and the lender to work out, even though the filing of the mechanic's liens would otherwise certainly be a title defect covered by the policy. If the lender were to advance funds to pay the unpaid mechanics, the title insurer would further argue that the payments

8. Construction Lending Agreements

were voluntary, not required by the loan documents, and created after the date the policy is effective—and so not covered. (Title insurance is in this respect retrospective, not insuring against future title defects.) The proper remedy here, insurers argue, is for the developer to supply the funds or to obtain another loan to cover the amount of the outstanding liens.

CHAPTER 9

Equity Financing and Investors

Entities for real estate development, including limited partnerships and limited liability companies (LLCs) treated for federal income tax purposes as partnerships, use a combination of partner equity and nonrecourse mortgage financing in order to acquire and develop real property.

In the 1970s and 1980s, whenever current mortgage interest rates were higher than those on outstanding mortgages, mortgagors were encouraged to have their mortgages assumed by would-be purchasers of their properties. Both residential and commercial mortgagees responded by inserting "due on sale" covenants into their mortgage documents. Such covenants gave the mortgagee the option of accelerating payment of the outstanding debt secured by the mortgage upon any "sale or transfer" of the secured property, in whole or part, by the mortgagor. These covenants were alleged to be unreasonable restraints on alienation and clogs on the mortgagor's equity of redemption. However, they were by and large held enforceable by the courts. By these means, mortgagees attempted to keep the interest rates payable on their mortgage portfolios current and in line with the rates they themselves were paying on their borrowed capital. These covenants also furthered the sale of mortgages lenders originated into the secondary market.

MEZZANINE FINANCING

In the 1990s, after the commercial real estate recession of 1990–1991, stricter underwriting guidelines for commercial mortgages and lower loan-to-value

9. Equity Financing and Investors

(LTV) ratios encouraged commercial developers/mortgagors to look for junior or second mortgages. Lenders responded with prohibitions on junior mortgages, often framed as "due on encumbrance" covenants, modeled on the due on sale covenants previously discussed and justified by recently encountered problems posed by junior mortgages in foreclosure and bankruptcy proceedings. Such problems were numerous: junior mortgagees might dispute a senior mortgagee's use of insurance proceeds or a condemnation award; they might pay real estate taxes and thus become senior to them to the extent of the payment; they might file for bankruptcy and thus stay any foreclosure proceedings by a senior mortgagee; and they might complicate any refinancing of a senior mortgage; moreover, the senior mortgagee will need the junior's approval upon any loan modification or workout.

Thus throughout the 1990s the use of junior mortgages sharply decreased, and commercial mortgagors searched for alternatives.

One alternative was mezzanine[1] financing. Typically mezzanine financing is a loan made in addition to a first mortgage loan and subordinated to it, but by agreement made senior in priority to both the mortgagor's equity in the secured property and the mortgagor's priority in the cash flow generated by the property.

Waterfalls for Commercial Real Estate

A cash flow waterfall is a method of dividing profits from a project among partners/venturers/members that permits their uneven distribution. Think of it as a series of pools that fill up with the cash flow from a project and once full, cascade down its excess cash into additional, lower pools. It permits equity investors to have the first or *preferred return* on their investments and then to reward the sweat equity of an LLC's managing members with a *promote* — an uneven, extra, disproportionate share of profits.

(1) The "*preferred return*" is the first claim on profits in the highest pool of a waterfall until a target return is achieved, and it is a first claim on profits before others are paid any distribution. It is a "preference" return hurdle that once met, allows excess profits to be distributed as agreed in the operating agreement.

(2) The *promote* is extra, uneven, and disproportionate share of profits that the developer receives when the project's cash flow is higher than expected, higher than (say) the IRR return (that is, as discussed in Chapter 6,

---

1. "Mezzanine" is a Wall Street term, referring to financing that is not investment-grade (as highly regulated institutions would require because their regulators require it) but not junk. It sits between secured and unsecured financing, between first priority mortgages and junior mortgages. The concept of mezzanine finance and equity investors was discussed in a preliminary way infra, Chapter 5, in the context of drafting an LLC operating agreement.

226

9. Equity Financing and Investors

the percentage rate of return earned on each dollar invested for each period it is invested). The IRR protects the investments of others — hence the phrase "return hurdle" — the rate of return that must be achieved before cash moves on to a different, lower pool and to the next hurdle within that pool. It is an equity investor's minimum acceptable rate of return on its investment — a/k/a, the hurdle rate. It is often the discount rate an investor uses to run a DCF (as discussed in Chapter 8) analysis for the project (recall that the higher the discount rate, the lower the value of the project) and the rate that triggers the disproportionate profit splits. Often the IRR or equity multiple is the return hurdle. The equity multiple is the sum of all equity invested + all profits divided by the total equity invested. That equity can be that of both the developer and the investor(s), the investor(s), or the equity alone.

All this is typically provided for in an LLC's operating agreement.

Examples

Example I

What are the key issues in setting this preferred return hurdle?

Explanation

Key issues are

(1) What the rate of return? Historically it has been between 8 and 12%.
(2) How is the preferred return collateralized? By the developer or by the LLC's membership in the project? If the sponsor is really eager for the investor's money, guaranties are not unknown, but not typical.
(3) Who gets it? All equity investors or some number of them?
(4) Is the preferred return cumulative or noncumulative? When is this issue relevant? When in a given year or payout period, there is not enough profit to satisfy it in a given year? If not, will it (if cumulative) be added to an investor's balance for the next period until it eventually paid?
(5) Is the nonpaid cumulative return compounded at the preferred rate of return when not paid out?
(6) If it is compounded, with what frequency will that occur?

The look back provision. At the end of the deal, when the project is sold, what if the investor has not recouped its preferred rate of return? Will the investor get to "look back" over the project's life and look at the amounts earlier given to the project developer, forcing the developer to disgorge amounts that give the investor its promised preferred rate?

Or . . .

227

9. Equity Financing and Investors

The catch up provision. This gives 100% of profits to the investor until the return hurdle is achieved in every payout period with any excess going to the developer.

Examples

Example 2

What do you see as the difference between a look back and a catch up provision?

Explanation

One is a variation on the other. The difference is who gets to hold the money over the project's life—with the look back, it's the developer, and with the catch up, it's the investor.

Example 3

Would developers prefer one over the other?

Explanation

Yes. Developers prefer the look back provision (because they get to use the money even if they might have to disgorge it later) while investors prefer the catch up provision (because she gets paid first and won't have to ask the sponsor to write the disgorgement check).

The Position of the Mezzanine Financier

The waterfall puts mezzanine financing in the sandwich position—between the senior mortgagee and the mortgagor/borrower/owner. In the traditional

9. Equity Financing and Investors

sense, it creates unsecured debt, "secured" by a pledge of the equity interests in the entity holding title to the project property and entitling the mezzanine lender to the cash flow from the project property left over once the mortgage lender is paid. Thus its security is, not the property itself, but the equity interests of the developer/owner; it is personalty,[2] not realty; it is only indirectly secured by real property owned by an intermediate entity owned in turn by the developer/borrower.

This security interest is adaptable: it can take the form of either an assignment, a pledge of cash flow, or an entity membership interest. If the borrower is a corporation, it may be an assignment of corporate shares, the dividends of which are sufficient to repay the loan. If the borrower is a partner or a member of an LLC, it may be a pledge of the borrower's partnership share or company membership—or an assignment of part of the cash flow in a preferred position. In any event, the mezzanine lender will typically require the personal guarantee of the debt by the borrower and be able to seize the shares or other ownership interests more quickly than if foreclosure (of any type) was required. Meanwhile, although a second mortgage would have to be carried as a liability on the balance sheet of the corporation, partnership, or LLC, the mezzanine loan is carried not on those entities' books, but on the books of the borrower. Mezzanine financing is off-balance sheet financing.

Just as with junior mortgages, mezzanine financing first was often used for (1) renovating commercial properties, (2) upgrading and repositioning a property in its market, (3) capturing the value of built-up equity in a property without the income tax liabilities of selling it, or (4) obtaining seed money for the developer's next project.

As experience was gained with mezzanine financing, it was used more widely to permit a developer achieve greater leverage—that is, a higher LTV ratio for all its land acquisition and development loans. For lenders recognizing that its security is not the property but its cash flow, mezzanine financing offers a higher rate of interest than do junior mortgage loans. Thus mezzanine debt is more expensive than permanent, take-out, or junior mortgage debt, but still not as expensive as other institutional investors' equity debt. Lenders engaging in such financing are usually seasoned real estate investors capable of evaluating the equity value that the developer/borrower has in a property. Mezzanine lending is unlikely if the developer's equity is not 20% or more of appraised value.

The typical mezzanine transaction has two to three components: (1) a promissory note, perhaps with a mortgage, unrecorded; (2) a pledge or

---

2. As personalty, the foreclosure process of the Uniform Commercial Code, Art. 9, applies to it. See Lenne R. Dunn & Peter Dopsch, Mezzanine Loan Foreclosure: U.C.C. Sales of Equity Interests under Revised Article 9, 18 Real Est. Fin. J. 5 (2002).

229

9. Equity Financing and Investors

assignment of entity interests; (3) an intercreditor agreement between the senior mortgagee, consenting to the mezzanine loan, and the mezzanine lender. This agreement seeks to eliminate the delays the senior mortgagee may encounter in foreclosure[3]: it provides (a) for notice of defaults and an opportunity to cure defaults in the senior mortgage and (b) for defining the relationship and priorities of the two parties in foreclosure, sometimes permitting the creditworthy mezzanine lender to step into ownership of the project property.

Other provisions of the intercreditor agreement will be urged by the developer as a mezzanine borrower.[4] Just as the senior mortgagee seeks to eliminate the delays it might encounter in foreclosure and speed up the foreclosure process, the mezzanine borrower will seek to slow down the mezzanine lender/investor's UCC foreclosure process by (1) providing for longer periods between the notice of foreclosure and the process itself, (2) lengthening the time required between the auction sale of the equity interest in the developer's LLC and the closing of the sale, (3) enabling the developer to bid at the sale, and (4) lowering the deposit amounts a winning bidder must post at the sale. See UCC § 9-603. Mezzanine investors/lenders will resist, wanting to preserve the typical rights conferred by the UCC—a 30 day notice, a 10% deposit, and a 24 hour period between the sale and the closing. See UCC §§9-604, 607. Likewise, developers who are mezzanine borrowers might ask the investor/lender to forswear the re-possession provisions of the UCC. See UCC § 9-609. Whatever the final resolution of these matters in the intercreditor agreement, reenforcing provisions should be inserted in the LLC operating agreement. Senior mortgagees should not routinely object to these developer-friendly provisions of the agreement. They seek to stabilize the three-party relationships in it by giving the developer time to preserve them, raise the cash to bid successfully at the auction sale, or find new investors.

Typical mezzanine borrowers will likely be an LLC, special-purpose entity (SPE) that will own only the secured property, will conduct its business independently, and is bankruptcy-remote (often by promising not to file for bankruptcy or with the existence of a lender-controlled director, partner, or member who is not an obligor under the financing agreement and who will vote against the filing).

Repayment may also be guaranteed by the developer as the managing member or partner of the SPE, or by SPE's parent company or entity. This

---

3. Recall that the mortgage is likely to be nonrecourse, focusing the lender's attention on achieving a speedy foreclosure.

4. Recall that the equity investors' interests are personal property, governed by the Uniform Commercial Code, Art. 9 (secured transactions). For Article 9 purposes, the equity investors are lenders, here mezzanine lenders. See Caroline Harcourt, Lynn A. Soukup. & Jacob A. Axelrod, Distressed Real Estate During COVID-19: Conducting a Mezzanine Loan Foreclosure, http/www.pillsbury.com (last viewed 3/1/2022).

9. Equity Financing and Investors

financing might also include a participating interest available on default (at a slightly higher than first lien interest rate, plus a contingent return based on cash flow) or a shared appreciation feature based on an equity event (such as sale, condemnation, refinancing, or revaluation, etc.). These inclusions are drafted to avoid recharacterization as a common law clog on alienation,[5] which usually results from lender control or lender participation in management decisions after a default, pledge and participation rights, conversion options, and equity kickers. Anti-clogging affidavits are also required from the borrower, and sometimes an anti-clogging endorsement from a title insurer, with the insurer that issued the endorsement in turn requiring an indemnity agreement from the borrower.

Additional intercreditor agreement provisions are drafted to avoid the financial pressure points found in the senior note and mortgage: that is, any balloon payment or refinancing dates in the senior mortgage will not occasion similar obligations for the mezzanine borrower, lest the double pressure of the two loans tip the borrower into insolvency. See Wells Fargo Bank v. Cherryland Mall LP, 812 N.W.2d 799 (Mich. Ct. App. 2011) (finding that the failure of an SPE to remain solvent triggers a full liability carve-out in a nonrecourse loan). In a similar vein, the mezzanine financing will have a term longer than the senior note and mortgage, tending to make mezzanine lenders look long and hard at the long-term prospects of the property. The mezzanine lender will have a right to cure defaults in the senior mortgage. The mezzanine lender and the senior mortgagee will agree on how to handle disputes that arise on leasing the property. One such dispute might arise, for example, when a mezzanine lender would willingly accept higher rents and a lower credit rating in tenants while the mortgagee might want lower rents and a higher rating. When the mortgage has been used as collateral for a secondary market bond or other instrument, this type of dispute means that the senior mortgagee will require that the mezzanine lender obtain written confirmation from a rating agency that enforcement of any of the mezzanine lender's proposed remedies will not adversely affect the credit rating given to the instrument sold to investors in the secondary market.

The disadvantages of mezzanine lending are that (1) a 10 to 15% decrease in fair market value will erode the borrower's equity and put the

---

5. "The principle is this: a mortgage is a conveyance of land . . . as a security for the payment of a debt or the discharge of some other obligation for which it is given. This is the idea of a mortgage: and the security is redeemable on the payment or discharge of such debt or obligation, any provision to the contrary notwithstanding. That, in my opinion, is the law. Any provision inserted to prevent redemption on payment or performance of the debt or obligation for which the security was given is what is meant by a clog or fetter on the equity of redemption and is therefore void. It follows from this, that 'once a mortgage always a mortgage.'" See Stanley v. Wilde, 2 Ch. 474 (Queen's Bench 1899) (a leading explanation for the mortgagor's equity of redemption.

9. Equity Financing and Investors

lender at risk, and (2) the costs of underwriting and due diligence are high compared to the amount of the loan. So investigation of the market is crucial and risky, and this increases negotiation costs. See Andrew R. Berman, Risks and Realities of Mezzanine Loans, 72 Mo. L. Rev. 993 (2007).

A mezzanine borrower responding to a senior mortgage lender who, when discovering mezzanine financing has been or will be used, feels insecure and threatens to declare a default of the senior mortgage, might make any of the following offers: (1) offer a "lockbox" agreement, which would require tenants on the property to pay rents and profits constituting the cash flow from the property directly into an account controlled by the senior mortgagee, who would then pay the mezzanine lender out of cash flow in excess of amounts needed to make payments due on the senior mortgage; (2) also offer to put the management of the property in the hands of an agreed upon property manager; and (3) further offer the senior mortgagee a "carry guarantee" for that mortgage, guaranteeing to cover the project's operating costs after the completion of construction or during the lease-up period of a project, covering such items as its day-to-day management fees, taxes, and insurance premiums; or (4) offer to purchase the senior note and mortgage upon default.

When mezzanine financing is used, title insurers should be consulted as additional issues with the borrower's title policy arise. Consider three that might arise. (1) Recall that claims on a title policy require a showing of damages "sustained or incurred"—that is, actual damages. The mezzanine lender, however, will want to get at the proceeds of a claim sooner, even though its loss will be contingent and may never arise by the time the claim is payable or paid. So an endorsement for this will be necessary. (2) Exclusion 3(b), giving the insurer a defense to a claim based on knowledge of the insured, may be a problem. Thus affidavits from all the participants in the due diligence underwriting for the mezzanine loan will be required, to the effect that they know of no matters, rights, claims, or interests affecting the property that are not represented in the application for insurance. (3) A Condition 1 or continuation of coverage problem may arise when the memberships in the borrowing entity change: this, too, will have to be the subject of an endorsement.

Examples

Example 4

Equity investors as mezzanine lenders have concerns about capital calls and contributions on their funds, and propose as follows:

> The [investors] will deposit $3,000,000 into the capital account of the LLC upon the approval of all applications for land use, building, and construction

9. Equity Financing and Investors

permits and thereafter (1) will deposit $1,000,000 at the closing of a construction loan, and thereafter (2) such monies as are needed, up to a total of $2,500,000 as necessary to stabilize the project.

The developer responds with the following:

At the execution of the operating agreement, the [investors] will deposit $3,000,000 into the capital account of the LLC and thereafter as called on, deposit as much as $3,500,000 when in the sole and absolute discretion of the management, all land use permits are received by management.

How would you advise the developer to compromise these versions?

Explanation

What are the basic factors? Amount, timing, and conditions precedent. The developer wants a larger investment, earlier, and without conditions. The amount of the contribution, the developer insists, should not be timed to the construction loan closing. Rather, the equity investors are to contributing a percentage of the total development costs, minus the principal of the construction loan. An investor wants to delay to give the developer time to have skin in the game, a financial stake in the outcome, typically in the 10 to 20% range. To this end, the developer proposes to contribute land and intangible personal property — the land contract, planning studies, the plans and specs, services, etc. Thus the investors will likely seek a profits interest rather than a capital interest, because the profits interest has a precondition that there are profits, while a capital interest only gives an immediate right to the value of all LLC assets. A profits interest is the most common of the two. It "incentivizes" the developers to do well. It lets the developer reduce his capital risks. What will the developer expect in return? Assumption of liabilities by the entity. What will the investors then likely want? Representations and warranties about the entity similar to those in the land contract.

Example 5

Equity investors' provision in an LLC's operating agreement often call for additional contributions of capital as a project is completed or matures. They naturally ask the developer when he thinks the extra money might be necessary. The developer replies that either an expansion of the successful project, or cost overruns, might occasion additional capital calls. What do you think are the initial attitudes of developers and investors?

9. Equity Financing and Investors

Explanation

(a) Investors think, "didn't we rely on your promised expertise in running the project?" (b) Developers think, "stuff happens," the budget is not a guarantee, it is reasonable estimate—developers want additional contributions to be mandatory, when necessary in its sole discretion, and in the same ratio as with initial contribution.

Example 6

Was the developer's two-pronged reply—as to project expansion and cost overruns—made in the prior Example, a smart one?

Explanation

Investors will seldom agree to a mandatory contribution for an expansion of the LLC's business. Why? They made their initial calculation to invest based on the initial proposed operation of the project, and probably wouldn't agree to recalculate based on an unknown future proposal. As to the prospect of cost overruns and their twin situation, operating deficits, equity investors will initially propose "no obligation to contribute whatsoever," but if the contribution is to be made, it is (a) made only after overruns and deficits are covered by the developer's fees or interests, (b) covered when the developer also contributes, and that (c) the developer's contribution is subordinate to the investors' capital position—that is, after the investor is paid its full initially promised return. Of these three investor responses, the developer likely to resist (b) most strongly. Why? Because (b) requires additional capital from the developer. After all, the investor is liquid, the developer is not.

Example 7

Any proposal by the developer for a unilateral right to call for additional capital runs afoul of the idea that equity investors bring a dispassionate, third party eye on the project. However, the developer will want remedies for a failure on the part of the equity investor to make a required, previously agreed to, contribution. What remedies is the developer likely to ask for?

9. Equity Financing and Investors

Explanation

Arranged in the order of their seriousness, the remedies typically used are (1) the loss of rights granted in the operating agreement, including voting rights, (2) the LLC's right to offset the defaulted amount against cash or property distributions, (3) the LLC's right to buy out the defaulter's interest, (4) the loss of the developer's promote (if the developer is in default), and (5) recalculation of the defaulting member's share of profits.

Example 8

Equity investors often want to vote in or have a veto power over major management decisions of the operating LLC. What if they propose that they have a veto power over the following management decisions, as follows?

The execution of leasing guidelines and standard form leases; the approval of brokerage and management contracts; alteration of land use restrictions; any signage or advertisement affecting the exterior of the project; the settlement of any lawsuit affecting the project; operating budgets; any agreement, including but not limited to letters of intent, to increase the gross square footage, floor area ratio, or acreage of the project; any commercial lease whose premises are more than 10,000 gross square feet.

And the developer responds:

The execution of an option or contract to increase the gross square footage, floor area ratio, or acreage, of the project; or any lease for commercial use of more than 10,000 rentable square feet if the average annual net rent generated during the first five years of its term is less than $20.00 per square feet.

How would you advise the developer to compromise these two proposals?

Explanation

By eliminating the brokerage, signage, and advertising elements of the investors' proposal. They are ancillary to the other elements, and then singling out the basic components of each version. For instance, the lease approval elements vary as to scope — the investors want to approve any lease and the developer only wants them to review major leases. Getting the investors to focus on giving meaning to what is meant by major decisions, defining them as leases with more than a certain rentable square footage and square foot rent will turn the discussion to objective criteria. These criteria are

235

9. Equity Financing and Investors

particularly important to both the developer and the equity investors in the early years of the project, when its mixture of leases and a rental pattern are being established.

Example 9

What if in addition the developer also proposes the following?

> . . . excluding any action required by law, municipal ordinance, or federal statute, including but not limited to the payment of all real property taxes and assessments; any action consistent with leasing guidelines and brokerage and management contracts previously approved; the settlement of any lawsuit for an amount less than $100,000; and operating budgets for the project.

How would you predict that the investors will respond?

Explanation

By asking for more control over other types of management decisions. For instance, they might also ask for participating on or a veto of any of the following decisions: the sale of the project, its refinancing, renovation, expansion or contraction; the admission of new LLC members; the selection or replacement of the LLC's manager; its filing a bankruptcy petition; its amendment to its operating agreement, re-purposing its business, or stepping out of the ordinary course of business; dissolving or merging with another entity; demolition of the project; settling a lawsuit or claim by third parties; any tax election resulting in entity taxation, leasing, approval or annual budgets; alteration of the LLC's land use permissions; establishing cash reserves, hiring legal counsel or accountants, or violating the terms of the operating agreement. To which of these might to the developer agree?

Explanation

The parties might find a source of likely agreement in the admission of new LLC members, any decision affecting the cash flow of the project, and the expansion, contraction, repurposing of the business. The developer will want these decisions couched, not as the investors' veto right, but as a voting right in them. Likewise, the operating agreement should expressly prohibit the investors from taking independent action or compelling the developer to take any affirmative action, although the 2007–2008 real estate recession brought equity investors to the point of asking for such provisions. Many of the other management decisions would also be of

9. Equity Financing and Investors

such concern to mortgage lenders that the developer might hide behind lender concerns or invoke the due on encumbrance covenants in the lender's mortgage. In this regard, the project's refinancing, renovation, expansion or contraction, the admission of new LLC members, the selection or replacement of the LLC's manager, its filing a bankruptcy petition—all will require documents that arguably involve a "sale or transfer" of an interest in the title holding LLC. The rest require attention in the LLC's operating agreement, defined either as major decisions or excluded from that category.

Example 10

Four years after his project is stabilized, the developer wants to refinance. The equity investors have approval and veto rights over any refinancing—and they refuse to approve the refinancing as well as the operating budget for the project. The project LLC's operating agreement typically addresses this situation: it generally locks in the equity investments for a period of time after the investment is made or the construction of the project is complete; it then provides for a cool off/negotiation period of 30 days and a budget approval carryover after the 30 days. "What should I do?", the developer asks. What's your advice?

Explanation

You might make two points. (1) You might explain why the developer wants to refinance. A new permanent loan with a higher principal, a lower interest rate or a longer term will capture project equity. Carrying a lower risk for the mortgagee, it would not have to be personally guaranteed by the borrower; so the loan will lock in a high level of cash flow for LLC members, and produce loan proceeds enabling a partial return on capital. (2) Upon their refusal to approve or veto you might advise the consideration of buying the protesting investors out after the 30 day cool off period expires.

Example 11

After the 30 day cool off period in the prior Example, what if the operating agreement contains a push-pull/ buy-sell procedure for use by either the developer or the equity investor(s) -- that is, any buy-out offer is also an offer to sell—and any offer to sell out is also an offer to buy. Who does this buy-sell procedure favor?

237

9. Equity Financing and Investors

Explanation

Almost always the equity investors. Why? Because their liquidity is greater and because it will take longer for the developer to arrange third party financing. How might the investors hurry the process up? Yes, with a "drag along" procedure, as follows: one party (either the investor(s) or the developer) obtains an offer to sell their LLC interest to a third party at the buy-sell price and terms, and agrees to have the third party buy the other out at the same price and terms. This is all terrifying: the uncertainties of the situation often produce further negotiations and settlement.

Example 12

Is a drag along method implicit in the buy-sell procedure?

Explanation

Yes, but this might take litigation to establish.

Example 13

What happens if the developer refinances without the equity investors' approval?

Explanation

If the applicable agreements don't handle such a situation, the developer will be consumed with the dispute, to the detriment of the management of the project. If the mortgage lender hears of the dispute, its loan committee is likely to invoke the business covenants in the mortgage, further complicating the developer's management and control of the project.

9. Equity Financing and Investors

Example 14

Equity investors propose the following regarding their right to ask that the LLC's manager be removed: "Management may be removed for cause, whether for malfeasance, misfeasance, violation of a fiduciary duty, self-dealing, or any adverse material effect on the operating budget and credit of the LLC." How should the developer respond?

Explanation

Under the investor's proposal, the developer/manager might fear going into the office. The developer might respond with the following counter-proposal for insertion into the operating agreement: "Manager may be removed for intentional fraud, criminal violations not related to permits and permissions given by governmental officials, the bankruptcy of the LLC, or other willful misconduct resulting in the liability of the LLC for more than $100,000." The developer might also propose that the trigger for the investors' right to ask for a manager's removal be an annual or periodic audit of management compensation and fees or an annual audit of all management compensation and fees "in excess of 10% of total development costs or 10% of total annual rents payable under project leases." Annualizing this trigger will give some stability to management and an opportunity to resolve whatever dispute is in prospect.

Example 15

A commercial mortgage lender, envious of the higher rates of interest given mezzanine lenders, offers a mortgagor a reduction of the principal amount of the loan secured by an outstanding mortgage in exchange for becoming a mezzanine lender in the amount of the reduction. What problems do you foresee with this offer?

Explanation

Those associated with a participating and convertible mortgage, because that's what is being offered. See Wonderland Shopping Center Venture LP v. CDC Mortgage Capital, Inc., 274 F.3d 1085 (6th Cir. 2001). The participation in the secured property's income might be measured by either its gross or net income, the latter being more typical of mezzanine loans, payable either periodically or deferred until the property is sold. It may either insulate the mezzanine lender from inflation or disappear if the property is unprofitable. Its payment may be reliant on the developer's management decisions and incentivize the lender to ask for a say on major decisions. The offer might indicate that the lender regards the cash flow of the property

239

9. Equity Financing and Investors

as unstable and require an appraisal and due diligence before acceptance. Acceptance might mean more cash flow for investors and an earlier return on their contributions. Careful analysis is required.

Example 16

A mortgage lender originates a new project's mortgage loan with an unstable but promising net operating income (NOI). The loan documents provide that if the debt service coverage ratio (DSCR) is not 1.2 after three years of operation, the loan will be "re-sized": that is, its principal amount will be reduced to an amount at which the DSCR is in fact 1.2. The difference in loan amount will, at the mortgagee's option, be either paid in cash by the mortgagor or the mortgagee will lend the mortgagor the amount of the difference with a mezzanine loan giving the mortgagee a 25% equity interest in the project. The project does not achieve the three-year, 1.2 DSCR. The mortgagee proposes to re-size the mortgage loan and elects to provide the mezzanine loan. The mortgagor objects, tenders the difference money in cash, and argues the mezzanine loan is a common law clog on the equity of redemption and an unreasonable restraint on alienation. Will the mortgagor's argument be successful?

Explanation

Probably not, although there is no clear answer in the case law on this subject. Cf. HH Mark Twain LP v. Acres Capital Servicing LLC, 2020 N.Y.L.J. LEXIS 1021, **5-6 (N.Y. Sup. Ct. June 17, 2020) (finding that the clogging claim has not been litigated on the merits, but finding the claim sufficient to issue a preliminary injunction). The purpose of the clogging doctrine is to prevent a mortgage lender from acquiring ownership of the secured property by any means other than foreclosure. The equity of redemption likewise guarantees that every mortgage contains by implication a right to repay the debt before it is foreclosed. The re-sizing provision in the loan documents provides options for the mortgagee, but the option exercised here is at the lender's discretion. The provision applies when the loan documents are executed; this is often evidence of a clog on the mortgagor's equity of redemption. Likewise, a mezzanine loan is typically held by a lender different from the mortgage lender for a project; here, both the mezzanine lender and the mortgage lender are the same. This argues in favor of finding the re-sizing provision is a clog. However, a mezzanine loan attaches to the ownership interests in the entity holding title to the project real estate, not to the real estate itself; it results in a Uniform Commercial Code (UCC) Art. 9 security interest, not a mortgage. On the other hand, controlling membership interests in an entity that controls the real estate might be regarded, as a practical matter, as control of the real estate. However, when the parties are

240

9. Equity Financing and Investors

sophisticated and well counseled, the form of the transaction chosen by the parties should control and this situation is close to a clog, but not quite.

Provisions like the re-sizing provision in this Example are used when a mortgage loan is pooled and sold into the secondary market to investors in bonds whose income must be stable.

Example 17

What types of federal income tax problems might arise for mezzanine lenders?

Explanation

The purpose of the loan is to replace part of the owner's equity ownership in the property with the mezzanine lender's right to repayment. Equity ownership is the subject of the loan, and the lender then generally wants to be treated as an owner for tax purposes — that is, to be taxed at capital gain, not ordinary income rates. (1) To gain this treatment, the Internal Revenue Code's crucial factors are the purpose of the investment, the frequency of sales, and the management of the property. See IRC §1221. So the more rights the mezzanine lender has to take over and manage the property, the more he will look like a real estate developer in the ordinary course of business and be denied capital gains treatment. Thus the lender wants the right to hire a management company, rather than manage directly — the right to be exercised on default by the borrower. (2) Another route to capital gains treatment is to characterize the loan as equity (and so a capital asset), not debt. See IRC §385. The right to designate SPE members or directors, the avoidance of a fixed maturity or repayment date, and the lack of a sinking fund or an obligation to repay, make the case for equity classification stronger and avoid the appearance of debt.

Additional protection of mezzanine lenders is provided by the UCC. Under its revised Article 9, the mezzanine borrower's pledge is either an "investment property" or a "general intangible." See UCC §9-102(42) and (49) for definitions. The former may be perfected by control (evidenced by possession or the right to possess in an assignment), by filing a financing statement, or (when certificated with a security under UCC §8-301) by possession. The latter may be perfected by filing. See UCC §§9-308, 9-310. Among interests perfectible by filing, the earliest to file has priority. Title insurers often offer either an endorsement for their loan policies or a UCC policy, insuring the Article 9 status of the lender's interest, but sometimes an attorney's opinion accomplishes the same result.

The UCC's protections are premised on the ability of the foreclosing lender to sell the property — but standard procedures for either such a sale

241

9. Equity Financing and Investors

have not developed. Why? Because potential purchasers cannot easily know what they are bidding on. Often it is a pledge or assignment of an interest in a single asset entity that owns the realty involved, and so the lender is one or two levels removed from the source of the cash flow upon which his loan was predicated. If the real estate is in trouble, the entity is in trouble and his cash flow is in double trouble.

Example 18

The senior mortgagee begins foreclosure. If the mortgagee succeeds, what is the mezzanine lender left holding?

Explanation

An equity interest is in an entity with no assets, other than the surplus realized at the foreclosure sale over and above the outstanding amount of the senior note. The lender is subordinated to every secured creditor of the borrower so that any surplus is unlikely to reach him—and in a severe market downturn, it is unlikely that there will be a surplus. If the note for the mezzanine debt was accompanied by a mortgage, so far unrecorded, now is the time to record it. The mezzanine lender will in the meantime be under extreme pressure to realize some portion of the debt through assertion of his UCC rights.

Example 19

The mezzanine lender avoids the senior's foreclosure by assuming the senior note and mortgage. What did the lender purchase?

Explanation

The senior mortgagor's rights, subject to the covenants in that mortgage. Those covenants might include (among others) a due on sale or encumbrance clause, specifically tailored for this situation and restricting further sale of the secured property. This tailoring is likely if the property was to collateralize a bond sold to investors in the secondary market; rating agencies have insisted on this covenant as a means of stabilizing the investments made in the bond.

In the context of a senior mortgagee's foreclosure action, the mezzanine lender will realize that he lacks the protections afforded by the common law

9. Equity Financing and Investors

to mortgagees, even junior mortgagees: the right to record, the right to a receiver, a cause of action in waste, protections on the equity of redemption that the junior would receive, and the fact that the rights of the mortgage holder run with the land, binding subsequent purchasers. Indeed, his transaction was structured specifically to avoid these protections, and the law does not have equivalent protections for him. He is left with an action in debt on the contract to lend against the borrower.

Any slight downturn in real estate market values causes many mezzanine loans to become delinquent. The downturn that occurred in 2007–2010 was not slight: commercial real estate in many markets lost more than 25% of its fair market value in those years.

Securities Acts' Exemptions for Equity Investors

Large partnerships and LLCs must, as discussed in Chapter 5, register with the federal Securities and Exchange Commission (SEC). Real estate project entities generally follow and use the "safe harbor" exemptions provided in §4(a)(2) of the Securities Act of 1933. See 15 U.S.C. §77(d)(a)(2) (exempting from SEC registration requirements "transactions by an issuer not involving any public offering"). Section 4(a)(2) exempt offers to invest are not subject to SEC filing, registration, and disclosure requirements.

Whether an investment offer is part of a public offering requiring registration is a question of fact. It depends on the number of offerees, their relationship to one another and to the issuer, the number of investments offered, and the size and manner of the offering. See SEC Release No. 33-285, 1935 SEC LEXIS 485 (Jan. 24, 1935) and SEC Rule 506(b), Regulation D.

These exemptions are often called "private placement" exemptions. They involve qualifying equity investors as either "accredited investors" or sophisticated but nonaccredited investors. They involve nonpublic investment offerings, unlimited in amount offered in a 12-month period, or offerings (1) not sold to more than thirty five (35) nonaccredited investors (and an unlimited number of accredited investors); (2) made with restrictions on resale; and (3) made without any public or general solicitation or marketing of the investment. See SEC v. Ralston Purina Co., 346 U.S. 119 (1953).

Accredited investors must have at least $1,000,000 in assets and a $200,000 annual income (or $300,000 when considered with a spouse or spousal individual). Nonaccredited investors must (1) have enough knowledge and experience in business and financial matters to be "sophisticated investors," or be able to bear the investment's economic risks, (2) have access to the type of information normally provided in a SEC registration statement, and (3) agree not to resell the investment to the public.

9. Equity Financing and Investors

Developers generally avoid filing SEC documents, particularly forms issued under authority of Rule 506(b), because the filing for an exemption can take as long as the registration process itself. Instead, they generally comply with the requirements for a formal private placement exemption but rely on the fact that the offering is not a public offering of an investment security.

Compliance with federal law for a private placement exemption does not preempt state securities laws and regulations. They must be separately consulted.

CHAPTER 10

The Permanent Mortgage

The documentation of a permanent mortgage loan is much the same as any commercial note and mortgage. There are differences, however, and these differences are often a matter of emphasis and the result of more protracted negotiation than would otherwise be the case. In addition, because these mortgages are usually nonrecourse, leaving foreclosure as the permanent lender's exclusive remedy, negotiators often turn to the assignment of rents and pre-foreclosure remedies.

AN ASSIGNMENT OF RENTS

After the granting clause, a mortgage often will include language such as "together with all . . . rights, appurtenances, and rents." This language is insufficient to assign the right to collect rents, particularly in a lien jurisdiction where applicable law does not permit the mortgagee to have possession or rents before a default or some later date.

When a permanent mortgage secures a project and the mortgagor depends mostly on its rents to repay the debt, or once foreclosure is recognized as a slow and cumbersome remedy, then an assignment of rents in the mortgage (essentially a mortgage on the rents) is one solution. It is often contained in a covenant in the mortgage, but sometimes it appears as a separate document. Attorneys disagree on which is preferable.

With such an assignment, the mortgagee, without going into possession and assuming the liabilities that might entail, may with notice to the tenants

245

10. The Permanent Mortgage

collect the rents and apply them to the outstanding debt. It is intended to prevent a mortgagor short on cash from stiffing the mortgagee, paying late, or milking the property. Its use has been widespread since the 1990s, when mezzanine lending replaced junior liens and senior mortgagees looked for further assurances of repayment.

The assignment needs to be effective "before the ink is dry" on the mortgage. An assignment of rents is a document delivering the right to possess the rents—a present, absolute, and unconditional transfer of the rents, with the mortgagor retaining a license to collect rents until a default. See Freedman's Sav. & Tr. Co. v. Shepherd, 127 U.S. 494, 502-503 (1888) (Harlan, J., approving an absolute assignment), and LaPlace Indiana, LLC v. Lakeland W. Capital XXIV, LLC, 96 N.E.3d 661 (Ind. Ct. App. 2018) (enforcing license revocation upon default). The rationale for the license is in part to make clear to tenants that the mortgagee is not in possession and has not taken over the mortgagor's reversion and has not ousted him for all purposes.[1] To do so would give the junior interests the right to either attorn or vacate, and because most leases will be junior to the mortgagee's lien, the prospect of tenants vacating a property is not a happy one. Further, in many senior mortgage documents, the senior mortgagee often insists that a future, junior mortgagee become, by subordination or otherwise, junior to all lessees. This is another way of assuring itself that a junior mortgagee, either foreclosing or in possession, will not give lessees an opportunity to vacate their premises.

A substantial majority of jurisdictions enforce an assignment of rents according to its terms when it is executed contemporaneously with or is contained in the mortgage. Depending on whether they are lien or title[2]

---

1. If it fails as an assignment for any reason, then it is sometimes treated as a pledge (an offer of property as security for a debt) or a bailment of rents; for both, delivery of possession is necessary to complete it, giving then possession for a limited purpose and not involving a transfer of the mortgagor's title or interest.

2. At common law, a mortgage was a conditional conveyance of the legal title to the mortgagee (the lender). He was vested with the legal title to the property securing the loan, subject, however, to the condition that the lien could not be foreclosed after the loan was repaid. Thus the lender or mortgagee had a defeasible or conditional fee simple absolute: "to the mortgagee so long as the loan is unpaid"—defeasible fee language—or "to the mortgagee, but if the loan is repaid, to the mortgagor"—a fee simple, subject to a condition subsequent. The mortgagee holds the legal estate, and the mortgagor the equitable one. The mortgagee's title was a legal estate subject to an equitable right of redemption—the right to repay the debt before foreclosure. This is the title theory of mortgages. Today it has some lingering effects on the law of mortgages. A second theory of mortgages is the lien theory of mortgages. Under it, the debt is the principal obligation and the mortgage a collateral agreement to secure the debt. The mortgage becomes a lien on the secured property, not a common law estate in it. Both types of mortgages were subject to the equity of redemption. Most states and jurisdictions have adopted the lien theory of mortgages, and the title theory is used in only a few states today. However, the two theories are just that—theories—and when applied to particular documents, the distinctions between them become blurry.

10. The Permanent Mortgage

mortgage jurisdictions, jurisdictions differ on when the assignment is effective between the parties and "perfected" against third parties (such as the tenants). Contemporaneous or early effectiveness is possible in title jurisdictions, but effectiveness is postponed in lien jurisdictions because the lien of the mortgage was neither "choate" nor perfected. For bankruptcy purposes, effectiveness and perfection are achieved when the assignment is filed for record. See 11 U.S.C. §552(b).

Earlier cases held that it was unperfected in lien jurisdictions until rents were actually collected, foreclosure started, or possession taken — but in many jurisdictions those cases have given way to a rule of absolute assignment, meaning that it is in effect a sale of the rents, or the creation of a security lien in them, giving rise to what is in effect a title theory mortgage for them. In some jurisdictions, the assignment is rendered absolute by statute or effective upon recording by the adoption of a provision from the Uniform Assignments of Rents Act, which also makes later activation or enforcement possible by a notice to either the mortgagor or the tenants.

Examples

Example 1

A mortgagee holds a mortgage containing an assignment of rents covenant and secured by the mortgagor's racetrack. Are the gate proceeds subject to the assignment?

Explanation

No. There are many cases holding that the proceeds are not rent, as they do not give the payor the right to occupy any predefined space within the track enclosure or in the stands. Instead, they provide a license related to the activities offered at the track akin to what tickets to the theater or golf course fees provide — a type of entertainment. The Restatement of Property (Third), Mortgages, §4.2 (1997), however, goes further and includes the proceeds of licenses as rents, reasoning that an all-inclusive definition will provide the law with needed certainty.

Example 2

After an assignment is activated or otherwise enforced, the mortgagor refuses to turn the rents over to the mortgagee. The mortgagee sues the mortgagor for waste. In this suit, what result, and why?

247

10. The Permanent Mortgage

Explanation

Judgment for the mortgagee. After activation or other enforcement, it is waste for a mortgagor to withhold or refuse to turn over the rents to the mortgagee. The measure of damages is the rents that would otherwise have been collected but were not applied to the mortgage debt. This is not a suit for waste involving the property itself, so the mortgagee need not show that it is insecure in order to bring the action.

Example 3

Why might a mortgagee prefer that an assignment of rents be in a separate document instead of in a mortgage covenant?

Explanation

A separate document might highlight it for the mortgagor and later persuade a court to enforce it more readily by encouraging the court to construe it as a standalone document not collateral to the mortgage. It can set out notice procedures for the mortgagor and tenants, procedures for paying rent, and even require that the mortgagor execute letters to tenants rerouting the rents to the mortgagee. Finally, it permits separate recording to provide notice to third parties. Following is such a document, given the form of a deed—a form that should provide you with a way to think about what should be included.

ASSIGNMENT OF RENTS AND REVENUES

As consideration for the debt evidenced by the Note executed along with this assignment, _____ (Borrower) absolutely and unconditionally assigns and transfers to _____ (Lender), all rents and revenues of the Property securing that Note, including those rents and revenues now due, past due, or to become due by virtue of any lease or other agreement for the occupancy or use of all or any part of the Property, regardless of to whom they are payable. It is the intention of Borrower and Lender that this assignment be absolute, not an assignment for lien security only. This assignment binds its parties and their successors and assigns and is made for the Property secured by a Mortgage, executed simultaneously with it and the Note and describing the property as follows: _____.

---

10. The Permanent Mortgage

This assignment is made together with the following: Borrower hereby authorizes Lender to collect said rents and revenues and directs each tenant of the Property to pay such rents to Lender, provided that prior to Lender's written notice to Borrower of the latter's breach of any covenant in the Mortgage, Borrower shall collect and receive all rents and revenues of the Property as trustee for Lender and Borrower, applying them to the sums secured by the Mortgage in the order described therein, with the balance, until such breach occurs, to the account of Borrower.

Upon a breach of any covenant in the Mortgage, Lender shall give written notice thereof to Borrower and then, without Lender's having to enter and take possession of the Property in person, by agent or by a court-appointed receiver, Lender shall be entitled to possession of such rents and revenues. This notice shall reference Lender's exercise of its rights under this assignment and its termination of authorization of Borrower's right to collect rents and revenues. Upon delivery of such notice, Lender shall make written demand that each tenant of the Property make such rents and revenues payable to and pay same to Lender.

Borrower warrants and covenants that (1) Borrower has not executed any prior rents and revenues assignment and has not made or done any agreement or act which would prevent Lender from exercising its rights under this assignment, (2) there is no anticipation or prepayment of any rents or revenues for more than one month prior to their due dates and Borrower will not hereafter collect or accept payment of any such rents or revenues more than one month prior to their due dates. Borrower also warrants that all leases pertaining to the Property are in a form previously submitted to the Lender for approval.

Executed this day _____ of _____, 20_____,

_____
Borrower

[Borrower's Acknowledgment attached.]

_____
Lender

Example 4

Would it be prudent to include the following in this document? "Borrower further covenants that Borrower will execute and deliver to Lender such further assignments of rents and revenues of the Property as Lender may from time to time request."

10. The Permanent Mortgage

Explanation

Maybe not, because, depending on applicable state law, this might indicate that the assignment is conditional, not absolute, and so might be treated as an executory contract for Bankruptcy Code purposes.

Example 5

What other procedures might reinforce a lender's concern to have the assignment construed independently of the mortgage?

Explanation

A provision for tenants' paying their rents into a "lockbox," with distributions from the box to the mortgagee/lender for mortgage payments and to the mortgagor/borrower for the residue.

MORTGAGEE IN POSSESSION

Today, when a mortgage document is silent about the mortgagee's right to possession, the mortgagee still has the right to bring a cause of action in waste to prevent the physical deterioration of the secured property. The typical mortgage covenant states that the mortgage "will not permit the property to deteriorate or commit waste" thereon. The mortgagee may, as a result of a judgment in this action, gain the right to take possession of the property to the extent necessary to prevent waste.

A mortgagee in title states is entitled in theory to possession to secure the debt after the mortgage is executed ("before the ink is dry on the mortgage," according to one wag); in other states, this right arises upon default. See 140 Reservoir Ave. v. Sepe Investments, 941 A.2d 805, 811 (R.I. 2007). However, in lien states, it arises only after foreclosure. Because most states

10. The Permanent Mortgage

today regard themselves as lien jurisdictions, mortgage covenants often provide the mortgagee with an express right to have a receiver appointed or to possession upon default. See Taylor v. Brennan, 621 S.W.2d 592 (Tex. 1981), discussed at 60 S.M.U. L. Rev. 579, 590 (2007). The mortgagee's interest in its right to possession is keenest in the earlier years of the typical mortgage when the debt to equity ratio is highest. The Restatement of Property (Third), Mortgages, §4.1 (1997) embraces the lien theory of mortgages on this issue.

No matter when this right arises, however, few mortgagees wish to go into possession. If the property is subject to leases, they have little desire to collect rents or manage the premises. On the other hand, if the business conducted on the premises is one in which the mortgagee has experience, they may be less reluctant on that account. In any event, the mortgagee in possession must exercise reasonable care, being responsible not only for the rents and profits actually collected, but also in some jurisdictions for those that a prudent owner would collect. This prudent owner standard of reasonable care also applies to the expenditure of funds for operation and maintenance of the property. It arises in many jurisdictions out of the duty of a mortgagee in possession to account to the mortgagor; accounting is an equitable action, and as such discretion is accorded a court to whom it is brought. A mortgagee in possession may have to guard against vandalism on the property but at the same time may have to take care that expenses incurred in guarding it are prudent. For purposes of environmental statutes on hazardous wastes, the mortgagee in possession may also incur liability for cleanup costs.

When the property is subject to leases, a mortgagee in possession has no right to disturb senior leases (those executed before his mortgage). Why? Because only the reversion of the landlord was bargained for and mortgaged to the mortgagee as security. So long as a senior tenant pays rent due under the lease and keeps its covenants, that tenant is secure in the possession of the premises for the term of the lease. That tenant could even prepay the rent under the covenants and would be secure from a claim for a second payment by the mortgagee in possession. Absent a special consent provision in the mortgage, the mortgagee in possession would have to evict the mortgagor-landlord and take over the reversion before being able to reach a senior tenant's rent payments.

A junior lessee, on the other hand, will be forced to recognize the mortgagee in possession and must "attorn" in the language of the common law. Thus a mortgagee will be able to take possession of a junior's leased premises unless the lessee attorns, and to relet because, as to junior lessees, the mortgagee bargained for the security of letting the premises in the future. (Until taking possession of the junior lessee's premises, the mortgagee cannot reach the rent.) Thus the mortgagee can agree on a new lease with an existing junior lessee. The easiest agreement on this score will be to relet

10. The Permanent Mortgage

at the existing rent to the junior lessee, but in a rising rental market, the mortgagee may (and probably will) ask for more. Such increased rents are part of the security for which the mortgagee bargained when executing the mortgage.

The mortgagee's rights when taking possession are analogous to those of a foreclosing mortgagee. Thus a junior mortgagee in possession has the right to oust nonattorning junior lessees, but no such right with regard to senior lessees. Against the latter, the most that a mortgage may give is the right to collect the rent due.

Courts have generally shown a reluctance to impute incidents of ownership to mortgagees in possession before they purchase at a completed foreclosure sale. See Case v. St. Mary's Bank, 63 A.3d 1209 (N.H. 2013). No mortgagee becomes the owner of the secured property by taking possession: foreclosure is still necessary. Likewise, courts are quick to imply an agreement permitting the mortgagor to remain on the secured property pending foreclosure, sometimes attempting to categorize the mortgagor as a tenant.

Examples

Example 6

For leased property, will the mortgagee in possession be affected by preexisting landlord tenant law?

Explanation

Yes. New York & Suburban Fed. Sav. & Loan Ass'n v. Sanderman, 392 A.2d 635 (N.J. Super. Ct. Ch. Div. 1978) (as to providing security for tenants). Thus, reforms in ejectment, eviction, and summary possession procedures will apply.

Example 7

A mortgagee erroneously declares a default in the mortgagor's mortgage, and the mortgagee orders the mortgagor to vacate the property. The mortgagor then sends the keys to the property to the mortgagee and vacates. Is the mortgagee now a mortgagee in possession?

10. The Permanent Mortgage

Explanation

No, so long as mortgagees activities are limited to paying utilities, taxes, and insurance premiums, it might be said to be in constructive rather than actual possession. See In re Dupell, 235 Bankr. 783 (Bankr. E.D. Pa. 1999). This sort of legal fiction is particularly likely in a lien state for mortgages where the mortgagee's right to possession is deferred. The mortgagee might take the mortgagor's sending the keys as authority to list the property for sale and as an agreement to cooperate with the listing and selling brokers, but further communication with the mortgagor will be necessary in order to close the sale, so the mortgagee does not yet have the rights and duties of a possessor. See Kubczak v. Chemical Bank & Tr. Co., 575 N.W.2d 745 (Mich. 1998).

RECEIVERSHIPS

A receiver is a court-appointed officer or representative, appointed to preserve, control, and manage property that is the subject of prior agreement or litigation. Thus, if a mortgagee does not wish to go into possession, he has an alternative — a court-appointed receiver. In a market in which real estate values have turned downward (where the mortgagor is, in common parlance, "under water" — that is, owes on a mortgage for an amount higher than the fair market value of the secured property), a receiver is particularly likely. See New Haven Sav. Bank v. General Fin. and Mortgage Co., 386 A.2d 230, 231 (Conn. 1978). For any mortgagee, however, a receiver has several more advantages. First, the receiver can act as a stakeholder when the amounts due are in dispute. Second, a mortgagee in possession has a duty to account, which a receiver does not. Third, the mortgagee in possession is subjected to tort liability from which a receiver can provide a shield. Fourth, the appointment of a receiver does not terminate existing leases on the mortgaged property, because the receiver has duties to both mortgagor and mortgagee and is the agent of both; the distinction between junior and senior leases can be obviated on that account.

The receiver, being a court-appointed person, is typically regarded as a mutual agent, not as (more important) the agent of the mortgagee. Where the income flow from leases is important to the mortgagee, the possibility that a mortgagee's taking possession will be construed as an ouster of the junior lessees is sufficient to make the mortgagee consider a receivership more desirable than taking possession. And, by the same token, many mortgagees will also consider an assignment of rents clause in the mortgage more valuable than a right to a receivership, and for the same reason: that assigning the rents provides one more step before the mortgagee need take possession.

Thus a junior lessee does not have the right to vacate when the receiver takes over. In most courts that have considered the issue, the receiver is permitted to hold junior lessees to their lease obligations.

Receiverships are equitable in nature. This means, among other things, that a court, in considering a petition for the appointment of a receiver, is not bound by the covenants of the mortgage. Standards for the appointment of a receiver vary from state to state, but a petition for appointment will be heard only after a default.

A mortgagee seeking a receiver must establish (1) waste, (2) a default, and (3) insecurity. Insecurity can mean several things. First, that the fair market value of the property is insufficient to cover the outstanding debt—in parlance common when real estate values turn down, the mortgage is "under water." Second, that the remedies otherwise provided are inadequate—that is, that the mortgagor is insolvent so that the legal remedies on the note are inadequate, that the property securing the debt is threatened with loss or destruction, or that waste is being committed on the property. See Union Guardian Trust Co. v. Rau, 238 N.W. 166 (Mich. 1931) (holding that nonpayment of taxes constitutes waste and justifies a receiver's appointment). Waste is perhaps the most commonly required element of proof necessary to justify a receivership. The grounds for a receiver are little different in title and lien jurisdictions, although perhaps the remedy traditionally has been granted more readily in lien theory jurisdictions (which means just about everywhere).

The rights of a mortgagee to have a receiver and take possession of the secured property depend on the distinction between title and lien mortgages. With a title mortgage, the mortgagee has a continuing right to the possession, rents, and profits of the secured property. With a lien mortgage, that right arises only after a default—at the earliest. Some lien jurisdictions put the mortgagee off until after the start of foreclosure.

A junior mortgagee is entitled to a receiver when the senior mortgagee has not yet petitioned for one's appointment, even when the senior mortgage contains a covenant currently entitling the senior to a receiver. That senior covenant is viewed as executory until the senior affirmatively acts upon it. Before the senior does so, the junior can have a receiver collect the rents and, once collected, cannot be forced to disgorge them if the senior later has a receiver appointed, although the senior's receiver will thereafter have a superior claim to receive the rents and in effect trump the junior receiver's right.

Receivers are often appointed *ex parte*—on the sworn affidavit of the mortgagee. Such procedures have been challenged on due process grounds, but were upheld as constitutional in Friedman v. Gerax Realty, 420 N.Y.S.2d 247 (N.Y. App. Div. 1979), so long as it is judicially supervised with an opportunity for a prompt hearing on the grounds for appointment.

10. The Permanent Mortgage

Examples

Example 8

A developer executes a brief but enforceable mortgage in favor of Big Bank (BB). The security for the mortgage is a large office building. The developer also executes a junior mortgage on the same property in favor of Local Bank (LB). In a title jurisdiction, is BB entitled to the rents if the developer/mortgagor is not in default on the repayment of the mortgage loan?

Explanation

Yes. BB is entitled to a receiver or to possession upon a showing of good cause (either waste, default, or lender insecurity) upon the execution of the mortgage, and of course he is entitled to file a petition later, at the time of a default in repayment.

Example 9

Would your answer in the prior Example be the same in a lien jurisdiction? If so, how should BB react to the difference?

Explanation

The answer would be different. In a lien jurisdiction, where the date on which BB is entitled to go into possession or to petition for the appointment of a receiver is either (1) the date of default, (2) the date of filing for foreclosure, (3) the date of the decree, or (4) the date on which the decree is confirmed. In a lien state, the mortgagee derives the right to the rents from the right to enforce the lien upon default. At the time of default, he is subrogated to the mortgagor's right to collect the rents — stepping into the mortgagor's shoes to do so. In reacting to the difference, BB should insist on an express covenant assigning the rents to him on default. Such a clause does not give the mortgagee a right to possession, and an entry to collect the rents may not be made unless a demand for them is first made of the landlord-mortgagor. Such a clause is one of the covenants distinguishing a commercial mortgage from a residential one. In a lien state, the courts sometimes treat such a covenant as an executory contract, executed upon

255

10. The Permanent Mortgage

default. Its subject is a lien on the rents, postponed until default and foreclosure is commenced.

Example 10

Consider the Explanation to the prior Example. Even if BB is entitled to go into possession, would it want to? What if the leases for the offices in the building were made during the construction lease-up period and prior to the execution of BB's mortgage? Would that affect your answer?

Explanation

No. BB may not want to run the risks associated with being a mortgagee in possession, particularly if going into possession would constitute an ouster of existing lessees. Here, however, senior lessees cannot be disturbed. Once in possession, the mortgagee is held to the standard of care of a prudent owner. This standard applies to profits ME should make and expenses ME might reasonably incur.

Example 11

In the Examples in this set, will LB's remedies differ from BB's?

Explanation

A junior mortgagee like LB may have a broader right to a receiver than BB does. Why? LB is more likely to be able to show insecurity. LB's right to a receiver is independent of BB's. It can be exercised even though BB has not petitioned for a receiver. At the same time, once LB's receiver is in possession, he cannot just devote the rent roll just to repayment of LB's debt. Why? Because if he does not first devote the rent receipts to (say) the payment of real estate taxes, a resulting tax lien might trump BB's lien or otherwise render BB insecure; then BB might itself petition for its own receiver. Likewise, if LB's receiver does not reasonably repair and maintain the office building, he may be liable in waste.

256

10. The Permanent Mortgage

Example 12

Is the authority of a receiver, pending foreclosure, generally broader or narrower in a lien jurisdiction than it is in a title jurisdiction?

Explanation

Broader. When the mortgagee files a foreclosure action, equity, regarding as done what should be done, will give the receiver broader powers while the action is pursued diligently and in good faith. Equity's doctrine of equitable conversion is at work here, regarding the appointment of a receiver as a mechanism for giving the a mortgagee what he will be entitled to upon the completion of foreclosure — repayment of the debt; and the same can be said of the other pre-foreclosure remedies discussed in this chapter — a mortgagee's taking possession and an assignment of rents.

Example 13

If during foreclosure either BB or LB has a receiver appointed, how long does the receivership last?

Explanation

Until the period of statutory redemption ends, or until any decree in foreclosure is absolute.

Example 14

If LB petitions for a receiver to hold the office building, and the building generates more proceeds than necessary to satisfy LB's debt, is BB entitled to the surplus? If not, to whom does the surplus go?

Explanation

No. BB would get more than its original bargain if such were the case. The surplus goes to the mortgagor. See Sullivan v. Rosson, 119 N.E. 405, 4 A.L.R. 1400 (N.Y. 1918). The junior mortgagee should be rewarded for its diligence, but not given a windfall.

Example 15

If after the mortgagor's default in mortgage payments, the mortgagor and the senior and junior mortgagees work out an agreement on the allocation of future mortgage repayments, should their title insurers be a party to the agreement?

Explanation

Yes, when each holds a title policy, the agreement affects the lien priority of each. In a loan policy, that priority is the primary matter insured against.

Example 16

If the mortgagor is using one of the offices in the building for use by its building manager when the mortgage was given, does the mortgagor have to surrender that office to a receiver?

Explanation

No. Even though mortgagor's partial possession of the secured property decreases the security offered the mortgagee for the debt, a mortgagee who takes the security on that basis is entitled to no more security than was bargained for. See Holmes v. Gravenhorst, 188 N.E. 285 (N.Y. 1933) (holding that the mortgagor-occupant need not pay a reasonable rent to a receiver). Furthermore, even if the occupying mortgagor agrees to pay rent to any receiver appointed under the mortgage covenants, that agreement may not

10. The Permanent Mortgage

authorize the mortgagor's eviction for nonpayment of the rent—eviction must await foreclosure. Id. And see Carlin Trading Co. v. Bennett, 264 N.Y.S.2d 43 (N.Y. App. Div. 1965), noted in 17 Syracuse L. Rev. 774 (1966).

Following is a covenant that might be included in a mortgage governing the mortgagee's right to a receiver.

> Upon Borrower's breach of any covenant in this Mortgage or Borrower's breach of any material covenant of Borrower as lessor under any lease, Lender shall be entitled to the appointment of a receiver for the Property, without further notice to Borrower. This appointment shall be by agent or court-appointed receiver and may be made regardless of the adequacy of Lender's security or waste of the Property. Upon appointment, the receiver or agent shall enter and take control of the Property in order to operate and maintain it and shall have the right to cancel, modify, or execute leases and occupancy and use agreements for the Property, collect all its rents and revenues, enforce or carry out any provision of any lease, repair the Property, and maintain, terminate, or execute agreements providing for its management or maintenance, all on such terms and provisions as are best to protect the security of this Mortgage. Borrower hereby expressly consents to such receiver or agent's appointment. The receiver or agent shall be entitled to a reasonable fee for so managing the Property.

Example 17

When, as in this covenant, the receiver is given "the right to . . . enforce or carry out any provision of any lease," is the mortgagee liable as a landlord and the receiver's principal, for any duties imposed under applicable state landlord tenant law?

Explanation

Yes. So it might be wise to add to the foregoing: "Lender shall not be liable to perform or discharge any obligation to be performed or discharged by Borrower under said leases of the Property and Borrower shall indemnify Lender in the event Lender, its agent, or receiver, performs or discharges such obligations."

LOAN PARTICIPATIONS

The permanent lender may seek other lenders to help it fund its loan. Once a lender decides to enter into a participation, it should do so before the

10. The Permanent Mortgage

closing and funding of the loan. Selling parts of the loan shares of the risk of default, raises capital to meet its loan closing and funding commitments, and shares the benefits of the long-term investment. If the loan is particularly large, regulatory requirements may require sharing the risk of default with third-party participants. This also puts dispassionate eyes on the underwriting of a loan. Loan participants are in effect partial assignees of a funding lender's status as a mortgagee.

The nature of the assignment is the subject of an agreement called the participation agreement. It is drawn up between the original lender, often called the lead lender, and the participating lenders. The lead lender is often classified as either (1) an assignor of an interest in the mortgage lien itself—the most common characterization—or as (2) the agent of the rest of the participants, (3) a debtor of the participants (who are its creditors), (4) a joint venturer for the purpose of making the loan, or (5) a trustee. The plethora of descriptions gives some idea of the complexity of the relationship established. Each classification not chosen should be negated in the agreement. This is particularly true when the lead lender is identified as the "trustee" or as "holding the note and mortgage in trust for participants." Without more, many courts are unlikely infer that the lead is a fiduciary of the participants. See Encore Bank v. Bank of Am., NA, 918 F. Supp. 2d 633 (S.D. Tex. 2013).

To distinguish a true participation from a loan to the lead lender, the transaction should involve (1) an advance of money by the participants to the lead lender, (2) a participant's right to repayment arising only when the lead lender is paid, and (3) only the lead lender having recourse against the borrower. On the other hand, when the lead lender guarantees repayment, the participation lasts for a shorter or longer time than the underlying loan, has different payment arrangements, or a different interest rate, these three factors indicate that the transaction is something other than a participation— and is perhaps a loan. See Rothenberg v. Oak Rock Fin., LLC, 2015 U.S. Dist. LEXIS 44032, **27-28 (E.D. N.Y., Mar. 31, 2015).

In a true participation, the lead lender continues to hold the note and the mortgage securing the project property. See S. Pac. Thrift & Loan Ass'n v. Sav. Ass'n Mortgage Co., 82 Cal. Rptr. 2d 874 (Cal. Ct. App. 1999).

Absent an agreement otherwise, buying a loan participation is the purchase and sale of an undivided interest in the note itself—but not an interest in the lien, with the consequent right to enforce the lien should that become necessary. Hence, for this purpose, the loan participant is described as an assignee. The alternative is describing the participant as one with the right to receive mortgage payments passed along by the lead lender; this description creates contract remedies in the participant but leaves the right to deal with the mortgagor exclusively with the lead lender. The legal title to the lien is retained by the lead lender, and the latter has the only recorded interest in the secured real property. Because it is rights in the note that are assigned, participation agreements are not customarily recorded.

10. The Permanent Mortgage

Absent an agreement otherwise, the participants and the lead lender are presumed to share in the proceeds of the loan on a pro rata basis. When the proceeds of the loan are insufficient to repay each participant its agreed share, each participant and the lead again share what proceeds are the available on a pro rata basis. This is the majority rule. (A minority rule, used in a few states, provides that the order of assignment controls: first to participate, first in right.)

Two exceptions to the pro rata rule arise. The first occurs when the lead lender provides a guaranty of repayment to all participants; then only the participants share pro rata, before the lead is repaid. Thus, participants go first, pro rata, followed by the lead lender. Two computational variations on this first exception exist: The pro rata computation preceding distribution does, or does not, include the lead's share. The second exception occurs when the participations mature at different times. Then, the order of maturity determines the priority of each participant's pro rata distribution.

The participation agreement will normally require the lead lender to share all information provided by the mortgagor with the participants, but precludes the latter from dealing directly with the mortgagor. Sometimes the mortgagor is required to send information to the participants, who nonetheless can only communicate back through the lead.

The lead lender generally warrants ownership of the loan, regulatory compliance of the loan, and the insured status of the loan and the property. Most loans are assigned on a nonrecourse basis, except as to any specific warranties given by the lead lender in the participation agreement. Further assignment of the loan participation is restricted, as is further modification in the loan documents, without the approval of (respectively) the lead and the participants. See Penthouse Ltd. v. Dominion Federal Sav. & Loan Ass'n, 665 F. Supp. 301 (S.D.N.Y. 1987), rev'd, 855 F.2d 963 (2d Cir. 1988), cert. denied, 490 U.S. 1005 (1989) (where the assignment of a participation provoked litigation when the deal collapsed).

Courts are reluctant to find a fiduciary duty owed by the lead lender to the participants. The participation agreement is sometimes said to control this matter, and a fiduciary duty will not be inferred from an otherwise silent agreement. See First Citizens Fed. Sav. & Loan Ass'. v. Worthen Bank & Tr. Co., 919 F.2d 510 (9th Cir. 1990). Seldom are agreements silent, however. Most will expressly negate such duties and any warranties concerning the loan (except those warranties previously mentioned).

The primary duty of the lead lender is to continue to service and administer the loan, including the collection of payments, interest, and fees, the maintenance of insurance, the payment of taxes, the review of financial information, and the oversight of the physical condition of the insured property. From the right to administer the loan, one court has found an implied right to modify its terms or renew it. See Baybank v. Vermont Nat'l Bank, 118 F.3d 30 (1st Cir. 1997). However, most courts considering the

261

10. The Permanent Mortgage

issue have not found that the lead has any further fiduciary duties to participants. See Den Norske Bank v. First Nat'l Bank of Boston, 75 F.3d 49 (1st Cir. 1996). For this continuing administration the lead receives a fee and, absent agreement otherwise, has the right to retain interest on any escrowed funds. In the normal course of things, this arrangement is little problem for the participant, but the participant's right upon the mortgagor's default is critical and often is the subject of negotiations between the lead and the participants. If the lead lender is severely restricted in its rights in dealing with the mortgagor, the latter will not be able to efficiently work out any default. For example, the right of the lead lender to draft and accept a deed in lieu of foreclosure is sometimes unclear in these agreements. Other potential conflicts between the lead and participants might involve waivers of the terms of loan documents, the lead's right to exercise pre-foreclosure remedies, the lead's right to buy out participants, and, of course, express limitations on the lead's liability to them.

Examples

Example 18

As counsel for a lead lender, how would you seek in the participation agreement to limit potential litigation problems?

Explanation

You might seek to spell out that: (1) the lead lender undertakes only the duties express in the agreement, making it liable only for willful misconduct and gross negligence; (2) when the lead lender relies in good faith on the judgment of consultants and experts, it has no duty to verify their opinions and is not responsible for any consequential damages arising from its reliance; (3) when a majority of the participants concur in a matter presented to them, the lead lender is completely exculpated from liability. The overall aim of the lead lender is to deal with the borrower as it would with its own borrower, leaving to the independent underwriting process of the participants the business and credit risks of the loan. Finally, the right to resign as lead lender might be expressly reserved.

Example 19

Your client, a lender proposing to "participate" a large loan, asks you whether it, as the lead lender, should be given the power to accept a deed-in-lieu of foreclosure. What is your advice on this matter?

262

10. The Permanent Mortgage

Explanation

Because accepting a deed-in-lieu will not wipe out junior liens as would a foreclosure, the lead lender should not accept such a deed without a title search and insurance assigning its mortgage lien first priority at the time the deed is delivered. If the participation agreement is unclear, the lead lender should have the permission of the participants before accepting such a deed: it brings with it ownership obligations that the participants did not expect.

Example 20

A permanent lender's commitment letter proposes that a permanent loan be "participated" to five other lenders before the loan in closed and funded. The lead lender has assembled four, creditworthy participants. Should the closing and funding proceed?

Explanation

No. Such a condition on closing is customary enough that the loan should not be closed without a modification in the loan commitment letter. Why? Once the four participants now underwriting the loan find out about the discrepancy, litigation may follow. Here the number of participants affects the risk each bears.

263

Leasing the Project

CHAPTER 11

This chapter explores topics involved in leasing a developer's project once it nears completion or is built. Commercial leases are long and complex documents. They require specialized knowledge and drafting skills. For the developer's attorney who has just shepherded a project through construction, they also require a shift in professional focus. Heretofore the focus have been on avoiding the risks inherent in construction; now the focus shifts to the income stream that leasing the project will generate, and in particular, to shifting the operating costs of the project to its lessees (hereafter tenants), stabilizing the rent flow over time so that it will support both the mortgage debt required to service the project's permanent mortgage, the developer's operating costs for repairs, renovation, and maintenance, as well as the developer's promised return to the equity investors and himself.

Experienced real estate brokers specializing in commercial premises will have knowledge of the law affecting commercial leases. They will market the project to attract prospective tenants. The developer's attorney has two functions, acting (1) sometimes as a back-up in negotiations over a lease, reviewing the broker's work, and (2) sometimes marketing and directly negotiating a lease.[1]

---

1. Guidance in drafting a commercial lease is available and excellent. See John B. Wood & Alan M. DiSciullo, Negotiating and Drafting Office Leases (Law Journal Press, 2007); Milton R. Friedman, Friedman on Leases (the late Patrick A. Randolph, Jr., Ed., 5th ed., 2005); and Mark A. Senn, Commercial Real Estate Leases: Preparation, Negotiation, and Forms (Aspen Publishers, 4th ed., 2011). All are excellent. The Wood treatise tends to be landlord friendly. The Randolph treatise is less so. The Senn treatise is a practical one. Taken together, all three should be consulted for a comprehensive approach to particular provisions of a lease.

265

11. Leasing the Project

Either way, the attorney must keep in mind that the project should be leased (1) at or above market rents, (2) as soon as possible, and (3) with an eye on the permanent lender, equity investors, and sales into the secondary mortgage market for mortgages similar to the developer's. The attorney's approach will have an impact both on the early success of the project and its longer term stability. No lease should be so complex that the business purpose underlying it is lost.

This chapter deals primarily with two types of commercial leases — the shopping center and the office building lease. Commercial leases of either type might deal with single tenant or multi-tenants projects.[2] Both retail and office leases are different in many ways from residential leases. Unlike residential leases, commercial leases in these settings tend to be negotiated by attorneys and brokers for both landlords and tenants; they also involve more money and have longer terms than residential leases. The typical office lease has a five-year term, often with a right to renew.

Commercial tenants bring their own operating budgets to these lease negotiations. They want the operating costs of their businesses to stay within their present and projected budgets over the term of the lease. Overall, they want to tailor the premises to the use they expect it to have and have the rents stable and predictable over the term of the lease. These objectives are less constraints than they are reasons many businesses want to lease rather than buy real estate. Business persons want to run their businesses, not operate those businesses on real estate for which they are primarily responsible. Similarly, they want their employees to grow the business, and not focus on the needs of the premises where that business is located. Its location need only be adaptable enough as the business grows or changes focus.

Commercial leases are best seen as a contract, but many reforms in the residential landlord-tenant relationship using contract law have not been applied to commercial leases. For example, in the residential context, an implied term of the lease is the implied warranty of habitability (IWH): Many of its protections do not apply in the commercial context. See Knapp v. Simmons, 345 N.W.2d 118 (Iowa 1984); Muro v. Superior Ct., 229 Cal. Rptr. 3d 383 (Cal. Ct. App. 1986); Restatement (Second) of Property §5.1, at 176 (Reporter's Note). Only a few jurisdictions have an IWH for commercial leases. See Davidow v. Inwood North Professional Group — Phase I, 747 S.W.2d 373 (Tex. 1988) (finding an implied warranty of fitness for a particular use by a built-to-suit commercial landlord).

---

2. A third type of commercial lease (not dealt with in this chapter) is the warehouse or industrial lease. The more intense uses made by tenants here require the attorney to deal with environmental, health, and safety, and "externalities" issues such as noise, pollution, and other issues affecting nearby parcels and neighborhoods. A law student will most likely encounter these issues in courses on environmental law.

11. Leasing the Project

Other areas of the law of commercial leases are subject to a split in the authorities. Whether the landlord has a duty to re-let after the tenant abandons the premises, whether the landlord's duty to mitigate a tenant's damages can be waived by the tenant, and whether the acts of one tenant give rise to the constructive eviction of another — these three issues are unsettled in many jurisdictions. See Allen v. Harkness Stone Co., Inc., 609 S.E.2d 647 (Ga. Ct. App. 2005).

SHOPPING CENTERS

The American shopping center is a unique form of land development that dates from the early 20th century. Some of the early ones, in the 1930s and 1940s, were built to serve as downtowns for established suburbs or to serve communities yet unbuilt. All along, so-called strip centers were built beside suburban roads and highways. In the 1950s, the first enclosed malls were built. As they grew larger, they often required both public and private financing. The largest today is the Mall of America, in Bloomington, Minnesota, with 9.5 million square feet (the equivalent of 78 football fields).

OFFICE BUILDINGS

The steel-skeleton office building, first developed in the last decades of the 19th century, then replaced freestanding stone and masonry structures, making the centralization of economic activity possible in central business districts of our cities. Such a building, at its most visible and dramatic, is a skyscraper. Electric lights, elevators, and telephones made such structures livable.

As with shopping centers, the value of commercial office buildings to developers, owners, and mortgage lenders is generated by cash flow — the rents and profits — generated by tenants. Whether the lease is executed for shopping center or office building premises, it is the product of three perspectives: that of the landlord, the tenant, and the mortgage lender who is financing that center or building. The lease must be "financeable." The premises have little value to lenders other than as the source of the cash flow used to repay the mortgage loan. Thus, most commercial lenders take an intense interest in the leases their mortgagors execute. A mortgagor thus wants flexibility to enter into whatever lease he wants, while the lender wants a cash flow that is stable, predictable, and within the guidelines of its underwriting practices. Between the goals of flexibility and financeability lie the compromises that the landlord and tenant reach. For each lease to

267

11. Leasing the Project

become a stable source of cash, it must be enforceable, and if upon a default in repayment the lender becomes (after foreclosure) a successor landlord, he will then ask which provisions of the lease will apply to him.

The Parties to the Lease

Identifying the parties is not just a matter of naming them. One or both is likely to be a special purpose entity (SPE), typically formed as a limited liability company (LLC) and in the landlord's best case, a creditworthy corporation. Inserting "XYZ LLC" in the lease's granting clause shouldn't suffice: the state in which the entity is registered or formed should be added. Accuracy in this respect enables the landlord, for example, to check the tenant entity's good standing and ability to do business in both the jurisdiction of formation and the jurisdiction in which the premises are located. Over the term of the lease, this accuracy will affect the landlord's ability to enforce the lease's provisions — and vice versa, affecting the tenant's ability as well.

Accuracy of name is also a prerequisite for checking the credit of the tenant. If that is found wanting, then the lender will likely insist on the lease naming a guarantor of the tenant — typically a high net worth individual or entity presenting financial statements once and on an ongoing basis satisfactory to the landlord — and again, the name, address, and affiliation to the tenant, and reference to a guaranty agreement incorporated by reference and attached to the lease. The guaranty should, from the landlord's perspective be for both payment of rent and performance of the tenant's obligations under the lease.

At this point, the guarantor will push back, seeking a cap on the guarantee during the term or the lease or during any particular period during the leasehold term. The guarantor may also seek to restrict the scope of the guaranty to the monetary obligations of the tenant. The landlord's actions against the guarantor must be stable and predictable over the leasehold term: they (1) should not affect the lease's continuing validity, (2) may be pursued both before and after the landlord takes action against the tenant, and (3) are not affected by any subsequent lease amendment or modification.

The Premises

The space that the tenant is to lease and occupy is, in the granting clause of the typical lease, called "the premises." A lease is the grant of an exclusive right to use the premises for a term. In short, it is an exclusive right of

11. Leasing the Project

possession. It can be described, in a multi-tenant building, as (for instance) "Suite 201" or as "Suite 201 as referenced on the attached floor plan." When attached to the lease as an exhibit referenced in it, the floor plan alone might suffice. If the premises are in a multi-tenant building, reference to the common areas of the building should also be identified—the lobby, elevator space, maintenance rooms, restrooms, rooftop garden, etc. Likewise, retail space can be similarly described and when located in a shopping center, a floor plan of the center along with inventory and parking spaces, serves the same purpose—that is, of specifically describing the premises that are the subject of the lease.

The rights to use common areas are nonexclusive rights—that is, rights shared with other tenants—and located either in the building or on its site. Common areas like the entry lobby are of particular concern to the landlord in a multi-tenant building.

Examples

Example 1

Your client reports that he has leased "20,000 square feet in the Acme Building." Are the premises located with reasonable certainty?

Explanation

No. See Sovran Bank, NA v. Creative Industries, Inc. 425 S.E.2d 504 (Va. 1993). Where in the building are the 20,000 square feet? The Statute of Frauds requires a precise location within the building. See Millennium Park Joint Ventures, LLC v. Houlihan, 948 N.E.2d 1 (Ill. 2010). And where is the building?

Example 2

What if the premises are described with certainty up to the end when the phrase, "being 10,000 square feet, more or less," is used. Is a lease using these phrase enforceable?

269

11. **Leasing the Project**

Explanation

Yes. It is. It renders the lease description neither vague and indefinite or unenforceable under the Statute of Frauds. See Hart v. Vermont Inv. LP, 667 A.2d 578 (D.C. 1995). When the phrase is used, however, a court is likely to permit a substantial shortage in square footage and still enforce the lease. For instance, the *Hart* opinion permitted a 20% shortfall. See Wohl v. Owen, 580 N.Y.S.2d 854 (N.Y. Civ. Ct. 1992). Thus the phrase "more or less" or the word "approximately," allocates the risk of a shortfall on the tenant.

Example 3

You propose that a commercial office lease begin: "In consideration of Tenant's agreement to pay rent, and subject to the provisions, terms, covenants, and conditions in this Lease, Landlord hereby leases to Tenant and Tenant hereby hires and leases from Landlord, those Premises described in section ____ of this lease." Please comment on this opening language.

Explanation

(1) Should a reference to rent appear in the premises? It establishes that the lease is given for consideration, and is thus a contract. Assuming that another section of the lease sets out the first year's annual base rent and any subsequent annual modifications to it, it might be better to cross-reference the rental provisions of the lease expressly, in order to satisfy the Statute of Frauds (requiring that the price, the parties, and the property—or Premises—be in writing). The language here might make the tenant think that the lease's right of exclusive possession and the rent are dependent covenants. This thinking is a "luxury" because the landlord will attempt in the lease's other provisions, expressly to deny this dependency. The language is traditional, but could be more explicit.

(2) How about the phrase "provisions, terms, covenants, and conditions"? Wouldn't one word, provisions, do as well? Yes, it would, since a string of terms raises interpretative issues. Does the first or the last word used in the phrase encompass the others? Who's to say? And as you will recall from first year property, "covenants" can be either personal or real, and "conditions" may either be precedent or subsequent. Since detailed cross-referencing to other sections of the lease would be prolix, "provisions" will suffice at this point.

(3) What about the verbs the parties are using to transfer and receive the lease? That the landlord "leases" his interest to the tenant denotes that the tenant receives an exclusive right to use and possess the premises and that the lease is a conveyance of that right. That the tenant, for its part, "hires" the

11. Leasing the Project

premises means that the tenant has a temporary right to use and possess the premises for compensation; the word also refers to the lease as personal property, as in a bailment of the premises. Words of transfer and conveyance thus have common law meanings that confuse the nature of the lease: better to use one verb alone and provide that the landlord "leases" and so does the tenant.

Example 4

The language proposed in the prior Example might continue: "***The Premises described in section _____ of this lease are substantially as shown cross-hatched on the attached Exhibit A, which Exhibit A is made a part of this lease. These premises are located on the <u>third</u> floor of the building named in the Exhibit A, in the City of ____, County of _____, and State of _____, on the land described on Exhibit B.

Explanation

As you will recall, a contract is vague and unenforceable if not adequately describing the premises. Since the lease will likely have a term longer than a year, the Statute of Frauds requires that its description be in writing (along with the parties and the price). The elements needed to locate the Premises are falling into place with this language. A mailing address for the building, the office suite number in the building, and the certification of the surveyor providing Exhibits A and B might be added. If the land on which the building is located is not the property of the landlord, the ground lease should be referenced as well: the legal as well as the physical location of the lease should be identified.

Example 5

Your client, a prospective tenant in a multi-story office building, notices that the ceiling in the space it proposes to rent, is a drop ceiling—one below the structural ceiling of the building. Knowing this, what advice might you give?

Explanation

You might advise that your client doesn't want to assume liability for what it cannot see and readily inspect—any asbestos, code violating wiring, etc.

271

11. Leasing the Project

Rent and Square Footage

As the prior section demonstrates, any commercial lease will have a complex method for describing the premises,[3] often beginning with a point on a vertical plane (for an office building), and continuing (or starting, for a one-tier shopping center) along a horizontal plane. Further description is often the square footage shown cross-hatched on a floor plan or sketch for the office building or center. The square footage is important, because rent is typically charged on a square-foot basis, and a tenant searching for premises on competing properties will want to compare square foot charges. Square footage is, however, a complex term. It may be *carpetable*, in which case you can walk on it; *useable*, that is, including somewhat more area than you can carpet; and *allocated*, which means that a portion of the utility areas serving the useable area, plus a portion of the lobby and common areas such as hallways, have been added on a pro rata basis. All told (and added up), the rentable area is often what's carpetable, useable, and allocated to particular premises. See Hart v. Vermont Invest. LP, 667 A.2d 578 (D.C. 1995) (holding that the risk that the square footage was less than what was actually leased by a factor of 14% was on the commercial tenant).

Not only will the rentable area's square footage be a basis for calculating the rent, it will also be used to apportion common area maintenance charges, building services, and other fees passed along to tenants in a so-called net lease. Thus, a "triple net lease" in an office building is typically meant to refer to a landlord's ability to pass through real estate taxes, utilities, and insurance costs to tenants.

Lenders want the square footage computed as of the execution of the lease and not changeable thereafter. They also want the totality of leases in a multitenanted building to encumber the totality of the coverage of their mortgage lien on the building.

Examples

Example 6

Your client reports that he has just leased "10,000 rentable sq. ft." using a triple net lease for his medical office. Can he use that number to order carpets for the office?

---

3. Nationwide, the most used standards for describing the premises of a commercial lease are those of the Building Owners and Managers Ass'n (BOMA), Standard Method for Measuring Floor Area in Office Buildings, variously issued. The 1996 standards are generally considered to be the most tenant-friendly. There are also BOMA standards for other types of properties, e.g., for retail store areas. In contrast to BOMA's standard approach, New York City and Washington, D.C., have their own standards. In N.Y.C., the Real Estate Board of New York (REBNY) promulgates standards emphasizing the rentable square footage as the most useful to prospective tenants. In D.C., the Greater Washington Commercial Association of Realtors likewise has its own standards.

272

11. Leasing the Project

Explanation

No, probably not without further investigation. As discussed previously, leases customarily use several terms in descriptions of the premises' square footage. *Rentable square footage* doesn't fluctuate in its definition lease to lease in an office building, but it gathers dust. In some leases, the comparable term in some leases might be *gross square footage*. It is the square footage that is measured by penetrating any special vertical or horizontal surfacing materials, such a paneling, furring strips, or carpeting. (The square footage including such penetrations is known as the "finished surface.") It makes allowances for "major vertical penetrations,"[4] e.g., stairs, vertical ducts, pipe and elevator shafts, deducting them from the calculation. It is the square footage area on which the tenant's rent is calculated. Thus when the 10,000 square feet is part of a 100,000 square foot building, tenant has rented 10% of it. That percentage — 10% of the square footage in the common areas in the building — is generally included in the rentable square footage chargeable to the tenant.

What the client needs to know is the *useable square footage* of his office space — in some leases, the comparable term might be *net square footage*. It is the occupiable area. However, useable does mean useful; that depends on the placement of furniture, partitions, windows, and building columns and supports in the tenant's premises. Thus if a tenant wants 10,000 square feet of usable area, it may have to rent 12,000 square feet of rentable area. The difference is known the "load factor" or "loss factor."[5] A prospective tenant may negotiate to exclude major "loss factors" such as the atrium of a building. The useable square footage will fluctuate, depending on the location of the premises within the building. The useable square footage might also change when the premises are renovated.

From building to building, the definitions of all these terms might differ, although the Building Owners and Managers Association (BOMA)[6] has pioneered the terms *rentable square footage* and *useable square footage*. These two

---

4. However, "major vertical penetrations" does not include structural columns or openings for electrical or other utility lines.

5. The loss factor is computed as a percentage derived from a fraction, the numerator of which is the square footage area that results from subtracting the useable area from the rentable area, over the denominator, the rentable area.

6. BOMA is located in Washington, D.C. See http://www.boma.org. Various iterations of its measurement standards have been promulgated by this group. Its "ANSI/BOMA Z65.1 1996 Standard" is generally reported to be the most tenant-friendly. The term sheet for a lease and the lease itself should identify the year the applicable BOMA standards were promulgated. BOMA also classifies office buildings: a Class A building has a downtown, central business district location, and competes for prime tenants, a Class B building brings an average rent for the area, and a Class C building bring a below average rent. Thus the premises should not be described as "being in a Class A building" unless a reference to a BOMA standard is intended.

273

11. Leasing the Project

terms are the predominant standard ones used in both the United States and Canada.

All things considered, however, the useable square footage of the premises is only a very rough guide. Your tenant client should take an old fashioned or laser measuring tape and do his own square footage computation when ordering carpet and computing the *carpetable square footage*. (And, in a lease for premises in a just constructed building based on lease-up sales plans, the measurement should be taken twice, at the execution of the lease and after construction.) The tenant's taking its own measurement of the square footage of the premises should be considered reasonable due diligence: after all, it's easily done, within the tenant's control, and prevents later disputes over any misrepresentation.

Example 7

Landlord (LL) and tenant (T) execute a triple net lease describing the taxes, utility charges, and insurance costs apportioned and passed through to, and to be paid by T as "additional rent." Why are these payments described this way?

Explanation

Such a description is useful to LL because, upon T's default in payment, the LL may quickly and cheaply recover the payments in a summary possession action. Such an action may only be brought to recover the rent due the landlord at the time the action is brought. In this type of action, the landlord recovers possession of the tenant's premises and back rent, but may not recover consequential, expectation, or other types of damages — computing such damages requires fact finding and so must await a suit in ejectment and a full-blown trial. In a summary possession action, on the other hand, all the landlord need allege is a lease, a default, and the right to possession. Thus, the greater the number of T's monetary obligations under the lease described as rent, the greater the recovery in summary possession.

Example 8

Landlord (LL) and tenant (T) execute a triple net lease describing common area maintenance charges as "additional rent" and providing that "the premises shall be returned at the end of the lease in good order and condition." Relying on these two provisions of the lease, LL then charges T

274

11. Leasing the Project

a portion of the costs of resurfacing the building's parking lot. Are these charges legitimate?

Explanation

No. When the "premises" are shown as a square footage cross-hatched on a floor plan, premises refers to interior space of the building, and not to its surrounding land and appurtenances. See South Road Assocs., LLC v. Internat'l Business Machines Corp., 826 N.E.2d 806 (N.Y. 2005).

Example 9

When the square footage of the lease is described with certainty up to the end and there the words, "the square footage is deemed to be 10,000 sq. ft." What is the impact of these words when also used in the rent covenant of the lease?

Explanation

Again, this phrasing is useful for landlords. The landlord might argue that he needs to use this phrasing because the "deemed" square footage is the basis for computing the tenant's rent in order to make the rental profitable for him. Thus the phrase "deemed to be" might mean "as if" the square footage was something different from what it actually is. A sophisticated tenant might be taken to know this. See Wohl v. Owen, 580 N.Y.S.2d 854 (N.Y. Civ. Ct. 1992). Such phrasing also is likely to mean that the landlord cannot be taken to have represented or warranted that the square footage is as stated. See S. R. Leon Co., Inc. v. Towers, 599 N.Y.S.2d 53 (N.Y. App. Div. 1993).

Example 10

You discover that, for a multi-lease office building, the triple-net lease your client is about to sign does not include the landlord's representation and warranty that it has used the same definition of rentable and useable square footage in all other tenant's leases. Why might such a warranty be important?

275

11. Leasing the Project

Explanation

This warranty is important where common area maintenance (CAM) charges are levied on and passed through to tenants. Tenants with such leases pay for every square foot of a building and the premises of each tenant are allocated a percentage share of the common areas. Thus the rental of 10,000 square feet is "grossed up" by the percentage of the rentable square footage leased. If this gross up is more than that percentage, the landlord has an opportunity to recover more than the maintenance expenses for the building's common areas. Typically, the gross up is more than the percentage leased, since the building's operating expenses include more than just the expenses of maintaining the common areas. Thus square footage measurement standards must be similar for all tenants in a multi-tenanted, triple-net leased building; this is why BOMA's objective standards are needed and used.

The landlord's warranty is also just as important for other pass through charges in a triple-net lease — for the allocation of real estate property taxes to individual tenants.

This warranty is just as important in retail leases as it is in office building leases, but the retail tenant is in addition concerned with locational attributes of the premises, e.g., its visibility, adjacency to stores reinforcing its business, and traffic and parking availability.

Example 11

Besides affecting the rent the tenant pays, what other considerations might the square footage of the premises affect?

Explanation

It might affect the utility of the HVAC (heating, ventilation, and air conditioning) system of the building. The HVAC system might, for instance, be designed to air condition, say, one person per 100 square feet of space. Or the tenant might be paying a portion of the maintenance staff wages for the building — the New York City term for this is the "porter's wages" — based on the square footage of the premises. Generally speaking, the terms premises and square footage might, in any later dispute, control the extent of the tenant's liabilities.

11. Leasing the Project

Example 12

Your client proposes to lease the top floor of a multi-story office building. The client wants to be able to use the roof for office parties and other functions. How should premises' rentable square footage be computed?

Explanation

By including the entire footprint of the building, as if a tape measurer was wrapped around it. Landlords sometimes resist including the air rights to the building and access to the roof in a description of the premises; they might for instance wish to locate utilities and HVAC facilities on the roof.

Example 13

Tenant's lease requires, as do most commercial leases, that as to any monetary covenant in the lease, time is of the essence. Tenant is two days late in paying the monthly rent in a large shopping center. Landlord declares the lease forfeit. If you represented the tenant, what is your response to the declaration of forfeiture?

Explanation

That a landlord's right to declare a forfeiture is to be strictly construed and is not unlimited when the breach is a trivial and non-material one; that this two day breach is trivial unless the landlord shows material damage or injury. Showing a material breach requires a weighing of factors showing both materiality and that the forfeiture would not be a penalty in the circumstance of the case. See Foundation Dev. Corp. v. Loehmann's, 788 P.2d 1189 (Ariz. 1990) (a comprehensive opinion on this situation).

Possession and the Commencement of the Term

A lease is the transfer of an exclusive right to possession. When a tenant takes possession of the premises, the obligation to pay rent arises, so attention

277

11. Leasing the Project

should be paid to defining "possession" in the lease. It can be simply defined, as the date on which the tenant is given the keys, or the date on which occupancy permits are available or issued, or some date defined in the work letter agreement for the construction fitting the premises for the tenant's proposed use ("a build out," being either a standalone agreement or an exhibit attached to the lease). See Bates Advertising USA, Inc. v. 498 Seventh, LLC, 850 N.E.2d 1137 (N.Y. 2006). See generally Rhonda E. Schwartz, How to Draft Delivery of Possession Clauses in Leases, Prac. Real Est. Law. (May 1999), at 9.

A tenant's possession of the premises should also correspond to some other obligations, such as obliging the tenant to carry insurance. Because new tenants are often moving an established business into a landlord's premises, tenants are likely concerned with lease remedies when possession is delayed. Landlords most readily consent to rent abatement as a sole remedy, but tenants will often seek additional damage remedies and a right to cancel as a means of giving the landlord an incentive to deliver possession on time.

In commercial leasing, the tenant's taking of possession of the premises and the commencement of its "term"—meaning the description of the duration of the lease—should be simultaneous events triggering the tenant's rental obligation. The time between the execution of the lease and the time the tenant becomes obligated to pay rent are distinct. This interval is known as the "contract interval" or in law Latin, the *interesse termini*. At the execution of the lease, the tenant typically has an obligation to present plans for its use of the premises. The contract interval is the time during which the tenant uses those plans to "build out" the premises, installing fits and finishes necessary to conduct it business. Typically the landlord provides the funds to build out premises. These funds are known as a tenant improvement allowance or TIA. Payment of the TIA is usually completed before the commencement of the term and the taking of possession.

During this interval, the tenant will bargain for the right to inspect the premises without obliging itself to pay rent; however, any unauthorized use of the premises—such as the installation of furniture or fixtures—may bring the contract interval to an end, begin the lease's term, and trigger the obligation to pay rent.

The contract interval also gives the tenant a covenant of quiet enjoyment. This is a covenant implied for the tenant's benefit once the lease was executed, but before the tenant was in possession. Under it the landlord promises to either (1) put the tenant into actual possession of the premises when the term commencs or (2) support the tenant's legal right to possession when the term commences.

The initial term of the lease often includes options to extend it.[7] No new lease is required. Such options are necessary because courts do not

---

7. There is a distinction between an option to extend a lease and an option to renew it. See McClellan v. Britain, 826 P.2d 245 (Wyo. 1992). A renewal is the execution of a new lease: it

11. Leasing the Project

generally favor perpetual leases. See Pope v. Lee, 879 A.2d 735 (N.H. 2005) (noting an exception when the intent of the parties is clear). Unless a lease has notice and other requirements for a tenant's exercise of an option to extend, remaining in possession and paying rent effects an exercise of the option. See Ellis v. Pauline S. Sprouse Residuary Tr., 280 S.W.3d 806 (Tenn. 2009). In commercial leasing, however, notice and preconditions to exercising an extension are commonplace, and strict compliance by the tenant is required. Substantial compliance is insufficient. See Langer v. Bartholomay, 745 N.W.2d 649 (N.D. 2008) (a comprehensive discussion on many issues in this section). Time is of the essence with both extension and renewal options. The courts only provide relief for slight delays in their exercise, ones without prejudice to the landlord or injury to the tenant (e.g., not resulting in a substantial loss of the tenant's improvements). See Fountain Co. v. Stein, 118 A. 47 (Conn. 1922) (a leading case). See also Annot., 27 A.L.R.4th 266, (circumstances excusing lessee's failure to give timely notice of exercise of option to renew or extend lease (1984)).

Because commercial leases may include options to extend or renew the initial term, the term is not usually the subject of prolonged dispute. Terms of three to five years are commonplace. The landlord wants this time to assess the tenant's fit in a retail setting and its reliability as an office building tenant; likewise, the tenant can seldom see much beyond the business cycles encompassed by the three to five year initial term. When a landlord, for instance, proposes a five year renewal option, a tenant unsure of its needs over time might prefer successive renewals for shorter periods of time. When a tenant is a business whose operations are expanding, the tenant may bargain for an option to expand the premises to adjacent space; such expansion options raise many of the same issues involved in options to extend or renew. See infra, this chapter.

---

requires more than a holding over and the payment of rent. An extension is a continuation of an existing lease. Some jurisdictions make this distinction as matter of law. For instance, a renewal may implicate a leasing broker's right to an additional commission, while an extension requires no new commission. Likewise, an extended lease need not be re-recorded, but a renewed lease must be. Other jurisdictions conflate the terms. See Homestead Enters. v. Johnson Prods., Inc., 540 A.2d 471 (Me. 1988), and Rehoboth Mall Ltd. v. NPC Int'l, Inc., 953 A.2d 702 (Del. Super. 2008). Options to renew in an existing lease are not a violation of the Rule Against Perpetuities. It is an option within a lease and so must be exercised if at all within the lease's initial term, and so long as that is less than 21 years, it arises within the period permitted by the Rule. See Symphony Space, Inc. v. Pergola Prop, 669 N.E.2d 799 (N.Y. 1996), and Citgo Petroleum Corp v. Hopper, 429 S.E.2d 6 ((Va. 1993). Options to renew and to extend are real covenants; they run with the land. Both are subject to specific performance.

11. Leasing the Project

Examples

Example 14

A landlord proposes that the term of your client's lease begins when the premises in a newly constructed office building are "substantially complete." Your client counters that the term should begin when "all permits are in place." What further advice should you offer on this issue?

Explanation

"Substantial completion" is often used as the standard to measure the commencement of the term of a lease, but it is subject to attack as a violation of the common law Rule Against Perpetuities.[8] It also lacks both objectivity and specificity. In a multi-tenanted building, "completion" should include completion of the lobby, common areas, corridors, stairways, elevators, and any facility permitting access to your client's premises. The "all permits in place" standard is a better one, but won't your client want notice of their issuance as well as a period of time to prepare to occupy the premises?

Example 15

Having defined to your client's satisfaction when the term commences, should you also advise that the term have a definite expiration date?

Explanation

Courts differ on the necessity for an expiration date. At common law, a term for years expired automatically. This is still the law in many jurisdictions. Providing for the lease's expiration may save it from the charge that it is a Perpetuity when the lease is for a term more than 21 years. However, when the commencement of the term depends on an event or non-event— substantial completion or obtaining all permits—and there is a delay in commencement, will the lease's term be extended by the time occasioned by the delay. When the delay is the fault of the tenant, landlords typically insist that the term commences and ends on the date set in the lease. For other delays, the drafting issue is more complex and landlords may extend the term for the time occasioned by the delay. The mortgage lender for the

---

8. Most recent decisions on this matter have, however, not voided to lease *ab initio*, but used as "wait and see" or a reasonable time approach to the application of the Rule.

11. Leasing the Project

project typically has the final word on this issue: they need to know what the income stream and the debt service coverage ratio[9] of the project will be, and an expiration date in all leases makes that computation possible. See Town & Country Shopping Ctr. v. Swenson Furniture Co., 110 N.W.2d 525 (Minn. 1961).

Example 16

Your client has executed a lease for a suite in an office building. On the day the lease's term is to begin, the previous tenant is holding over, refusing to leave the premises. What is your advice to the client?

Explanation

Your advice in this situation depends on the law of the jurisdiction in which the premises are located. The covenant of quiet enjoyment applies during this contract interval, but its effect is either to require the landlord to put the tenant into actual, physical possession of the premises (the so-called "English rule"), or to give the tenant only the legal right to possession (the "American rule"). The difference in the two rules is their allocation of the burden of litigation with the holdover: the landlord has it under the English rule, the tenant has it under the American rule. The English rule is the law in a majority of American jurisdictions. See, e.g., Adrian v. Rabinowitz, 186 A.29 (N.J. 1936). Few incoming tenants will want the obligation to sue the holdover, so many commercial tenants bargain for an abatement of rent and damages, or the right to terminate the lease and damages, while the landlord takes care of the holdover problem. See Matthew J. Heiser, What's Good for the Goose isn't Always Good for the Gander: the Inefficiencies of a Single Default Rule for Delivery of Possession on Leased Premises, 38 Colum. J.L. & Soc. Probs 171 (2004). The American rule is our minority rule. See, e.g., Hannan v. Dusch, 153 S.E. 824 (Va. 1930). You probably studied either *Adrian* or *Hannan* in your first year property course. Once in possession, your client will have to deal with trespassers under either rule, and both rules are subject to waiver when the negotiated lease so provides.

---

9. As discussed in Chapter 6, the debt service coverage ratio (DSCR) is the net operating income of the building over its debt service amount, converted to a ratio greater than 1.0, meaning that the income is more than sufficient to cover the debt service. A DSCR greater than 1.3 is typically required and less than that is often a default event in the developer's mortgage.

281

11. Leasing the Project

Example 17

A prospective tenant bargains for a right to extend its lease in an office building. Your client, the landlord, agrees to an extension option but wishes to set some conditions precedent to its exercise. What preconditions would you suggest to the landlord?

Explanation

You might suggest (1) that the tenant give some adequate prior written notice to the landlord—say, three months in advance of exercising the option, (2) that there be no (past or) existing default[10] in the lease on both the date of the notice and the date of its exercise,[11] (3) that the rent on the existing lease be paid in full on both dates,[12] (4) that the tenant warrant that there are no continuing (monetary) disputes over the interpretation of the lease covenants on both dates, (5) that the tenant is on both dates occupying at least ___ (say, 80%) of the rentable square footage of the premises, (6) that the tenant warrant and represent that it has neither assigned nor subleased the premises, (7) that the tenant pay an additional security deposit when giving notice to extend the lease. Finally, if the law of this jurisdiction might interpret this extension as a renewal of the lease, that the tenant pay an increased rent in consideration of the renewal. (Note: when there is any increase in the rent beyond the initial term, this fact itself might be interpreted as a renewal.) As you might think from the length of this Explanation, landlords give options to extend or renew the lease only to its best tenants.

Example 18

Your client agrees that an option to renew its lease will contain an appraisal method to determine the fair rental value of the premises as of the date of the renewal. Your client has made substantial improvements by installing valuable fixtures to the premises during the initial term of the lease. Should the value of the improvements be included in the appraisal?

---

10. If the tenant were to be in default, absent this precondition, the common law gave the tenant the right to extend or renew the lease on the basis of the doctrine of independent covenants.

11. See Annot., Right to exercise option to renew or extend lease as affected by tenant's breach of other covenants or conditions, 23 A.L.R.4th 908 (1983).

12. See Hieb v. Jelinek, 497 N.W.2d 88 (N.D. 1993).

11. Leasing the Project

Explanation

The landlord will argue that since the improvements become his at the expiration of the lease, they should be included in the appraisal. Your client might agree that this is the law, but argue that it shouldn't be required to pay twice for the improvements—once when they are installed and again through the increased rent. This double payment would result in the landlord's unjust enrichment. When the lease is express that all such improvements are the landlord's at the expiration of the lease, the landlord's position is stronger but not dispositive on that account.

Rent

In a commercial lease, rent comes in more than one form. The "base rent" is the minimum amount of rent a tenant is required to pay. It is payable in the first year of the term and thereafter when the lease contains no rent escalators. It is generally calculated on a square foot basis and will be (say) "thirty dollars and fifty cents ($30.50) per rentable square foot." It is expressed as a promise to pay or a covenant, not a condition precedent to the tenant's continued occupancy of the premises. If it were to be expressed as a condition, it would not survive any assignment or sublease of the premises.

In a quadruple net lease, a tenant's "prorated share of taxes, utilities, insurance, maintenance and repair costs, and other charges," is also paid as "additional rent." Absent an express provision to this effect, rent would not include such items. "Additional rent" might be defined as "all sums of money required to be paid by tenant under this lease." In other words, the landlord seeks to characterize as many of the carrying charges for the premises as additional rent. Why? Because, at common law still applicable to commercial leases, the rental covenant is an independent covenant: the tenant's obligation to pay rent is effective regardless of the landlord's other obligations to the tenant under the lease. This (again) ensures that, for non-payment of rent, the landlord has the right to an action for summary possession or procedure—an accelerated cause action in which most of the tenant's defenses under the lease are unavailable, resulting in the landlord's quick repossession of the premises.[13]

Additional rent will often be paid "without offset or deduction." This phrase is useful to landlord's because it gives them decision making authority to decide what "other charges" might be included in the term "additional rent."

---

13. One exception to the landlord's desire to characterize payments as rent is the tenant's security deposit; the landlord might ask that, as security, that the tenant pre-pay (say) 6 month's worth of rent. Such a deposit, when characterized as rent, would be ordinary income to the landlord; however, as a security deposit, it might be treated as a capital gain whose taxation can be deferred.

11. Leasing the Project

All forms of rent are payable in advance. At common law, the rent was due at the expiration or termination of the term. See DeVore v. Lee, 30 So. 2d 924 (Fla. 1947). It is typically also payable at the landlord's office. Again, this is to reverse the common law rule that it was payable on the premises as and when the lease provides. See Williams v. Aeroland Oil Co., 20 So. 2d 346 (Fla. 1944). These reversals of common law rules reenforce the idea that, when the tenant takes possession of the premises, the landlord is quit of any preconditions to the payment of rent in whatever form.

Landlords also often ask for "hell or high water" rental covenants in commercial leases. Such covenants require that the tenant guarantee that it will pay the base rent, additional rent, and all other moneys due under the lease, of whatever kind and without restriction. See ReliaStar Life Ins. Co. v. Home Depot USA, Inc., 570 F.3d 513 (2d Cir. 2009) (holding "hell or high water" covenants enforceable).

Examples

Example 19

The most desirable tenants will of course push for a comprehensive list of items included in the term "additional rent." How would you formulate such a list? What assurances will those tenants have that the list is used fairly by the landlord?

Explanation

Such a list might include: materials and supply costs for maintenance of the building, repair and maintenance costs, the costs of replacing worn out or outdated equipment, management fees and direct overhead costs, accounting professional's fees, consulting fees, contractors' fees, utility service charges, water and sewer charges, electrical utility taxes and charges, telecommunications charges, real property taxes, special district assessment charges, and property and casualty insurance fees, but not including debt service amounts, the costs of alterations and tenant improvement allowances (TIAs) for other tenants, the landlord's brokerage fees and the costs of negotiating lease with other tenants, the landlord's income tax liabilities, transfer tax liabilities, franchise tax liabilities not based on the value of the building, the costs of correcting design and construction defects in the building, the costs of capital expenditures, and the costs of compliance with municipal and state building codes, ordinances, and statutes.

The more specific and exclusive the list of operating costs is, the more likely it will be tenant-friendly. On the other hand, landlords will want a non-exclusive list including a catch all phrase like "all costs of operating the project."

284

11. Leasing the Project

What items on the foregoing list are likely to attract desirable tenants' attention? Tenants will negotiate for more specific definitions involving two items or issues: (1) the compliance costs with codes, ordinances, and statutes, and (2) capital expenditures vs. replacement, repair, and maintenance costs.

As to capital expenditures, this scrutiny is based on the tenants' idea that if the landlord owns the building, it most benefits from these expenditures and so should both bear their costs and recoup them in future rents. A landlord's response? It might be that some expenditures are not readily translated into rent increases because the market and not the landlord controls the rental rate.

As to compliance with laws, the tenant's assumption is that the non-compliant features of the project are most likely the landlord's fault.

Back-up covenants in the lease can assure proper implementation of any list of operating expenses used in calculating additional rent: these are a tenant's right periodically to audit the landlord's books and a warranty and representation by the landlord that those expenses are "reasonable, customary, necessary, uniformly administered to all tenants, competitively priced, actually paid, and currently deductible by the landlord under the Internal Revenue Code."

Finally, the tenants' attorney should advise the client that no calculation of operating costs and additional rent will be entirely fair, e.g., one tenant will inevitably use more air conditioning than another.

Example 20

Your client, a creditworthy, desirable tenant, has learned that some business tenants in the office building in which it rents a suite are minority-owned such that they qualify for an abatement on the building's real property taxes. You advise the client to discuss this matter with the landlord when the operating costs and additional rent calculations are next audited. Frame this discussion for the client.

Explanation

What you can say about this matter is not necessarily good news for your client. Property taxes are based on a project's assessed valuation. The abatement here follows the building's assessment. When the list of operating costs is next reviewed, the client will want to know if the item for such taxes is based on a "taxes assessed" or "taxes collected" basis. The issues becomes whether the taxes included as additional rent include amounts that were abated? If the abatement was computed based on the value of the tenant's premises, it should lower only that tenant's additional rent. When computed on the value of the building, then the abated taxes should reduce

285

11. Leasing the Project

your client's additional rent. "Taxes assessed" may include the value of the abatements; "taxes collected" does not.

Rent Escalation Covenants

Landlords, seeking to maximize profits, include rent escalation covenants in a lease, and the longer the lease, the more often the landlord will push to include such covenants in it.

Rent escalation covenants provide for either automatic rent increases—for example, "the base rent shall increase two dollars ($2.00) per square foot on the fifth and tenth anniversaries of the rent commencement date," or "the base rent shall increase three percent (3 percent) per year on each anniversary of . . . " The rent covenant may provide for increases tied to indices of local wage rates, the consumer price index (the CPI), or some fair rental value appraisal method, often with a maximum amount of increase in any one year, stated as a percentage of the initial or base rent. See George Backer Mgmt. Corp. v. Acme Quilting Co., 385 N.E.2d 1062 (N.Y. 1978). The uncertainty about the economic risks of entering into a lease with escalating rents is generally handled by reducing the lease's primary term and inserting options to extend or renew for several secondary terms. Likewise, maintenance charges can also be subject to predetermined escalation covenants based on local cost indices.

An index using local wage rates—for instance, porter's wages in New York City—is based on the assumption that labor costs and building operating costs rise in tandem. More commonplace is the use of the CPI, or even more common, some percentage of the CPI's annual increase, as an index for rent escalators. The negotiated percentage of the CPI customarily used is 30 to 40% of the whole yearly increase.

The cost-of-living CPI index has largely replaced step-ups (stated as a percentage of the base rent) as a measure of rent increases after the base rent year; it has become a staple of commercial leasing. This replacement has been largely landlord-driven and a response to the idea that step-ups are inadequate to compensate for changing economic conditions over recent decades.

The CPI is a basket of statistics about consumer price rises over time.[14] Some of these statistics are relevant to the landlord's expenses, but some are not. A developer/landlord's attorney would be wise to point out the differences. Further, the CPI is based on inflation in consumer prices, and

---

14. The CPI $= \dfrac{\text{cost of the basket in the current year}}{\text{cost of the basket in the base year}} \times 100$

The CPI is published monthly by the U.S. Dept. of Labor's Bureau of Labor Statistics. There are both national and regional CPIs, as well as CPIs for our largest metropolitan areas. There are also CPIs "for Wage Earners and Clerical Workers (CPI-W). The CPI-W index typically favors tenants since wages respond more slowly that consumer prices to inflation.

286

11. Leasing the Project

that assumes that the tenant's income can keep pace with inflation—that the tenant's services and products can keep pace by being passed through to customers and consumers. When inflation is steeply rising, so will the tenant's rent—and that can produce "rent shock" for the tenant, particularly for the tenant whose business is depressed in inflationary times. These disadvantages to the CPI as an index has led to the common use of a percentage of the CPI's cost-of-living increase, instead of using 100% of the CPI

How the CPI is used can also be a matter for a landlord tenant debate. Two methods are common. They differ in effect, diverging most over a longer term lease: the longer the term, the more the divergence.

The first, so called "prior year method" would be described in a covenant providing as follows:

> "At the anniversary of the execution of this lease, the Base Rent payable will increase in an amount equal to the product of then current Base Rent multiplied by a number equal to the percentage increase in the CPI over a 12 month period, calculated by using the most recently published CPI and the CPI published 12 months earlier."

A second calculation (the so called "base year method") changes the last six words of this covenant to provide ". . . the CPI published at the end of the first year of the term of this lease." The effect is to aggregate all of the annual changes in the CPI over the term of the lease into the most recent calculation of the Base Rent then due. With inflation rising each year, this produces greater rent increases each year after the commencement of the term. It does this by comparing the current CPI to the lease's first used CPI. It is the analogue of calculating compound interest, while the "prior year method" is like a calculation of simple interest based on the prior year's base rent.

For an attorney for a tenant, particularly a tenant with a newly established business, the "base year method" may produce rolling "rent shocks" with each successive year of lease's term. Protection against this is achieved with a cap, say of a 3 to 4% increase in rent in any lease year. Any prospective commercial tenant, however, will need its attorney's assistance in negotiating a rent escalator. The formulae for escalations are complicated—so complicated that one attorney has said that "no one understands them. This is not merely a cynical remark: it is rather a truism." See Theodore H. Hellmuth, Missouri Practice, Real Estate Law, §450 (1991 Supp.).

Percentage Rents

In shopping center leases and for retail stores, rents are typically based on a base rent and a percentage of the gross or net sales of the tenant. The base rent is subject to escalation after the first year of the term, but the

287

11. Leasing the Project

percentage rent typically is not. See Joseph Muccio, The Commercial Leasing Market & E-Commerce: Is E-Commerce Causing Commercial Leases Trouble and What Could be Done to Fix It?, 38 Rev. of Banking & Fin. L. 799 (2019).

Landlords typically want to negotiate short terms, anticipating higher rents on renewals or extensions. Tenants, however, want terms long enough to amortize their trade fixtures and TIA improvements. The compromise has traditionally been percentage rents.

The most common dispute over a percentage rental covenant is the percentage itself. Traditionally, the greater the rentable square footage of the premises, the lower the percentage is likely to be. Over time, the percentage has been lower when items sold are high volume/low margin items, such a food. The percentage is higher for low volume/high margin items, such as jewelry and art works.

Where a particular line of goods falls on this spectrum requires local knowledge and experience. How about a parking lot? The lot is mostly unimproved, but the spaces are limited. This might argue for a higher percentage. A motion picture theater? The space is improved but the seating is limited. This might argue for a lower percentage than for a parking lot. On and on, by the type of retail.

Some retailers sell many types of items. Supermarkets sell food, but they also sell many other non-food items, and often today include a pharmacy. Thus the percentage rent should blend the types of items sold. The supermarket owner may object that accounting for every type of item is a difficult task, but a landlord might insist on different percentages for high volume/low margin food items (say, 1%), for lower volume/higher margin non-food items (say, 3%), and for its pharmacy (say, 5%).

The next most common dispute over a percentage rental covenant is whether an item of sales income is included in the gross sales calculation for the premises. Landlords typically prefer that the percentage rent is calculated on gross sales, tenants on net sales. They argue that gross sales as a measure of rent is more easily computed and audited. Tenants argue that net sales is more reflective of the actual income stream of their businesses.

Typically it is "gross sales" that measures the percentage rent. "Gross sales" might include "all sales, cash or credit, made by tenant and originating in, from, on, or through the premises," with the landlord having the ancillary right to periodic reports from a tenant (often these are made quarterly), and a right to inspect the cash register tapes and tenant's sales records. All of the prepositions in this initial, basic definition are intended by the landlord to cover the possibility of salespersons redirecting customers off-premises, possibly to a warehouse or another store. Thus sales of returned items, sales discounted for employees, family and friends, the full price of an item as opposed to its wholesale price, and the full price of an item sold on an installment sale basis, might be included, whether or not the price is collected. If the price is collectable, it is included. Net sales typically will include none of these.

11. Leasing the Project

Some tenants might bargain for a list of exclusions from the definition of gross sales, as follows "Gross sales" typically excludes: (1) fees for special services from pay toilets or pay phones; (2) sublease rentals to licensees, accounted for in the base rent or in a payment in lieu of percentage rent; (3) sales made outside the premises; (4) sales taxes or taxes on gross receipts; (5) sales of exchanged items; (6) refunds on returned items; (7) sales in any cafeteria for employees.

Examples

Example 21

When might a net sales percentage rent be used?

Explanation

"Net sales" might be used for a high volume, low margin, discount store or outlet. It might also be used for a consignment shop tenant who agrees to share the sale price with the consignee. Likewise, a tenant selling lottery tickets who receives a commission for the sale but remits the balance to the jurisdiction running the lottery, a tenant making widespread use of discount coupons, or a tenant who is a furrier accepting trade-ins as partial payment for a new fur coat—all make a good candidate for a lease using net sales as the measure of the percentage rent.

Example 22

Your client, a developer/landlord of a retail tenant in a shopping mall, has proposed to a high-end, national retailer, a lease defining gross sales as "all sales made by tenant and originating on or through the premises." The tenant is a desirable, creditworthy one. What further advice might you give to expand this definition without giving offence?

Explanation

"All sales" might be expanded to "all revenues from sales, rentals, or services." This expansion takes account of fees charged by personal shoppers, rental services for bridal dresses, and rent-the-runway clothes. "Made by tenant" might be expanded to read "made by tenant or any licensee, subtenant, assignee, concessionaire, or vending machine." This expansion accounts for sales income from specialty and designer shops within the premises, but excluding the rents paid by such parties. After all, you might explain, the income attributable to the licensee's (etc.) sales, as opposed to

289

11. Leasing the Project

the fees paid to occupy part of the premises, are what the landlord expects to be included within the percentage rent. Likewise, the preposition "through" the premises might be expanded to include sales "whether or not and sales were delivered on the premises and sales made off the premises but delivered on the premises." Other issues that might be raised with this prospective tenant are the inclusion of "sales made, performed, or fulfilled by telephone, email, catalogue, internet, whether or not made by present or future electronic means."

Example 23

You have just passed the bar exam and are unsure of your future professional income as you build your law practice. Should you rent an office using a base rent plus a percentage rent?

Explanation

No, not without researching the matter first. An attorney's splitting fees with a non-attorney is most likely a violation of the canons of professional ethics, and the percentage rent arrangement in this lease may be such a violation.

Example 24

You check into a hotel. You buy traveler's checks at the front desk. There you receive a discount coupon for dinner in the hotel's restaurant and another coupon for a free drink in the hotel bar. You go up to your room with two keys: One unlocks the door to the room and the other a locked cabinet in which there are snacks, sodas, and other foods, available for an extra charge. You select a cable movie on TV, knowing that this will add $6 to your bill. The hotel is operated under a percentage lease on "gross sales and receipts." Which of the foregoing purchases, coupons, and extra charges should be included in the calculation of gross rents and receipts for purposes of calculating the percentage rent due?

11. Leasing the Project

Explanation

Answers are provided by the cases. See Papa Gino's of America, Inc. v. Broadmanor Assocs., Ltd., 500 A.2d 1341 (Conn. App. Ct. 1985) (permitting a tenant to deduct used restaurant coupons from gross sales); McComb v. McComb, 155 N.W.2d 860 (Mich. App. Ct. 1967) (holding that the sale of traveler's checks was included). The locked cabinet approach to a refreshment bar in the room emphasizes that the refreshments are not part of the room charge. See Cocke v. Pacific Gulf Dev. Corp., 594 S.W.2d 545 (Tex. Civ. App. Ct. 1980) (holding that the TV rental was included).

Expansion Rights

Every developer wants to rent to successful tenants. Their success often means that they need to expand their premises. This is particularly a problem in office buildings. For instance, a law firm or an accounting firm is likely to add more attorneys or accountants, while a retailer is less often to ask for more square footage on its selling floor. So a tenant might ask for "a right of first refusal (ROFR) to lease the remaining space on the tenth floor as available and on terms acceptable to third parties." To this the landlord might make several objections. What if the tenant decides to take less than all the available space on that floor, leaving the landlord with an unacceptably small area to rent to a third party? What if the tenant decides to rent only during the last several years of its primary lease, and plans to use the additional premises as a warehouse, or for a term that isn't as long as a third party would accept because the expansion term only extends to the end of the primary lease? The rights to expand and to extend the term are economically linked in the landlord's mind as he calculates his overall rent roll.

From the landlord's perspective, any less-than-all-the-floor ROFR lease needs to leave marketable premises on the floor. It also needs to have a term that is suitably long or that triggers an extension of the primary lease so that it and the ROFR lease terminate in tandem. In addition, the ROFR itself should end after the first several (say, three) years of the primary lease's term: in this regard, the landlord might offer to (1) hold space open in a new building for a short time following the commencement of the term and (2) require that the tenant expand its floor space within the same short time. In the back of the landlord's mind is the idea that expansion covenants decrease the value of the ROFR space on the office building's floor or in the adjacent spaces in the shopping center or mall. To limit this decrease in value, a landlord will bargain that the expansion space be contiguous with a tenant's existing premises.

291

11. Leasing the Project

If the tenant was procured by a leasing broker, the listing agreement should be checked to determine if the ROFR triggers a right to an additional commission, and if so the expansion covenant should allocate its payment. Finally, in an existing building, extending an ROFR should not interfere with the renewal and expansion rights of existing tenants. When such tenants are identifiable, they should be named. Generally, the landlord might be wiser to give instead a right of first negotiation.

Typical ROFRs are to be accepted or refused by written notice within as short a time as (say) five business days. Strict compliance with the procedures for exercising the rights in the expansion covenant is generally required. A tenant cannot exercise an expansion right conditionally. Its acceptance must mirror the terms offered, conforming exactly to them. See Central Nat'l Bank v. Fleetwood Realty Corp., 441 N.E.2d 1244 (Ill. App. Ct. 1982). A right not exercised is lost, although some tenants might bargain for a continuing right of first offer (ROFO). When the primary lease's rent covenant is subject to an escalation clause, the ROFR should make clear whether the expanded lease starts from scratch or at the escalated rate. If the lease contained a "rent-free" period during the time construction on the premises under the TIA and its work letter was performed, it should make clear whether that would apply to the expanded lease too.

A landlord will bargain for a rent that does not distinguish between primary and expanded premises. Altogether, an expansion right should define the ROFR premises, the ROFR lease term's length, the rent calculation, tenant improvements, the time the ROFR is effective, how it affects brokerage commissions, and its effect on existing leases.

Examples

Example 25

In a rising market for rents, a commercial landlord client of yours is wary of offering expansion rights to his successful tenants because they are "in the way" of deals with prospective tenants offering to pay higher rents. The landlord is dissatisfied with the way his ROFR provisions are working. What alternatives might you suggest to him for future leases?

Explanation

In lieu of suing the tenant who is interfering in bad faith with a prospective advantage (a long shot), you might suggest a right of first offer (ROFO) be offered to future tenants. Here the landlord is able to offer an existing tenant with expansion rights an expanded lease at current market rates before offering it to third parties. If the tenant refuses, he is quickly "out of the way." If he accepts, the landlord receives no less than he would be accepting a third-party tenant. An ROFO might even encourage third parties to bargain more seriously. The disadvantage to the landlord is that the tenant

11. Leasing the Project

may quickly accept and then bargain harder for better terms, knowing that the third party has been eliminated. In this regard, the ROFO should be sharply distinguished in future leases from a right of first negotiation. To take account of this, the third party might be given a right to make an improved counteroffer. So a ROFO might prove more acceptable to some landlords than a ROFR.

Contraction Rights

Much less often, a tenant is given a contraction right. These are less frequent than expansion rights because mortgage lenders often object to them well before they are offered. However, when present, the same drafting issues apply: clarity as to the times they must be exercised, the procedure for doing so, the effect on the rent covenants, the requirement that the contracted space be contiguous and accessible to common areas (usually a corridor in the building), and if the premises are on more than one floor in a building, a requirement that all the space on one floor be surrendered before any contraction occurs on another.

Contracting the premises is in effect a partial termination of the lease. This analogue often raises issues as to the quality or condition of the space at the time of the surrender and the penalties for holding over once the contraction date has passed.

SUBORDINATION AND NONDISTURBANCE

Mortgage lenders for shopping centers and office buildings want a first lien on the property securing the loan. At the same time, they realize that on the successful foreclosure of a senior mortgage lien, junior liens and other interests, including leases, are extinguished.[15] See Applebee's Northeast, Inc. v. Methuen Investors, Inc., 709 N.E.2d 1143 (Mass. App. 1999). They also realize that a center or building with no tenants is a profitless enterprise that will not attract foreclosure sale or resale purchasers.

---

15. Because the lease might in some jurisdictions be regarded as a conveyances or a sale of the premises for a term, this extinguishment of junior leases is not always automatic; some jurisdictions require that the tenant be joined as a party to the foreclosure, some don't. Some jurisdictions have further variations on this problem, e.g., Illinois distinguishes between foreclosing a mortgage (the tenant must be made a party in order to extinguish a lease) and a deed of trust (extinguishment is automatic). See Mark A. Senn, Commercial Real Estate Leases at p. 25-3, n. 2 (2d ed.2000). Thus decisions by the foreclosing lender must often be made tenant-by-tenant—one good reason for clarity in an SNDA.

11. Leasing the Project

These realizations lead lenders to enter into Subordination, Nondisturbance, and Attornment Agreements (SNDAs). An SNDA is an agreement between the lender and a tenant relating to the tenant's lease. Often the developer/landlord is a party to it as well. It spells out the relationship that the tenant and the lender as a successor landlord will have if the lender forecloses. It obligates the tenant to treat the lender and any purchaser at the foreclosure sale acting as a successor landlord, in the same manner as the tenant treated the original landlord. Its provisions also address any matters otherwise unclear in applicable law. Both tenant and lender gain predictability about their futures as a result. See Andrew N. Jacobson, Reviewing Subordination and Nondisturbance Agreements from the Tenant's Perspective, 30 Prac. Real Est. Law, No. 4, at 9 (2014).

An SNDA has four major provisions:

(1) *Subordination.* The tenant agrees that (a) the lease is junior to and so subordinate to the lender's lien and (b) the terms of the mortgage control the terms of the lease. There is little litigation about this provision outside California and New York because, as a practical matter, lenders do not wish to extinguish a lease in foreclosure unless a tenant occupies some crucial space at a below-market rent; lenders prefer tenants who steadily pay rent to having to find new tenants. See CW Capital Asset Mgmt., LLC v. Chicago Props., 610 F.3d 497, 502-503 (7th Cir. 2010) (Posner, J.) (collecting authorities on SNDAs).

(2) *Nondisturbance.* The lender, in exchange for the subordination, agrees not to disturb or disrupt the tenant's possession of its leased premises after foreclosure so long as the lease is not in default at that time. At minimum, this aspect of the agreement is back-stopped by the implied covenant of quiet enjoyment. Because the purchaser at the foreclosure sale acquires no greater rights than the foreclosing lender had, the nondisturbance provision means that a new purchaser (a) will not disturb the tenant, and (b) will also recognize the terms and conditions in the tenant's lease and (c) if the lender disturbs the tenant's possession, the lease becomes prior to the mortgage again. Without a nondisturbance agreement, the lender or new purchaser may require the tenant to vacate the premises. See KVR Realties, Inc. v. Treasure Star, Inc., 445 N.E.2d 641 (N.Y. 1983) and 49 Am. Jur. 2d, Landlord and Tenant, §999 (2018).

(3) *Attornment.* In return for the nondisturbance provision, the tenant agrees to recognize (or to attorn to) any new purchaser as its landlord. In total, then, an SNDA is a defeasible subordination, one that lasts only so long as the underlying nondisturbance and attornment agreement lasts. See Dime Sav. Bank v. Montague St. Realty, 664 N.Y.S.2d 246 (N.Y. 1997).

(4) *Carve-outs.* These are provisions of a lease that a new purchaser/ landlord is not bound to recognize. Security deposit provisions, work letter agreements regarding a tenant's fixturizing the premises, tenant alterations provisions, and rent prepayments are often the subject of carve-outs.

11. Leasing the Project

The lender's mortgage lien, made prior to the possessory interest of a tenant under the terms of the SNDA, still requires the project property to be in continuous use. Moreover, the lender making a loan expects that the premises will be leased. Indeed, the mortgagor not leasing is arguably committing economic waste on the property. Thus, an SNDA in effect makes a foreclosure of commercial buildings a partial foreclosure—that is, the foreclosure of the unrented and common areas of the building.

When foreclosure is not used, as when the mortgage default is resolved by a conveyance of the secured property in a deed in lieu of foreclosure, or the default is settled by a preplanned bankruptcy proceeding, no SNDA is needed because the leases will not be extinguished. Nonetheless, many SNDAs provide that a deed in lieu or a mortgagee's taking possession does not extinguish a subordinated lease.

In order for the SNDA to be enforceable by the lender, the landlord, and the tenant, each against the others, it should be executed by each; this establishes privity of contract between them.

The lender who cannot convince a major tenant to execute an SNDA may nonetheless convince that tenant to agree to provide an **estoppel certificate** or letter (in a form attached to the agreement) to any new purchaser of the mortgagor/landlord's interest.

An estoppel certificate is a statement executed by a party, such as a tenant, affirming for a third's party's benefit that certain facts are correct. It is a widely used device in the sale of property involving leased property.[16] Such a certificate affirms that the attached lease is the full and complete agreement between the landlord and tenant and that there are no unwritten or sidebar agreements. It prevents the tenant from raising claims for a lease default known at the date of its execution but not disclosed in the certificate. See K's Merchandise Mart, Inc. v. Northgate LP, 835 N.E.2d 965 (Ill. Ct. App. 2005), further discussed in Urban Sites of Chicago, LLC v. Crown Castle USA, 979 N.E.2d 480 (Ill. Ct. App. 2012). The certificate addresses the lender's concern that the landlord and tenant may later connive to reduce either the landlord's collateral or the value of the secured property in foreclosure. See Carteret Props. v. Variety Donuts, 228 A.2d 674 (N.J. 1967) (holding that a tenant's possession is itself notice of its rights), and Martinique Realty Corp. v. Hull, 166 A.2d 803 (N.J. Super. 1960).

Major tenants will be the least likely to connive and so are usually most willing to execute an agreement to provide this certificate. Estoppel certificates are also a good method of flushing out problems, but to encourage the tenant's returning them, they should be tenant friendly: short, using

---

16. Estoppel certificates are also used in mortgage loan assignments, where they enhance the marketability of the loan sold or assigned, by stating that there are no defenses to the mortgage. See Hammelburger v. Foursome Inn Corp., 431 N.E.2d 278 (N.Y. 1981).

11. Leasing the Project

a true/false format, not requiring legal conclusions, and making all or some answers "to the best of tenant's knowledge." They should, however, not permit answers that incorporate the tenant's lease by reference: The object is for a landlord or lender to learn what the tenant thinks the lease provides.

Examples

Example 26

T executes a lease to be a major tenant in O's office building and, once moved in, negotiates for an SNDA agreement with L, O's permanent mortgage lender. In negotiations for the SNDA, L insists that T provide CERCLA indemnities to L and O for the benefit of any purchaser at a future foreclosure sale. T refuses. What arguments might you use on T's behalf?

Explanation

If no such indemnities are provided in T's lease, L is using the SNDA to renegotiate its terms. L is entitled to be as secure as the lease makes it, not more so. Lenders frequently ask for environmental indemnities, restrictive assignment clauses, or financial reporting not required by the lease, and tenants who ask, "Why, if it's so important, is it not in the lease?" typically end the discussion there. The SNDA's purpose is in part to reconcile inconsistencies between the lease and the mortgage—so if, for example, the use of insurance proceeds to repair or restore the secured property if damaged can be clarified in the agreement, that clarification is a proper subject for negotiation.

Once O has executed the lease and the loan agreements, the negotiations for an SNDA may go badly, particularly when, as here, T is a major tenant. Why? Because both L and T have done the principal piece of business they set out to do, both have bargaining power and may tend to drag their feet or just be stubborn—and all this leaves the landlord O caught in the middle. Better to negotiate the SNDA before the lease and the mortgage loan agreements are executed.

Example 27

During SNDA negotiations, T insists that the nondisturbance provision of the agreement apply automatically to L when foreclosing and to any new purchaser of the property. L refuses. What are the arguments that you might make on L's behalf at this point?

296

11. Leasing the Project

Explanation

Lenders seldom agree to automatic nondisturbance provisions. Why? Because if the rents and profits prove insufficient and are the cause of the mortgage default, either the lender or the new purchaser may want to reposition the property in its rental market. So they will want the leases in effect at the time of foreclosure to meet certain financial criteria. T in response would be wise to insist that those criteria be objective and nondiscretionary on L's part. Thus the qualifying lease should have a maximum term and a minimum rent, be executed in a form that the lender has previously reviewed, and have no sidebar agreements. The latter criteria are important because lenders will be concerned about landlord-tenant sidebars concerning rent prepayments, most likely to be made when foreclosure is imminent.

Example 28

Why might a tenant in SNDA negotiations insist that the nondisturbance provision expressly include nondisturbance before foreclosure as well as afterward?

Explanation

Because preforeclosure remedies, such as a suit in waste or for a receiver, can equally affect a tenant's rights. Also, the law applicable to the lease may be unclear as to whether the covenant of quiet enjoyment is implied in all leases. A tenant would not want to find out later that it had given up the right to quiet enjoyment damage claims. Thus a nondisturbance provision should preserve the covenant and so "include claims based on the covenant of quiet enjoyment, regardless of whether the tenant vacates the premises." (Recall that vacating premises was a common law precondition to asserting a breach of the covenant and constructive eviction.) See Eugene Grant, Disturbing Concepts: Quiet Enjoyment and Constructive Eviction in the Modern Commercial Lease, 35 Real Prop. Prob. & Tr. J. 57, 65-67 (2000).

Example 29

Why would a lender want an SNDA's attornment provision to incorporate by reference a separate agreement on T's part to agree to execute a new lease (albeit on the same terms as the original one) directly with the purchaser at the foreclosure sale, or with any new purchaser?

297

11. Leasing the Project

Explanation

Because the deed to any foreclosure sale purchaser may convey only the mortgagor/landlord's reversion and so some direct privity between the tenant and the purchaser may be needed under applicable law for that purchaser's benefit. Establishing such privity is one reason why an SNDA should be a three-party agreement between the lender, the tenant, and the landlord, although the latter is not a necessary party for other purposes.

TELECOMMUNICATIONS ACCESS

In the past, landlords wired their office buildings for telephones. Today tenants need more specialized wiring and may even shift telecom carriers and providers during the term of a lease. The federal government's policy of fostering competition among providers has also forced landlords to provide multiple types of access. In practice, a landlord's agreement to permit one provider access to its building and tenants means that comparable access will have to be given to all competing providers.

A tenant who executes a lease without considering telecom problems may have to make unexpectedly large expenses should its telecom needs change during the term of the lease. Suppose an existing tenant suddenly needs a rooftop antenna. What the landlord might have provided for free as a component of the TIA during the lease negotiation may now cost the tenant extra money once the landlord realizes that the tenant is in a captive market for such things.

With regard to an individual tenant, telecom needs may be so specialized that the riser space in a building may quickly fill with wires of various types. Fire and electrical codes in some jurisdictions require the removal of abandoned cables. In any event, landlords typically negotiate an option to elect to keep or remove wiring at the end of a lease. They want this option provided as a right, but not an obligation. (The cables and wiring may turn out to be valuable fixtures, giving the landlord a competitive edge in re-renting the premises.) This option should survive the end of the lease's term, otherwise a tenant may refuse to perform or pay for the wires' removal. In the same vein, the landlord will bargain for the tenant to pay for removal and will also want to decide who will remove the wires—and even to have the tenant pay for it when the landlord does it. The landlord will want to be reimbursed for the removal from the tenant's security deposit, but this reimbursement right should not be limited to that deposit.

In the alternative, if the landlord elects to keep the wires, the landlord may require the tenant to warrant their good condition, transfer any

11. Leasing the Project

warranties and service contracts to the landlord, and certify that they are free of mechanic's liens or other encumbrances.

ASSIGNMENTS AND SUBLEASES

Generally an assignment occurs when the tenant conveys all or part of its rentable space to a third party for the remainder of the tenant's term. A sublease occurs when the tenant conveys all or part of its rentable space for a period of time that is less than the remainder of the tenant's term.

Landlords will customarily want tenants to agree not to execute any assignment or sublease without their consent. They will further want to treat any change of control of the tenant's legal entity as an assignment and want the tenant to deliver on request an estoppel and warranty letter to the effect that the control of the entity is unchanged from the time the lease was executed to the present. They will want this prohibition to be all-inclusive as to the type of entity (even if unknown at the time).

"Change of control" or similar language is preferable to naming changes to particular types of entities, and it also might include a transfer of assets in an entity or its merger or affiliation with other entities of the same type (although that too should be made explicit). It is unwise to name particular entities when a tenant might then easily argue that its LLC is functioning as a partnership or is like some other entity.

Tenants, faced with a landlord's request for a blanket prohibition on assignments and subleases, will respond with a proposal that any assignment (or sublease) be "conditioned on the landlord's written consent, such consent not to be unreasonably withheld." A tenant's counsel, reviewing this language might propose to the client that the consent not only be "not unreasonably withheld," but also that it "not be unreasonably conditioned, withheld, or delayed." In a situation in which time is of the essence, consent "conditioned or delayed" might just as well be denied. Tenant's counsel might also add that the landlord's refusal to consent should not be based on its "convenience, personal or religious beliefs, or economic interest." Thus the landlord's personal distaste for the proposed assignee, the assignee's race or religion, or because the proposed assignee might compete with the landlord's existing tenants, are not grounds for refusing consent. Likewise, the landlord may not refuse consent unless the tenant's rent is increased. Typically, the landlord's refusal should be based on terms within the four corners of the existing lease and be "commercially reasonable." See 1010 Potomac Associates v. Grocery Mfrs. of America, Inc., 485 A.2d 199, 209 (D.C. App. 1984) (collecting cases). The burden of proof is on the tenant to establish otherwise.

On the other hand, when the landlord is not presented with any information on the financial condition of a proposed and famously creditworthy

11. Leasing the Project

assignee, the landlord might reasonably believe that (1) the proposed assignee would not be successful occupying the premises, or (2) the percentage rent would substantially decrease when the existing business was not maintained by the proposed assignee; in either event, the landlord has a commercially reasonable basis for refusing consent. See B.M.B. Corp. v. McMahon's Valley Stores, 869 F.2d 865 (5th Cir. 1989) (collecting cases).

Paramount in the landlord's decision to consent or refuse is the financial responsibility of the proposed assignee. When the existing lease is guaranteed but the assignee's is not, when the assignee is undercapitalized and provides no rent guaranty, when the use of the premises substantially changes the services required of the landlord or impacts the common areas of the building, when the legality of the proposed use is questionable, or when the anticipated volume of business (in a percentage rent lease) is less than the existing business generates, the assignee's financial responsibility is in play.

A landlord's unreasonable refusal to consent may give rise to a frustrated tenant suing for the interference with a contract, and when the tenant was attempting to avoid a lease default in rent, to a claim that the landlord failed to mitigate the damages flowing from the default. In response to such potential liabilities, a landlord's attorney might insist on eliminating a tenant's damage remedies. Such a limitation on remedies will not of course prevent the frustrated assignee or leasing broker from suing, but the tenant will be left with a suit for a declaratory judgment and/or a mandatory injunction.

Assignments and subleases are more litigated in retail and shopping center settings than in office buildings. This is because the use to which a proposed assignee puts retail premises implicates the "mix" of tenants a landlord needs to maximize the income stream of its project, whereas the office building tenants' uses are more likely than not, compatible with one another.

Examples

Example 30

A prospective tenant is presented with a lease effectively prohibiting an assignment or sublease of premises. The tenant objects and writes a substitute provision stating that the tenant has the right to assign or sublet all or part of the premises, subject to the landlord's prior consent, which the landlord agreed not to unreasonably delay or withhold. The handwritten provision is initialed by both parties, and the lease is executed. Later, when presented with a suitable subtenant, the landlord refuses to honor the provision. The tenant informs the landlord that the lease is cancelled. Is the tenant justified in doing this?

11. Leasing the Project

Explanation

Yes. The tenant's objection, the substituted provision, and its acceptance by the landlord prior to the lease's execution all show that the provision was essential, inducing, and so material to the tenant's executing the lease. A material breach by one party excuses the other of further performance and once excused, relieves the other of liability for further damages incurred by the breaching party.

Example 31

A tenant agrees in its lease "not to assign or sublet without the landlord's consent, such consent not unreasonably to be withheld." The tenant then executes a mortgage of the leased premises. Is the anti-assignment covenant violated?

Explanation

No. A court would likely find that if an assignment or sublease involving a transfer of possession is not involved, then the freedom of contract and free alienation of property rights dictates that no violation be found, a restriction on alienation not being a favorite of the law. The difficulty with a blanket prohibition on mortgaging is that it might actually encourage tenants to sublease a portion of the premises, or discourage a tenant from financing improvements to them; likewise, a tenant might attempt to finance its fixtures. The landlord will of course attempt to include all of these situations within the definition of an assignment or sublease when it thinks that the new mortgage might get in the way of paying the rent. Any modification of an approved sublease or assignment, any retaking of possession by the tenant, and any further assignment or subletting by any approved assignee or sublessee should also be bargained for.

Example 32

The tenant in the prior Example is leasing in a very desirable, highly sought-after building. He proposes to assign its lease to another tenant of the landlord's, in the same building, at a rent less than the current market rate. The proposed assignee is just as creditworthy as the present tenant, but the landlord knows that the latter is pocketing the difference between the contract

301

11. Leasing the Project

and market rate in a lump sum discounted to its present value. May the landlord refuse to consent?

Explanation

This is a difficult question that might take litigation to resolve. It suggests that the landlord should bargain in future leases for a prohibition on any assignment or sublease to another of the building's tenants, perhaps even to a tenant occupying another of the landlord's buildings within the same market or within a specified neighborhood.

Example 33

The landlord in the prior two Examples has never refused to permit an expansion to one of his tenants holding such rights. The tenant in the prior Examples now proposes to assign to another tenant, now leasing on the floor just below the assignor but without expansion rights in his lease. The proposed assignee has just won a lawsuit against the landlord. Would the landlord be justified in refusing consent?

Explanation

Is the downside of winning a piece of litigation not being able to expand its premises? Is punching a hole in the floor a sufficient ground for refusal? If the integrity of the building is compromised, it might be. But it might take litigation to find out. Refusing just on account of the lawsuit is probably an insufficient ground for the landlord's refusal to consent. Again, from the landlord's perspective, it is better to expand the anti-assignment prohibition to cover this situation in future leases.

Example 34

After contentious bargaining over a tenant's right to sublease premises in a rising market for rents, the landlord proposes a "recapture provision" for the lease of commercial office building space. A recapture provision would permit the landlord to take the lease back upon its assignment or sublease. What advice might you gives the tenant at this point in the negotiations?

302

11. Leasing the Project

Explanation

The landlord is proposing that the tenant lose some or all of the market value of the lease upon an assignment or sublease. A recapture provision has been found not to be an unreasonable restraint on the alienation of the lease. See Carma Dev. (Cal.), Inc. v. Marathon Dev. Cal., Inc., 826 P.2d 710 (Cal. 1992). You might advise the client to turn to its leasing broker. The broker will report as follows: some landlords want to take the lease back if the tenant even proposes its transfer to another. Some propose that the tenant lose that value permanently by terminating the whole lease. Others propose that the tenant loses rights in the space assigned or subleased only during the term of the assignment or sublease. You might propose that the tenant share the appreciated rent paid by the assignee or subtenant with the landlord on an agreed basis (say, 50-50).[17] Tenant might object that if it bears the risk that the premises will decrease in rental value during the term of its lease, it should have the benefit of the up-side appreciation in value. If the tenant proposes to improve the premises, the up-side value attributed to those improvements should be computed before any sharing occurs. If this sharing is applied to a sublease, a further issue might be whether the up-side value is applied over the term of the sublease or the remaining term of the tenant's lease.

WORK LETTERS AND TENANT IMPROVEMENT ALLOWANCES

In new buildings, the first tenant will probably find out exactly what the developer landlord is offering for rent by reading a document attached to and incorporated into the lease and describing the design and construction process for fitting out the premises. This attachment is called the "work letter." It describes the work that either the landlord or the tenant will perform to install the fixtures, fits, and finishes that will make the premises operable for whatever use the tenant plans to make of them. It will describe the electricity in terms of the power delivered to the premises, the HVAC system and where its components are ready to connect it to the premises, as well as fire alarm systems, water, waste, and other equipment. Reading it with attention to what's not described lets the new tenant know how far into the building's

---

17. In contrast, a tenant of retail lease for premises operated by a chain of stores will likely reject any sharing provision as it will decrease the fair market value of the chain to any prospective purchaser.

303

11. Leasing the Project

shell the tenant will have to reach to make the premises operable. What is described is often given in terms of building-based standard materials that the landlord will provide to fit out the infrastructure already on the premises.

Major tenants will do their own work, with plans their architects have designed, but subject to approval by the landlord or his architect. These tenants may even have their architects and construction consultants review the suitability of competing premises before a lease is executed. Other tenants will typically rely on the landlord's work, with the landlord's plans subject to review by the tenant or his architect; then the work letter will describe the work the landlord will do and set a maximum dollar amount, called a tenant improvement allowance (TIA) funded for a first tenant by the construction loan agreement. See Tech Ctr. 2000, LLC v. Zrii. LLC, 363 P.3d 566 (Utah Ct. App. 2015). For any tenant, the prudent thing to do is to design the layout, plans, and specifications prior to executing the lease. This permits the identification of any nonstandard jobs and materials before they add unexpected costs. It also facilitates bargaining over a TIA.

Examples

Example 35

L and T execute a lease with a work letter describing the premises as accessible by an opening off an east/west hallway. What more would a tenant need to know about this matter?

Explanation

Access usually means a door, but a door has a frame, hinges, and hardware, a threshold, doorknob, doorjambs, and a "door"—which may be a standard size or not. Each component's cost, and the labor needed to install it, should be allocated by the work letter.

Example 36

L and T execute a retail lease with a five-year primary term, subject to two options to renew for five years each, a work letter, and a TIA. The premises need extensive work to make them operational for the tenant, but the improvements will be difficult to remove at the end of the lease and are considered fixtures under applicable law. Do you have any tax advice in this situation?

11. Leasing the Project

Explanation

L would like to be able to amortize the improvements over the term of the lease, but can only do this if T is found the owner of the improvements. If L is the owner, he must depreciate their cost according to the IRC's longer depreciation schedule—over a life of 39 years. Thus L's tax benefits are greater with lease amortization than with property depreciation, and L should make sure the tenant owns the improvements. Landlords and tenants often negotiate hard about this matter. L has a strong incentive to claim T owns the improvements, and similarly T has an incentive to claim L owns them. If T owns them, T must treat the TIA as income and depreciate the improvements over 39 years. Generally speaking, the IRS uses a benefits and burdens of ownership test to allocate the tax consequences.

IRC §110 provides a benchmark for the tenant in this dispute: If the TIA is a "qualified lease construction allowance for short-term leases" the landlord will be considered the owner for federal income tax purposes. To qualify, the TIA must be (1) paid in cash or rent reduction, (2) made in a lease with a term of 15-years or less, (3) paid to improve "qualified, long-term real property" used for trade or business and reverting to the landlord at the end of the lease, and finally (4) spent in the year received. See Treas. Reg. §1.110-1 (2000). Thus L will want to extend the lease term beyond 15 years and will not accept language saying that the TIA is "for the purpose of improving qualified, long-term realty for use in the tenant's trade or business conducted on the premises."

COMPLIANCE WITH STATUTES, LAWS, ORDINANCES, ETC.

A landlord, or any property owner, has a common law duty to comply with all laws pertaining to the property. See Polk v. Armstrong, 540 P.2d 96 (Nev. 1975), and 1 A. James Casner, Am. L. Prop. §3.80 (1952). A landlord will thus have an incentive to have a tenant assume this duty—or as much of it as its attorney advises a court will countenance.

When a tenant executes a lease with a covenant that provides it will "comply with all laws affecting the premises," most courts would not thereby impose on the tenant a duty to so comply when the cost of doing so is substantial. See Glenn R. Sewell Sheet Metal, Inc. v. Loverde, 451 P.2d 721 (Cal. 1969) (a leading case), and Dennison v. Marlowe, 744 P.2d 906 (N.M. 1987). If the compliance cost involves (a) structural alterations to the premises, (b) a law enacted after the date of the lease's execution, or (c) a law enacted toward the end of the lease term when the benefit of compliance favors the landlord rather than the tenant, the cost will likely be allocated to

11. Leasing the Project

the landlord. See Milton R. Friedman, Friedman on Leases, §11.1 (Patrick A Randolph, Jr., ed., 5th ed. 2005).

Don't expect that a developer/landlord's attorney won't attempt to reverse all or some of these rules by negotiation, attempting to have the tenant assume some or all compliance costs. As you might expect, courts will then assess whether to enforce a compliance covenant according to its terms by examining a welter of factors, including those suggested by the Randolph treatise. See SDC/Pullman Partners v. Tolo, 70 Cal. Rptr. 2d 62, 68-69 (Cal. Ct. App. 1997). They might also ask (1) whether the costs of compliance are attributable to the tenant's peculiar use of its premises, (2) whether compliance is required or applies to all tenants in the building or all owners of real property, (3) whether the costs are substantial when compared with the total cost of the lease to the tenant, (4) whether the parties anticipated or intended this type of compliance, or (5) whether the cost relates to a part of the premises the landlord or the tenant is expected to maintain. This list of inquiries is (of course) not an exclusive one and is only limited by the creativeness of counsel.

When complying with the law involves some change in the premises, the compliance covenant is closely related to the covenant involving repairs and maintenance, the quality of the premises, as well as the covenant involving alterations to the premises.[18] Issues resulting in litigation are likely to involve compliance with environmental laws or asbestos removal, particularly when the tenant is leasing a whole building.

A tenant's attorney might ask for (1) a cap on compliance costs in any one year or over the term of the lease, with the right to terminate the lease if the cap is exceeded, (2) warranties and representations from the landlord as to a building's full compliance with all laws as of the date of execution of the lease, or (3) a proviso limiting the tenant's compliance obligations to nonstructural components of the building exclusively used by the tenant on its premises.

Examples

Example 37

Considering the three (3) tenant "asks" in the paragraph immediately preceding this Example, which would you think a mortgage lender reviewing a lease would find most and least objectionable?

---

18. It is likely that the landlord will initially want to prohibit all alterations to the premises, but the tenant bargaining over the alterations covenant might well succeed in obtaining a limitation on a prohibition on alterations for those the landlord consents to in writing. The issues following a "such consent shall not be unreasonably withheld" clause track those arising with assignments and subleases of the premises.

11. Leasing the Project

Explanation

The right to terminate the lease in the first request is the most objectionable since it threatens the rent roll of the building. The least objectionable is the third request. It is a proviso, coming after and counterbalancing the enumeration of costs for which the tenant assumes responsibility.

Example 38

The jurisdiction in which you are practicing uses an objective standard in interpreting contracts, including leases. Representing a project landlord in upcoming lease negotiations for a project office building, you have been asked to devise objective standards for enforcing a "compliance with laws" covenant. What standards might you suggest?

Explanation

You might suggest that a tenant "shall not occupy or permit anyone to occupy the premises and cause or permit any (1) violation of the certificate of occupancy for the premises or the building, (2) liability for harm or injury on the premises, (3) inability to obtain property, casualty, or any other insurance from a reputable insurance company for the premises or the building, or any component therein, (4) impairment of the reputation, character, or appearance of the building as a Class A office building, (5) nuisance, public or private, to other tenants, (6) legal, economic, or equitable waste of the premises or the building, (7) violation of any law, statute, ordinance, or regulation of any governmental body, (8) breach of any covenant in a mortgage or deed of trust secured by the landlord's interest in the building." The foregoing all contain references to either documents, judgment liabilities, insurance policies, trade association standards, or the common, case and regulatory law of the jurisdiction.

LEASING SHOPPING CENTER SPACE

The negotiations for leasing space in a shopping center or mall can often start with a simple letter of intent, such as the following.

307

11. Leasing the Project

> June 1, 2022
> Louie Lessor
> 1234 Mall Parkway
> River City, Maryland
>
> Dear Sir:
>
> In response to your request that we express our interest in leasing space in the White Heat Mall, a shopping center to be constructed by you at the intersection of Urban and 150th Ave., River City, please be informed that we have a definite interest in such a lease on satisfactory provisions, including (but not limited to) the following:
>
> 1. The space shall be approximately ___ in area.
> 2. The minimum monthly rent shall be one-twelfth of $ ___ per square foot, multiplied by the number of square feet in the premises.
> 3. This minimum rent shall apply against the percentage rent of ___% of gross sales.
> 4. The term shall be ___ years.
>
> The provisions of the lease shall be subject to the review and approval of our legal counsel. This letter is not intended to be contractual in nature but is only an expression of some of the major terms that we would discuss with you before entering into a lease.
>
> Very truly yours,
> Theresa Tenant CEO, Super Drugs, Inc.

Some other provisions might include a flexible rent commencement date, a delivery condition, and sign requirements. The letter might also provide for electricity, possibly stating that it be provided at "12 watts per square foot" delivered to a tenant's direct meter, or at the "landlord's annualized kilowatt hour cost, with increases at landlord's actual cost"; or for HVAC performance standards, to the effect that the HVAC should be "sufficient without supplements to operate at 72°F during business hours."

The letter calls for a percentage rent. This term might also be expanded. A percentage rent is added to a base, fixed rent, and is typically calculated as a percent of a store's gross sales.[19] The base rent is intended to set a floor and reduce the landlord's overall risk; it is based on an appraisal of the lease's fair rental value. The percentage rent is intended to allow the landlord to participate in the tenant's success in a rising economic and rental market, and to some extent is a hedge against inflation. (In a depressed market, percentage rent is one way to remarket foreclosed rental properties.) The relationship between base and percentage rent plays off the landlord's need for a secure cash flow — to make taxes and mortgage payments — against her desire to share quickly in the equity built up in a successful shopping center, and the tenant's need to have fixed costs against his willingness to share profits with the landlord.

---

19. Percentage rents are used in hotel industry leases, too, and are there expressed as a (different) percent of the hotel's room, beverage, and food revenues.

11. Leasing the Project

Percentage rent may be computed as a percent of either gross or net sales. The latter is the industry standard because it reduces the landlord's need to be involved in the tenant's accounting procedures otherwise used to establish the difference between net and gross sales. Most tenants concur in this standard because they do not want their landlord to know the extent of their profits. The landlord in negotiating this rent is pushing for the broadest definition of gross sales — for example, one including the full amount of cash and credit sales, catalogue sales, discount sales, layaway sales, installment sales, sales made to employees at deep discounts, vending machine sales, franchise sales, returns, and charge account sales. As to any exemptions from a broad definition, the landlord might insist that they be capped at some dollar amount. The percentage is typically also subject to periodic recomputation, and for this purpose computing the percentage during the Christmas shopping season makes no sense; similarly misleading will be picking the low point in a tenant's sales cycle — the middle of the summer in the Sun Belt, the dead of winter in the Frost Belt.

Letters of intent, sometimes referred to as "term sheets," can typically range from 3 to 4 pages to 15 to 20, depending on level of planning in which the tenant has engaged. The more planning, the more likely there will be no costly disputes later.

Examples

Example 39

How long should Theresa Tenant's term be? How should it be stated?

Explanation

Landlords are likely to resist terms longer than five years, so a short primary term, followed by several options to renew the lease, is the norm.

Example 40

Shopping centers typically open in either the spring or the fall. What problems arise because of this fact?

309

11. Leasing the Project

Explanation

The rent cannot be annualized on the basis of the first months of operation. (The landlord will likely want the percentage rent paid more frequently than annually.) This is particularly true if the opening is in the fall, because the Christmas shopping season starts during those first months. Perhaps a special base rent should be negotiated for the startup period.

Example 41

Shopping center leases are typically "triple net" leases. This means that taxes, insurance, and utility costs and all increases in these costs are passed along to the tenant. Your client, a landlord with long experience in the field, is about to retire and asks you to make sure that his future leases are as "pass through" (and so as trouble free for him) as possible. What is your advice?

Explanation

As to taxes: The landlord will be able to provide a list of taxes paid over the last several years and will know to whom they were paid, asking that a prospective tenant verify the list. The resulting lease provision might list the anticipated taxes and make plain whether special assessments, and other substitutes for real property taxes, are included as well. If the center is under construction, the date on which the landlord can start to pass through the taxes will become important. The billing period for the pass-through is important as well: Will the taxes be passed along as levied, or in anticipation of the levy, or after it? And how will the tenant's pro rata share be computed—on a ratio of the tenant's square footage to the total square footage of the project, or according to the value of the lease as a portion of the landlord's rent roll?

As to utilities: Should the landlord negotiate for the right to provide electricity to each tenant? The landlord might find that the surcharge added to the utility charges for the provision is worthwhile when passed along to the tenants. But maybe not. If the landlord provides such services, the further issue is whether the landlord undertakes (expressly or implicitly) a duty to provide a certain level of service, so any such duty should be negated in his leases. Should the tenant seek to obligate the landlord to provide a certain number of kilowatts? The modern office

11. Leasing the Project

or commercial space requires a good deal of computers and electronic equipment that, at some minimal level, should never be completely without power and that require a controlled range of temperatures in order to function.

As to other charges: The landlord will want to pass along maintenance charges as well. He will want to define maintenance as broadly as possible: "All costs and expenses of every type and nature, including appropriate reserves." If the center is an enclosed mall, the landlord will want to include a charge for the depreciation of the HVAC system. If the previously quoted language were used, it would remain unclear whether a depreciation charge, a charge to pass through the administrative expenses for billing and collection of common area charges, or a bad debt reserve would be permitted, so such issues should be resolved in the leases.

Example 42

Whether the pass-through is for taxes, insurance, utilities, or maintenance, a tenant's charge is computed as a fraction of the total charged the center. This fraction has the gross leasable area of the tenant's premises as its numerator. The denominator will be either the gross leased area or the gross leasable area of the center. Which denominator will the tenant typically prefer? Which the landlord? And what is at stake in the discussion?

Explanation

The landlord will prefer the gross leased area and the tenant the gross leaseable area. (These labels can get confusing, so remember that the tenant is negotiating to pay the smaller fraction of the total cost, while the landlord is negotiating to have the tenant pay the larger fraction.) At issue is the question of who bears the burden of vacant space in the center, a matter vital to the survival of the project as a whole.

Example 43

A net lease has become more common as the shopping center industry has grown. How can a tenant induce efficiency in a landlord offering such a lease?

11. Leasing the Project

Explanation

The tenant should negotiate a cap or dollar amount ceiling on the amounts that the landlord can pass through in any computational period. Thus the landlord will be given an incentive to stay within the limits imposed.

USE COVENANTS

In an office building, the landlord may forbid retail uses, uses generally disruptive, equivalent to common law waste or a public or private nuisance, but is otherwise unconcerned about the use made of the premises. For instance, use covenants typically do not forbid smoking or pets on the premises. See Hanson Natural Res. Co. v. Automated Commc'n, 926 P.2d 176 (Colo. Ct. App. 1996) (permitting dogs in leased offices is a "general office use"). So landlord's and tenant's attorney might agree to describe the tenant's use as "any general office use" or "any legal use." "Any legal office use" easily allocates the risk of noncompliance with applicable zoning ordinance and land use statutes to the tenant. See Custer Envt'l Inc. v. 9305 Georgetown Road P'ship, 691 A.2d 1336 (Md. 1997) (tenant obliged to cure noncompliance with zoning). The latter is in the best position to assess the legality of its own use and is also in the best position to cure any noncompliance.

Whatever restrictive language appears on the lease, from the landlord's perspective, it cannot be precatory (that is, construed as a statement of purpose), thus statements that the premises "are being leased for" or "may be used for," or "will be used primarily for" general office use is not a restriction on use; they are merely descriptive or illustrative. Prohibitory words such as "shall be used solely for" or "used only as" are necessary. Once found to be restrictive, a use covenant is a real covenant and "runs with the land," binding successive holders of the lease. Likewise, a statement that "the premises shall be used only for lawful uses," does no more than restate the common law.

Just as a number of jurisdictions imply that a landlord act reasonably in consenting to assignments and subleases, a restrictive use covenant acts as a backstop to protect a landlord denying such consent.

Because the use of the premises implicates its alienability, a basic feature of any estate or interest in real property, any lease covenant restricting the use of the premises will be strictly construed against the landlord; likewise, the least restrictive reading is the preferred one. Absent a restrictive use

312

11. Leasing the Project

covenant, a tenant will not forfeit its lease even for an illegal use of the premises, except for the commission of waste or a nuisance. See Restatement (Second), Property, Landlord & Tenant, §12.5 (1977). Moreover, the use of the premises is "one of the most important determinants of a tenant's profitability at a particular location." See Alan M. DiSciullo, Negotiating a Commercial Lease from a Tenant's Perspective, 18 Real Est. L.J. 27, 28 (1989). Restrictive use covenants pit that profitability against the landlord's desire to protect other tenants. Thus an office building landlord might however be concerned when the tenant is (say) an accounting firm, that the premises be limited to "an accounting firm of no more than five accountants and seven support staff."

Often a tenant's use rights are restricted by a separate lease covenant concerning the building's general rules and regulations incorporated into the lease and applicable to all tenants in the building. Thus prohibited uses might be described as "any use unreasonably causing a nuisance or interfering with another tenant's business or injuring the reputation of the building as a Class A office building." In that vein, prohibited uses might also be expressly described in a nonexclusive list as any government office, any office open to the public generally (e.g., an entertainment or sports ticket broker's office), or a massage parlor.

Examples

Example 44

You are negotiating a project lease with a large law firm. You propose that the premises be operated for "use as a law firm." What objections might be anticipated from the managing partner negotiating this lease?

Explanation

Several objections. What if the real estate partners want to open a real estate closing company or a title insurance agency? What if the land use attorneys in the firm want to employ urban planners? What if the tax partners want to employ an accountant? What if the firm wants to merge with a small banking law firm? Or start up a lobbying firm? It is unlikely that expanding what you have proposed by four words, i.e., " . . . and other incidental uses" will satisfy the managing partner. More specificity is needed.

* * *

In contrast to the general office building landlord, a shopping center developer or landlord is very concerned about the particular use a tenant makes of the premises. He has two concerns. A first type is common to all tenants. He is concerned that their business hours be the same, that their sales be

313

11. Leasing the Project

conducted together, that they observe the same holidays, and that the signs they use be similar.

A second concern is that the stores in the center generate the greatest possible number of shoppers, and a sales volume sufficient to make the center a success. Thus he wants the stores to complement, and not compete with, each other, except where competition generates a greater sales volume overall; moreover, he wants its major tenants — such as a department store or a big box electronic, household goods, drug, supermarket, or grocery store (all known as an anchor or magnet store) — to attract shoppers to the center's smaller stores.

To achieve this optimum mix of tenants, the landlord pays close attention to the use covenants applicable to each. These use covenants define the use to be made of the premises and restrict the tenant to the operation of that use; they sometimes grant a major or anchor tenant an exclusive use covenant, which gives the tenant the exclusive right to operate that use in the center. Such covenants are often expressly effective "so long as the tenant is operating as [whatever the exclusive use is] on (say) 90 percent of its premises" and provide that "no other portion of the shopping center shall be used for [that use] by any store leasing more than (say) 300 square feet of sales areas for [the use]." Exceptions might be made for supermarkets, variety stores, or department stores, or existing named tenants, their assignees, and subtenants.

Smaller centers are often anchored by a supermarket. However, defining a supermarket as premises for the sale of food, and granting the operator an exclusive use covenant in its lease, is a mistake that few landlord/developers are likely to make. Today, a drugstore, a chain discount store, or even a clothing or sporting goods store is likely to sell some type of food. Similarly, an exclusive use for a restaurant might define the use

(1) by type (e.g., fast food, pizza, to-go bakery, coffee shop, fine dining, French cuisine, Italian cuisine, etc.),

(2) by products sold (e.g., sandwiches (including but not limited to hoagies, heroes, submarine, and cheese steak sandwiches), such as meats, processed meats, lettuce, tomato, with butter, mayonnaise, dressing, or savory spreads between two pieces of bread or rolls),

(3) by naming its prohibited competitors (for fast food (say), McDonald's, Wendy's, Burger King, Panera Bread, etc.) (a) operating (say) within 1,000 feet, (b) on a particular wing of a mall, or (c) within a food court,

(4) with exclusions (for, e.g., anchor stores, stores selling competitive products for not more than (say) 20% of gross sales, or existing (named) lessees).

The exclusive use covenant should last as long as the tenant operates the use on the premises — no longer. It ceases when the tenant holding it ceases operations, except perhaps when the lease is assigned or sublet to a retailer restauranteur, or user approved by the landlord.

11. Leasing the Project

The landlord granting an exclusive use is betting on the success of the user. The lease must be drafted in such a way that the user's business can evolve over time, so it must not be too narrowly drawn; on the other hand, it must not be overly broad lest it unduly restrict the landlord's future tenants' businesses.

Once having granted an exclusive, the prudent landlord will include a prohibition on that use in succeeding leases, and maintain a running list of exclusives both to keep track of them and to attach the list to succeeding leases; so exclusive use covenants should expressly state that they are effective only against future leases. A tenant negotiating an exclusive use should thus be responsible for investigating the businesses of existing tenants. Excepting prior leases by both name and use may similarly aid the landlord in avoiding future disputes among tenants.

Permitting one tenant an exclusive use encourages others to ask for the same. When a radius clause is employed in the definition of the exclusive, or if competitors are named, then the holder of the use should indemnify the landlord if it becomes liable thereby under fair trade or antitrust laws and statutes.

Defining the type of business — for example, retail, not wholesale, and not discount — avoids future disputes but will have to be dovetailed with other covenants, such as the one involving signs. Adding a general prohibition on operating for any other purpose should signal the end of the use's definition. From the developer/landlord's perspective, defining an exclusive type of business, rather than providing an exclusive on certain types of goods, will provide the landlord with greater flexibility in future leases.

Some tenants with an exclusive may also request the power to enforce it, but landlords typically resist this — better that the landlord police other tenants, armed with the option to terminate the lease of any other tenant intentionally violating the covenant. (Lenders reviewing the lease will likely resist this latter "option to terminate" remedy.) A less objectionable remedy might be liquidated damages computed as rent abatement pro rated for the exclusive use holder's showing of decreased income or sales.

Exclusive use covenants are not for every lessee; indeed, some would not benefit from one. Some types of businesses — dress shops, shoe stores, and jewelers — may not be as profitable standing alone; they may do better with surrounding competitors. It is up to the landlord to select the mix of tenants that will maximize consumer traffic for every lessee and create multi-stop shopping for many consumers. Often the selection of the anchor and other major tenants will determine the best types of surrounding lessees.[20] For a new center, selection of most lessees will occur during the

---

20. The idea of working the leasing process backward applies here as well as when negotiating permanent and construction loans for a project. The higher rents are paid by the smaller tenants, so that the landlord's profit margin is typically higher when renting to a card shop rather than to a department store. The latter "leases in bulk" at an annual square footage rate that may even be a loss leader for the developer. Those losses will have to be made up so that

315

11. Leasing the Project

"lease-up" period, occurring in advance of the center's takeout or permanent mortgage loan closing.

So a use covenant might state that "this lease is executed so that, during its term, and the term of any renewals and extensions thereof, the tenant will occupy, use, and operate the business of a drugstore on the premises, and no other use whatsoever." This would not prohibit the lessee from providing, for example, a vending machine, or a video game, so long as it is a use incidental to the primary business conducted on the premises. Similarly, an exclusive use clause for a "sandwich shop" would not prohibit the landlord from leasing to the operator of Bert's Burritos. See White City Shopping Ctr., LP v. PR Restaurants, LLC, 2006 Mass. Super. LEXIS 544 (Mass. Super. Ct. Oct. 31, 2006) (finding that a burrito is not a sandwich)

Restrictive and Exclusive Use Covenant Remedies

Suppose that a shopping center developer leases premises to a large pharmacy, giving it an "exclusive right to maintain a pharmacy" and promising not to lease to another pharmacy. Forty years later, fearful that its largest anchor tenant is about to go bankrupt and close its store, the developer landlord attempts to buy out the anchor lease and proposes to lease the premises to a discount pharmacy. The large existing pharmacy sues for an injunction to prevent the buy-out and new lease of the anchor space. At the hearing for a temporary restraining order, the landlord argues that damages can be measured and are an adequate remedy, so the injunction should not issue, then or ever. The landlord's argument is an instance of (what you learned in contracts as) the doctrine of efficient breach.[21]

However, the issuance of an injunction is the result of balancing the equities, of weighing the advantages and disadvantages of doing so. The advantages of an injunction are that (1) it shifts the cost of measuring damages from the court to the parties, (2) it can be written in a clear, prohibitory manner not requiring continuing jurisdiction, (3) the resulting negotiations have a narrow focus, whereas the litigation over damages would turn into an expensive battle of expert witnesses who can as easily battle it out in private negotiations as in court, and (4) the negotiations can consider noneconomic as well as economic costs, and irrational as well as rational factors. Thus the benefits of the injunction trump its costs — and

---

the project achieves overall profitability at the expense of the other, smaller lessees. Thus some initial square footage is typically set aside for small, specialized shops.

21. "The duty to keep a contract at common law means a prediction that you must pay damages if you do not keep it, and nothing more." O.W. Holmes, The Path of the Law, 10 Harv. L. Rev. 457, 458 (1897).

316

11. Leasing the Project

the restraining order and injunction should issue. See Walgreen Co. v. Sara Creek Prop. Co., 966 F.2d 273 (7th Cir. 1992) (Posner, J.), noted at 20 Cardozo L. Rev. 321 (1998), and J.C. Penney Co., Inc. v. Giant Eagle, Inc., 813 F. Supp. 360 (W.D. Pa. 1992).

Tenants might negotiate for rent abatement if and when a landlord breaches an exclusive use covenant. See Red Sage LP v. DESPA Deutsche Sparkassen Immobilien-Anlage-Gasellschaft mbH, 254 F.3d 1120 (D.C. Cir. 2001) (upholding such a covenant as a liquidated damages provision). In the alternative, tenants might bargain for an option of first refusal to (say) add a type of service, goods, or menu to their line before the landlord leases to another tenant offering those services or goods.

In a similar vein, shopping center developers often provide that the lease "shall be forfeited upon any violation of a covenant contained herein." Thus a developer landlord may be given an injunction, barring the tenant's continued sale of a line of goods violating its restrictive use covenant. The lease's express terms, draconian though they may be, imply that lesser and less draconian remedies are included within it.

In each instance, the injunction is a way of giving leverage in ensuing negotiations, giving either party the option of short-circuiting them by enforcement of or compliance with the injunction.

The more general question remains. Why don't landlords negotiate leases in which some defaults work a forfeiture, but other defaults give rise to a claim for damages? Landlords don't; they seem to want the lease arranged so that, with any default, the tenant is subject to eviction. This is explained by the leverage landlords have in negotiating a lease, but it is also the result of landlords knowing that equity abhors a forfeiture, and so courts will treat trivial, technical, inadvertent, and nonprejudicial defaults as immaterial and giving no grounds for a lease's termination and a tenant's eviction.

A violation of a use restriction is a good place within a lease to provide something less than forfeiture. See Ray-Ron Corp. v. DMY Realty Co., 500 N.E.2d 1163 (Ind. 1986).

Once a shopping center is built and leased, the landlord's continuing ability to control the mix of tenants will depend on her ability to control subleases and assignments; thus a tenant's subleasing and assigning the lease will usually depend on the landlord's consent, "such consent not unreasonably to be withheld," as the common clause used in leases has it. See Warmack v. Merchants Nat'l Bank of Fort Smith, 612 S.W.2d 733 (Ark. 1981) (finding that a shopping center landlord's desire for a good tenant mix is a proper reason for withholding consent). Thus, in the context of the shopping center, there is a close connection between use restrictions and subletting-assignment clauses. A broad right to assign or sublease may eventually be rendered much less valuable if accompanied in the lease by a narrow use covenant.

11. **Leasing the Project**

Continuous Operation Covenants

Retail landlords have a horror of having premises "go dark." That gives the appearance of failure and economic gloom, particularly in a shopping center. Thus landlords traditionally bargain for continuous operation of the use on the leased premises during the time the center is open for business. A restrictive use covenant, even when mandatory, does not alone imply a duty to operate continuously. Thus landlords have to bargain for this covenant expressly. An example of this express covenant might provide that the "tenant agrees to operate" for a set number of years, or during the term of this lease, 100% or some lesser percentage "of the leased premises with due diligence and efficiency," and "carrying and stocking merchandise of such character, quality, and quantity, that will produce the maximum gross sales and return to the landlord and tenant." See Berkeley Dev. Co. v. Great Atl. & Pac. Tea Co., 518 A.2d 790 (N.J. Super. Ct. Law Div. 1986) (even when a base, fixed, or minimum rent is substantial, tenant is liable for discontinuing operations when to do so would only inflict economic injury and not serve the tenant's business purpose, as with a sublease to an assignee whose motive for taking the assignment is to curtail competition with other stores in its chain).

Without an express covenant in a lease for continuous operation of the tenanted use, such a covenant is not traditionally implied in a shopping center lease, even when the tenant is given an exclusive use covenant in its lease restricting the landlord from leasing to another to operate the same use. However, if in addition the ability of the tenant to assign or sublease is severely restricted, a continuous operation covenant has been implied. The implication is all the stronger when the tenant is in addition an anchor tenant, because the anchor tenant is needed to draw shoppers to the other tenants' stores and make the center as a whole an economic success. Even in a strip center, without an anchor store, a principle of mutual dependence might be used to draw the same conclusion. Moreover, when a tenant is paying a low base rent and high percentage rent and the lease's term is long, the implication grows stronger still. See Lagrew v. Hooks-SuperX, Inc., 905 F. Supp. 401 (E.D. Ky. 1995). However, with so many preconditions to making this implication, it is little wonder that most courts considering the matter have refused to imply a continuous operation covenant. See Sampson Inv. v. Jondex Corp., 499 N.W.2d 177 (Wis. 1993), and Mercury Inv. Co. v. F. W. Woolworth Co., 706 P.2d 523 (Okla. 1985) (refusing to imply such a covenant from an express covenant "to operate diligently," even when sales have flatlined for a substantial period).

318

11. Leasing the Project

Examples

Example 45

Suppose that Super Drug, Inc., signs a lease in a shopping center that has one major anchor tenant, a department store. The Super Drug lease called for a term of 15 years, with five options to renew the lease for 5-year renewal terms and a minimum rent of $200,000, with a percentage rent based on gross sales, triggered annually by sales of $400,000 during the first 15 years and $300,000 after that. The only other relevant provision of the lease provides that the premises are "to be used and operated as a drugstore and for no other purposes whatsoever." Business is bad, and Super Drug seeks to cease operations but is willing to pay the minimum rent and look for a sublessee. Can the developer insist that Super Drug continue operations?

Explanation

No. Super Drug is not the anchor tenant and thus not a magnet to attract customer flow into the center. No implication of a duty to operate can be taken from the percentage rental, in part because the base rent does not seem insubstantial or nominal. See Walgreen Arizona Drug Co. v. Plaza Ctr. Corp., 647 P.2d 643 (Ariz. Ct. App. 1982). If the base rent were nominal and the tenant an anchor, the answer might be different. See First American Bank & Trust Co. v. Safeway Stores, Inc., 729 P.2d 938, 940 (Ariz. App. 1986) (insubstantial base rent implied a duty to operate), and Ingannamorte v. Kings Super Markets, Inc., 260 A.2d 841 (N.J. 1970) (duty to operate implied for lease of anchor tenant paying percentage rental). Thus, when the base fixed rent is substantial, no implied covenant to operate continuously is likely to be found, whereas if the fixed rent is insubstantial in comparison to the percentage rent, an implied covenant is more likely.

Consider whether the parties could indicate an intent to agree otherwise by the landlord's first making improvements to the premises and then agreeing to a substantial fixed base rent, with a comparatively small percentage rent. The possibility of implying a continuous operation covenant rises with the landlord's helping out with the improvements. If the landlord financed the improvements for the tenant, on the other hand, your answer would probably stay the same. See R. Schoshinski, American Law of Landlord and Tenant 234 (1980).

11. Leasing the Project

Example 46

The Super Drug lease prohibits its assignment without the express written consent of the landlord. The parent company for Super Drug decides to reposition itself in its market and to close all of its Super Drug stores. The lease provisions give Super Drug the right to discontinue operations at any time by sending a notice to that effect 90 days in advance; within 90 days after the mailing of this notice, the developer could then elect to terminate the Super Drug lease. (As previously discussed, the landlord's right to terminate is often called a "recapture" provision.)

Super Drug provides the developer with the 90-day notice of its intent to discontinue operations, but the developer does not elect to terminate the lease within 90 days after its receipt of the notice. Super Drug then agrees to sublease to Disco Drug, another drugstore chain wishing to establish a presence in the center's market area. Super Drug informs the developer that it will exercise its second and third options to renew in a timely manner. The developer refuses to renew Super Drug's lease or recognize its sublessee and sues to terminate Super Drug's lease, known here as "the head lease." In this suit, what result?

Explanation

Judgment for Super Drug. If the sublease to Disco is distinguishable from an assignment, the right to sublease remains in Super Drug's arsenal of leasehold rights. If the developer did not elect to terminate, the cessation of operations does not destroy that right to sublease, not otherwise restricted in the lease. See Joseph Bros. Co. v. F.W. Woolworth Co., 844 F.2d 369 (6th Cir. 1988).

Example 47

If the Super Drug lease contains a provision that permits (but does not require) the landlord to relet the premises after the tenant abandons them, does the presence of that provision affect the landlord's rights? How?

11. Leasing the Project

Explanation

Yes. The permissive reletting provision is inserted by landlords who wish to make it plain that they are reletting on behalf of the tenant and not on their own behalf. The clause is thus a method of preserving the landlord's right to sue on the lease for damages. At the same time, however, the clause is also a basis for a court's declaration that the landlord has an implied duty to mitigate the tenant's damages. See Sandor Dev. Co. v. Reitmeyer, 498 N.E.2d 1020 (Ind. App. 1986).

Example 48

If Super Drug takes more than 90 days to remove its fixtures to prepare the premises for Disco, is that a breach of an implied duty to operate the premises found in the restrictive use provision?

Explanation

No. Assuming that the court would imply a duty to operate out of the restrictive use provision, the right to redecorate or ready the premises for a sublessee is incidental to the right to sublet and should be protected on that account. See Monmouth Real Estate Inv. Trust v. Manville Foodland, Inc., 482 A.2d 186 (N.J. Super. Ct. App. Div. 1984), cert. denied, 491 A.2d 722 (N.J. 1985).

Example 49

The developer and Super Drug settle their several disputes by inserting an express covenant for continuous operation into the lease. Prior to the effective date of the lease amendment, the parent company of Super Drug changes its corporate policy of geographic expansion and decides that henceforth it will not operate in the area of the shopping center. Super Drug files suit for an injunction, asking the court to decide whether it may assign its lease to an otherwise suitable assignee because of the change in policy. In the suit, what result, and why?

321

11. Leasing the Project

Explanation

Super Drug may not assign its lease. See Steel LP v. Caldor, Inc., 850 F.2d 690 (4th Cir. 1988). A mandatory injunction is the typical remedy in such a case, but what is the whole remedy? May the developer also have damages? See Hornwood v. Smith's Food King No. 1, 772 P.2d 1284 (Nev. 1989) (holding yes when the tenant is an anchor tenant). The loss of value for the shopping center developer during the time the tenant's portion of the center is "dark" is a consequential damage that the tenant could reasonably foresee and for which it is liable. The "economic interdependence of all tenants" justifies extending the rule of Hornwood to all tenants in a center. See Slater v. Pearle Vision Center, Inc., 546 A.2d 676 (Pa. Super. 1988).

Example 50

Over several lease renewals and extension, RX Drugs has operated in River City Mall and recently invested in the installation on its premises of facilities to engage in compounding drugs (combining medications, as opposed to retailing brand name and generic drugs, to fill prescriptions). RX Drugs' lease has never contained an exclusive use covenant. The mall's landlord now proposes to expand the mall and execute a lease with another drug store for part of the expanded mall space competing with RX Drugs for its compounding business. RX Drugs seeks a judicial order enjoining the second lease as a breach of the landlord's implied covenant of good faith and fair dealing. Will RX succeed?

Explanation

No. Finding a breach of the implied covenant of good faith and fair dealing is a backhanded way of rewriting RX Drugs' lease to incorporate an exclusive use covenant into it. A commercial lease is above all a contract, negotiated by savvy persons who know their own business interests. Implying a covenant into such a lease lessens the premium on careful negotiations and protects persons from their own inattention. RX wants a benefit for which it did not negotiate. Why give it a second bite of the apple? RX now seeks a more valuable lease than it negotiated. That the mall space for the second drug store is in a location not part of the mall when RX executed its lease might mean that the landlord now thinks as a business matter that the expanded mall can support two drug stores. Since an exclusive use covenant restricts trade and restrains alienation, it is not favored, and, assuming that the covenant that RX seeks was implied, its reach should not encompass these facts. Both the nature of the implied provision and the manner in which it is sought argue against RX Drugs here. See Horton v. Uptown Partners, LP, 2006 Iowa App. LEXIS 1719 (Iowa Ct. App. 2006).

322

11. Leasing the Project

The implied covenant of good faith, the fair dealing, might be a darling of the law of contracts generally, but absent some indication of bad faith by the party against whom it is employed, its use in the context of commercial leasing is unwise.

OTHER LEASE COVENANTS

As long as this chapter has been, it does not exhaust the range of subjects that a commercial lease typically covers. It is not unusual for such a document to run to 30 to40 pages of typescript, single spaced. Length of course is no measure of quality, but the length makes assessment of the bargains struck in it virtually impossible. Who's to say which right, remedy, or obligation was traded for which? Sometimes the interplay between various covenants is apparent, sometimes not.

The continuing quality of the premises; their maintenance, repair, restoration, and alternation; the building and project services; the consequences of fire, casualty, and condemnation of the leasehold; insurance by landlord and tenant; the consequences of default and the remedies following on default, all are likely the subject of separate covenants in addition to those discussed in this chapter.

As to **quality**, once the tenant accepts possession, subject to the TIA, work orders, and/or landlord's improvements, tenant typically "agrees to maintain the premises in good order, repair and condition, and to surrender the same at the expiration or termination of the lease." A few jurisdictions have an implied covenant of habitability for commercial leases. Most imply a covenant of quiet enjoyment into commercial leases. Otherwise, the law governing eviction, constructive eviction, waste, and nuisance controls the lease, subject to negotiated modifications.

As to the **maintenance, repair, and restoration**[22] of the premises, the longer the term of the lease, the more landlord-friendly these covenants are likely to be. On the other hand, the longer the lease, the more likely the tenant will be able to alter the premises to accommodate its changing needs; but then the ability to alter the premises might be regarded as ameliorative waste— waste that adds value to the reversion but physically changes the premises. See Two Guys from Harrison-N.Y., Inc. v. S.F.R. Realty Assocs., 472 N.E.2d 315 (N.Y. 1984). If the landlord is to shift the costs related to these covenants to the tenant, the lease must do so clearly. See Restatement (Second), Property, Landlord & Tenant, §5.6 (1977).

---

22. For a discussion of these terms, see Seoane v. Drug Emporium, Inc., 457 S.E.2d 93 (Va. 1995).

11. Leasing the Project

Litigation over these covenants often takes place when the term of the lease nears its expiration: then the tenant is less likely to want to spend money on repairs, and the landlord is looking to retake possession of any tenant improvements made during the term. See Fisher Props., Inc. v. Arden-Mayfair, Inc., 726 P.2d 8 (Wash. 1986) (discussing end-of-term disputes).

The less detailed these covenants are, the more likely the landlord's sole remedy will lie in the law of waste. To avoid the charge of waste, the tenant will have to perform its maintenance obligations lien-free. Even a statement that the tenant "maintain the premises in good repair" requires more than the law of waste does. Less detail about these matters means that the landlord will attempt to allocate all the unspoken costs of maintenance, etc., to the tenant.

All such covenant breaches will likely have to be reported to the landlord, cured at the tenant's sole cost, and when the tenant fails to cure, cured by the landlord, with reimbursement by the tenant.

When the lease is silent on particular matters, courts compare (1) the cost of the work to the remaining contract rent (see, e.g., Second United Cities Realty Corp. v. Price & Schumacher Co., 151 N.E. 150 (N.Y. 1926)); (2) the length of the term and the comparative benefits of the work received by the landlord and tenant (see Scott v. Prazma, 555 P.2d 571 (Wyo. 1976)); (3) the structural/nonstructural nature of the work (see Baxter v. Ill. Police Federation, 380 N.E.2d 832 (Ill. Ct. App. 1978)). They will also consider (4) the likelihood that the parties contemplated the work, and (5) the degree of interference to the tenant's use of the premises while the work is done. These five factors are similar to those that courts consider when interpreting a "compliance with laws" covenant.

As to **building and project services**, a prospective tenant will likely be presented with a list of services that the landlord intends to provide. Such services might include the provision of utilities, trash and garbage disposal, window washing, landscaping, parking, elevator service, and janitorial and lobby services. A tenant's attorney might then query the client as to the services it needs and then consider: (1) how often and when (24/7 or during business hours?) they will be provided; (2) how they will be paid for; (3) how increases in their cost will be paid for, and (4) the remedies available when they are not provided. If a service is not listed and not provided, but necessary for the tenant's use of the premises, will the tenant be able to claim a constructive eviction from the premises? Not necessarily. Not providing a service must first be found a material breach of the lease. Compare Sims v. Mason, 281 N.E.2d 608 (Mass. 1972) (deprivation of cleaning and HVAC services held no constructive eviction), with Charles E. Burt, Inc. v. Seven Grand Corp., 163 N.E.2d 4 (Mass. 1959) (deprivation of heat resulting in damaged business equipment held a constructive eviction).

Except in a few jurisdictions, not providing a service is not a ground for abating or withholding rent: the common law doctrine of independent

11. Leasing the Project

covenants here still applies. Unlike a residential tenant, a commercial tenant likely need not abandon premises in order to assert that it was constructively evicted: instead, filing an equitable bill for a declaratory judgment or an action for damages would suffice. Needless to say, the covenant of quiet enjoyment and the doctrine of constructive eviction is no substitute for bargaining over the tenant's remedies when promised services are not provided. Partial abatement of rent is the sole remedy that landlords are likely to grant. Landlords typically raise strong objections to alternative remedies. For instance, both landlords and lenders object to any right to terminate the lease and jeopardize the landlord's cash flow, and a self-help right might affect the building's reversionary value. Moreover, whatever services the landlord undertakes to deliver, they will typically be delivered only to the premises. When the tenant is leasing a whole building surrounded by grounds or other facilities, it is advisable to check the definition of the premises in the lease to make sure the building isn't surrounded by a weed patch or a services desert.

As to **fire, casualty, and condemnation,** the common law rule is that the landlord is under no obligation to restore the premises after a fire or casualty event. The lease is here regarded as a conveyance, and once that conveyance occurs the landlord is free of any further obligation to restore. Most office building leases reverse this rule and obligate the landlord to restore after a fire or other casualty. However, any express reversal in a commercial lease will be strictly construed; remember, the default rule is that the landlord has no such obligation.

Mortgage lenders have encouraged this reversal, hoping to preserve the security value of a building in order to secure repayment of their loans. Landlords therefore typically agree to restore, but are then interested in the definition of "restoration" and the timing and extent of their obligation to do so.

(1) No lease that provides the landlord will restore "forthwith" after a casualty should satisfy the tenant's attorney. A schedule for the restoration is necessary. Is the tenant entitled to rent abatement while the restoration is underway? Such a remedy assumes that the lease is not terminated. When should the assumption be otherwise? Suppose the premises are destroyed by fire and the lease provides that if the restoration would take more than 90 days, the landlord can terminate the lease; the landlord estimates that the restoration would take more than 90 days and terminates the lease. That estimate might still be tested in litigation and proven wrong with proof that restoration could have taken less than 90 days. See Restaurant Operators v. Jenny, 519 A.2d 256 (N.H. 1986) (awarding tenant five year's lost profits in this situation). As to the timing of when and what restoration is required after a casualty, landlord and tenant might better agree that the tenant's obligation to restore begins when the landlord has restored what damage occurred to common areas or to utilities and infrastructure that the tenant's restoration can build out.

325

11. Leasing the Project

(2) Is the landlord obligated to restore premises to the condition the tenant found when the tenant first took possession? Are up-dates in order? The lease must be express on the matter. No general obligation on the landlord to "maintain and repair" the premises will suffice to impose any obligation to "restore" them in an updated manner after a casualty. These quoted words have separate and distinct legal meanings. Likewise, the landlord may reserve the right to elect either to restore or terminate the lease, but if the landlord elects restoration, it must complete the work in a "workmanlike manner." What that means should be cross-referenced with the "compliance with laws" covenant.

The condemnation of a leasehold, or more likely, the condemnation of the developer's ownership or entity interest in the project, presents unique problems of deciding who can participate in the condemnation proceedings and then allocating the proceeds of the condemnation award.

As to **insurance**. No two lease covenants are as closely related as are the covenants for fire and casualty and the covenant for insurance. The most obvious connection is an express one: that the events covered in the fire and casualty covenant are the same events required to be insured against in the insurance covenant.[23] Obtaining property insurance and liability/casualty insurance are concerns of both landlords and tenants. Exclusions in the standard comprehensive general liability (CGL) policy generally exclude claims that might be made under other types of policies: i.e., policies for contractual liability, crime and vandalism coverage, business interruption, rent loss, workers' compensation, and environmental pollution. CGL policies are offered either on a claims made or occurrence basis. The former is preferable because it permits a claim if either the injury or event occurred during the period of coverage, whether or not the claim is made during that period.

In recent years, coverage for terrorist attacks has been removed from many generally available property and liability policies, but may be separately insured. Landlords typically obtain rent insurance. (Lenders insist on the latter.) Tenants are more likely to obtain business interruption insurance, but landlords might benefit from such coverage too. See K.C. Hopps, Ltd. v. The Cincinnati Ins. Co., 2020 U.S. Dist. LEXIS 144285 (W.D. Mo. Aug. 12, 2020) (denying an insurer's motion to dismiss a suit claiming coverage under a CGL policy for Covid-19 effects on tenant's premises).

At common law, there is no duty imposed on a tenant to insure its interest, just as a life tenant need not insure premises for remaindermen or other future interest holders. Both landlord and tenant have separate insurable

---

23. Insurers issuing property and casualty insurance policies are constantly changing coverage and amending policy provisions about handling claim. The attorneys for both landlords and tenants are prudent when they employ insurance brokers they trust to keep then up to date on such matters.

11. Leasing the Project

interests in the leasehold. Absent a lease provision, no law compels either to obtain insurance for the benefit of the other; so neither party has a claim on the other's policy. A lease often requires the tenant to name the landlord either a beneficiary or third-party insured[24] on the tenant's insurance; when the tenant's policy does not name the landlord in either capacity, a court might infer otherwise and confer the required status on the landlord. However, once named either, the landlord assumes no obligation to pay the premiums on the tenant's policy.

When both landlord and tenant carry separate insurance policies, each insurer will waive claims against each other for damages to their respective interests, being sure first that the waivers do not violate their own insurance policies. These waivers except the intentional acts of each, and apply to property damage but not personal injuries. These will in turn require that their insurers waive their rights of subrogation against the other insured party — this is done in order to prevent each carrier from becoming the insurer's insurer. When the tenant has signed a lease with a hell-or-highwater provision, it will need to carry business interruption insurance. Likewise, if the lease provides that rent will abate during any business interruption, the landlord will need to carry rent loss insurance.

For claims, losses, liabilities, suits, actions, proceedings, or expenses involving personal injuries, landlords and tenants typically cross-indemnify and hold each other harmless, whether for negligent, willful, or tortious conduct. One exception might be for a single tenant building for which the tenant carries all the liability insurance. Since each party is likely a legal entity, the indemnity should cover the indemnitor's employees, agents, and contractors.

Landlords generally ask that the tenant periodically provide evidence of insurance coverage by supplying a certificate[25] to the effect that all premiums are paid and that coverage is in effect.

As to **remedies and defaults**. Here the covenants of the lease control, since the common law remedies are likely incomplete or slow. (This discussion is likewise incomplete as the combination of remedies for particular defaults is vast: considered here are remedies following an early lease termination.) At common law, neither the landlord nor tenant could terminate a lease, absent a covenant in the lease conferring that power. By statute in most jurisdictions, and by an express covenant in most commercial leases, a

---

24. The difference in the landlord's being named a third-party insured, as opposed to a beneficiary, under the tenant's policy is that the landlord has the right to deal directly with the insurer when a claim arises. A beneficiary has no such right and must rely on the tenant's negotiations with the insurer.

25. Standard form property and liability policies are promulgated by the Ass'n for Cooperative Operations Research Development (ACORD), ACORD also issues standard form certificates of insurance. The latter forms provide that they create no enforceable right for their holder and are informational only.

327

11. Leasing the Project

landlord may reenter the premises, recover possession, and terminate the lease for a material breach. Because the re-entry is typically seen as the landlord's terminating the lease, a right to re-enter and terminate the lease for a material default is sometimes supplemented by a lease covenant accelerating all contract rent remaining after the default, becoming due and payable at the date of the default.[26] Such acceleration covenants are scrutinized by most courts as they would a liquidated damages remedy. See Aurora Business Park Assocs., LP v. Michael Albert, Inc., 548 N.W.2d 153 (Iowa 1996).

Landlords will thus want every default to be material and become a basis for termination of the lease. Tenants will consider only monetary defaults material, resulting in termination. The difference in these positions is likely to result in material defaults being subject to a written notice and cure period and a limitation on remedies for tenant breaches that can be monetized by the landlord's recovery of a high default rate of interest and late charges on the breach — and, upon early termination of a lease, landlords might recover TIA amounts paid, rent concessions and abatements, and brokerage commissions. Material defaults include nonpayment of rent and common area charges, bankruptcy, abandonment, and subleases and assignments without consent.

As to the basic list of material defaults, (1) landlords often insist that events indicating an impending bankruptcy, insolvency, shutting down business on the premises, or any substantial decrease in a tenant's net worth, become a material breach; (2) tenants often insist that, upon a tenant's abandonment, a landlord's damages be subject to a set-off when the landlord fails to re-let in reasonable manner (this set-off is really an affirmative defense in the landlord's action for damages); and (3) landlords often insist that the tenant's remedy for a landlord's unreasonable withholding of consent to a sublease or assignment be limited to injunctive relief.

A landlord's termination remedy can be limited in various ways: it can be subject to a tenant's right to an injunction, a stand-still agreement, an agreement to arbitrate, or a waiver of a jury trial. Once in litigation, a landlord might be denied a right to terminate the lease for even a material breach that is one-off, inadvertent, trivial in relation to the rent due or the value of the lease, and non-prejudicial, even when the right is express in the lease, while a court considers *de novo* the manner of the breach as well as its materiality.

---

26. Such a covenant has provoked litigation over whether the landlord has a "duty" to mitigate the tenant's liability in a damage action to invoke it: most courts have decided that the tenant in such an action is entitled to have a set off amount for the contract rent involved in any re-letting. Five jurisdictions enforce the covenant as written. See, e.g., Stonehedge Sq. LP v. Movie Merchants, Inc., 715 A.2d 1082 (Pa. 1998). However, thirteen would not and would permit the set off amount. See, e.g., Austin Hill Country Realty v. Palisades Plaza, 948 S.W.2d 293 (Tex. 1997). Permitting the landlord to recover rent due after it recovers possession might also be seen as unconscionable and a penalty by a court. But see Elliott v. LRSL Enterprises, Inc., 589 N.E.2d 1074 (Ill. Ct. App. 1992) (a minority view). Whether a tenant could waive its right to this offset amount also varies by jurisdiction.

CHAPTER 12

Planning to Exit a Project

Many developers are optimists, and confident that a project, once complete and with a stable cash flow, will continue to appreciate in value, rewarding good management with increased profits as the years pass. Many believe that adding a project to their portfolio of projects will further result in increased wealth for themselves, their investors, and their families in the long run.

Countervailing beliefs, some equally strong, require developers to plan to sell a project. He or she may have a desire to diversify one's assets: real estate has traditionally been a laggard in the economy, following rather than leading its trends, so selling a project can enable investments in other, faster growing, markets. Moreover, a developer's family may not share a passion for development, may be more risk-averse, and may want a life pursuing other professions. Further, over time, real estate market values go up and down. In 2005, the market for commercial real estate was up; in 2009, down; and in 2021, up from 2009, but not robust. If one can identify when values are high, selling at the top of a market creates opportunities for reentry and other investments.

Holding a stable project for a time is a hedge against seller's remorse. Stability of course is a relative matter — a 10% return on equity is very different from a 25% return, the former being a sell signal and the latter being a hold signal to a developer. Likewise, a low cap rate for a project is a sell signal, a high cap a hold signal. No one signal is likely to control a hold-or-sell decision.

Most developers choose to hold a project for a long enough period of time to evaluate the risks and rewards of doing so — an experienced developer with substantial liquid assets may hold longer than one just starting

329

12. Planning to Exit a Project

out. (In contrast, residential subdivision developers "break bulk" and sell as quickly as possible.) A developer's confidence in the original planning for a project bolsters his choosing to hold onto it. If a developer's interest rate on a project's long term, takeout, adjustable rate financing is lower than current rates, a developer may hold a project so long as he is confident that the project's rents will keep pace with any future rise in interest rates.

A developer's decision to hold or sell is seldom taken alone. Equity investors may have, under the partnership or LLC membership agreement, to consent to any decision to sell. Takeout lenders may, under the covenants in the mortgage, (1) prohibit the prepayment of a mortgage during a "lock-in" period of three to five years at the beginning of the term of the loan; (2) restrict or make prohibitively expensive prepayments thereafter; (3) accelerate the loan principal repayment on a sale or transfer of a project[1]; (4) prohibit further encumbrances or mortgages on the project; (5) invoke a carve-out exception to any nonrecourse clause[2] in the mortgage for dealing with the property in such a way as to make the lender's foreclosure remedy less secure. Moreover, the amortization period of a takeout loan may be different from its term: that is, the repayment schedule for the loan may be longer than its term, resulting in a substantial balloon payment being due at term's end. Investors and lenders, moreover, may take a dim view of a build and sell developer, taking it as a lack of confidence in the initial planning for the project sold: once investing and lending, they may want investment stability for a while longer than the developer.

In this interim (however long), the developer's attorney serves both to gut-check the developer's beliefs and find the best strategy for either holding or selling.

---

1. As discussed in previous chapters, a "due-on-sale-or-encumbrance" covenant in a mortgage permits a lender to accelerate a loan's repayment when the covenant is breached without the lender's consent. A sale or transfer of any interest, however small, without the consent of the lender, breaches such a covenant. Likewise, a mortgagor's encumbering the secured property with a second mortgage, or the sale of further equitable partnership or LLC interests in it, no matter how small in relationship to the outstanding loan amount, accelerates the full amount of debt. Starting in the 1980s, courts have found such covenants enforceable, not an unreasonable restraint on alienation, nor a penalty for an unreasonable amount of liquidated damages.

2. As discussed in previous chapters, a nonrecourse covenant, customary in a commercial mortgage, excluding the mortgagor (and typically any guarantor of the debt) from personal liability for any remaining debt upon default in repayment, leaving the mortgagee's remedy solely to repossession or foreclosure and denying the mortgagee any right to a deficiency judgment after foreclosure. Carve-out exemptions from this covenant might include any conversion or diversion of the cash flow, rents, insurance or condemnation proceeds arising from the secured property; any waste or deterioration of the property; failure to pay taxes; any fraud or misrepresentation in the administration of the loan, etc. Lenders have over time developed a long list of carve-outs. Mortgagor/borrowers seek to limit carve-outs to intentional ones.

12. Planning to Exit a Project

Examples

Example 1

Mortgage interest rates for long term takeout mortgage loans are the lowest they have been in over a decade. A developer with an office building financed at these rates is thinking about selling. Should he?

Explanation

If the developer believes that (1) the cash flow from the building will continue to exceed the debt service so that the debt service coverage ratio (DSCR) will also rise and stay above (say 1.3) for the predictable future; and (2) the developer's equity in the building, measured by a falling loan-to-value ratio, will continue to rise, holding on to such a project is advisable. It might even be refinanced with a loan with a longer term and amortization rate. The likely weak point in this analysis is the stability of the cash flow on which the DCSR depends. Some developers would, however, see the favorable financing as a saleable commodity, bringing a higher sales price for the building: even residential mortgagors in the 1980s saw a low interest rate loan as an assumable commodity, following the general rule that lower interest rates mean higher sales prices. (This perception led to the drafting of tighter due-on-sale covenants in mortgages.) As in any hold-or-sell decision, not one factor will control, but perhaps the most common factor in a decision to sell is the developer's need for cash to respond to changing market conditions affecting his portfolio of projects or other investments.

Example 2

A developer's long term, takeout, permanent mortgage is nonrecourse, with a carve-out to the effect that any violation of its due-on-sale covenant renders the loan fully recourse and accelerates the outstanding loan amount as of the date of the violation. The developer agrees to sell the secured property to a third party in an arm's length transaction and proposes to offer the proceeds of the sale to the mortgagee. Is the carve-out enforceable?

Explanation

Yes. A sales contract is a clear violation of the due-on-sale covenant; it diminishes the lender's security and its foreclosure remedy. These in turn trigger the carve-out, rendering the loan fully recourse: the developer thus becomes personally liable for its repayment. Filing for bankruptcy and an unauthorized transfer of the secured property are the most common "full liability" carve-outs in commercial lending, resulting in personal liability for the full amount of the outstanding debt. See Weinstein v. Park Funding Corp.,

331

12. Planning to Exit a Project

879 P.2d 462 (Colo. Ct. App. 1994). That the secured property might be sold in an arm's length transaction, that the developer offers to cure the breach that triggered personal liability, and even that no harm resulted to the lender, is of no consequence. See CSFB2001-CP-4 Princeton Park Corporate Ctr., LLC v. SB Rental I, LLC, 980 A.2d 1 (N.J. Super. Ct. 2009). The developer is held to its bargain. Moreover, the nonrecourse carve-out is not a provision for liquidated damages that might be scrutinized by a court and found to be a penalty. A fully recourse loan provides for personal liability; it does not set damages, and if it did, it provides a certain basis for calculating them—the outstanding amount of the loan provides that certainty. See *SB Rental LLC*, op. cit.

Many of the cases following *SB Rental* involve a developer filing for bankruptcy, thus violating a carve-out for such a filing: that the bankruptcy case is later dismissed does not cure the breach of a carve involving filing for bankruptcy. Once triggered, the carve-out cannot be un-triggered. See United States Bank Nat'l Ass'n v. Springfield Prairie Props., 2009 U.S. Dist. LEXIS 31975 (C.D. Ill. Feb. 28, 2019).

In a hold-or-sell decision, then, consultation with a developer's lender is a must before making and acting on any decision to sell.

Example 3

As in the prior Example, a lender proposes that some carve-outs extend beyond so-called traditional "bad boy" exceptions to the application of the nonrecourse covenant. "Bad boy" carve-outs might involve, e.g., fraud, misapplication of insurance proceeds or a condemnation award, or the application of a super lien for environmental liability to regulators. The lender also proposes that other carve-outs involve (1) any developer behavior involving the misapplication or conversion of tenants' rents or security deposits; (2) a failure to turn over insurance proceeds or a condemnation award; (3) the removal of personal property or fixtures without replacing them; or (4) the negligent or unintentional misrepresentation by the developer to the lender. How should you, as the developer/mortgagor's attorney, respond to the lender's proposal?

Explanation

While a lender will insist on and is unlikely to negotiate over "bad boy" carve-outs, the lender's additional proposals might be limited by negotiation; that is, some of them might subject the mortgagor to personal liability to the lender for the loss the lender incurs as a result of (say) the developer's misapplication of rents or security deposits or a failure to turn over insurance proceeds or a condemnation award. Such "loss liability" carve-outs do not accelerate the full amount of the debt, but are easily remedied by the payment of money or property denied the lender.

332

12. Planning to Exit a Project

Example 4

As in the prior two Examples, the lender proposes carve-outs involving: (1) any failure to pay real estate taxes or insurance premiums for the secured property; (2) common-law waste of the secured property or a failure to maintain it; and (3) anything destroying or diminishing the value of the secured property. Again, how would you respond to these further proposals for carve-outs?

Explanation

These proposals will be harder to negotiate away. Why? First, a failure to pay taxes might result in a lien superior to that of the mortgage lender. Since the primacy of its lien is all important to a lender, a lender is unlikely to yield on this first item. Second, the measure of damages for common law waste might be either restitutionary or ameliorative, and measuring the damages before the lender's remainder or reversion is possessive is a matter of debate in some jurisdictions. Third, any event resulting in a diminution in the value of the project property as security might be measured by (1) an amount that preserves the original loan-to-value (LTV) ratio as of the time of the event, or (2) an amount that equals the amount of the lender's original loan-to-value cushion at the inception of the loan, or (3) an amount that restores the loan-to-value ratio at the time of the loan's execution. A lender will insist that it expected the LTV ratio to fall and its equity cushion to increase as the loan is repaid. The uncertainty in the amount of the damages in the lender's last two proposals will mean that the lender would not accept a "loss liability" carve-out in place of a "full liability" carve-out unless the "loss liability" measure of damages is defined with more precision.

Example 5

As a developer's attorney, in reviewing a mortgage lender's proposals for carve-outs in a nonrecourse note and mortgage, you find that your client's contesting any future foreclosure will result in full personal liability for the debt. Is this carve-out enforceable?

Explanation

Yes. See F.D.I.C. v. Prince George Corp., 58 F.3d 1041 (4th Cir. 1995). Since foreclosure is the lender's remaining remedy in a nonrecourse loan, its efficiency as a remedy is all the more important to the lender and it can be protected from being protracted by the mortgagor's raising defenses to it.

333

12. Planning to Exit a Project

Example 6

In negotiating a permanent, takeout loan, what should the developer's attorney do to facilitate flexibility for the client in timing the sale of a stable, completed project?

Explanation

(1) Eliminate or shorten any lock-out period for prepayment of the loan (perhaps substituting a prepayment schedule for shortening the lockout). (2) Limit the equity investors veto power over any sale once the project net operating income (NOI) is stable and in accord with their expectations. (3) Negotiate carve outs to due-on-sale-or-encumbrance covenants in the mortgage: these might include the sale to a purchaser meeting defined qualifications as to business experience and financial condition equal or better than the mortgagor's, along with that purchaser's right to assume the existing permanent mortgage; the mortgagor's substitution of collateral whose value is equal or higher than the secured property's; or a sale that "breaks bulk" — that is, sells vacant land not needed to operate the project at a predetermined release price of so-much per acre.

THE SALES CONTRACT

A developer's sale of a project involves more legal relationships than the acquisition contract did. In any sales contract, the selling developer will typically warrant that it will operate the project up to the closing "in accordance with its past practice" and not enter into any new leases or amend existing ones "without the prior written consent of the purchaser who may consent or not in its sole and complete discretion." While this might amount to a stand-still agreement for the project, the purchaser may reasonably insist on having the developer explain any change in the business.

If the sale is to be successful, it must transfer an up-and-running business, not just the real property involved in the project. Thus the existing leases should be assigned to the purchaser, along with the developer's accounts holding the tenant's security deposits. Other non-realty assets of the project might include leasing broker listing agreements, project management contracts, tangible and intangible personal property, project contracts for servicing the project (e.g., the contract for trash and garbage removal, the maintenance contract for the HVAC, electrical, technology,

12. Planning to Exit a Project

and communications systems, as well as the project's intangible assets), the assignment of architectural and construction plans and specifications, construction and systems' warranties, and the trademark of the project's name, are examples. The developer will want to specify precisely what is assigned, the buyer will want sweeping mop-up clauses covering all other personal and intellectual property associated with the project.

Examples

Example 7

A developer desirous of selling a project may want to protect the jobs of personnel managing a project for a period after the closing. Why would a prospective purchaser agree to extend such protection?

Explanation

The purchaser might want the same employees to sign nondisclosure agreement about the business practices and finances of the project once their employment ends. Protecting these employee's jobs for an interim period protects the project's business and prevents the employees from "going away mad," likely to immediately sign up with a competing developer, or disclosing any trade secrets.

Example 8

A prospective project purchaser indicates a desire to have the sculpture in the lobby of the project moved to a different location. The sculptor is a world famous artist, living in New York City. Should the artist be consulted first?

Explanation

If the artist has rights under the Visual Artists Rights Act of 1990 (VARA), 17 U.S.C. §101 et seq., then yes. VARA's coverage includes a "right of integrity" for exhibited sculpture of "recognized stature" to prevent both its destruction or a change in how the work is presented to the public. The rights created by VARA last so long as the artist is alive, but are transferable and may also be waived.

12. Planning to Exit a Project

Example 9

When negotiating a purchase contract for a project, the purchaser insists on seeing the existing leases. Why? To assure that the leases are consistent with the financial data and the rent roll presented by the developer. The purchaser also insists on a right to terminate the sale contract if an inconsistency is found. How should the developer's attorney respond?

Explanation

By inserting in the sales contract materiality, substantiality, and knowledge qualifiers to the developer's warranties and representations as to the leases when presented to the purchaser, and by tendering tenant estoppel certificates confirming that the leases presented the purchase are the true and valid agreements between the parties thereto.

The point of sale for a project is the time when the developer's attorney proves to a certainty that he or she has added value to the project through anticipating the vagaries of the real estate market and drafting flexible documents right up to the sales contract removing the project from the developer's portfolio. This proof is the best evidence that a developer should continue to employ the attorney in the future.

Deed in Lieu of Foreclosure

Often when a project becomes unprofitable and is facing foreclosure, giving the secured property to the lender or investors is the simplest way to exit the project — that is, by delivering to the lender a deed in lieu of foreclosure. This is the least complicated form of workout. In form, a deed in lieu of foreclosure looks like any other deed. See Johnson v. Wilmington Sav. Fund Soc'y, FSB, 2020 Bankr. LEXIS 231 (E.D. Tenn. Jan 29, 2020) (holding that a deed in lieu must sufficiently describe the property transferred). It has the same components, but its special purpose is to memorialize an agreement by the developer/mortgagor with its mortgage lender to avoid a foreclosure action. It is in effect a friendly foreclosure — one achieved by contract. This special purpose, however, raises several problems. Its preliminary recitals outlining the effects of the transfer, might be as follows:

1. A statement specifying the default(s)
2. A statement of the consideration — the lender's forbearance from foreclosure
3. A statement that the deed is freely given, is not an equitable mortgage, is made in lieu of foreclosure, and is made at the request of the

336

12. Planning to Exit a Project

mortgagor, with the express intent of terminating the mortgagor-mortgagee relationship

4. A statement that attached and incorporated by reference are a current appraisal, the results of the title search, and (if true) a statement that no junior liens exist
5. A statement that the parties have been represented in the course of the transfer by independent legal counsel
6. A statement that the parties intend to effect mutual releases of all liability on the debt by means of the transfer, but do not intend to merge the lien of the mortgage with the fee simple absolute and, further, do not intend to benefit third parties (such a guarantors) and expressly reserve their rights against third parties

The first part of this sixth statement will likely encounter the greatest resistance on the part of the mortgagee: many will insist on keeping the note effective, since the mortgage (not merged here) will exist so long as the note does. See C. Phillip Johnson Full Gospel Ministries, Inc. v Investors Fin. Servs., LLC, 12 A.3d 1207 (Md. 2011) (for a deed in lieu with preliminary recitals).

The advantages of a deed in lieu are several. The lender/mortgagee avoids the high costs of a foreclosure action. The deed can provide a resolution of disputes that otherwise might arise during the foreclosure action: actions for a deficiency judgment; attacks on the foreclosure sale; allegations of fraud, duress, and so forth. The potential for time-consuming squabbles between the parties is considerable in a foreclosure action. In contrast, successful negotiation over such a deed can provide an amicable termination of the mortgagor-mortgagee relationship, and when that relationship was longstanding, the deed serves to keep a business relationship alive for the future. For a developer and the lender, this may be important. Equally important may be keeping the details of the transaction as confidential as possible so that as little damage as possible is done to the business reputations of the parties. Embarrassment and an impaired credit rating might otherwise result. Finally, the deed may remove the secured property from the bankruptcy estate of the mortgagor.

The disadvantages of using such deeds are also numerous. A foreclosure of a senior lien will wipe out the lien of a properly joined junior mortgagee, but the transfer of a deed in lieu has no such effect. Not only that, the lender/mortgagee may also be giving up rights ancillary to the mortgage transaction — rights to a deficiency judgment, to guarantees of the debt, and so forth. See GMAC Mortgage LLC v. Dyer, 965 N.E.2d 762 (Ind. Ct. App. 2012) (a promise not to pursue a deficiency judgment sufficient to release mortgagor from all liability for the mortgage debt). Moreover, the developer/mortgagor may later have a change of mind and seek to attack

337

12. Planning to Exit a Project

the transfer for any one of a number of reasons or to avoid the transfer by filing for bankruptcy. From the developer's perspective, a bankruptcy liquidation is a second bite of the apple and moreover may be perceived as bringing more money for the property than a foreclosure sale. This prospect may be justified because the trustee in bankruptcy will not auction the property but instead will appoint a real estate broker to handle marketing and sale, making it appear more like a standard purchase and sale. Further, the purpose of bankruptcy may not be liquidation of the assets of the bankrupt, but the reorganization of debts as well, depending on which chapters of the Bankruptcy Code are utilized.

An alternative to the voluntary deed in lieu is abandonment of the property. Abandonment requires an intent to abandon and acts evidencing that intent, such as a failure to perform vital maintenance, to pay property taxes, insurance premiums, or utility charges — or, of course, giving a deed in lieu. Such acts will do far more damage to a developer's reputation than a deed in lieu would. In any event, for federal income tax purposes, an abandonment is treated just like a sale or other disposition by deed. See Arkin v. Comm'r, 76 T.C. 1048 (1981).

Examples

Example 10

An owner of a commercial office building is in default on his mortgage, and listens to his attorney as she recites the advantages and disadvantages of a deed in lieu. Then he asks: "Why don't I just mail the mortgagee the keys to the building?" How would you respond?

Explanation

Mailing the keys is not the equivalent of a delivery of the deed in lieu, and proving abandonment has its own difficulties. So mailing the keys back achieves nothing.

The mortgagee who accepts a deed in lieu not only avoids the high transaction costs associated with any type of foreclosure but also, when the fair market value of the property exceeds the debt, acquires the equity of the developer/mortgagor built up in the property. At the time of the mortgage closing, however, a deed in lieu cannot be placed in escrow for the benefit of the mortgagee because the establishment of the escrow, with delivery of the deed conditional upon the mortgagor's default in payment of the mortgage debt, would be a clog on the mortgagor's equity of redemption.

There must be a consideration for the granting of the deed in lieu that is separate from that realized in the original mortgage transaction — otherwise

338

12. Planning to Exit a Project

the equity is clogged. A mortgagor cannot release or waive the equity as a part of the original transaction, but that is no bar to its subsequent release. Thus, a deed in lieu cannot be executed at the time of the original mortgage transaction; even a provision for one in the original loan documents is likely to invalidate the later deed. Because this equity of redemption is in fact a right of late payment, it does not arise, and so cannot be released, until there is a default that gives rise to the mortgagee's right to foreclose. What is the drafting consequence for a deed in lieu? It is the inclusion, in such a deed, of a recital concerning the prior default.

As to including a recitation in the deed of the consideration, that is also advisable but does present a problem of its own. Not stating a consideration leaves a court free, later, to infer that factors involving fraud and duress induced the transfer. So it is better to state some consideration, even though a conveyance (of any type) does not require such a statement.

A conveyance made "in full satisfaction and release of the debt evidenced in the note and mortgage" is, from the developer/mortgagor's standpoint, the best that can be obtained. Perhaps the word "satisfaction" is better than "cancellation," unless the mortgagee produces the cancelled note and mortgage, or those two documents are attached to the deed and referred to there. And, when there are junior liens on the property, the word cancellation should be avoided to prevent a merger of the lien and the fee that would promote the junior's status to senior lienholder. For the lender/mortgagee, accepting the deed is the equivalent of collecting the debt, but only to the extent of the fair market value of the property at the time of the deed's execution. This may or may not make the mortgagee whole. Thus, an appraisal of the property at the time the deed is delivered should establish that value and determine the extent to which the note might remain enforceable.

What if the mortgagor is not liable on the note? In other words, if the note is nonrecourse and the mortgage lien has been granted by one not liable for the debt, how should the consideration be recited? Consideration other than the release of the debt will have to be found; that consideration might be the monetary value of avoiding a foreclosure.

From an income tax perspective, when the sole consideration is stated as the discharge of some portion of the debt, the conveyance by deed in lieu will be treated as a sale to the lender/mortgagee for the amount of the debt released. Assigning a monetary value to the consideration is thus important for documenting the tax consequences of the sale, for often the consideration will have other elements besides whole or partial release from the debt. See Comm'r v. Spreckels, 120 F.2d 517 (9th Cir. 1941).

The deed in lieu has, as its purpose, the termination of the mortgagor-mortgagee relationship. Ending that relationship is the reason for reciting

339

12. Planning to Exit a Project

that the deed satisfies and releases the debt. Further, the rationale for any continuing relationship between the parties should be closely scrutinized. The mortgagor's continued possession of the property, his option to buy the property, or his lease of the premises after giving the deed all increase the risk that the transaction may be recharacterized as an attempt of the parties to continue their preexisting relationship.

Examples

Example 11

A mortgage lender requires a mortgagor to deliver a deed in lieu into escrow, the deed to be delivered to the mortgagee upon default in repayment of the mortgage loan. The mortgagor defaults. The mortgagee demands the deed from the escrow agent. The mortgagor objects. The agent files an interpleader action[3] to determine whether the deed should be delivered. Should it?

Explanation

No. The execution of the deed in lieu contemporaneous with the execution of the mortgage is an attempt to avoid the mortgagor's equity of redemption and void as a common law clog on the equity. The equity of redemption is not subject to waiver: a mortgage cannot be made irredeemable. See C. Phillip Johnson Full Gospel Ministries, Inc. v. Investors Fin. Servs., LLC, 12 A.3d 1207 (Md. 2011) (collecting authorities). The mortgagee must first afford the mortgagor an opportunity to repay the outstanding mortgage debt before foreclosing its lien. The deed is only valid if delivered after separate negotiations subsequent to the execution of the mortgage.

Example 12

What are the remedies of a junior mortgagee against the property that has been conveyed to a senior mortgagee by means of a valid, separately negotiated in a workout, deed in lieu of foreclosure when the senior's note has not been released?

---

3. This is a civil action that allows a plaintiff (here the escrow agent) to file a lawsuit in order to compel other parties (here the mortgagor and mortgagee) to litigate a dispute (here the right to the deed which when the plaintiff holds on another's behalf), when the plaintiff does not know to whom the deed or other property should be transferred.

12. Planning to Exit a Project

Explanation

Its remedies are much the same as those of a junior mortgagee (whose loan is in default) omitted from the foreclosure of the senior lien. These remedies are twofold. First, the junior can foreclose his own mortgage, and second, the junior can redeem the senior mortgage by paying the amount of the outstanding mortgage debt. Because the second remedy may involve a large cash outlay, it is seldom employed. The first remedy, of foreclosure, is more likely, but if the junior mortgagee seeks foreclosure, the priority of the junior lien may move up to senior lien status. It could do so if the senior lien is merged with the mortgagor's title. The doctrine of merger provides that when a mortgagee's lien and the underlying fee come into the same hands, the lien is merged with the fee and is extinguished. To avoid merger, a senior mortgagee accepting a deed in lieu should release the mortgagor from personal liability on the note but not cancel the note, thus preserving the mortgage lien too. Thus, if and when the junior forecloses, the purchaser at the sale takes the property subject to the senior lien.

Example 13

After workout negotiations, a mortgagor in default to Big Bank delivers a deed in lieu to the Bank as the mortgagee. The Bank accepts the deed. Another division of the Bank, without knowledge of the deed, forecloses. A junior mortgage lender on the same secured property argues that the acceptance of the deed preserves its lien (which would normally be extinguished upon foreclosure) and moves it up to senior status. Will this argument be successful?

Explanation

No. In some jurisdictions, there is a presumption that upon acceptance of a deed in lieu by a mortgagee, the title transferred in the deed is not merged with the lien. See Decon Group, Inc. v. Prudential Mortgage Capital Co., LLC, 174 Cal. Rptr. 3d 205 (Cal. Ct. App. 2014). If a merger were to occur, the lien would be extinguished: the lesser interest, the lien, would be merged into the greater interest, the title to the secured property. For this reason, a prudent mortgagee, wishing to preserve the mortgage for future enforcement in foreclosure, would agree in writing with the mortgagor delivering the deed that no such merger resulted from the deed's acceptance. This agreement is founded on the generally accepted rule that merger is a matter of intent and is subject to any agreement otherwise. Moreover, the generally accepted rule is that acceptance of the deed is not presumed to be a waiver of the right to foreclose.

341

12. Planning to Exit a Project

Example 14

Considering that one advantage of a deed in lieu is often its confidentiality, one might want to avoid a recital of the details of the underlying transaction on the deed itself because the grantee will want to record the deed in the public records. How should this matter be handled?

Explanation

By inclusion of the recitals in an affidavit accompanying the deed, but retained by the title company or legal counsel, rather than on the face of the deed itself.

Example 15

Ben develops commercial properties. One of them is the Big Ben Building. It is 75% leased a year after its completion. The loan for its construction costs was provided by Builder's Bank, but hard times made the large insurance company once committed to the building's long-term permanent financing walk away. Builder's Bank then provided a long-term note and mortgage, for 20 years, at a variable rate of interest 3 points over its prime rate, for 75% of the fair market value. The mortgage contains a covenant authorizing the use, upon default, of a power of sale foreclosure. Ben's four most recent payments have been late, and he has been assessed late payments on these in the amount of 5% of the late payment amounts of principal and interest due. Ben would like to continue to attempt to lease the building until it is 90% leased. He is willing to deposit a deed in lieu into an escrow pending completion of this last effort. If he fails, he would like to continue to manage the property, perhaps giving a deed with an option to buy the property back, but Builder's resists this idea. Ben and the bank's attorneys are negotiating the terms of a deed in lieu of foreclosure. Ben has other real property interests that are not in distress. As the bank's attorney, what should concern you?

342

12. Planning to Exit a Project

Explanation

Your first concern might be whether there are any outstanding junior mortgages or mechanic's liens filed against the property. Will the junior lien get senior status when the mortgagee of the senior lien takes a deed in lieu? Will a mechanic's lien do the same under similar circumstances? May a quitclaim deed be used as a deed in lieu? If you don't have ready answers to such questions, consult the Banks's title insurer about continuing the lender's coverage as a mortgagee in possession. This might be a good case for giving the lender a deed when Ben has a 25% equity in the building, its rental market's vacancy rate is low, and there are no junior liens. Perhaps Ben can offer to continue to manage the property after the deed in lieu is transferred, with an option to buy it back before the end of the maximum amount of time that the bank under applicable government regulations, can hold the title to real property in its own name. The right to manage can become consideration for the deed and pegging the option to the length of time the bank can hold property shows a business purpose for the transaction and so avoids its re-characterization. Ben's management offer puts the best light on Ben's having to deliver the deed in lieu.

Example 16

In the prior Example, suppose Builder's Bank is willing to accept a deed in lieu, but is unwilling to release the note. How would you advise Ben to respond?

Explanation

Ben might ask the bank for a covenant or agreement not to sue on the retained note, subject to carve-outs for fraud, misrepresentation, Ben's filing for bankruptcy, and other bad acts. Rather than a release of the debt, the bank might want to preserve the right to a deficiency judgment if the fair market value of the property drops or has been misrepresented in the negotiation for the deed.

343

12. Planning to Exit a Project

The Sale-Leaseback

This transaction—involving a sale of the title to a project and leasing it back—is encouraged by its income tax advantages. It is a partial exit strategy. It leaves the developer in control of the project, leaves his management team in place, does not affect the rental stream from the project, but disposes of some of the tax advantages of ownership.

Examples

Example 17

Developer gives a deed to a project to a buyer, who, at the moment he accepts the deed, becomes a lessor and gives the developer back a lease. Thus developer becomes a lessee. Possession of the property does not change hands. The developer continues as before, now in possession of the premises as a tenant, often with an option to repurchase the title in the future. What are the legal and tax consequences of these two transactions?

Explanation

There are at least two. First, the buyer-lessor becomes the titleholder. He gets to depreciate the improvements on the property. That in itself is quite a tax benefit. Second, the developer-lessee gets to deduct 100% of the rent as a business expense.

As a general proposition, the IRS does not like to see a market for tax benefits develop. If one taxpayer decided to collect all the tax benefits of his neighbors and claim them on his own return, the IRS would disallow the claim. If, however, taxpayers do a sale-leaseback transaction as in this Example, the trade is just as real but perfectly legal from an income taxation standpoint. Some taxpayers will likely take each of the deductions, so what does it matter who? The answer is, it doesn't matter if (and this is a very BIG if) both buyer and seller are taxed at the same marginal rates or take the depreciation according to the same schedule. But if these assumptions don't apply, it will matter from the IRS's perspective.

So, here is the basic, benefit-trading sale-leaseback. The two transactions take place in close sequence, at the same closing. The advantages to the initial owner are greater than those involved in a mortgage loan transaction, and are substantial. Consider:

1. As a lessee, the developer receives the lump sum purchase price or has the equivalent of 100% loan to value financing; as a mortgagor, he would have to pay a down payment, loan closing costs, and so

344

12. Planning to Exit a Project

forth. In exchange, without an option to repurchase, the lessee gives up any appreciated value that property has gained by the end of the lease—that is, the lessor has the reversion after the term for years.

2. As a lessee, to the extent he doesn't receive a lump sum, all payments are deductible as rental business expenses; as a mortgagor, only interest payments are deductible. The payment amounts are negotiable.

3. As a lessee, the developer may avoid[4] the onerous acceleration clauses found in mortgages and gains the many protections extended to tenants after the revolution in landlord/tenant law that has occurred during the 1960s and 1970s. On the other hand, as a lessee, he loses the statutory protections available to a mortgagor in the jurisdiction's foreclosure code.

Other differences between using a lease and a mortgage are the following:

Lease	Mortgage
Lessor depreciates property	Mortgagor depreciates property
Usury limits inapplicable	Usury applicable
Summary process available	Foreclosure available
Lessor has control of any sublease or assignment	Due on sale covenant applies

Instead of a deed, the buyer could buy using an installment land sale contract. Its long executory period might give him time to comply with securities or environmental regulations when the use of an executory purchase and sale contract would not, but might strike the Internal Revenue Service as a sham mortgage, subject (as will be discussed in the next section of this chapter) to being recharacterized as such. To avoid recharacterization, the transactions comprising the sale-leaseback must be at conventional market rates and terms, each party bearing a share of the business risks involved.

A leading case. In Frank Lyon Co. v. United States, 435 U.S. 561 (1978), a bank wanted to build itself a headquarters office building. It initially proposed to finance the project with bonds, but usury laws prevented the bank from bringing the bonds to market at current rates. Banking regulators also objected to the bank's holding title to all of that real property, but preapproved a sale and leaseback in which (1) the titleholder would be an independent third party, and (2) the bank would have a repurchase option after

---

4. This avoidance is not a sure-run thing: the developer has "transferred" an interest in the secured project property, but the mortgage lender is not less secure on account of this transfer. While a technical violation of a due-on-sale covenant, the no-less-secure lender is unlikely to withhold consent.

345

12. Planning to Exit a Project

the 15th year of the leaseback. After a series of bids to finance the project by several investment bankers and negotiations with several of them, the bank choose Frank Lyon Co., whose principal business was not banking, but rather the retailing of major appliances. Lyon negotiated with the bank, agreed to a rent reduction, and invested $500,000 of its own money.

After construction was begun, Lyon engaged in a sale and leaseback with the bank and, after that, assumed in its own name a construction note and mortgage and later a permanent mortgage for the office building. The transaction proceeded in five steps:

1. Title to the office building was transferred from the bank to Lyon. The bank retained title to the underlying land.
2. Lyon assumed the note and mortgage obligations and became personally responsible for payment of the debt that they represented. The debt was further secured by an assignment of Lyon's interest in the lease and the bank subordinated its interest in the ground to the permanent mortgage.
3. The bank leased the land to Lyon, reserving a ground rent at a nominal level for a 25-year term, but after 25 years, the rent level, starting at $100,000, jumped up in $50,000 increments every 5th year.
4. Under the leaseback of the building, the rent was just sufficient to pay off the permanent mortgage note as the debt it represented came due over the first 25 years of the lease term; after that, over each 5 years of the lease, the annual rent was reduced to $300,000 — a 50% reduction.
5. The bank had, in its lease for the building, an option to repurchase the building after the 11th, 15th, 20th, and 25th year of the term, at a fixed price equal to the unpaid, outstanding balance due on the permanent mortgage note, plus Lyon's initial, $500,000 investment, plus 6% interest on that investment.

In sum, Lyon held the fee simple to the building and the air rights, the bank held the fee to the land, while Lyon held a lease to the land.

The IRS said that the transaction was a disguised mortgage and denied Lyon a depreciation deduction. The federal circuit hearing the case on appeal ruled in favor of the IRS, looking at the documents involved in the transaction alone. Meanwhile another circuit had looked in its cases beyond the documents at the economic substance of the transactions and in effect held for Lyon. Thus, there was a conflict among the federal circuits, and on that basis, the Supreme Court granted certiorari and upheld the transaction.

The Supreme Court's primary factor validating the transaction was that, first, Lyon was primarily liable on the note and mortgage, first to the construction lender (a commercial bank) and then to the long-term, or permanent, takeout note and mortgage. So the sale-leaseback was in substance an

12. Planning to Exit a Project

extension to the bank of Lyon's creditworthiness. But the opinion also goes on to consider additional factors.

Second, Lyon undertook a risk that the rental value of the building would recoup its investment, noting that the decreasing rent under the ground lease would not. That is, the return to Lyon on his initial investment was contingent on the bank not exercising its option to repurchase in the building lease.

Third, the opinion notes that the IRS was likely to lose little revenue because of a sale-leaseback. Someone was going to take the depreciation deduction at issue in this case, so what did it matter to the IRS whether it was Worthen Bank or Lyon? That is, the arguments of the IRS seeking to recharacterize a sale-leaseback must overcome an initial preference that the parties be allowed to cast a transaction as they wish, particularly when the Treasury will not likely lose revenue if the Court decides for the taxpayer. If the transaction is a wash as far as the public treasury is concerned, why should the IRS pierce the veil thrown over the deal by the documents used to close the transaction? This suggests that the bank traded its depreciation and mortgage interest deduction to Lyon, in exchange for its rent deduction taken as a business expense; this trade, however, was made on the assumption that if the bank continued to hold the title, it would lease some of the building. If the taxpayers involved in the sale-leaseback are taxed at different marginal rates, however, this trade is not a wash so far as the public treasury is concerned. And if the sale-leaseback is a wash, why do it? Answering this question is what sent the Court in search of a business purpose for the transaction. In the tax-wash transaction, the documents control and the parties to it are to be permitted to structure it the way they see fit; the burden on the government to upset the transaction as documented will be great.

Fourth, the transaction here was not the simplest, two-party type of sale-leaseback, and the opinion makes much of the three-party nature of the transaction. Such a transaction has an economic reality check—the presence of a third-party, institutional mortgage lender—built into it, so it is less likely that the sale portion of the transaction would be for an inflated price and that the lease payments would be insufficient to cover Lyon's mortgage payment liability. The Court was not saying that two-party transactions are more likely to be recharacterized than three-party ones. It is the reality check rationale that makes the distinction important. So if the lease had contained high initial rental payments, which tapered off at the end of the term, and the lease permitted the lessee to exercise an option to purchase the title for a nominal sum at the end of the term, such a lease should be considered a contract of sale for the property. That is, the IRS argued that the lessee would be considered less than rational if he did not exercise the option; he would be under an economic compulsion to do so—thus argued the IRS, unsuccessfully in this case.

347

12. Planning to Exit a Project

The *Lyon* opinion holds:

> [W]here, as here, there is a genuine multiple-party transaction with economic substance which is compelled or encouraged by business or regulatory realities, is imbued with tax-independent considerations, and is not shaped solely by tax avoidance features . . . , the government should honor the allocation of rights and duties effectuated by the parties.

The Court is generous in its holding. Few transactions are not "encouraged" by business motives and few transactions will be "solely" driven by the tax code. The holding encourages third-party loans to finance sale-leaseback purchases. With such financing present, the IRS was given a high burden of proof for future litigation.

Lest anyone think that any one factor is dispositive, read the full paragraph of the opinion in the footnote below.[5] This reading should free you from the mistake of relying on any one factor. Still, the holding is capable of

---

5. This paragraph recites the factors the Court found important:

> We . . . find . . . [the Court of Appeals opinion] incompatible with the substance and economic realities of the transaction: the competitive situation as it existed between Worthen [Bank & Trust Co.] and Union National Bank in 1965 and the years immediately following; Worthen's undercapitalization; Worthen's consequent inability, as a matter of legal restraint, to carry its building plans into effect by a conventional mortgage and other borrowing; the additional barriers imposed by the state and federal regulators; the suggestion, forthcoming from the state regulator, that Worthen possess an option to purchase; the requirement, from the federal regulator, that the building be owned by an independent third party; the presence of several finance organizations seriously interested in participating in the transaction and in the resolution of Worthen's problem; the submission of formal proposals by several of those organizations; the bargaining process and period that ensued; the competitiveness of the bidding; the bona fide character of the negotiations; the three-party aspect of the transaction; Lyon's substantiality and its independence from Worthen; the fact that diversification was Lyon's principal motivation; Lyon's being liable alone on the successive notes to City Bank and New York Life; the reasonableness . . . of the rentals and of the option prices; the substantiality of the purchase prices; Lyon's not being engaged generally in the business of financing; the presence of all building depreciation risks on Lyon; the risk, borne by Lyon, that Worthen might default or fail, as other banks have failed; the facts that Worthen could "walk away" from the relationship at the end of the 25-year primary term, and probably would do so if the option price were more than the then-current worth of the building to Worthen; the inescapable fact that if the building lease were not extended, Lyon would be the full owner of the building, free to do with it as it chose; Lyon's liability for the substantial ground rent if Worthen decides not to exercise any of its options to extend; the absence of any understanding between Lyon and Worthen that Worthen would exercise any of the purchase options; the nonfamily and nonprivate nature of the entire transaction; and the absence of any differential in tax rates and of special tax circumstances for one of the parties—all convince us that Lyon has far the better of the case.

431 U.S. at 582-583.

348

12. Planning to Exit a Project

two interpretations: (1) the documents control, unless there is no business purpose; or (2) when a business purpose is present, the documents control.

Avoiding Recharacterizations How can the purchaser-lessor avoid recharacterization? The following methods are useful, but not one of them standing alone will be determinative.

1. By the lessor's not exercising a great deal of control over the business of the lessee.
2. By reciting that the transaction is not a mortgage, nor a loan, nor a joint venture, but indeed a sale and leaseback. Reciting the business purpose for the transaction can't hurt either.
3. By not using the terms of mortgage law — for example, interest rate, prepayment premium, escrows, and so forth.
4. By avoiding any duty to repurchase on the developer-lessee, untying the repurchase price from the initial amount of the consideration for the deed by pricing the property at the then-fair market value by some recognized method of appraisal and by giving third parties an opportunity to bid for the repurchase, with the developer-lessee having an option or right of first refusal after that bidding. The holding in Lyon sanctions the use of small repurchase prices when the business reasons for the sale-leaseback are substantial.
5. By requiring extra types of collateral or security, personal guaranties, or letters of credit by the lessee. Such techniques are sometimes referred to as credit enhancements. The Supreme Court appeared impressed by them in Lyon.

TAX-FREE EXCHANGES

If the developer/taxpayer's existing property is long held and very valuable, a tax-deferred exchange may be the needed exit strategy. IRC §1031. IRC §1031(a)(1) provides that no gain (or loss) will be recognized when the owners of like-kind properties, held for business or investment uses, exchange them. Section 1031 is a well-worn exception to the rule that taxpayers must recognize income gains or losses realized from the sale of property in the year realized. See Teruya Bros., Ltd. v. Comm'r, 580 F.3d 1038 (9th Cir. 2009) (giving background for this section).

Internal Revenue Service regulations about what constitutes a like-kind property are quite liberal. "Like-kind" property may be of any type — an office or apartment building may be exchanged for a shopping center, timberland, or unimproved land, and vice versa. There may also be more than one property on each side of the exchange: A taxpayer might trade 10 rental houses for a shopping center, or an office building for 20 rental

349

12. Planning to Exit a Project

houses. In each instance, the only requirement is that both the relinquished or exchanged property, and the replacement or target property, be held for business or investment purposes. One caveat: the 2017 Tax Reform Act provides that real property cannot be exchanged for personal property of any kind.

A developer looking to retire might want to exchange property he now owns for property in the Sunbelt, or for property that requires less time and expense to manage but that has an equivalent value. Further, deferred exchanges, in which the properties to be exchanged are not precisely identified at the time of the agreement to exchange properties is executed, are possible. See Starker v. United States, 602 F.2d 1341 (9th Cir. 1979), sanctioned by IRC provisions enacted in 1984 (imposing two requirements: identification of the property within 45 days after the agreement and receipt of the title within 180 days).

Starker deferred exchanges are the most used type of exchange. Their success depends on irrevocably escrowing the exchange property's sales proceeds so that those proceeds are beyond the actual or constructive receipt of the exchanger.

Aside from those already suggested, some other purposes for using either a direct or a deferred like-kind exchange are to (1) use the equity in the exchanged property to acquire a larger property, (2) avoid financing the replacement property with a mortgage loan, (3) acquire exchange property with a larger depreciable basis, to take advantage of unsolicited offers to purchase without paying capital gains taxes, (4) acquire more readily marketable replacement property, or (5) increase the value of the developer's decedent's estate without paying capital gain taxes.

The last purpose is possible because, while the developer carries over her basis on the exchanged property into the tax treatment of the replacement property (an exchange is a tax deferral method, not a tax reduction or avoidance method), his heirs will receive a "stepped-up" basis in the replacement property, measured by the value of the property at the date of the developer/decedent's death.

If the use of all the proceeds of the sale of the relinquished property is not needed to purchase the replacement or target property, then that part of the proceeds will be transferred to the developer, and that amount will then become taxable. To tax attorneys, such an amount is known as "boot."

Examples

Example 18

Suppose that the IRC is amended to raise the rates at which income in the form of capital gains for investment properties will be taxed. Is such an action more or less likely to encourage §1031 exchanges?

350

12. Planning to Exit a Project

Explanation

More likely. Viewed another way, the closer capital gain and ordinary income rates of taxation are, the less incentive there will be to use §1031, and when federal capital gain rates slip below ordinary income rates, there is a likelihood that more taxpayers will sell their real property investments than other types of assets.

Example 19

A young developer owns four adjoining houses and has lived in one of them for the past five years. The total fair market value is about $500,000 divided equally among them. If he decides to move into another market, may he sell them all at market value and claim a "§121 exemption"[6] on income from the sale of a residence?

Explanation

If the house in which he has lived has been his principal residence for two of the past five years and the profit on its sale is $250,000 or less, the profit on his $125,000 home is exempt. This exemption does not apply to his other three houses. His personal residence is not business or investment property and does not qualify for a §1031 exchange.

Example 20

What further advice might you give the young developer?

---

6. Internal Rev. Code §121 provides that a seller who has owned and occupied a primary residence an aggregate of two years out of the last five years before the sale, qualifies for a capital gains tax exemption of $250,000. A married couple has a $500,000 exemption from capital gains. Only one spouse need hold the title — occupancy is all that is needed to qualify, and the exemption survives divorce. It can be used repeatedly — but not more than once in 24 months. It applies only to a taxpayer's primary residence, not to second or vacation homes or rental property. To use this exemption, a taxpayer must have occupied the property for an "aggregate" of 24 months out of the 60 months (five years) before its sale — the months need not be continuous. See Alan Tarr, Sell Your Home Tax-Free, Prac. Real Est. Law. (Sept. 1998), at 25. Section 121 replaced roll-over rules of IRC §1034 (still in the Code). In order to obtain the benefits of §121, however, the taxpayer need not buy a new residence Section 121 is discussed further, infra, in this chapter.

351

12. Planning to Exit a Project

Explanation

He might engage in a *Starker* exchange of properties. The Internal Revenue Service will treat his sale as two transactions, the sale of the principal residence and the sale of the other three properties, here for a market value of $375,000. Thus, he needs to find property worth that amount and exchange them for his current properties. This will defer, not eliminate, tax on this portion of the profit. He may sell the three houses, place the proceeds of the sales in escrow, and use the proceeds to buy replacement properties. The escrow agreement must place the proceeds beyond his actual or constructive possession or control, and also be part of the implementation of a plan to acquire like-kind property. He must designate the like-kind property to be acquired within 45 days after the sale and close the purchase of the designated property within 180 days. IRC §1031(3). The designated property need not be three houses; it might be an apartment building.

Example 21

A developer sells an apartment project on April 30 for a profit. By prior agreement, his attorney immediately escrows the proceeds of the sale for use in a §1031 exchange. He takes title to an office building, a property otherwise qualifying as replacement property on May 30 the same year. May he qualify for a §1031 tax-deferred exchange?

Explanation

Yes. No identification of the target is needed when the taxpayer completes both identification and the exchange within the earlier, 45-day deadline. The early receipt of title is a *per se* identification of the target property.

Example 22

A developer sells an office building on May 1 for a profit. His attorney immediately escrows the proceeds of the sale (again by prior agreement) for use in a §1031 exchange. She then identifies an apartment building and some vacant land as target properties suitable for his §1031 exchange in July, and uses all of the proceeds to close his transaction to purchase

12. Planning to Exit a Project

the apartment building in September. Should the capital gain from the sale of the office building be subject to federal income tax during the current year?

Explanation

Yes. He met the 180-day deadline, but not the 45-day identification deadline. A failure to meet the 45-day identification requirement defeats the whole exchange as far as the IRS is concerned, even if the deed to the target property is received within the 180-day deadline. See Dobrich v. Comm'r, 188 F.3d 512 (9th Cir. 1999). The IRS requires strict adherence to its timetables for these exchanges.

Example 23

Would it matter if a developer has designated the replacement properties to be acquired before the purchaser is identified for the sales of his existing properties?

Explanation

No. This is a "reverse *Starker* exchange." Where the exchanging taxpayer finds new replacement or target property before finding a purchaser for his existing property, the exchange requirements are still met. There must be an intent to complete the exchange and an integrated plan for completing it, but identifying the exchange properties earlier than the sale of the existing property need not defeat a showing of either of these elements. Reverse exchanges require that the escrow agent or intermediary take title to the replacement property temporarily, unless the exchange property is sold. This is called "parking" the title with the agent.

Example 24

Setting up a *Starker* escrow puts the risk that the escrow agent will embezzle the proceeds on deposit on the exchanging taxpayer. How can this risk be reduced?

353

12. Planning to Exit a Project

Explanation

Two methods might be considered: (1) a letter of credit callable upon any embezzlement, or (2) the exchanger's retaining a mortgage lien on the existing property. The mortgage should probably (1) include an agreed-on amount for this lien (that will enable the exchanger to bid at any later foreclosure sale), (2) include also a subordination of the lien to future mortgages (necessary to facilitate the acquisition of the existing property by a third party replacing owner), (3) be nonnegotiable and nonassignable (to prevent the exchanger from realizing income from or cashing out of the exchange), and (4) be interest-free. Any interest paid to the exchanger during the exchange process is likely to be challenged as cashing out and resulting in nondeferrable income. Such provisions make the take-back mortgage into a part of the integrated exchange plan.

Example 25

Upon completion of a §1031 exchange transaction, the owner of Blackacre (the relinquished property) transfers the obligation to pay off an existing mortgage on Blackacre to its new owner and uses the cash that his equity in Blackacre generates to purchase Whiteacre. Whiteacre qualifies as replacement property, is identified as such within 45 days, and its deed is delivered and received within the 180-day deadline. What further advice should the owner receive?

Explanation

Advise him that, not only may "boot" be cash proceeds, it may also be the amount of any mortgage liability of which he is relieved during the course of an exchange. So the transfer of the mortgage obligation, when assumed by the transferee, will be treated as cash received, and upon receipt taxable as such. Either cash or mortgage relief may be considered boot. Any such boot becomes taxable. The rationale for tax deferral is that disposing of one property and acquiring a replacement or target property results in a continuous investment, and so should not be a taxable event. However, the purpose of §1031 is to defer taxation only when a taxpayer's assets are as illiquid after the exchange transaction as they were before it, but when boot is present, the taxpayer has the wherewithal to pay the tax and should do so. The cash that he would have used to pay off the mortgage can now be devoted to paying the tax. All this is not to say that a taxpayer should not refinance either the relinquished or target property before or after the exchange—it's just not advisable to do so during it. An exchange of equally valuable properties, in both property value and net equity, will be a tax-deferred exchange.

354

12. Planning to Exit a Project

Example 26

A developer sells Blackacre on July 15 for a $1 million profit. His attorney immediately escrows the proceeds of the sale (again by prior agreement) for use in a §1031 exchange. He then identifies Whiteacre and Greenacre as target properties suitable for his §1031 exchange at the end of July. The attorney disburses $250,000 to him in August and uses the rest of the proceeds—$750,000—to close his transaction to purchase (the otherwise qualifying target property) Whiteacre in December. Is the capital gain from the sale of Blackacre subject to federal income tax?

Explanation

Yes. The $250,000 disbursal shows that he could have directed his attorney to disburse all of the proceeds to him, even if the express terms of the escrow agreement says otherwise. So he is deemed to be in constructive possession of all those proceeds, and they are taxable to him, even if the transaction to purchase a qualifying target property closes in December.

Example 27

After selling a developer's exchange property (to which he held title individually) and locating the replacement property, he applies for a mortgage loan to finance the purchase. The mortgage lender, as a result of losses it suffered recently, insists that the replacement property's title be held by a legal entity that is "bankruptcy remote." That is, the lender wants to be sure that the titleholder cannot voluntarily file for bankruptcy and avoid the obligations of the loan. The very presence of the entity means, however, that the title to the property won't be held just by the exchanger in his individual capacity, and the IRS requires that the same taxpayer who held the exchange property receive the replacement property. How do you think this problem should be handled?

Explanation

By forming a limited liability company for the exchanged property with two members. The first one is the developer, the second is another legal entity (say, an LLC) wholly owned by the developer and controlled by (say) two persons, including a representative of the lender. The developer would have the right to all the profits and losses of the company, but the LLC would have the right to control (by unanimous vote) any decisions about filing for bankruptcy, borrowing more money, going out of business, mergers, changing the entity further, or amending its certificate or membership

355

12. Planning to Exit a Project

agreement with regard to any of the previous matters. The company is thus made "bankruptcy remote." And the company will be disregarded for purposes of determining whether the developer is the sole owner of the replacement property. See IRS, Private Letter Ruling 1999-11033 (Mar. 19, 1999), 1999 WL 148569 (IRS PLR).

Converting Business Property into a Residence

As previously discussed, federal taxation is postponed until sale or other disposition of the property, but the Code also offers many sellers of residential real property nonrecognition of gain in the following two, fairly common situations: first, if a transfer of property is made to a spouse, or to a former spouse when the transfer is incident to a divorce. IRC §1041 (this section applies to nonresidential property as well). Such a transfer is treated as a gift, and the transferee receives the property with the adjusted basis of the transferor spouse.

The second nonrecognition situation occurs when the sale of a "principal residence" is followed by the purchase of a new residence. IRC §121(a) provides: "Gross income shall not include gain from the sale or exchange of property if, during the five-year period ending on the date of the sale or exchange, such property has been owned and used by the taxpayer as the taxpayer's principal residence for periods aggregating two years or more." This exemption is limited to $250,000—or $500,000 for a married couple filing a joint tax return. The period that is "aggregated" within the five years before the sale may be two continuous years (giving a vendor time to rent the residence in anticipation of the advent of a better market), or five months in each of the past five years. The baseline for measuring the exempted gross income is either the tax basis computed under the former buy-up, roll-over rules, or the basis of the property computed under amended §121. This section may be used by a taxpayer once every two years and results in exempt or "forgiven" income along with deferred taxation.

Examples

Example 28

Your parents retire while both are still active. Your father has been handy all his life and tells you now that they have spotted a house down the street that they plan to move to so that he can fix it up for resale. You are his sole heir. What do you think? Is he squandering your inheritance?

356

12. Planning to Exit a Project

Explanation

Assuming that the house is saleable, he may have found a wonderful retirement occupation. Buying a fixer-upper for resale, when he lives there as his principal residence as he is restoring it over a two-year-plus period, will upon resale result in income forgiven by §121. He can move from house to house free of capital gains, taking the exempt income into their next project or investing it in ever more valuable property. He can move from property to property, buying, improving, and reselling indefinitely until his death, at which time the basis of the property he owns at death will be your "stepped-up" basis under §1014(a). This means that the home's basis will be its fair market value on the date of death, so that when you inherit it, you will pay a tax on very little capital gain.

Example 29

Dick and Jane, husband and wife, own their residence outright and also own a beach house. The beach house has appreciated greatly in value recently, so that its sale today will result in a profit of $400,000. May they move into the beach house, live there two years, and then sell it, claiming that the profit is exempt under §121? What if they lived there with a lessee?

Explanation

So long as the beach house is their principal residence for the two years before the sale and the profit is within the exemption ($500,000 in the instance of a married couple filing jointly), it does not matter for §121 purposes that it was bought initially as a second or vacation home. Sharing residential occupancy of the property with a lessee would not affect the result.

Example 30

Harry is 45 years old and has owned his home for the last decade. A year ago, he married Wanda and made her a concurrent owner of the home (actually, Wanda became a joint tenant with a right of survivorship), after living with her there for a year. They then sold the home for a profit of $450,000. Is this sum exempt under §121?

357

12. Planning to Exit a Project

Explanation

There are two elements in the two-year aggregate test in §121. First is an ownership test, which only one spouse must meet. Harry has owned the property for the required two years. Second is an occupancy test. Both spouses must meet it, and both do: Harry obviously, and Wanda also, even though for one of Wanda's two years there she was not an owner but an occupant—so the full $450,000 profit is exempt.

A related scenario involves divorce. What if Harry and Wanda owned their residence in joint tenancy, but later divorced, Wanda remaining on the property and using it as her principal residence for two years before the property was sold, five years after the divorce? All this occurred while the title to the residence remained subject to the joint tenancy. This scenario yields the same result: The occupying ex-spouse qualifies regarding the occupancy element, while both continue to qualify for the exemption as to the ownership element. So both Harry and Wanda would qualify for the exemption claimed after their divorce.

Example 31

Same facts as in the prior Example, but Harry and Wanda decide not to sell right away. Harry later dies and soon afterward Wanda sells, at a time when the home is worth $800,000 and their joint tax basis was $200,000. How much of the $600,000 profit is exempt?

Explanation

Wanda has two interests in the residence. Her initial co-ownership interest yields a $300,000 profit, so the amount over her $250,000 exemption— $50,000—is taxable at the long-term capital gain rates. The ownership share in the home received through the right of survivorship is entitled to a tax basis stepped up to its fair market value at the time of Harry's death, or $400,000, so her profit is measured by the amount received over that amount—and probably is within the exempted amount of income. (For community property states, Rev. Rul. 87-98 gives the surviving spouse approximately the same result and a stepped-up basis in a community property residence.)

Example 32

Twenty-five years ago, a developer purchased Blackacre for $100,000 and resided there until two years ago, when he moved into a condominium and rented Blackacre to Ted, the developer's son, who has lived there for the last two years. Ted is about to take another job in a distant city and the developer

358

12. Planning to Exit a Project

wishes to sell Blackacre, now valued at $400,000. What tax advice would you give him?

Explanation

He can either (1) sell Blackacre and, because he has lived in the property for two years out of the last five years, take the §121 exemption of $250,000 for a single taxpayer on the sale of a personal residence, and then pay a capital gains tax on the $50,000 nonexempt proceeds of any sale, or (2) sell Blackacre and, because Ted's rental now qualifies Blackacre as the developer's business or investment property, complete a §1031 *Starker* exchange. The developer did not have this second option two years ago—no personal residence at the time of the exchange can be either an exchange or a replacement property. After selling the exchange property, the sale proceeds should be held in an irrevocable, third-party escrow account with a secure lockbox feature preventing him from obtaining them, and he should then acquire a like-kind property within the timetables provided by IRS regulations. Either option offers tax savings.

* * *

In this chapter on exit strategies, the final word goes to a well-known developer of the mid-20th century. He claimed to be the first to use it—and he called it the Hawaii Technique—so named because, he said, he thought of it fishing on a beach in Hawaii.

In the final decade of his career as a New York City real estate developer, William Zeckendorf (1905–1976) wrote an autobiographical memoir. Part way through his memoir, he related his developing and selling a building on Park Avenue. See William Zeckendorf, *Zeckendorf* 144-148 (Holt, Rinehart, and Winston, N.Y.C., 1971). Zeckendorf's exit strategy for the building was as follows.

It was a Class-A office building in a prime downtown location and earned its developer a million dollars a year in rental income. The building's fair market value is $10 million—that is, its rental income was 10% on an annual basis, and its capitalization or cap rate was 10.[7]

---

7. Recall that the capitalization or cap rate is the ratio of net operating income and the fair market value of the asset. So an asset's NOI divided by its fair market value (FMV), or

$$\frac{NOI}{FMV}$$

is its cap rate. It can be used to compare the returns from different assets—a higher cap rate might mean a better investment when an investor is a potential buyer. A cap rate in a particular real estate market might also indicate a trend of real estate prices. If the rates of various assets are decreasing, it may indicate that the value of the properties is increasing, and

359

12. Planning to Exit a Project

One quarter or 25% of the rental income can be attributed to the building's underlying land parcel—or $250,000. (Historically, 25% of a land parcel attributed to the underlying land isn't a bad estimate, but the actual percent would depend on an appraisal.) If that $250,000 were capitalized at 5%, the land parcel would be worth $5,000,000. If the land parcel was subject to a senior mortgage with an LTV of 60%, the principal amount of the mortgage would be $3,000,000 and, at an interest rate of 4%, the annual debt service would be $120,000. That would leave $130,000 of the land parcel's income; capitalizing that $130,000 at 6.5% would yield a fair market value of $2,000,000—the value of the land parcel encumbered by the senior mortgage. Then the land parcel could then be sold outright for that $2,000,000.

The $1,000,000 income on the building, now reduced by $250,000, leaves $750,000 in earnings still available to the developer. Since the land parcel was worth $5,000,000, the other $5,000,000 of the annual rental income can be attributed to the building.

After all this, the developer still owns the building, not free and clear, but subject to the ground lease. So he can now think about what to do with it. In a matter similar to his treatment of the land, he might think about splitting its value—or breaking bulk again—in the expectation that the parts might be worth more than the whole, undivided fee simple absolute in it.

Example

As the owner of the Park Avenue building, the developer has the task of marketing it, soliciting tenants, negotiating its leases, and managing it. Commercial real estate brokerage firms are interested in doing some or all of this. Based on the numbers so far assembled, how should the developer proceed?

Explanation

Any manager signing up to do these tasks would receive $1,000,000 in rental income, pay the developer $750,000—that is, $1,000,000, minus the $250,000 in income derived from the underlying land parcel and due to the ground lease lessor—and keep $250,000 each year. If the manager could increase the rental income derived from the negotiation of future leases, his "keep" would be even greater. The developer would then receive $750,000 in rental income, pay $250,000 to the owner of the land parcel, and keep $500,000 for himself.

---

their market is a rising one. If cap rates for an asset are increasing, their real estate market is falling—all other things being equal—which of course they never are. For one thing, a reliable cap rate requires a stable NOI.

12. Planning to Exit a Project

Example

With the $500,000 in hand from the prior Example, what might the developer do next?

Explanation

If the building's $500,000 income might be capitalized at the rate of 5% and then mortgaged, the principal amount of that leasehold mortgage would be $3,750,000. If this mortgage were extended on an interest only basis of interest for 15 years, the debt service annually would be about $250,000. If this mortgage was extended on a constant amortization basis, at an annual rate of interest at 7.5%, there would be an additional $100,000 of debt service, but this would leave $150,000 in the developer's hands.

Example 33

What might the developer do next?

Explanation

The developer still has three options: (1) selling the building outright to a new owner, (2) capitalizing and then mortgaging its remaining value to him, or (3) selling the building and financing its buyer through a take back mortgage. In any event, he has increased the $10,000,000 value of the building, just by "breaking bulk," by dealing with each component of the building's operational value separately—in Zeckendorf's terms, slicing the Hawaiian pineapple horizontally. Keeping what's left of his rights in the building, he would still be considered its owner for tax purposes, taking for instance, the IRC's depreciation deduction for it. In the end, the developer either has the proceeds of each third-party mortgage loan in hand, or, if he financed each mortgage as take back financing, the mortgage payments as each mortgage is repaid. The loan proceeds might become seed money for his next project, or the loan repayments might support his business or personal expenses, or become income for his heirs at his death.

361

Index

Acquisition of Land, 1–14
  Leverage in a purchase, 1
  Seller's Remorse, 1
Architects, See Construction

Builder's Risk Insurance, 185–186
Brokers, See also Leases

Choice of Entity, 111–112. See also Limited
        Liability Companies
  General and Limited Partnerships, 115–116
  Investment Trusts, 132
  Sub-Chapter S Corporations, 116–117
Construction, 147–190
  Agreements for, 162–164, 170–173
    Conditions in, 173
  Architects Fees, 150
  Architectural Design, 149–152
  Documents Used for, 148–149
  Fast Track Design, 188–190
  General Contractor for, 160–168
    Selection of, 161
  Inspections of, 161–162
  Lending for, See Construction Lending
  Mechanics Liens, 175–181
  Planning for. 149-151
  Preparation of Plans and
        Specifications, 152–160
  Subcontractors, 173–175
  Surety Bonds for, 181–185
    Bid Bond, 181
    Payment Bond, 181
    Performance Bond, 182
  Warranties for, 168–169
Construction Lending, 191–224
  Appraisals for, 196–197
    Hard Costs in, 194
  Business and Financial Covenants
        for, 219–224
  Commitment Letters, 200–205
  Lenders, Types of, 192–196
  Loan Agreements, 296–212

Notes and Mortgages, 212–213
Mortgages, 213–218
  Permanent Mortgages, 245–264
    Assignments of Rents in, 245–248
    Sample Assignment of Rents, 248–249
  Permanent Lenders, 194–196, 245–264
    Buy-Sell Agreements of, 195–196
  Reverse Engineering, 206
Contracts of Sale, 15–45, 334–336
  Anti-Assignment Clause, 41–42
  Break Up Clause, 20–21
  Contingencies, 16–17
  Drafting, 15–16
  Due Diligence Period, 18–19
  Due on Sale Covenant, 331
  Executory Period for, 16
  Marketable Title Clauses, 34–39
  Purchase Price, 19–20
  Subject to Clauses, 16
    Subject to Financing, 22–29
    Subject to Rezoning, 31–34
  Time of the Essence Clause, 39–41
  Remedies for Breach, 42–45
  Warranties and Representations
        therein, 29–31

Deed in Lieu of Foreclosure, 336–343
  Recitations in, 339

Endangered Species, 67
Environmental Hazards, 66–68
  Asbestos, 66–67
  Lead, 67
  Radon, 67–68
Environmental Laws, 47–68
  Audits under, 59–61
  Brownfields, 65–66
  Clean Up Costs, tax treatment, 65
  Comprehensive Emergency Response,
      Compensation and Liability
      Act, 50–56
  Defenses under, 62–65

363

Index

Environmental Laws (continued)
    Owner Defenses, 64–65
    Facility, application to, 42
    Owner or Operator of, 52, 55
    Objectives of, 51
    Potentially Responsible Parties,
        defined, 51–52
    Liability of, 52
  Contracts of Sale Disputes, 47–49
  Enforcement of, 61
  Hazardous Substances, 50
  Indemnity Agreements, 56–57
  Insurance for Violations, 57
    Policy Terms, 57–59
  Mortgage Disputes Regarding, 49–50
Equity Investments, 225–244
  Capital Calls in, 125, 232–234
    Defaults in, 234–235
  Clog on Alienation, 231
  Developer Refinancing Decisions, 237
  Disadvantages of, 231–232
  Inter-Creditor Agreements, 229–231
  Investors, 225–226
  Management Decisions, 235–239
    Negotiations for Vetoes, 235–236
  Mezzanine Finance, 228–232
  Securities Acts Treatment, 243–244
  Taxation of, 241–243
  Waterfalls, 225–228
Exit Strategies, 329–361
  Conversion of Business Property into a
    Residence, 356
  Deed in Lieu of Foreclosure, 336–343
    Timing, 340
  Equity of Redemption, 231, 340
  Hawaii Technique, 339–361
  Holding or Selling a Project, 329–331
  Section 121, 356–358

Federal Income Taxation. 133-146
  Business and Investment Property, 136, 139
  Deferring Gain, 136
  Depreciation, 137–138
  Passive Losses, 138
  Tax Events, 133–134
Fiduciary Duties, 128–130
Financial Analysis, 140–144
Foreclosure, 340–341
  Cash Flow and, 145–146

Green Buildings, 187
Ground Leases, 82–97

  Anti-Merger Clause, 92
  Lessee's Option to Purchase, 92, 97
  Mortgaging of, 92
  Negotiations for, 83–87, 93–96
  Sample of, 87–88
    Comments on, 88–93
  Subordination of, 92, 98–101

Implied Covenant of Good Faith, 322
Installment Land Sales Contract, 69–82
  Bankruptcy, treatment in, 74–75
  Closing of, 75–76
  Forfeiture Clauses, 70–72
  Legislation on, 81–82
  Mortgaging, interest in, 73–74
  Remedies, 75
    Measure of Damages, 76
  Sample Contract, 78–79
Investment Trusts, 132

Leases and Leasing, 265–328
  Assignments, 299–303, 320
  BOMA standards, 273–275
  Brokers, 265
  Building Services Covenant, 324–325
  Commencement of Term, 277–279
  Compliance with Laws, 305–307
  Continuous Operation Covenants, 318–319
  Contraction Rights, 293
  Expansion Rights, 291–293
  Finished Surface, 273
  Fire, Casualty and Condemnation
    Covenants, 325–326
  Insurance Covenants, 326–327
  Load Factor in, 273
  Material Defaults, 328–329
  Office Building Leases, 267–268
  Parties to, 268
  Premises, 268–271, 275
  Possession and Commencement of
    Term, 277–281
  Remedies, 327–328
  Rent, 272, 283–286
    Additional Rent, 274–275
    Escalation Covenants for, 286–287
      Base Year Method, 287
      Prior Year Method, 287
    Percentage Rents, 287–289
      Gross Sales, 288–290
      Net Sales, 288–289
    Rentable Square Footage, 273, 277
  Shopping Center Leases, 266–267, 307–323

Index

Subleases, 299–303
Subordination and
        Non-Disturbance, 293–298
Supermarkets, 288
Telecommunications Access, 298–299
Tenant Duty to Maintain Premises, 323
Treatises on, 265
Triple Net Lease, 274–276, 310
  Taxes, 310
  Utility Charges, 310–311
Use Covenants, 312–316
  Exclusive Use Covenants, 316–317
Usable Square Footage, 273–274
Work Letters and Tenant Improvement
      Allowances, 303–305
Letters of Intent, 3–7
  Agreement to Agree, 5
  Confidentiality Clause, 3
  Consideration, 6–7
  Enforcement, 4–6
  Exclusivity Clauses, 3, 5
    Carve outs, 3
  Statute of Frauds, 3
Limited Liability Companies, 111–132
  Compared to
    General Partnership, 115
    Limited Partnership, 115–116
      Agreement, 117
    Sub-Chapter S Corporation, 116–117
  Formation of, 117–118
  Operating Agreement for, 117, 123–127
    Contributions, 123–124
    Waterfall Agreement, 124–125
    Preferred Return Hurdle, 125, 127
  Taxation of, 121–122
Loan Participations, 259–263

Mechanics Liens, 175–181
  Scope, 177
  Stop Notice, 177
  Enforcement, 177
Mortgagee in Possession, 250–252
Mortgages, 197–199, 200, 212–218, 245–264

Nonrecourse Provisions, in 197-199, 330
  Carve Out Exceptions to, 332–333
Permanent Mortgages, 245–264
  Loan Participations in, 259–263
Mortgage Workouts, 341

Options to Purchase, 7–11
  Attachment of Contract to Buy, 10
  Call Option, 7, 11
  Extension of Time, 7
  Land Assembly, 8
  Recordability, 9
  Specific Performance of, 9

Permanent Mortgage, 245–264

Receivership, 253–259
Right of First Offer, 12
Right of First Refusal, 11–14

Sale Leasebacks, 344–348
Sample Agreements
  Assignment of Rents, 248–249
  Ground Lease, 87–88
  Nonrecourse Covenant, 197–199
Securities Acts, 130–132
  Exemptions from, 243–244
Subordination, 98–101
  Sample, 99
Supermarkets, 288
Surety Bonds, See Construction

Take-Back Financing, 97–98
Taxation, 133–146. See also Federal Income
    Taxation
  Tax Free Exchanges, 349–356
    Boot, 354
    Like Kind Property, 349–350

Visual Artists Rights Act, 335

Work Letters, 303–305
Workout Negotiations, 341

365